T0338164

An Editor for Oregon

▲▲▲

An Editor for Oregon

▲▲▲

Charles A. Sprague and the Politics of Change

by

Floyd J. McKay

Oregon State University Press
Corvallis

The paper in this book meets the guidelines for permanence and durability of the Committee on Production Guidelines for Book Longevity of the Council on Library Resources and the minimum requirements of the American National Standard for Permanence of Paper for Printed Library Materials Z39.48-1984.

Library of Congress Cataloging-in-Publication Data

McKay, Floyd J.

An editor for Oregon : Charles A. Sprague and the politics of change / by Floyd J. McKay. — 1st ed.

Includes bibliographical references and index.

ISBN 0-87071-439-2 (alk. paper)

1. Sprague, Charles A. (Charles Arthur), 1887-1969. 2. Governors—Oregon—Biography. 3. Newspaper editors—Oregon—Biography. 4. Oregon—Politics and government—1859-1950. 5. Oregon statesman (Salem, Or : 1916). I Title.

F881.S68M38 1998

979.5'043'092—dc21

[b] 98-30120

CIP

Oregon State University Press

101 Waldo Hall

Corvallis OR 97331-6407

541-737-3166 • fax 541-737-3170

www.osu.orst.edu/dept/press

Contents

Publication of this book was made possible in part
by a contribution from
Wallace A. Sprague
The Oregon State University Press is grateful for this support

To Dixie Ann McKay,
who shared it all,
and to
those who cherish the memory
of
The Oregon Statesman

Foreword

Soon after I became editor of the *East Oregonian* at Pendleton in 1951, an adviser cautioned me to avoid editorial comment on any aspect of religion. He said, "There's only one editor in Oregon who can write about religion without fear of being challenged or contradicted. Only Charley Sprague can do that."

He was speaking of Charles Arthur Sprague, editor of *The Oregon Statesman*. While some readers didn't agree with all that he wrote, they respected him and his opinions.

A longtime resident of Salem confided, "I wouldn't think of going to the polls without Mr. Sprague's editorial advice."

As I adjusted to the responsibilities of being editor of a daily newspaper, I examined what other Oregon editors were doing and found that I wanted to emulate Charles Sprague. As he did, I wrote a daily column and editorials and participated in public affairs. I sensed that I couldn't sit at a typewriter and preach to readers; that I must become involved in seeking solutions of community problems.

It was Charles Sprague's concern with statewide issues that led him to become a candidate for governor. He felt that editorializing on those issues wasn't enough. That he must do more.

During twelve years of service on the state Board of Higher Education, I frequently went to Mr. Sprague for advice. I knew of his involvement in public school education before becoming an editor and I found that his advice regarding some problems within the State System of Higher Education was immensely valuable.

As an editor he supported both Republicans and Democrats and took editorial positions on issues without regard for their partisan political origins. I thought that conservative Republicans seriously erred in not supporting him for re-election as governor because they thought him too liberal.

Of all the editors of Oregon newspapers I have known since beginning as a reporter at *The Oregonian* in 1933, I have most wanted to be like Charles Arthur Sprague. I cannot adequately convey my respect and admiration for him.

I commend Floyd McKay for undertaking this biography. His subject will have a lasting place in the history of Oregon government and journalism and for that we are indebted to Floyd McKay.

J.W. Forrester

Preface

American journalism in the nineties is a corporate product, traded on the Stock Exchange and packaged like breakfast food after careful consultation with pollsters and marketers. As readership declines, the corporate planners urge their editors to practice what some are calling "public journalism," in which editors and even reporters become part of the solution to community problems rather than merely the chroniclers.

To one who came of age in a time when there were still outposts of individual ownership, and editors who invested themselves in their communities, this approach is obvious. Personal commitment makes a newspaper (or a broadcast station) a citizen of its community, and its readers can relate to it on a personal rather than corporate level.

It was my good fortune to work nearly three decades for individual owners, all of whom have been replaced, sadly, by corporate owners. In 1960, I became a reporter at *The Oregon Statesman*, owned by Charles A. Sprague. Sprague lacked the common touch, but he brought to his newspaper distinction of a sort not rivaled in my experience. Sprague was for me neither friend nor mentor; he was the boss. Nearly half a century his junior, I had little contact with Mr. Sprague, as he was uniformly called, until his last years, when I was assigned to the Capitol. Even then, our relationship was formal.

I began this project in part because I wanted to tell a story of individual ownership, of media before the corporations. But most of all, I wanted to find out about Charles A. Sprague. I was basically ignorant of his life, and I wanted to find out more about the man many consider the outstanding Oregon journalist of the century. As I interviewed those who knew him, beginning in 1989 with Cecil Edwards, and as I read and reread his editorials and columns, a man began to emerge to accompany the public persona, a man who underwent incredible change in his lifetime, while maintaining his basic values.

Along the way, I received both financial and personal support. My wife and I are indebted to Wendell Webb and Charles A. Sprague for welcoming us into the family that was the *Statesman*. The Sprague children, Wallace Sprague and Martha Sprague Hurley, assisted with the costs of my research and readily answered my questions. They did not ask for, or receive, permission to review copy, and this work is entirely that of the author. Western Washington University helped with a faculty research grant and professional leave for Fall 1996.

Tom and Marguerite Wright, who were as close to Sprague as any of his employees, are in many ways godparents of this book. Tom Wright,

Don Scarborough, and Al Jones helped with photographs, and the families of Henry Hess and C. E. Ingalls searched for photos of these men important to Sprague's life. J. Wesley Sullivan shared interview tapes and thoughts from his own research on Sprague. The late Robert Sprague, the editor's nephew, provided business records, as did Judy Ashard of Newport. This material, and other miscellany collected during my nine-year quest, are identified as "author's collection" in footnotes.

Researchers always owe a great deal to library and archive professionals, and that is certainly the case here. Sprague's papers are at the Oregon State Archives and Oregon Historical Society, where I invariably received ready and expert help. Papers of other important figures and agencies are from the University of Oregon, Reed College, Princeton University, and the Federal Archives Center. Newspaper archives at Salem Public Library and Oregon State Library were also invaluable. Counsel and editing from Warren Slesinger and Jo Alexander of the Oregon State University Press was invaluable.

Because Sprague was active in nearly every facet of his community, including church, school, business, and civic work as well as his political life, choices had to be made as to which areas would be pursued in depth in these pages. I emphasized those areas which Sprague addressed regularly in his column, and which might be expected to have wider interest.

The limits of time and energy prevailed against expanding the circle of interviews beyond those listed in the bibliography. To those I failed to reach, my apologies; to those who responded, my sincere thanks. Your recollections, advice and counsel helped shape this work. Any errors or omissions are the responsibility of the author.

Floyd J. McKay
Bellingham, Washington, 1998

◆◆◆

Introduction

It was called the Age of Reform, a restless, searching, idealistic beginning to a new century. It was a time of progressive politicians and muckraking journalists, who joined forces against ruthless corporate bosses and their bought political allies, and ushered in what publisher Henry Luce later dubbed The American Century, with wars hot and cold, a great economic depression, electronic communications and nuclear nightmares. Throughout the turmoil, progressives would draw on the reservoir of idealism from the moral crusade that was the Progressive Era.[1]

The dominant figure in that period was Theodore Roosevelt, rough-rider, trust-buster, big-game hunter and president of the United States from 1901 to 1909. By 1912, Roosevelt had split with his successor, William Howard Taft, and was mounting an insurgent campaign, pulling his forces from the Republican Party to form the ill-fated Progressive Party. In June of that year, Roosevelt spoke to a large group of five thousand followers in Chicago, on the eve of the Republican National Convention. He closed with a ringing call: "We fight in honorable fashion for the good of mankind; unheeding of our individual fates; with unflinching hearts and undimmed eyes; we stand at Armageddon, and we battle for the Lord."

Reflecting at half-century, Charles A. Sprague termed those years the "halcyon period."[2] Sprague was only a foot soldier in T.R.'s army of progress, but the values Sprague brought to the campaign he maintained throughout his public life. In 1912 Sprague was a local leader of the Progressive Party, and during his long life as editor and politician, even in the period when he was most faithful to the Republican Party, he spoke of T.R. with warmth and of progressive causes with approval. As editor, as governor of Oregon, as alternate delegate to the United Nations and in a host of other roles, he was for over half a century a progressive. Analysts may disagree on the extent of Sprague's influence, but from 1943 to 1969, no Oregon journalist approached his stature. He was continuity in an age of transition, for his values remained rooted in the Progressive Era of Theodore Roosevelt, for whom he cast his first vote. But he was also an agent of change, for his life was one of learning by doing, of education gained through public acts.

Charles A. Sprague was shy and reserved, an introspective man who climbed mountains and hiked wooded trails. He possessed a dry wit and a deep sense of loyalty, but throughout his life, particularly his life in politics, he was described as a cold fish, an aloof intellectual without the gift of small talk. He was a Republican partisan who had no use for many of the party's headline stars, yet for many years he loyally stuck with party regulars whose views were far to the right of his own moderate editorials. He first supported Democrats for state office in 1952, and in 1964 he broke with his party and backed Lyndon B. Johnson for president. Fiercely protective of moderate Republicans in Oregon, Sprague in his later years found little to support at the national GOP level.

Sprague was a man of contrasts. He was at home with Eleanor Roosevelt and Arthur Schlesinger, but he could also talk shop with printers, foresters, and farmers. Capable of deciphering the most complex tax legislation, he also was familiar with crop rotations and commodity prices. A man of deeply held religious beliefs, he opposed adding "under God" to the Pledge of Allegiance. Teetotaler and prohibitionist, he refused liquor advertising in his newspapers but tolerated without comment hard-drinking associates. As governor, he supported internment of Japanese Americans in World War II; as editor he became their strongest champion in the fevered climate of their homecoming.

Sprague was one of the last of the progressive editors, a contemporary of Walter Lippmann and a survivor of William Allen White. Lippmann wrote his last "Today and Tomorrow" column in 1967; Sprague's last "It Seems To Me" was in 1968. Sprague was a regional rather than national figure, but he was one of the few progressive editors to succeed, if briefly, in a political career. But it was as an editor that he wished to be remembered, and he was clearly the most influential Oregon editor of the 20th century.

Historians have wrestled with definitions of progressivism, but progressives may be broadly described as men and women of the great American middle class, whose interest was reform rather than revolution, who wanted to recapture the American values that they felt were being eroded by urban crowding and immigration, giant corporations and rising labor militancy, and corrupt political establishments at both the local and national levels. They were believers in the moderate virtues of small-town America, its middle class and its Protestant theology, its fear of bigness and foreign influence.

Progressives were well educated and heavily influenced by both natural and social science, but influenced as well by an evangelistic social gospel prevalent in mainstream Protestant churches. Readers, and often writers, the progressives followed Charles Darwin, William James, and John

Dewey, as well as the popular reform journalists of the day, the muckrakers. Sprague was influenced particularly by Darwin, often referring to him later in life; an enthusiastic letter home during college days brought the reply, "I suspect you will be an evolutionist before you have finished the study."[3] Sprague also accepted the social gospel and followed the writings of Elbert Hubbard, a flamboyant evangelist for a strange mixture of radical politics, old-fashioned individualism and the virtues of simple living. Hubbard influenced many progressives, particularly as he spoke against the forces of entrenched privilege.[4]

Progressives believed that government, properly democratized, could be a powerful tool against sloth and sin. Richard Hofstadter found that a distinguishing mark of progressives was activism; "they argued that social evils will not remedy themselves, and that it is wrong to sit by passively and wait for time to take care of them."[5] Carried to extremes, the movement instilled its sense of morality through Prohibition. Sprague remained a prohibitionist all his life, sticking to his position long after the great experiment had proven to be a disaster. But the progressive spirit also supported child labor laws, voting rights for women, and the regulation of monopolies; Sprague also supported these causes.

Inherent in the progressive view was a distrust of big-city corruption, often associated with the Democratic Party and immigrant voting blocs. Sprague was never at home in Portland (certainly one of the tamest of America's big cities), and it cost him his political future. Even as he grew more cosmopolitan in later life, he was not drawn to city life; he had all the amenities he needed in provincial Salem and its nearby mountains and streams.

In the area of race relations and civil rights, however, Sprague moved away from his progressive roots, beyond xenophobic Salem with its lack of racial diversity, and became a crusader for civil rights. Most western progressives were not racist in the Ku Klux Klan sense, but they accepted much of the less-violent discrimination of that time, used racial epithets in conversation and even in newspaper columns, and feared foreign influence other than the northern European stock of their ancestors. Sprague was no exception in these areas, and his discovery of other races is one of the fascinating aspects of his life.

Sprague was also a progressive in his outlook on conservation and environmentalism. A disciple of the progressive forester Gifford Pinchot, Sprague championed forest conservation and as governor passed what was at the time the nation's most progressive forest legislation. Reforestation and state ownership of the charred Tillamook Burn was his legacy, but like Pinchot he accepted a "wise use" view of conservation that was later at odds with the rising tide of protectionism inherent in national wilderness legislation. Historian Samuel P. Hays described the essence of the progressive view of conservation as "rational planning to promote efficient development and use of all natural resources." It was a view Sprague shared. His progressive views adapted to modern conditions, but he did not stray far from a path Pinchot and T.R. would have endorsed.[6]

Charles A. Sprague was the last of a breed in more than the progressive sense; he was one of the last of the personal editors, men who owned and edited daily papers and simultaneously sat on the councils that ran their cities, counties and states. By the time of his death in 1969, newspaper chains had entered Oregon, one of the last hold-outs, and both Portland dailies were chain-owned. Sprague distrusted newspaper chains as he distrusted concentrated power in many forms but his heirs sold his newspaper to the nation's largest newspaper group.

Too detached and aloof to be a good politician, Sprague took for his political platform the front-page column "It Seems To Me," which he wrote daily for a quarter-century. Personal journalism in every sense, the column was fueled by Sprague's civic life, whether he was at the United Nations, traveling in France, inspecting a forest nursery or visiting an old political friend. The man branded as too intellectual for politics never wrote down to readers; and he never completely set aside the role of schoolmaster, his first career after college.

The column was required reading for legislators of both parties, of whom it was said, "they waited for Sprague to tell them what they thought." That analysis is overdrawn; Sprague wound up on the losing side of many battles. But his presence could, and did, tip the scales, and to quote him in support was considered an important asset in debate. Sprague, said a contemporary, "had more influence through his column on state government after he was governor, than he ever had as governor." Another remarked that politicians and editors might not have always agreed with Sprague, "but they felt they had to cope with what he said. If those in power have to react to you, right or wrong, you have power."[7]

When Charles A. Sprague died in 1969, only weeks after writing his last front-page column, he was eulogized as the conscience of the state and its outstanding statesman. But the kudos were not always there, and Sprague's struggle to survive as a new publisher in the Depression, his political rejection, and his regret at having abandoned civil liberties under stress were also part of the molding of the statesman and his legend.

Like so many leaders of his generation, Sprague had been immersed in the waters of reform, and throughout his life he was a missionary for the cause. From those formative years there was implanted a fear of big cities, big business, big labor, and political bosses. For most of his career, he associated at least three of these forces with the Democratic Party, and remained a dependable Republican partisan.

His views were formed early and were strongly held. If consistency was their virtue, rigidity could be their vice. Sprague could cling to men and ideas long past their proper hold on his loyalty. He was able to discover virtues in the mundane and weak simply because they adopted the Republican label, a loyalty that was not always reciprocated. He clung to fiscal prudence when elderly widows and shoeless children were in need during the Depression. In two wars, his concern for order and support of authority allowed him to trample the rights of ethnic minorities. Yet at other times he was willing to be a lone voice against the crowd, standing on principle when others were expedient.

The human drama of Sprague's inner conflicts ultimately was revealed in print, for his life and experiences were the gist of his writing. A man who found it hard to meet the eye of a visitor and who could terminate conversations with jarring abruptness, he shared his fears and his delights with thousands of strangers through his writing. The ebb and flow of 53 years of printers' ink turned Sprague into a man who, in the eyes of his colleagues, epitomized the title of his newspaper: The Oregon Statesman. To follow his life is to take a voyage through the politics and journalism of 20th-century Oregon. Sprague's life is in effect the life of a state through Depression, war, and recovery, and into a new era.

1

◆◆◆

A Serious Young Editor

The tall, slender young man, sober in expression and serious in demeanor, looked anxiously on the dry and dusty main street of a small county seat in the wheat country of southeastern Washington. This day—October 21, 1915—marked his emergence at age 27 as editor and publisher of the struggling but pretentiously named *Washington State Journal and Ritzville Times*. As the new boy on the block, he was about to meet his neighbors and readers, the farmers and burghers of Adams County.

Charles Arthur Sprague went to meet his community in the way he would continue to meet his neighbors in half a century as editor, publisher, and political and civic leader in the Pacific Northwest: on the printed page:

Announcement

In announcing the policy of the new management we wish to state that it is our intention to make the Journal-Times distinctively a newspaper, featuring particularly the news of Ritzville and of Adams County. In a city and county as large as we have here there is a wide field for a local newspaper; and in developing this newspaper so that it will enter into and occupy this field we believe that the investment involved in capital, energy and time, will prove worthy and profitable. We confess therefore to the possession of ambition, the ambition to build the Journal-Times, so that it may become a more and more vital factor in the life of the community which it serves. We shall endeavor to keep our news columns open for the printing of all news of interest which is worthy of publication, reserving to the editorial page the expression of opinion. Politically the paper will continue to be free from partisan affiliations.

With reference to editorials there is no occasion for an announcement of policy, for we have none. We recognize that a community which has been established for any length of time has developed its peculiar channels of life and thought and that a newcomer must adapt himself to the community's habits rather than presume to project his ideas upon the public. In whatever comments we may make from time to time we shall endeavor to be fair and candid in our views and dignified in our expression of them. The day has passed when the newspaper, which ought to be a broad democratic institution, can be a narrow and controversial organ and succeed, either financially or as a reliable newspaper.

As promised, Sprague's first issue was generously laden with local news, in sharp contrast to the previous publisher who had borrowed heavily from other sources and ran stale reports on the European war. Sprague, whose sole journalistic experience had consisted of editing a college newspaper and working two summers as a reporter, clearly understood the nature of news. His pattern was established: an emphasis on local news and local people, an editorial page that provided thoughtful and well-researched views, a keen eye for the business of publishing, and an extraordinary personal commitment to the civic work of the community.

Journalism was not an accidental choice for Sprague, but it was not the only option he had considered as he pondered ways to live out his ideal of service, an ideal born of his staunch Presbyterian upbringing and his early interest in politics and a wide variety of literature. He wanted to be someone, and from his early years there is no evidence that he considered anything but some type of public career.

While still in college, he confided to his diary in 1909: "I am in a sore strait, betwixt two opinions, whether to go into teaching or journalism. Both are attractive to me."[1] In 1911, while working as a teacher and superintendent of schools in Waitsburg, the 23-year-old was confronted with a request to return to Iowa and help manage the family's feed and grain business. In a letter to his older brother, Wyatt, Sprague wrote:

I will confess that my ambitions lie along the lines of a public career. I should like to enter politics; but the problem is the nubbin hold. Law is the great avenue; but I rather dislike its practice. Journalism is good, provided one owns the paper. But I am persuaded that I must decide finally this winter and then go after it with tooth and toe-nail.[2]

Four years later, almost to the day, Sprague had made his decision, and was launched on the career that he would follow for 53 years, with notable side excursions into politics, education, and public service. In many ways Sprague's life direction was already beginning to take shape before the turn of the century, in the studies and interests of a young man growing up in a typical Iowa farm town still influenced by the drama of the Civil War.

The veterans of that war were very much a part of community life when Sprague was a child, and on patriotic occasions he would often paint word pictures of Independence Day, when the young boys jostled to see the aging veterans as they passed, marching to honor fallen comrades. As the band played the dead march, they filed two abreast to the cemetery. The battery of old Civil War pieces boomed out the military salute, and widows wept at the memory of men lost three decades ago. As evening drew down the young boys listened in the shadows while the old men gathered around the fife and drum corps and talked of the camp and march, the hardtack, the battles fought and comrades gone.[3]

There lived in Louisa County on Iowa's Mississippi River border some families who had not joined in the Union's cause. The dread word, "copperhead" (meaning a Southern sympathizer, usually a Democrat), was whispered still, a measure of scorn in a country where memories of Lincoln still lived. To come of age in Louisa County in the late 19th century was to be forever stamped with the passions, the divisions, the sense of Union that lingered from the late war. "I was born in the afterglow of the great Civil War," Sprague told a Memorial Day audience in 1924:

> *My grandfather [Austin Greene Sprague], a soldier of the 24th Iowa, was killed in the battle of Champion Hills in the siege of Vicksburg. Two of my uncles served in the war, and one was a prisoner at Andersonville. In my town it seemed that most of the men of mature life had been soldiers in the "late war," as my father would tell me. . . .*
>
> *Time had not assuaged the fierce animosities of that great struggle. The upper Mississippi Valley, which had given Lincoln and Grant to the Union, still cherished the intense feelings which the war had aroused. A Confederate soldier was still a rebel. The feelings of the elders naturally stirred similar emotions with those of the younger generations.*[4]

News of Sprague's grandfather's death had been conveyed to the 24-year-old widow by a fellow soldier, George W. Harbin, who informed Lucille Farley Sprague that on May 16, 1863, Austin Greene Sprague had been killed:

> *. . . while the 24th was gallantly charging a battery, Mr. Sprague fell by a cannister ball passing through him at the pit of his stomach. . . . The 24th was called on to charge a battery of four guns, and most gloriously did they do it, not a man flinching. They took the battery and all their gunners, at the same time putting to flight four times their number who were supporting the battery, but, on account of the most disgraceful failure in the coming up of the troops who were held as a support, our boys were flanked on both sides by a reinforcement of the rebels, and compelled to relinquish their prize and retreat, to avoid being all taken prisoners.*[5]

Harbin concluded by noting that although someone had taken the fallen soldier's pocketbook, Harbin had salvaged a letter written to Lucille shortly before Austin Greene's death, and a 10-cent stamp, "a little stained with blood." The Iowan was buried on a grassy ridge along with others of the 210 casualties of his regiment. Austin Greene Sprague left his widow with four young children.

Charles A. Sprague was descended from William Sprague, who arrived in Massachusetts Bay in 1629. Some of his family moved to Cape Cod and Rhode Island, later descendants to the Western Reserve (Ohio) after the Revolution. Direct ancestors founded the town of Marietta, Ohio, and then the next generation moved to Kansas and Iowa.[6]

Charles Arthur Sprague was born in Lawrence, Kansas, on November 12, 1887, but his parents, Charles Allen Sprague and Alice Caroline Glasgow Sprague, soon moved to the farming community of Columbus Junction, Iowa, where they bought a feed and seed business and a grain elevator.

The son was known in the family as Arthur, to distinguish him from his father, and would be so known within the immediate family all his life. In his later writing, Sprague recalled a typical Midwest upbringing, in a distinctly middle class home where the father operated a small business and the mother stressed reading the Bible and getting a sound education.

This idyllic setting was marred, however, by a dark side Sprague never mentioned in his writing or public utterances. His mother contracted tuberculosis while he was a child, and she died when Arthur was eight years old. His formative years would have been dominated by this illness and death, yet if he ever spoke of it as an adult, it was in private.

His father's mother, Lucille Farley Sprague, the Civil War widow, took over the role of raising Arthur, his brother, Robert Wyatt, and his sister, Mazie; they were respectively five and two years older than Arthur.[7]

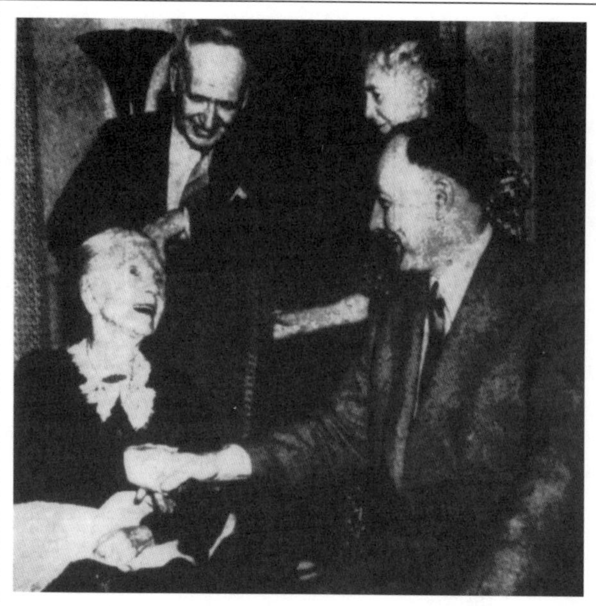

Left motherless when he was only 8 years old, young Charles Sprague was raised by his grandmother, widow of a Civil War soldier. In 1940, now governor of Oregon, Sprague visited the centenarian Lucy Sprague Brooks in Cedar Rapids (*Cedar Rapids Gazette*).

Charles Sprague's parents were Charles Allen Sprague (1856-1911) and Alice Carolyn Glasgow Sprague (1857-96), both descendants of early American families (Sprague Family Archives).

Striking a manly pose, 4-year-old Charles poses for an Iowa photographer in 1891 (Sprague Family Archives).

Sprague's sense of history and his references to the influence of the Civil War, particularly on his Republican political allegiance, may well be traced to an upbringing by a Union widow. Lucy Sprague subsequently remarried and lived into her second century, long enough to entertain a 1940 visit from her grandson, now the governor of Oregon.[8]

Young Arthur worked in the family feed store, and at least once rode a cattle car to Chicago, feeding the stock. Across the street was the weekly *Columbus Safeguard* newspaper office, and the boy would visit to watch the paper being printed; as a young man he worked briefly for the newspaper, and possibly for its successor, the *Columbus Gazette*.[9]

Nearly all of the 12,859 citizens of Louisa County in 1900 were native-born whites; only 2,170 had been born outside the United States, and the county had only eight Blacks, a single Chinese and no Indians. Most of the foreign-born were from Germany, Wales or Ireland. Columbus Junction, where C. A. Sprague had his grain elevator, was the largest settlement in the county; in 1900, when Arthur was thirteen years old, the town had 1,099 residents.[10]

The Spragues were active in the local Presbyterian church, and Arthur's older sister Mazie married a Presbyterian minister, Archibald Graham. The Presbyterianism lasted Arthur's lifetime and, although there is no indication he considered joining the ministry, he was active in the church and in statewide ecumenical work. His father, active in public affairs, was a Republican who later supported what was known as "the Iowa idea," a branch of the Wisconsin progressivism of Robert LaFollette.[11]

Family Republicanism was strengthened when Arthur enrolled at Monmouth College, on the edge of Illinois' Lincoln country. "It's true that one who lives in central Illinois and has any inclination toward history is pretty well steeped in Lincoln lore," Sprague told an interviewer late in his life.[12]

Monmouth College was a place for Sprague to pursue his interest in history and politics, and engage for the first time in journalism. He had been active in debate and theater at Columbus Junction, where he was one of five graduates in 1904; he was one of two who took the "Latin course" instead of the "English course" of study, and he delivered the class oration.

Arthur's college career was abruptly interrupted after two years, when financial problems at home forced him to drop out and teach school in Ainsworth, Iowa. Sprague, in what he later described as "my first real job—an interlude in my college course," taught all three high school grades and ran the four-room school in an old brick building.[13] He was apparently well liked, for the school board and town leaders wrote letters of support when he applied for a Rhodes Scholarship in 1908. It was a brash undertaking for a young man from a small college, lacking even his bachelor's degree and competing against a large state university and the prestigious University of Chicago. Arthur Sprague was one of twelve Illinois candidates for the Rhodes in 1908 and, although he failed in his bid, he did marshal an impressive body of support, including the entire Monmouth College Class of 1908. He returned to Monmouth and completed his degree in 1910, taking with him a "First Class" teaching certificate.

At Monmouth, Sprague took a heavy load of classes in Greek and Latin, including the study of Cicero, Virgil and Horace; and won honors in debate and declamation. He played on the Monmouth varsity football team, which won the Illinois collegiate title in 1905. "He was somewhat handicapped by his lack of weight," wrote O. C. Bell, athletic director, in a letter to the Rhodes committee, "but he made up for this by sincerity and hard work to such an extent that he was chosen for the position over his more bulky rivals." In 1909, Arthur secured a first-team position at right guard, but broke his leg in the team's third game.[14]

A supportive family awaited the young graduate back in Iowa, and plenty of opportunities to use his new teaching certificate, but he was still considering journalism. The summer after his graduation he worked as a reporter for the Monmouth *Review*, at $12 a week. Competitive juices were already flowing. "Got a good scoop today on the Atlas. We beat them on news right along," he wrote on one occasion. On another he recorded a bit of excitement: "I saw an aeroplane *fail* to fly at Monmouth in the afternoon, but saw it run on the ground—the first I have ever seen."[15]

If he had known in 1910 that his father would live only two more years, Arthur might have remained in the heartland. But he elected to follow his older brother, Wyatt, to Waitsburg, another farming area but on the frontier in southeastern Washington state. Wyatt Sprague had been teaching in the Presbyterian Waitsburg Academy, but by 1910 it had been sold to the public school district and Wyatt was ready to leave, to pursue banking in Seattle. Before he left, he wrote Arthur to tell him of a position in the public school system.

When Charles Arthur Sprague arrived in 1910 to take up duties as superintendent of schools, Waitsburg had a population of 1,237 people, second only to Walla Walla in Walla Walla County. Waitsburg had been a rest stop for Lewis and Clark; it was a spot known to the Nez Perce and the Whitman missionary families. It was on two branch rail lines, and boasted a flour mill, two banks, an opera house and hotel, an electric light plant and several stores, a weekly newspaper and four Protestant churches. With its tree-lined streets it was a green oasis quite attractive to visitors.[16]

The high school had six teachers, including Superintendent Sprague; the grade school had seven, including Principal Blanche Chamberlain. In a letter to Wyatt, Arthur described busy days and reported that he could do more work by eating less and keeping the temperature in his room at 62 degrees. He took an immediate interest in politics and the progressive movement, confiding to his diary after the 1910 elections that the Democratic landslide was "a popular rebuke of Republican reactionaries such as (House Speaker Joe) Cannon. The Progressive doctrine is not defeated."[17] Soon Sprague was caught up in the effort to elect Theodore Roosevelt on a Progressive ticket in 1912.

Sprague went without breakfast one April day in 1911 in order to arrive at a Spokane auditorium in time to get a good seat: "I heard T.R. in Spokane. He was great. I enjoyed the man, his personality and his address." Roosevelt met with Sprague's group of teachers and, a year later, Sprague enlisted as a soldier in T.R.'s army of reformers.[18]

Sprague also continued to entertain thoughts of newspapering, and he spent the summer of 1911 reporting for a newspaper in Aberdeen on the Washington coast. The town was dominated by forest and sea, and Sprague rode a logging train deep into the woods and sailed on a small ship to a new whaling plant at nearby Acosta. It was an experience he never forgot:

"I heard T.R. in Spokane. He was great. I enjoyed the man, his personality and his address." Sprague was probably in this audience, as Theodore Roosevelt took his Progressive campaign to Spokane in April 1911; the young schoolmaster became a T.R. disciple, and was deeply influence by the progressive movement (Spokane *Spokesman-Review*).

> *A small vessel made the rounds of harbor points. When it put into the small bay fronting the whaling station, the passengers quickly became aware of its presence. Summer tourists who had planned to stop off to see the attraction stayed aboard the boat, handkerchiefs to noses, eager for the captain to get the ship underway again. Having worked a good many summers candling eggs in Iowa, I was accustomed to high-voltage odors, so I debarked and spent most of the day around the plant.*[19]

Aberdeen was a rough-and-tumble town, considerably more so than the Iowa county seat where Sprague had been raised. One of his first stories was a colorful account of a fracas involving Wobblies, socialists and sailors on shore leave:

> *Given several score of jackies with shore leave till morning, add socialists, I.W. W.'s and a crowd of stimulating bystanders, lubricate well with "red eye and tarantula juice," and the mixture is one that is bound to effervesce. That was the combination and such was the result Friday evening on the down*

> *town streets. The whole affair bore in fact a metropolitan air that would do justice to Seattle or Frisco when the floating population is set adrift with a liquid cargo . . .*[20]

Back in Waitsburg, Sprague had found friends, including a Presbyterian minister who was a Union Seminary graduate and reader of Maeterlinck, Chesterton, and Shaw. Then there was his counterpart in education: "I have a good Tilacum [sic] in Miss Chamberlain," he wrote Wyatt. "She is principal of the other building and quite capable. We have some interesting and pleasant discussions."[21]

The Tillicum Club took its name from a Chinook word denoting friendship; as the school year progressed romance blossomed. Blanche was six years older than Sprague; at age 31 she was a handsome woman of imposing intellect, but nearing the age of becoming an "old maid school teacher." The age difference would have been an item of gossip in a small town, and in fact Blanche's age was kept secret for her entire life. Even her 1976 obituaries list her as five years younger than her actual age.[22]

Charles Arthur Sprague and Blanche Chamberlain were married on August 8, 1912 in Walla Walla, where her mother and stepfather lived. They honeymooned at Mount Rainier, and the bridegroom climbed the mountain, the first of several Cascade peaks he scaled in his lifetime. He noted the occasion fifty years later:

Waitsburg school teachers Blanche Chamberlain and Charles A. Sprague, about the time of their 1912 marriage (Sprague Family Archives).

> *There was no hotel in Paradise Park, only Reese's tent camp on a point not far from the present hotel. The inn was at Longmire's. Motor cars were allowed as far as the inn; horse-drawn vehicles carried freight and passengers from the inn to the tent-camp. For going-away (Blanche) had a lovely blue suit and wore a matching blue and white hat—I thought the outfit was charming then, and it is still so in memory. Its beauty, though, was short-lived. From Ashford to the inn we rode in an early-day motor stage, like an old-fashioned hack; unlike the surrey in "Oklahoma" it had no "fringe"—not even a canopy.*
>
> *After we got started the skies opened, evidently to give our marriage a christening. We had no umbrella. A man seated on the other side of (Blanche) did, and the water from his umbrella dripped into her hat with its upturned brim. Alas for wedding finery. The hat was ruined; the suit's white lining all stained—later it was traded to an Indian woman for a woven basket.*[23]

The bridegroom, perhaps responding to some advice from his older brother, observed that, "To me, the sex life is a function and I have no sympathy with those who make it a passion. We are here in the mountains for one purpose—to get a rest."[24] From the beginning, Blanche was Sprague's sounding board on all matters, and probably one of the very few people with whom he could really unwind. The couple did not often display affection, their children recalled, but there was a closeness and unity that left no doubt of their love.

Blanche Chamberlain, age 7, with parents John and Martha Chamberlain (Sprague Family Archives).

Blanche Chamberlain's religious roots were also deeply planted. She was born July 16, 1881, in the ranching country of northeast Oregon, where her father, John Byron Chamberlain, was a circuit-riding Methodist minister who had been a Yankee sea captain and whaler, making several trips around the world before he was ordained to the ministry.

John Chamberlain traced his roots to Edward Fuller, one of the passengers on the Mayflower; both Fuller and his wife died within a year of arrival at Plymouth Rock, but one of their descendants married a Chamberlain. For many generations, the family lived in New England. From Blanche's side of the family came two names that became familiar to readers of Sprague's newspaper columns: Mehitabel became Blanche's nickname, after a descendant of Edward Fuller; and the Spragues' river cabin in the Oregon Cascades was named Thetford, after the Chamberlain family farm in Vermont.[25]

The seafaring John Byron Chamberlain was born in 1826 in Rochester, New York and he married Martha Jane Gerking in 1879 in the ranching and farming country of Umatilla County, Oregon.[26]

John Chamberlain had a reputation as a fiery preacher. He toured the back country with a horse and buggy, staying away from the family home at Dayton, Washington, for weeks at a time to minister to the lonely farms and ranches. Blanche recalled a trip she had taken with her father, during which they crossed the Columbia River two or three times.[27] John Chamberlain died in Enterprise, Oregon, in 1905, making one of those lonely trips to officiate at a funeral.[28]

Martha Gerking Chamberlain was left a widow with a daughter newly graduated from high school and very little financial support. She moved to Waitsburg, Washington, to be near her sister. Blanche went to Pullman to begin school at Washington State College, and in her absence her mother renewed an old acquaintance with a childhood sweetheart, Louis Schmuck, who had become a prosperous farmer in Umatilla County. Martha Chamberlain and Louis Schmuck were married in September 1907, a marriage that was at first jarring to Blanche but later proved a blessing in many ways. She recalled late in her life: "It took me a year to be reconciled to the change in our family, but it became a very happy relationship. . . . My stepfather, Mr. Schmuck, was a wonderful man and did many things for me that my father could not have done because my father did not have the means."[29]

Schmuck, born in the Alsace-Lorraine region, was a Catholic, "which in my family was really something!" recalled Sprague's daughter Martha. She remembers the elderly farmer as possessing "an enormous hearing aid—a horn," and "drinking Postum noisily" at breakfast.[30]

Blanche was no longer teaching when the newlyweds returned to a swirl of activity in Waitsburg, but politics was heating up, and Sprague was quickly caught up in the excitement of Theodore Roosevelt's Progressive candidacy for president. Sprague took a leading role in the local campaign, speaking at rallies and plunging into the activity with enthusiasm.

October was a rainy month in Walla Walla County in 1912, but there was political excitement in the air, as the Progressive Party mounted its challenge. A Young Men's Progressive Club was formed, with Sprague as first vice president. At the Walla Walla organizational dinner, he shared the podium with U. S. Senator Miles Poindexter. Sprague was one of three speakers quoted, in addition to the senator:

> *The Democrats are attempting to destroy the big money interests and corporations of the country. What we want to do is to control them, not to destroy them. The problem before us is the regulation of wealth. The money of the country is at the present time in the hands of a very few. The social fabric which allows this is entirely wrong. It is the aim of the progressive party to destroy all this. . . . Today we are fighting for economical and social independence. We want human rights above property rights.*[31]

That philosophy, to be repeated in later editorials and columns, placed Sprague in the category of a Progressive who sought reform and fairness, but shunned socialism or other more radical cures for the nation's ills. T.R. did reasonably well in Waitsburg, polling 145 votes, compared to 190 for Democrat Woodrow Wilson, and 90 for Republican President William Howard Taft.[32] Statewide, Roosevelt won Washington's seven electoral votes.

Blanche's mother with her second husband, prosperous wheat farmer Louis Schmuck, about 1907 (Sprague Family Archives).

By 1924, as Senator Robert LaFollette mounted a last campaign for the presidency on a Progressive ticket, Sprague was back in the Republican camp. Although his father had been a follower of LaFollette a quarter-century before, Sprague scorned the Wisconsin senator for sitting out the 1912 Teddy Roosevelt campaign, while claiming his own bona fides in that crusade. His comments came in an editorial reply to a roasting of Republican candidates by Knute Hill, the Democratic candidate for Congress:

> *Mr. Hill says he is proud of being a radical. I am proud of being a liberal. I began politics as a liberal, an anti-machine republican. I continue to that faith. In 1922 [sic] I stood at Armageddon and "battled with Theodore Roosevelt for the Lord." And where then was Bob LaFollette? We soldiers of Progress in that day, with a glorious cause and a more glorious leader, looked all around for Fighting Bob of Wisconsin. Where was he? Why, he was skulking in his tent. He announced that he had always been a republican and would remain a republican. Who then was reactionary?*[33]

In many ways, the 25-year-old Sprague fit the profile of progressive activists in Washington state, men and women of the middle class rather than the underprivileged and more radical elements that supported Populism or Democrat William Jennings Bryan. Progressivism drew heavily upon the native-born, the moderately prosperous, and the better-educated elements of the state. The overwhelmingly middle-class nature of progressive politics meant the movement was dominated by men like Sprague, from native-born Protestant stock, often from New England ancestors and well educated, financially secure, with professional or business status in the community. Many were relatively new to the state, and were young.[34]

When most of the Progressives of 1912 moved back under the Republican tent, Sprague moved with them and stayed, although he was part of a Roosevelt Memorial Association committee in 1919.[35] But the 1912 campaign had for Sprague more than the temporary excitement of an election. It opened a new career vista.

In that same election, Josephine Preston was elected state school superintendent, the first woman ever elected to Washington statewide office. County superintendent for nine years in Walla Walla County, Preston invited Sprague to join her in Olympia, and the newlyweds packed up their limited belongings in January 1913. The Waitsburg *Times* noted that Sprague's service had been "very successful and satisfying."[36]

The state position offered an entirely new experience for the Spragues, and the prospect of living in a larger city. For Blanche, "One of the exciting things of going to Olympia was my stepfather giving us a check for 500 dollars and telling us to buy some furniture."[37] The young couple had also come into an inheritance with the death in 1911 of Charles Allen Sprague. The feed, seed and elevator business had been sold and the estate divided among the widow (C.A. Sprague had remarried) and three children, Wyatt, Charles, and Mazie Sprague Graham. Charles' portion came to some $3,966, a substantial amount in 1912 when the estate had been settled, and it helped the young couple build a house in Olympia, and eventually purchase a country weekly newspaper.[38]

Their enthusiasm was short-lived as it became apparent that Sprague and his new boss were badly matched. Preston, ambitious in school politics, was building an image for herself, using state funds for travel and other political necessities. Matters came to a head in June 1915 and, in a letter to Wyatt, Sprague noted that he "drank the hemlock" and had resigned, apparently to avoid dismissal. He had sided with office workers against the superintendent, and two colleagues apparently resigned with him.[39]

The internal battle, in which Sprague was no match for the superintendent's experience, apparently centered on office procedures, management style, and the use of public funds. In 1916, when Preston sought re-election, Sprague was involved in a campaign to defeat her, and probably wrote a circular criticizing her administration. Sprague asked the state auditor to examine Preston's office, receiving in reply a brisk note signed by a deputy, commenting that "charges of superficiality, lack of thoroughness and of politics are not justified by the facts."[40] Sprague accused Preston of "abusive treatment of women subordinates . . . a treatment which, in my judgment, was nothing short of cruel and inhuman, a treatment that was a disgrace to the womanhood of the state of Washington." He went on to accuse Preston of unauthorized travel using public funds, of administrative mismanagement and failure to come up with any educational initiatives.[41] It was a harsh attack, very much out of character with Sprague's usual restrained manner, and an indication of how bitter the split had been. But it was in vain, and Preston was re-elected, eventually serving three terms.[42] Preston served until 1928, and a history of Washington public education written 45 years later described her: "A large, positive person, with an approach to people and problems bordering on the puritanical, she was known (behind her back, to be sure) among staff members as the Duchess." She was also a consummate politician, the biographer continued, who "endeared herself to multitudes of parents and children by sending personal letters of congratulation, signed in her own handwriting, to every child promoted from eighth grade."[43]

It was the last time Sprague worked for someone else, and it was the end of his career in education. The fight with Preston had left him disillusioned and frustrated. Blanche recalled:

> *I realized Arthur was very unhappy. He had no opportunity to show any of the ability which he possessed and he resigned his position without any kind of a job, but set out with a meager sum of money. At that time his salary was $1800 a year. That was what we lived on, but we had saved some. He took our savings and set out to find a newspaper.*
>
> *He felt the greatest outlook for himself was to edit a newspaper. In the interval, his father had died, and he came into a small estate, not many hundred dollars, but we had been frugal and saved that, and after traveling through Washington and visiting the various papers which were in our reach to buy, he came home and told me about a possibility of a paper that we could buy at Ritzville for $5000, with $2500 down. We didn't have quite $2500, but again my stepfather came to our help and said, "I will do what I can," and he gave us the money to make up the amount. Arthur went back to Ritzville and bargained and bought the weekly county paper.*[44]

Sprague was enthusiastic, writing his brother that the Ritzville plant was worth easily $10,000 and he felt he could clear from $3,000 to $5,000 a year. Sprague was also encouraged by former Governor Marion Hay, a Republican during whose term (1909-13) most of Washington's major progressive legislation was passed. Hay advised, "Don't you sleep on it," and Sprague closed the deal the following day. Sprague wrote his brother, "The town is in the wheat region, is dusty and dry in summer, but aside from a strong foreign element the people seem of a fine class."[45]

The "strong foreign element" was one of the largest immigrant communities in the Northwest. Most were German-Russians, the "Volga Germans" who began moving into Washington's wheat country in 1883. The first party of eighteen German-Russian settlers came by wagon train from Nebraska, with Ritzville as their final stop in a 120-year odyssey across three nations and the American continent. They were descendants of farmers who had fled the Palatinate region along both sides of the Rhine from Cologne to Mannheim, after the Seven Years War ended in 1763. Lured by Catherine II's promise of free land and exemption from taxation and military service, a large colony of Germans moved to the

Volga region of Russia. A century later, as new Russian governments withdrew the exemptions from taxation and military service, the German-Russians began moving to America. Later in the century they were joined by other German-Russians from the Black Sea region, and finally by a colony of German Mennonites, many also from Russia.[46]

Ritzville's German-speaking community supported Lutheran, Methodist, Congregational and Mennonite congregations, and the German language was offered in the public schools and spoken in many businesses. The 1910 Federal Census reported 3,403 foreign-born or second-generation Germans and Russians in Adams County, nearly a third of the county's population of 10,920. The statewide average was 7.3 percent and no other county had more than 18 percent foreign stock of German and/or Russian heritage.[47]

Sprague made his accommodations with the large Germanic population, did business with them and claimed some as friends, but there were in fact two communities in Adams County: the Volga Germans and a native-born Anglophile community.

Wheat dominated Ritzville; merchants sold on credit, and received payment when the crop was harvested, the price sometimes dictating intense negotiations for credit extensions. J. C. Penney came into Ritzville during Sprague's tenure, creating somewhat of a revolution by selling its goods for cash.[48]

Sprague quickly picked up job printing as well as advertising. The community was on a main railroad line and it was a county seat. That meant a healthy job-printing market, and Sprague moved quickly to assure himself of capable printing help. He learned the machinery himself, but was never skillful at linotype or press, although he ran both in a pinch. His family recalled one emergency when their father caught his hand in the linotype one evening and had to call for help to get free; the middle finger on his right hand was always a little distorted as a result of the accident.[49] Early in his tenure, Sprague hired Claude Talmadge as lead printer, and Talmadge remained with him in Ritzville and Salem until his retirement. Blanche frequently helped with the press runs and in the office.

Sprague's first front page included five major headlined stories, all of local origin, and another eleven short articles under single-line headlines. The major stories announced the county's tax levy, completion of a new grain warehouse, residential building in the county, the Commercial Club's efforts to improve a highway, and a long story on a "dragnet" by county lawmen that brought in several men accused of illegal gambling and bootlegging. Inside, the single editorial discussed and praised a new, modernized budgeting system that accompanied the county's tax levy.

The approach was similar to that of subsequent issues of the *Journal-Times,* as the newspaper was known; Sprague clearly intended to publish a *news*paper. Although he later departed from his promise to be nonpartisan, and advanced Republican causes and candidates editorially and at times in the news columns, Sprague never abandoned his pledge to emphasize local news and to do so in a professional manner.

It was not an easy task. Printers and typesetters were often hard to attract to rural areas; Sprague did not have a car until 1918, so he gathered news afoot and by rail, as the small towns in Adams County were on a rail line. His daughter recalled him walking two miles into the country when a prominent farmer died, to gather details for the obituary. Sprague was raised in the pre-automobile age and knew how to ride a horse, but the family had none in Ritzville.[50]

Sprague's first car was a Liberty 6, an open car with eisenglass windows. On a trip to Walla Walla, the Spragues encountered freezing sleet and spread castor oil on the windshield to try to keep it from freezing solid.[51]

The *Journal-Times* never had a circulation above 1200, and in a county of only 10,920 people it competed with three other English-language newspapers and one German-language paper. But it was easily the largest and most important of the Adams County papers, it served the county seat's business and professional community, and as Sprague matured and became part of the civic establishment it increasingly became a voice for Adams County.

At the end of his first month, Sprague had cleared $700. He weathered the threat of a rival paper started by B. A. Leddy, the man who had sold the paper to him; Leddy could not attract advertising or subscribers, and his paper died after a few issues. The Spragues earned a steady profit from the newspaper and from job printing, and in 1916 they built a new plant across from the Ritzville train depot, which still functions as a newspaper plant today.[52]

The family was growing as well. Martha was born in 1915 and Wallace in 1918. The children grew up in a handsome Victorian house on Broadway, one of the nicest residential streets in Ritzville. They also spent time at the printing plant, and Martha later recalled their father's roll top desk, "littered with papers and correspondence, with more falling out of the pigeon-holes." For the children, the treat came in the smelly back shop, reeking of ink and melting lead:

> *There were two linotype machines, operated by one of the two printers—paid $25 per week! The paper cutter was great, for sometimes they would let one of us sit on the wheel as they turned it to tighten down the paper before lowering the blade to cut it.*

> *There was a low stand that just fitted a tray of type, with a gooey ink roller nearby, and we were sometimes allowed to take big block letters and make proofs of them, messy but not dangerous. There were tall chests with shallow drawers containing type to be hand-set, and on the other side of the room a mailing table. My father would go to the post office to get the mailing sacks and after the weekly printing fill these sacks for distribution to our own and the surrounding towns—people got their mail in boxes at the post office.*[53]

Sprague was putting his Iowa background to good use. From his father he had learned basic business practices and the language of grain and farming. The *Journal-Times* followed wheat prices, and remarked on the planting patterns of the county's farmers. Sprague himself bought a quarter-section of land for about $3,000, and held it until 1941, selling at the same price.[54]

Sprague also invested in a printing plant in Pasco and became a minority stockholder and director in the Ritzville State Bank, organized in 1921. He maintained his directorship in the bank through the Depression, as it survived the wave of closures.[55]

Wearing the multiple hats of editor, town booster, and landowner, Sprague involved himself in the efforts to bring irrigation to the Columbia Basin, but wound up on the losing side, backing a gravity-flow scheme known as the Pend Oreille Plan, from the name of the Idaho river where the flow would originate. He sided with entrepreneurs in the Spokane area, including Washington Water Power Company and the *Spokesman-Review*, against a group favoring a pumping system at Grand Coulee. The latter organization was spearheaded by dry-land farmers around Ephrata and promoted by engineer-publicist James O'Sullivan and the irrepressible *Wenatchee World* editor, Rufus Woods. Both plans were somewhat outrageous but backers became zealots and competition was intense. Adams County, including Sprague's land near Lind, stood to benefit more from the gravity flow idea, and Sprague supported it in several editorials and gave the promoters generous news coverage. The "pumpers" won in Congress when President Franklin D. Roosevelt sided with them in 1933.[56]

Massive engineering and reclamation schemes were part of the progressive agenda. Progressives generally had an optimistic outlook on life, and were vulnerable to appeals to patriotism and national pride. Sprague was no exception, and as the nation moved toward involvement in the European war, he was swept up in the emotions of the time.

Ritzville, with the largest Germanic community in the state, was torn. German families with sons in the Army were accused of "slacking" at home by failure to purchase their quota of war bonds; a pool hall argument brought criminal conviction against a German man who had held political office in the county for years; churches dropped the use of German, although older parishioners spoke little English. Everywhere, forces of patriotism clashed with cultural heritage and sometimes with common sense. Trying to establish himself with a clientele of advertisers and readers divided in their heritage and sometimes their loyalty, Sprague felt pressure from all sides.

The family attended an English-language Methodist church, and the children began their schooling in a public school where divisions of ethnicity mirrored those of the community. Martha recalled German youngsters ("they ate sunflower seeds") in her classes, but felt a social division in the school and community during World War I. She did not learn German in school—it was taught at the high school level only—and her father knew only a few phrases of the language. But the Spragues had German business associates and acquaintances, and some of these friendships continued throughout their lives.[57]

The family of Charles and Blanche Sprague about 1922, when Martha was 7 and Wallace 4 (Oregon Historical Society 98548).

By the time of U.S. entry into the war in April 1917, Sprague had moved into the ranks of community leadership despite his youth and relatively recent arrival in the community. Sprague's politics were compatible with feeling in Adams County, where a number of veterans of the Progressive campaign of 1912 lived. He was actively engaged in Republican politics from the outset; in 1916 he was named Republican state committeeman for Adams County.[58]

As 1916 unfolded, Sprague wrote occasionally of the war, but carefully avoided the tension building between the English and German elements of his community. He urged (June 1 and June 29) an end to discrimination against colored regiments in the Army, and agonized (July 27) over the issue of universal military service, his skepticism producing no recommendations.

President Wilson's declaration of a break in diplomatic relations with Germany occasioned Sprague's first mention of the tensions within the Ritzville community. On February 8, 1917, he called on the community for reason:

> *This is no time for jingoism, for invoking the resort to arms, and for the blare of militarism. Nevertheless, preparations for eventualities must proceed, for our peace is held by a delicate thread. Whatever be the outcome we must be ready for emergencies. If it be that we must enter the lists against Germany, we must be ready to do so, not in hate and not out of any national ambition, but because we feel that Germany's course will break down all the slowly built up restraints of international law and because we feel that military necessity is no justification for transgressing the rights of humanity.*
>
> *Particularly gratifying in this juncture has been the attitude taken by Americans of German birth and by the German-American papers. There is now no doubt, if indeed there ever was, that the Americans of German birth or descent will support the government of their adoption. We have every sympathy for the German-Americans, for the rupture involves a strain upon two loyalties, one to the land of their blood and race, the other to the land of their homes, their adoption, their children."*[59]

Sprague's reference to German American newspapers was to Ritzville's *der Beobachter*, which was widely read by the older generation of immigrants. Published from 1911 to 1918, with an estimated circulation of 825, it was the second German-language paper in the community; the

Washington Herold was published from 1906 to 1912. When World War I began in 1914, Washington state had thirteen German-language newspapers; only five survived the war.[60]

Despite the competition, Sprague refrained from any criticism of his rival, even in his frequent letters to Wyatt Sprague. And when, on the eve of U.S. entry into the war, *der Beobachter* published an editorial urging its readers to support the cause, Sprague reprinted the editorial in its entirety. It concluded:

> *The German-Americans who are citizens of this country must be loyal to America under all circumstances. Whether or not they approve of this war is of no consequence; they have sworn allegiance to the Stars and the Stripes and they owe it to their German ancestors, to their fellow-citizens and to themselves to strictly live up to their oath.*
>
> *Men and women of German extraction enjoy the reputation of being law-abiding and well disciplined citizens. The present predicament affords them an opportunity to prove that they are desirable citizens of the highest type, and, no doubt, they will do so.*

Sprague's own sentiments were reflected in his introduction to the editorial of his counterpart, in which he expressed pleasure at d*er Beobachter's* comments, but warned that native-born Americans "will not tolerate acts or words of disloyalty on the part of any Americans, and will insist that all aliens refrain from any words or acts of hostility to the United States."[61]

In the same edition of the *Journal-Times,* the tension building in the community could be seen in an advertisement for the German-American State Bank, which read:

> **Secrecy**
>
> *Our customer's relations with us are held in complete confidence. The amount of money you have on deposit with us—your business relations with us—are never disclosed to any one. Any person can secure information about OUR affairs, but when you carry your money here no one can obtain information about YOUR affairs.*
>
> *Your money and your business with us are both safe.*
>
> *German-American State Bank*
>
> *Ritzville, Washington*

The bank's security concern was but a small symbol of a larger phenomenon sweeping the nation, that of a buildup of hatred against anything German. It was a phobia that caused particular tension in Germanic communities such as Ritzville. For an editor trying to please readers, advertisers, public opinion and not least his own conscience, it was a difficult time. Upon Congress' declaration of war, Sprague addressed his German American neighbors directly, again extending both a warning and a hand of sympathy.[62]

Editorially, Sprague then withdrew from the field for several months, but his involvement in the war effort increased. Although at age thirty he was subject to the draft, as a young father he was covered by the dependency exemption, and he carried a Class 4 draft card for those with spouses and children. Sprague drilled with the community's young men, and was a member of a Committee for the National Defense, appointed in March 1917 to raise an infantry regiment if that should be requested (it was not).[63] Years later he recalled the young men going off to war:

> *They came through at night, train after train, solid Pullmans with blinds pulled down. We could hear them thundering in, pausing perhaps for water for the engine; perhaps not, just thundering on into the night. And we knew the 91st division was being moved from Camp Lewis across the country, thence across the water to the western battlefront. Sometimes it was daytime when the trains came through all loaded with young, khaki-clad soldiers, mere boys many of them, headed for great adventure. There might be chalk writing on the coaches: "Powder River"; or "Hang the Kaiser." Day time or night time, at intervals, the troops went through. Then, after harrowing months the troop trains came back; but some of those who went never returned.*[64]

Sprague's instincts appeared to be torn between the jingoism he had deplored and the intellectual approach with which he was normally more comfortable. As the war effort picked up speed, the contradiction was shown in separate editorials appearing on June 7. In "The lunatic fringe" Sprague resorted to a brand of name-calling and guilt-by-association seldom seen on his pages:

> *The lunatic fringe is the name applied to the radicals who make up the advance guard of political progressivism. To be a member one must be a college graduate with a bad case of yellow jaundice. The officers have to be sociologists or college professors, who have shown skill in throwing chills up and down the spine of the*

plodding middle classes. All they know about labor they read in a book. They haven't guts enough to be socialists. But whenever they get a chance they line up with the socialists, I. W. W.s, anarchists, and against government, employers, newspapers, churches, in fact everything that has been running for over two or three years.[65]

This outburst ran adjacent to an editorial, "The democratic crisis," in which Sprague worried about the very sort of jingoism in which he had just engaged: "It is America's opportunity to show that a Democracy can wage swift hard and successful war, without reducing the Bill of Rights to a 'scrap of paper,' and so abolishing freedom of speech, of assemblage and the press that the very shibboleth of the war becomes a hollow mockery." It was as if the editorials had been written by different people.

As the summer continued, Sprague's editorial voice became more strident, even as he attempted in his news columns to support the German American community. In coverage of a regional German Congregational Church meeting, he noted that the Zion church "was beautifully decorated in the Stars and Stripes." And a regional conference of the German Methodist Episcopal Church was given the lead position on the front page of August 23.[66] When one of his country correspondents slipped one of the ubiquitous German atrocity stories into a column, Sprague promptly retracted the item and apologized for the report.[67]

As with many progressives, the pressures of war were breaking down Sprague's equanimity in regard to opponents of American war policy. The war, noted Richard Hofstadter, had been justified in progressive rhetoric and the nationalistic jingoism of Theodore Roosevelt and others who saw the war as one to save democracy in Europe.[68] Justified as a moral crusade, the war effort engulfed Americans of progressive bent, and they accepted tactics of coercion and intimidation.

Sprague took a sharp turn toward intolerance in early 1918 when the Patriotic League chapter in Ritzville was first organized. The League became the leading edge of Adams County's efforts to enforce conformity, set and enforce quotas for the purchase of Liberty bonds, and organize patriotic displays.

At the League's organizational meeting on January 10, Sprague was temporary secretary and one of several speakers. Some 175 people joined at that first session, and the League's importance was underscored by the early closure of businesses and pool halls. The League's pressure point was Liberty bonds, and in his report Sprague described the approach the effort would take: "Mr. Lovell . . . said he could name a hundred people around Ritzville worth $10,000 or more who had only taken out $100 bonds or similar small amounts."[69] It did not take a great deal of imagination for League boosters to target the county's prosperous Germanic community. Describing the campaigns later in his *History of Adams County in the World War,* Sprague said of the Patriotic League pressure:

> *The property holdings of each individual were ascertained from county records, a fixed percentage of this was taken as the allotment for bonds, and the individual notified by mail of what he was expected to purchase. . . No subscription was accepted for less than the allotment unless a person appeared before a 'grievance committee' and was granted a reduction. At the end of the drive a 'slacker list' was published with the names of those failing to buy their quota of bonds.*[70]

The county subscribed $1,346,050 in Liberty bonds, with another $334,150 in postwar bonds in 1919.[71] The Spragues purchased bonds in at least the Second, Third and Fourth drives, and in 1920 still held at least $1,750 in Liberty bonds.[72] Sprague commented to Wyatt at war's end that, "It took hard plugging here because crop conditions were so bad the people didn't have the money. I was out soliciting for several days and helped land a few of the big ones."[73]

Although the town was deeply divided along ethnic lines during World War I, patriotic parades were popular as the town's civic establishment rallied behind the war effort (Ritzville Public Library, Bert M. Kendrick collection).

As important as Sprague's canvassing and his speeches to establish Patriotic Leagues in other Adams County towns was his willingness to publish lists of "slackers" who did not yield to pressure to purchase bonds, or even to sign a Patriotic League pledge and join the association.[74] The latter was announced in a front page box in the *Journal-Times* on March 7 and it typified the type of pressure that was becoming increasingly common as the war deepened:

NOTICE

It is the wish of the Ritzville Patriotic league that all persons who have received a post card containing the league pledge, sign and return the pledge within ten days from the publication of this request. The executive committee of the league wishes this list to be completed, that publication may be made March 21, 1918 of the membership roster and also a list of those who have been invited, by card, to become members of the league and have neglected or refused to do so.

C.H. Spaulding,
President Ritzville Patriotic League.

The tactics were a thinly veiled form of vigilantism; potential offenders were not given a list of proscribed activity and forms of punishment were equally vague. It was harassment, and in the threat to publish the names of offenders it pulled the newspaper and its editor squarely into the fray.

If Sprague had any misgivings about the campaign, he did not express them in letters to his brother, and certainly not in his editorial columns, which were silent on these incursions into the rights of his readers. On March 28, 1918, he published a letter from the League containing the names of over 220 Ritzville residents who had refused to sign the League's pledge. Predictably, the list was overwhelmingly made up of German names.

Then, on April 4, Sprague published his most strident editorial of the period, a direct attack on German Americans in the community who remained outside the war effort:

In this city on Monday a man, who had been run out of a neighboring city for peddling seditious literature, said: "I am a loyal American citizen and I have a perfect right to be pro-German if I want to be." There stands revealed the real pro-Germanism of many in this community and other communities. They claim to be "loyal" Americans, yet they are for the Kaiser

> *heart and soul. The only reason they do not become active is because they are afraid, though we sometimes wonder what they have to be afraid of. . . .*
>
> *How long is this thing going to keep up? Is America going forever to be a tolerant grandma to traitors and enemies? . . . When the death rolls come in the passions are going to rise. Then he who sneers at the flag and the cause will do so at his peril. We want no resort to violence or mob law. That would be a reversion to rank Prussianism, which we are fighting. But we do want loyalty and we do want action, in orderly ways, against pro-Germanism and anti-Americanism.*[75]

The editorial marked Sprague's total commitment to the war effort, as his news columns reported other pressures on the German American community. The German-American State Bank, one of the pioneer banks in the community, survived the war but was forced to shorten its name by dropping "German." Lutheran churches dropped German-language services and the teaching of German in Ritzville schools was curtailed.[76]

There was often irony in the news reports. Adams County's first soldier killed in action was Rudolph Stumpf, of apparent German heritage.[77] And in a celebrated case in the summer of 1918, a former pastor of the German Methodist Episcopal Church was arrested for allegedly hoarding six sacks of flour, and taken to Federal court in Spokane. The minister explained that he had never earned over $900 a year, and supporting a family of nine required buying in bulk. Not until the story's final paragraph did the report, reprinted from the Spokane *Spokesman-Review*, note that: "The minister broke down several times while he was addressing the court. He spoke feelingly of the trouble he had to support his family on the small salary and was deeply affected when he spoke of his *two sons in the army and the other one who is soon to go*." (author's emphasis)[78]

As the war neared its end, the threat of publicity came down for a second time on those resisting the Patriotic League. A full-page advertisement, purchased by "Twenty-four citizens who have purchased their Fourth Liberty Loan Bonds," listed some seventy "slackers" who had failed to "respond to the call of their government in the present crisis" by the purchase of bonds. Included was the minister of the German Methodist Church, and one farmer described as "owner of 2000 acres of Adams County land clear of encumbrance." The names of the ad's sponsors were not listed.[79]

Sprague had carried out the objectives of the Patriotic League, not in his news columns but in a letter from the League and in a full-page advertisement. He did print, in a front-page article on October 31, the objection of two men to being placed on the "slacker" list.[80] But his editorial pen was either supportive of the League or silent as the pressure was applied.

Assessing the period later in his *History of Adams County in the World War,* Sprague took great care to note the contributions of the German American community, noting that in the 1914-1916 period "feelings inclined very largely according to the racial derivation of the people. Those of German origin sided with Germany, while the rest, mainly of English origin, favored the cause of the Allies. In February, 1917, however, it was patent to all that it was to be America's war, and former affiliations had to be disregarded in loyalty to the United States. Henceforth it was **our** war." (original emphasis)[81]

Indeed, the county had only one arrest and conviction under the sedition laws, a prominent German American naturalized citizen who expressed his opinions too freely in a local pool hall.[82] In his summation of the war, Sprague noted that "There were in this county virtually no resorts to violence either against person or property, though at times there were loose threats when provocations were acute. When one considers the large element in the county who are of foreign birth, and considers, too, the brilliant record made by the county in all war lines, it is highly gratifying to know that this was attained by the democratic methods of education and fair treatment and not by mob violence or physical intimidation. The county was blessed by having leaders of sane counsel, devoted to the cause and effective in personal appeal to the rank and file of the people."[83]

When compared to the travails of German Americans in many communities during the war, Ritzville's ethnic community had emerged relatively intact. Whether it was because the size of the Germanic community made it difficult to label it a "minority," or whether there were in fact "leaders of sane counsel," incidents of violence against people or property appear to have been rare.

Sprague's Adams County war history glossed over the strong emotions of the time, including his own jingoistic editorials. Three-quarters of a century later, talk of this era in Ritzville can still produce bitterness, and surviving residents recall German Americans being harassed or worse. W. Walters Miller, whose father was county attorney during the war, recalled a threat to lynch a German-speaking minister, and the loss of several businesses during the war. But histories of the county do not mention the divisions, and in a photographic collection of Adams County families the descendants of the Volga German and Anglophile communities proudly and equally offer photographs of stern pioneers dressed for their official portrait.[84]

Sprague later recalled the "intense patriotism," and with it the injustices, including pressure against teaching German language in the schools, and against people with German names. "This we believe is one of the sorriest chapters of the war, the boycott and pressure and worse against many Americans whose only offense was that they were born in Germany."[85] If he felt he had been one of those to over-react, it was not mentioned.

The nature of the progressive easily turned to an excess of nationalism, and even jingoism and nativism; more than one leading progressive turned with a vengeance against German-Americans, socialists and radical labor leaders.

Sprague was more moderate, but he did respond to appeals to his patriotism and, if not a nativist, he worried that Asian races could not become assimilated into American society, a common view of progressives. He supported the old "gentlemen's agreement" under which Japan limited emigration, because he didn't feel that Japanese "fit" in American society. But he opposed the 1924 Immigration Act passed by Congress and directed against the Japanese, because of the manner in which it was done, and predicted it would further alienate Japan and could lead to war.[86]

He could be unintentionally racist in the manner of the times, but he never used an overtly racist anecdote or joke and, when accused by some German-Russians of careless use of the term "bolshevik," he went to great lengths to explain his intent and defend himself against the charges.[87]

A serious threat throughout the Northwest was a revived Ku Klux Klan, which in 1922 helped convince Oregon voters to ban parochial schools and elect a strong KKK contingent to the Legislature. Klan organizers were in Ritzville in 1924, organizing first in a Christian church with ministers speaking, then drawing a thousand people to a fiery outdoor rally featuring white-robed speakers and a brilliant electric cross. Sprague editorialized strongly against the KKK on at least three occasions, commenting in particular on their efforts in Oregon, but he failed to specifically condemn the large 1924 Ritzville rally. The Klan did not establish itself in the county, however.[88]

On other issues of the time, his editorial page took a progressive stance. Sprague editorialized during this period for national women's suffrage, against the Immigration Law of 1916 and its literacy test, and in favor of Federal action to settle a railroad strike. He reprinted a *New Republic* call for nationalizing the railroads and, after declaration of war, he urged Federal operation of the railroads, "at least for the duration of the war."[89]

In his approach to the International Workers of the World, which was active in the state at the time, Sprague deplored the violence and the anti-religious tone of the Wobblies, but was one of the few editors of the region to also point to grievances driving the radicals. He commented in November 1916 on the Everett dock clash, which left six dead and forty injured as Wobblies met deputies and armed townsmen:

> *To our mind the tragedy at Everett is not in the loss of life, but in the collapse of our industrial system at too frequently recurring periods when controversy culminates in violence, and in the general failure to provide any system for settling rationally such disputes. . . .*
>
> *The deeper issues lie in the causes for the two bodies facing each other behind blue barrels of pistols, in the social and economic situation from which such violent groups as the I. W. W. effervesce . . .*
>
> *There may be provocation at times of acute contention, but in our judgment the way to finally suppress I. W. W.s and other agitators is by disarming them of basis for argument by democratizing the industrial order, exercising some patience, and refusing to be stampeded at the utterances of the three offensive letters: I. W. W.*[90]

Despite his fear of radicalism and his consistent opposition to the I.W.W., Sprague maintained the view that violent reaction was the wrong approach. Commenting on violence in Oklahoma, he wrote, "Taking I.W.W.s, human beings remember, out of Tulsa, beating them with lashes over bare backs and giving them a coat of tar and feathers is a helluva way to encourage the German people to set up a democracy."[91] The language was unusually blunt for Sprague, who throughout his life was rarely known to utter a word as profane as "helluva." Through the worst of the anti-Wobbly campaigns in Washington in 1917 and 1918, Sprague maintained a demeanor of stern disapproval of the I.W.W., but he did not join in the violent rhetoric seen in many newspapers at that time.

But as the war continued and patriotism became a national religion, Sprague was increasingly willing to sacrifice individual liberty for the common good. Free speech was not a priority of the progressives, and editors who spoke strongly for reform in other areas often ignored the issue of free speech for radicals or other outsiders. Because progressives had access to public platforms in their communities, the issue of free speech and press was not their major concern; their concentration was on the restoration of traditional values and the re-establishment of popular government, which they assumed would be controlled by people much like themselves. Thus the I.W.W.s and pacifists, the neutralists and pro-German elements, were outside the progressive concept of community. An editor like Sprague could be on the one hand progressive and on the other repressive of civil liberties; the positions, deemed contradictory by later generations, did not seem so at the time.[92]

Sprague's acceptance of violations of civil liberties may also be explained by his personal situation at the time. Sprague arrived in Ritzville, an established community dominated by older business and professional men, a few days short of his 28th birthday. He had both editorial and political ambitions, and these ambitions demanded that he blend into community leadership. His intellect and scholarship were respected, but he was also careful to maintain interest in crops and roads, civic festivals and church meetings.

This drive for acceptance and success may be seen as a factor in his efforts to maintain relations with the German American reader and advertiser, citing instances of their patriotism and loyalty, while at the same time joining the Patriotic League's cry against "slackers" in the war effort. He was walking a thin line, and attempting to emerge from the war as a community leader.

He was successful in that effort. By the time he left Ritzville in 1925, he had helped found a bank, had served in key positions in the city's business association and in the Republican party, and played an active role in his church. But Ritzville restricted his ambition, and his daughter Martha's allergies also called for a different climate.

In 1925 the family set off on a camping trip to Oregon and wound up buying part of a newspaper. Blanche recalled that "on one side of the car was a commissary where we carried the food and at night we sought out an auto park where we could spread our tent." Sprague learned that he could buy an interest in a newspaper at Corvallis, and within a week, the deal was consummated.[93]

The result was a one-third partnership in the Corvallis *Gazette-Times* from 1925 until 1929, but it was a relatively uneventful period, with Sprague relegated to running the business side of the small daily. He learned much that was valuable to his role as publisher, but he yearned for a newspaper of his own, most particularly for an editorial page of his own.

The *Gazette-Times* gave Sprague an introduction to Oregon journalism and invaluable business experience with a daily publication, and he supervised the building of a new newspaper plant. He hired his wife's cousin, Sam Walters, "a man who had been in the Klondike—he

Claude E. Ingalls, conservative Republican editor of the Corvallis Gazette-Times and Sprague's partner, was also a collector of movie star photographs (Cathy Ingalls).

wore a black derby hat," and sent Walters out to convince the farmers around Corvallis to subscribe. The Sprague children worked at times in the paper's bindery, folding and stuffing inserts for job printing, "until my mother would find out that some unsuitable adult with a gossipy tongue or risqué stories had been hired to help, and we were promptly recalled," Martha Sprague recalled.[94]

Sprague served a brief school board term, began making contacts in Oregon higher education, and forged a close friendship with Claude Ingalls, the conservative Republican who wrote the newspaper's editorials and owned one-third of the paper; the other third was in the hands of Myron K. Myers, who directed the small news department. Shut off from writing, Sprague longed to have his own editorial column again. He had always liked Salem because it combined politics with the agricultural base he knew so well. It was also the state's second-largest city, home of a small university and the sort of community where he wanted to raise his family. When the opportunity presented itself, Sprague was quick to move.

2

◆◆◆

Rescuing a Pioneer Salem Newspaper

Embarking from Ritzville on the 1925 camping trip that took his family to Oregon to search for a newspaper, Charles A. Sprague told his young family, "I don't want to move again except to heaven or to Salem!"[1] Restless in Corvallis, with business responsibilities but no outlet for his writing, Sprague kept a sharp eye on developments in Salem, where an aging publisher was losing circulation and advertising to an aggressive competitor.

After nearly two years of on-again, off-again talks, Sprague acquired a newspaper in Oregon's capital city in 1929. The timing could not have been worse. He had barely settled in Salem before the Stock Market crashed, the nation was thrown into the Depression, and advertising revenues took a dive.

Thrown into an awkward partnership with a man almost completely his opposite, buffeted by the economic storms of the era, Sprague was forced to draw on all the business acumen he had acquired in Ritzville and Corvallis just to keep the tottering newspaper on its feet. *The Oregon Statesman*, the state's second-oldest daily, was a poor second in its market all through the thirties, and the era was one of struggle to keep its doors open, even as the new publisher tried to make a mark as an editorial force.

By the time of his surprise entry into the race for governor of Oregon in 1938, Sprague had rescued the floundering morning newspaper and put it on its feet. But the story of *The Oregon Statesman* in the thirties is one of financial turmoil despite a growing reputation for local news coverage and editorial leadership. The *Statesman* was not one of the 706 daily papers closing their doors during the period from 1929 to 1949, as Depression and then world war demanded a heavy financial toll.[2] But at times Sprague was hard-pressed to avoid a forced sale or merger.

Sprague had begun preliminary discussions in 1927 with R. J. Hendricks, publisher of *The Oregon Statesman*, but the paper was not then for sale. In April 1928, Sprague renewed contact with Hendricks; a series of letters and personal meetings followed, and Hendricks provided Sprague with financial data concerning the newspaper. He valued the paper's equipment, including the presses and other printing machinery, at $151,673 and the building and land at another $65,000.[3]

The newspaper was the major element of The Statesman Publishing Co., an operation that in 1928 included three monthly publications and a commercial printing shop. By far the largest income line was *Statesman* advertising; in 1927, it accounted for $144,337 of the company's $211,848 in receipts.[4] The newspaper's circulation that year was reported as 5,931 daily (Tuesday through Saturday) and 6,196 on Sunday.[5]

After two weeks of discussions, Hendricks broke off talks with a terse note to Sprague explaining only that, "I fear, for reasons that I cannot at the moment explain, that we will have to call off our negotiations."[6] The negotiations had broken down on price and because new buyers entered the field.

Sprague, in a letter to Salem banker William S. Walton, of the Ladd & Bush bank, explained that an inspection of the *Statesman* convinced him the property was not worth more than $180,000 and that his offer to that effect, with $40,000 down, had been rejected. Another party, Sprague added, was "willing to deal on the higher basis: $200,000 and assume the accounts." Sprague was unwilling to assume either accounts receivable or payable.[7]

By mid-summer a new player was on the scene: Sheldon F. Sackett, a brash and talented young newspaperman who had made a name for himself editing the weekly McMinnville *Telephone-Register*, which he

From 1918 until 1953, the Statesman was published on Commercial Street, Salem's main business artery; the venerable building had housed territorial government offices at one time (Sprague Family Archives).

owned jointly with H. B. Cartlidge from 1925 to 1928. In July 1928 Sackett and Earl C. Brownlee of Forest Grove entered into an agreement to purchase the *Statesman* from Hendricks and Carle Abrams, who held one-fourth ownership. Sackett and Brownlee obtained a $30,000 loan and were listed as co-publishers of *The New Oregon Statesman* (they added "*New*" to the masthead in an effort to separate the paper from its previous owner). By fall they were in financial trouble and casting about for a partner, even if it meant giving up control of the paper. Willamette University Law Dean Roy R. Hewitt alerted his friend Charles Sprague that Sackett was talking about selling his interest in the paper. Sprague immediately got in touch with Sackett.[8]

By December 15, Sprague had outlined a plan under which he would enter into a partnership, but not a tri-partnership. He suggested that Brownlee was more compatible in terms of age and experience (Sackett was only 26 years old), but as the month proceeded it was Sackett with whom the discussions were taking place.[9]

On December 21 Sackett forwarded to Sprague a five-page report on the *Statesman's* financial situation, circulation and advertising data. He confided that the problem he and Brownlee faced was paying for building renovations that had gone over budget and stretched their limited capital; a new press room and warehouse had cost $4,500, well beyond estimates, and other new equipment had added to the financial strain. The company was also behind on payments for linotype equipment.[10]

On January 2, 1929, Sackett proposed a two-thirds ownership to Sprague, with Sackett retaining one-third. Sprague accepted the following day and named Sackett managing editor and himself editor and publisher.[11] But Sprague suddenly had second thoughts, and on January 7 offered to outright purchase Sackett and Brownlee's interests for $26,600, with $180,000 to buy out Hendricks and Abrams. After two days of letters and telephone calls, Sprague relented and agreed to the two-thirds, one-third ownership pact with Sackett.[12]

The contract finally signed later in January by Sprague, Sackett, Hendricks, and Abrams settled on the $180,000 purchase price and established the two-thirds, one-third split. The down payment was $46,500 in cash, and financing extended through 1944 at 5.5 percent interest. Sprague and Sackett executed a separate agreement that gave Sprague the right to buy Sackett's interest for $15,000 after the first six months of their partnership, the price to be adjusted for profit or loss since the inception of the agreement. A third agreement cashed Brownlee out, at about $13,000.[13]

The Sprague-Sackett partnership was never a happy affair; the new partners were strong-willed and intelligent men, but of totally different temperaments and politics. Sprague was as patrician and aloof as Sackett was rumpled and profane. Both men were Republicans in 1929, but Sackett soon became one of the state's prominent Democrats. It was an odd-couple relationship, in which the partners had a mutual respect for each other, but were simply incompatible on a personal level.

The abstemious Sprague was offended by Sackett's drinking and irregular hours. A saving grace for Sackett was his second marriage, in 1931, to Beatrice Walton, sister of Salem banker William Walton. A woman of considerable charm and intellect, she later served on the State Board of Higher Education, and her family money helped Sackett as he engaged in a long series of financial adventures involving newspapers and radio stations up and down the Pacific Coast.[14]

Sackett was an Oregonian, born at Jefferson in Marion County in 1902, and graduated from Willamette University in 1922. He was a school principal at Raymond, Washington, from 1923 to 1925, when he bought part ownership of the McMinnville *Telephone-Register*. He was a Methodist, Republican, president of the Salem Kiwanis Club, active in the Chamber of Commerce; on the surface, his resumé was similar to that of Sprague.[15] But Sackett marched to a different drum.

Sackett was a large man, over six feet tall, raw-boned and blond, given to explosive outbursts. Associates almost uniformly described him as a sort of mad genius, given to profound mood swings in what was surely a form of manic-depression. Sackett, said J. W. Forrester, was "a genius, who bordered between being brilliant and being insane."[16] Forrester and other associates reported similar stories of Sackett in his manic phases,

Sheldon Sackett, flamboyant, irascible and often brilliant partner of Sprague for 10 years (1947 photo, Oregon Historical Society 014661).

wildly bidding for radio stations or newspapers and seeking men to run them. Over a period of years, he acquired and sold or lost a number of properties. A 1947 buying spree in Vancouver, Washington and in Portland and Seattle brought the attention of national news magazines, but he over-extended himself and the ventures collapsed.[17] At the time of his death in 1968, he owned the *World* and KOOS Radio in Coos Bay, Magic Valley Cablevision in Twin Falls, Idaho; and, in California, *The World of Sonoma County*, a weekly in Santa Rosa; Artcraft Printers and Publishers in Eureka; and Olympic Press in Oakland.[18]

While the frontier days of editors carrying weapons to defend themselves against angry readers were long past, *The Statesman*'s editorial offices in 1929 were easily accessible to foot traffic and a wide variety of drunks, drifters and offended readers were part of the day's work for the partners. Sprague moved in with Sackett on the ground floor of the old newspaper plant, their desks back-to-back and their office opening directly onto South Commercial Street. Cecil Edwards, whose father was a press operator for Sprague, recalled loud arguments between the partners, "shouting matches that you could hear out in the street." Veteran Associated Press writer Paul Harvey, Jr. remembered the partnership as volatile, exacerbated by the close proximity of their work spaces.[19]

Martha Sprague Hurley recalled Sackett six decades later: "I can see him now on South Commercial, his desk looking one way, father's the other, (Sackett's) long hanging foot dangling over the desk." A flamboyant character, so different from her father, Martha recalled, yet the latter's view was one of, "if their lives were cast together for a period of time, let's make the best of it."[20]

Sprague later described his partner as brilliant, bordering on genius, with a reporter's instinct for news. "Our temperaments were different," he noted, "I was conservative, satisfied with concentrating on The Statesman. Sackett had mounting ambition which led him through the years to recurring adventures in press and radio expansion, sometimes at severe loss, sometimes with real success." His old partner, said Sprague, "could be a most engaging companion. He was a good conversationalist, always with something to talk about, and always probing the mind of those he was talking with. But he was a man, too, of moods, as though with a divided personality."[21]

At the time, the partners made do with their disparate personalities, and pulled together in a struggle for survival. The *Statesman* was second in longevity only to *The Oregonian* among the state's surviving pioneer newspapers. Founded in 1851 by Samuel R. Thurston, Oregon's delegate to Congress, it was a Democratic response to the Whig *Oregonian*, which began publication in 1850. Asahel Bush, Thurston's editor, quickly became owner as well. Bush was leader of the "Salem Clique," which dominated Democratic politics during Territorial and early Statehood days, and he was an editor who gave no quarter. The "Oregon Style," a particularly virulent form of editorial rivalry, appears to have been started by Bush and *Oregonian* editor Thomas J. Dryer. Typical of their invective was Bush's 1854 description of his rival: "There is not a brothel in the land that would not have felt itself disgraced by the presence of the *Oregonian* of week before last. It was a complete tissue of gross profanity, obscenity, falsehood, and meanness. And yet it was but little below the standard of that characterless sheet."[22]

Bush left the paper in 1863 and in 1869 founded the Ladd & Bush bank, in which he remained active until his death in 1913. Following his departure, the paper moved toward Republican ranks, and when R. J. Hendricks took over in 1884 it was firmly established as a Republican organ.

Salem and Marion County were solidly Republican. Not since 1860 had Marion County voted Democrat for president, although two reform movements had made heavy inroads. In 1892 the Populist Party picked up 38.9 percent of the vote, barely behind the Republicans with 43.6 percent. And in 1912, Progressives garnered 23.7 percent of the vote compared to the 31.1 percent Republican vote.[23]

Salem's governmental center along State Street about 1930, with the Marion County Courthouse in foreground, Post Office behind it and the Capitol in background. The Capitol burned in 1935, the Courthouse was replaced; only the Post Office remains, moved to Willamette University's campus (*Statesman-Journal* photo files).

Salem's economy was based on agriculture and state government. State employment centered on institutions in and around the city: a prison, an "Institution for the Feeble-Minded" (later known as Fairview Hospital), the Oregon State Hospital for the mentally ill, state schools for the blind and deaf, a tuberculosis hospital, and the State Industrial School for Girls. At nearby Woodburn was a reformatory for boys. The state Supreme Court and a modest assortment of state agencies were housed near the Capitol, and in 1930 a new state office building was completed at a cost of $500,000. These agencies employed a considerable number of Salem residents, and had to be maintained even in the darkest days of the Depression.

Salem was clearly Oregon's second city; not until the post-World War II boom did Eugene match and then surpass Salem in size. The 1930 census placed Salem at 26,266 people, well ahead of Eugene's 18,901. Another 974 lived across the Willamette in West Salem, which was still a separate city. Marion County, the *Statesman's* home base, in 1930 boasted a population of 60,541.[24]

As a young man Hendricks was somewhat of an innovator; in 1893 the *Statesman* purchased the second and third linotype machines in Oregon (the first was at the *Morning Astorian*).[25] The *Statesman* joined the Associated Press in 1888; and when the modern AP was incorporated in 1900 the *Statesman* was one of 612 charter members.[26] But editorial outrage was not Hendricks's style. He was silent as the Ku Klux Klan ravaged state politics in the early twenties. Hendricks supported Klan themes, including the controversial measure to ban parochial schools, and it hurt his newspaper in the predominantly Catholic north of Marion County.[27]

In this setting of stability and promise of growth, the *Statesman* was a property with great potential, but plenty of room for improvement. It was a poor second in circulation; the *Capital-Journal*, guided by the courageous but irascible George Putnam, had moved ahead in circulation and influence as *Statesman* publisher Hendricks aged.

The *Capital-Journal* dated to 1888, "holding aloft the banner of true Republicanism and fighting for the principles of the noblest and greatest party that the world has ever known."[28] By 1929 the paper had switched parties; Putnam was a Jeffersonian Democrat and the C-J reflected that view.

George Putnam was a product of the E. W. Scripps newspaper organization, a champion of the common man. A Nebraskan, Putnam worked several years as an engineer before his off-season work as a reporter on the San Diego *Tribune* attracted Scripps's attention. In 1899 and 1900 Putnam served as Scripps's private secretary, and in 1901 he became Pacific Coast manager of the Scripps-McRae Press Association. He subsequently worked for Scripps as editor or publisher in Spokane and Eureka, and served a short stint as news editor on the *Oregon Journal*. In 1907 he purchased the Medford *Tribune*, merging it with the Medford *Mail* in 1910. In 1919 he purchased the *Capital-Journal*.[29]

Putnam had no patience with progressives and reformers, and his chief annoyance was Prohibition. Although a hard drinker himself, it was the entire idea of social engineering that offended Putnam. He expressed his views in a classic editorial in 1930:

> *A Progressive is one who believes that all that is necessary to reform humanity is to pass a law, and employ an army of officials to enforce it. A Progressive asserts that all governmental ills can be remedied by bureaucratic regulation. A Progressive holds that humanity must be standardized by coercion to conform with his own standards or those of the Utopia he visions through class legislation.*
>
> *Prohibition is the best example of Progressive legislation for the uplift. This attempt to standardize habits in conformity to ecclesiastical dogma has cost us hundreds of millions of dollars, filled our prisons to overflowing, and left us worse off than before—but it does provide jobs for tens of thousand of tax eaters at taxpayers' expense—that is the main objective of the Progressives.*[30]

Sprague, of course, was worse than a Progressive in Putnam's eyes; he was a prohibitionist and a teetotaler. When Sprague arrived, Putnam was Salem's leading editor, and a thirty-year rivalry ensued. Seldom associating socially, the men were a study in contrasts. Sprague was a tall and vigorous six-footer, a hiker and climber; Putnam was nearly a foot shorter, stooped and slow in movement, one of the old-time editors who wore the green-visored eyeshades used by copy editors. But what Putnam lacked in physical vigor, he made up with a tart and fearless editorial voice that neither asked or gave quarter. Sprague accepted the challenge; the men battled for three decades in their editorial columns, and the struggle began immediately.

Sprague's name first appeared on the *Statesman* masthead in the issue of February 5, 1929. Others may have written the editorials that day, but by February 10 Sprague was clearly in charge; an editorial called attention to an experience he had had in Ritzville.[31]

Sprague quickly made his mark, taking controversial stands on two important issues before the 1929 Legislature, and then wading into the political thicket at City Hall in a highly personal battle with the *Capital-Journal*. The campaigns marked his first appearance as an editorial voice in his adopted state. In all three cases, his progressive leanings surfaced and in all three cases he prevailed. The issues involved adoption of a state income tax, establishment of a single governing board for higher education, and political control of the Salem City Council.

Salem newspapers have always had a unique opportunity to influence Oregon legislation, simply by their proximity to the Capitol. With legislators meeting four blocks down State Street from his office, dining and socializing at the Marion Hotel across the street and in private homes in the city, Sprague had plenty of opportunities to meet the state's political leaders and observe their work. It was a major reason for his preference for Salem; he wanted more than a chance to observe, he wanted a place at the table.

The Oregon Legislature had only recently moved out from under the shadow of the Ku Klux Klan and its nativist legislation early in the decade. The Klan tide, peaking in the 1922 popular vote to ban private and parochial schools, had begun to recede, but the 1929 Legislature still had veterans of KKK days, including the felicitously named Kasper K. Kubli, Speaker of the House in 1923. In 1929 the House and Senate had only two Democrats each. Governor Ike Patterson of Eola, a farmer from across the river in Polk County, was a conservative Republican elected in 1926 over the populist Democrat, Walter Pierce. Patterson's opposition to an income tax, which was one of Pierce's major proposals, was a factor in his election, as the voters in the same election turned down two income tax initiatives.[32] It was clearly not a session to expect serious reform.

Despite the conservative climate, Sprague almost immediately rushed into the fray to promote two distinctive reform proposals, a graduated income tax and a single governing board for Oregon's feuding colleges and university.

The income tax flew in the face of repeated voter rejection; different forms of income tax had been defeated seven times since 1912. Only in a special election in 1923 had an income tax measure been approved—only to be repealed the following year. Clearly, it was an unpopular tax, and it was opposed by upper-income Republicans who were the dominant force in Oregon politics at the time.

A graduated income tax, however, matched Sprague's sentiments; the 1912 Progressive platform called for both a graduated inheritance tax and an income tax.[33] In his first week writing editorials, Sprague penned a "Primer of Taxation" on February 14, urging an income tax as recognition of the shift in wealth and also as a matter of simple equity. "Commerce or trade or manufacturing is really the source of wealth in this day and age and not inert lands," Sprague wrote. "The only way to reach this accumulation of wealth, and assuredly the fairest way, is by means of the income tax."[34]

Sprague, in a manner that would become his trademark, presented a logical argument in an editorial taking up only eight inches of double-column type. The income tax did pass, with modifications that Sprague did not favor but was willing to accept, and then was approved in the 1930 general election.

In supporting the income tax, Sprague flew in the face of past voter sentiment, and also the editorial views of powerful Oregon newspapers. *The Oregonian* and the evening *Telegram* railed against the bill as defying the expressed will of the voters; the measure was "impudent" said the *Telegram*, and *The Oregonian* asked, "Have the people no will?" Most outspoken was the *Capital-Journal*; Putnam wrote two editorials charging legislators with openly defying the will of the people. Sprague had help from the *Oregon Journal*, a Democratic paper often aligned with reform movements. In two editorials, the *Journal* urged legislators to attend to their duty to the state and pass the tax.[35]

In his other major foray of the session, Sprague weighed in strongly on legislation to consolidate the state's bickering colleges and university under a single board. He had made higher education contacts in Corvallis, and he put his knowledge to work. Sprague opened the debate February 19 with another "primer" of sorts, longer than his income tax editorial and detailed to a fault. Refusing to take sides on the legislative wrangling over budgets for Oregon State College and the University of Oregon, Sprague rejected as "smoke-screens" proposals to ban out-of-state students, to eliminate "duplicate" courses or departments, and to hire an outside expert. He urged, instead, a single board of regents. He followed his initial call with two more editorials for consolidation.[36]

College-town editors in Eugene and Corvallis waffled. The Eugene *Register-Guard's* Bill Tugman came out for the principle of consolidation but was clearly worried about the timing. Claude Ingalls in Corvallis agreed with Tugman that more study was needed. Both papers ultimately accepted the measure with misgivings, calling on Governor Patterson for quality appointments.[37]

Ultimately these measures, the income tax and a single board of higher education, became cornerstones of the Oregon system of government. At the time, Sprague and the *Capital-Journal* squared off on the value of the session, which a C-J columnist called an "asinine session," and Putnam blasted for its income tax and $5 daily legislators' expense account. Sprague labeled the session "constructive" and listed six major accomplishments, including the two he had championed.[38]

The division was typical of the way Sprague and Putnam approached government. Sprague offered praise whenever possible, particularly in the case of Republicans. Putnam was acerbic and biting, had no real party affiliation and remained outside the social circles of political leaders. Sprague understood the value of a bit of flattery, and if he took a politician to task he was also quick to defend him against an attack that he thought was unreasonable or venal. Manners and proper respect for authority were important to Sprague and he suffered fools and demagogues lightly.

Nor did Sprague take personal teasing or needling well. From his first day in Salem, he had trouble dealing with sharp-tongued *Capital-Journal* columnist Don Upjohn, who was frequently able to goad his controlled *Statesman* rival into editorial response. Upjohn saluted Sprague's arrival by noting: "We understand Mr. Sprague of Corvallis becomes boss of the Noo Statesman today. No doubt from now on it will be know as the Nooer Noo Statesman."[39] By fall, Upjohn and Putnam were in a name-calling battle with Sprague over control of City Hall.

Salem's city government was controlled by fourteen aldermen and a mayor. This unwieldy system was presided over in 1929 by T. A. Livesley, "the hop king," so named because he owned what was claimed to be the world's largest hop farm. A man accustomed to leading, Mayor Livesley ruled the City Council in league with a minority of aldermen and, according to *The Oregon Statesman*, the counsel and connivance of the *Capital-Journal's* city editor, Harry Crain. The power of Livesley and his band was considerable; there being no civil service, they hired and fired the city work staff.

Crain was a slight man who got around with the aid of crutches, due to a childhood illness. City editor from 1920 to 1948, Crain also reported most of the C-J's political stories. His reporting was colorful, accompanied by catchy headlines ("Insurgents Plan to Hog-Tie Mayor by Committees Grab"), and clearly partisan. Crain, referring to efforts by the council majority to strip Livesley of his power to appoint committees, termed the rebels "bolsheviks," and presented only the mayor's side of the dispute.[40] Putnam and Upjohn added editorials and columns in support of Livesley and his group of five committed votes.

Crain's counterpart on the *Statesman*, Ralph Curtis, got into the spirit of the fray, terming Livesley's faction "the Capital-Journal party" and labeling the C-J Livesley's "semi-official mouthpiece."[41]

Events reached their height with the insurgents pushing through a "Committee on Committees" to assume power previously held by the mayor. Crain, in a long and sarcastic bylined piece, "revealed" himself as "the Mussolini of Salem" and confessed that the *Capital-Journal's* sins in the affair had been to favor such "evils" as a modern sewage system, adequate fire protection and concrete bridges. Curtis's coverage, no more balanced than Crain's, at every turn linked the rival newspaper to the losing faction: "Heretofore the mayor has appointed the standing committees, and it has been intimated rather strongly that he has been advised in making those selections by Harry N. Crain of the Capital Journal, under a plan whereby Crain sought to control the council's policies."[42]

While their city editors were dueling, Sprague and Putnam had a turn at the melee, with Upjohn throwing caustic comments from the sidelines. On November 5 Putnam piled on the insurgents; the last straw was apparently the *Statesman*'s endorsement of wooden bridges instead of the concrete structures Livesley and the C-J favored. A backer of the new city manager form of government, Putnam termed Salem's system "an anachronism in this day and age, a survival from hick-town times . . ." Sprague responded that: "Half of it [the feud] may be directed at the mayor, and the other half properly charged to the Capital-Journal itself whose bully-ragging the council members finally tired of." The C-J stood accused of being a spiteful poor loser.[43]

Upjohn now completed the editorial triumvirate, in a stinging rebuke to Sprague as an interloper from Corvallis, whose "wooden bridge triumph is but a forerunner of what is to come. A symbol, or a banner as it were, of the Statesman-council combination hellbent for sliver decked bridges and retrogression . . . ."[44]

While Upjohn was chuckling, Sprague was seething; it was not the first, nor would it be the last time that the C-J wordsmith succeeded in getting under his rival's hide. In the case of the City Council imbroglio, Sprague fired back an indignant editorial defending himself and touting Corvallis as "one of the urban jewels of the Willamette Valley." "From Corvallis?" Sprague concluded, "Yes, we're from Corvallis; and proud of it. What is more, it is altogether safe for us to go back there."[45]

For the newspapers, by design or by accident, there was more at stake than prestige. The council majority, after stripping Livesley of his appointive powers, also switched the paid city notices to the *Statesman*; they had been divided equally between the papers. Putnam pointedly noted that the *Statesman* had only three-fifths of the C-J's circulation, so the council had made a bad deal economically as well as politically.[46] This time, there was no rejoinder from Sprague.

The whole affair was reminiscent of the "Oregon Style" invective that once flew between Asahel Bush and Thomas J. Dryer, toned down only slightly from the days when a rival could be libeled almost with impunity. Sprague loved an editorial duel, and throughout his career relished in quoting a counterpart and then refuting it with his own views. But the personal journalism of Upjohn went beyond Sprague's standards of good taste, and he was always vulnerable from that quarter, "totally unequipped" to deal with Upjohn's sarcastic digs, his son recalled.[47]

The year had contained more than a few news and editorial battles between the Salem rivals; the *Capital-Journal*, after coasting during Hendricks's final years as publisher of the *Statesman*, had met a formidable rival. In the decade just opening, the rivalry would be exacerbated by the financial difficulties of the Depression, when even Salem, with its insulation of government payrolls, had to tighten the belt.

After a successful first year, *Statesman* sales and circulation began to drop and profits all but disappeared for the next five years. Sprague jettisoned two of his three monthly publications in 1930, *The Pacific Homestead* and the *Oregon Teachers Monthly. Northwest Poultry Journal* lasted until 1938.

While Sprague established an editorial presence and tried to shore up business and circulation, Sackett churned out copy and built up the small news staff in an intensely competitive environment. A colorful writer, given to explosions of opinion in his bylined articles, Sackett was a whirlwind typist, his fingers flying as fast as his ideas.

Veteran printer Claude Talmadge joined Sprague at Ritzville, operated the newspaper briefly when Sprague went to Corvallis in 1925, and then followed Sprague to Salem, where he is shown in the Statesman composing room with his boss in 1938 (Oregon Journal, now Oregon Historical Society 014615).

Sprague and Sackett were seasoned newsmen but they were stretched to cover all the bases; despite the tight times, it was imperative that they expand and improve their staff. The job began almost at once. Hendricks had hired Ralph Curtis as sports editor and Isabel Childs as a reporter; Sprague and Sackett quickly added Steve Mergler as principal reporter.

Curtis and Mergler were workhorses of the Depression era and both stayed with the paper until the mid-forties. Quiet and competent, they covered all beats and managed the news desk. Curtis began in sports, took a brief turn publishing the weekly Stayton *Mail* (1934-36), then returned full-time as managing editor when Sackett moved to Coos Bay in 1936. Mergler covered news and politics. Soon they were joined by others.

The first to arrive was Lillie Madsen, free-lancing as a garden columnist and correspondent from Silverton. Her byline first appeared in 1931, with a jaunty picture of the young writer in a hat. Madsen became full-time in 1943, established herself as a legend at the Oregon State Fair, putting in long hours reporting judging results and fair highlights, and maintained her Silverton columns for forty years. Fiercely protective of her territory, Madsen worked tirelessly at her task and was a great favorite of Sprague's.

Arriving in 1937 was the team of Maxine Buren and Jeryme Upston, hired by Sprague on the same day and destined to work side-by-side until 1966, when Buren retired.[48] Buren became women's editor;

Lillie Madsen began a four-decade career with the Statesman in 1931, and from free-lancing moved to the permanent staff as farm and garden editor. With her in this 1951 photo is reporter and Valley Editor Les Cour (*Statesman-Journal* photo files).

Maxine Buren (at typewriter) and Jeryme Upston English (on phone) joined the Statesman staff in 1937 and served as a women's-page team for three decades. Also pictured is Florence Bell, librarian at the time of this 1951 photo (Statesman-Journal files).

Upston—newly graduated from Willamette University—began "Seen and Heard," a society column she wrote until 1977. Madsen, Buren, and Upston (who became Jeryme English after her 1939 marriage to Wheeler English) were *Statesman* stalwarts as long as Sprague lived. Others came and went during the thirties.[49]

Wallace Sprague joined the paper upon completion of graduate work in history at Harvard, writing news and editorials from mid-1939 until called to the Navy in 1941. He lived at home, and his father was hopeful that he would make the newspaper his career. Wallace was picking up knowledge that would benefit him in a publishing career, but that career was not to be in Salem.

On the business side of the paper, Robert Sprague was brought in to work with Ralph Kletzing, advertising manager. Robert was the son of Wyatt Sprague, Charles's older brother and confidant. After graduating from Whitman College he had taken a position in San Francisco with the Wine Institute. Neither his father nor uncle approved of alcohol, which may have been a factor in his coming to Salem in 1935 as business manager. He was one of the stalwarts still with the paper at Sprague's death; others were Mary White and Phil Gilstrap, advertising; Hunt Clark, circulation manager; and Wendell Wilmarth, controller.[50]

It was Clark who brought Al Lightner aboard in 1941, originally to increase newspaper sales in Polk County. Lightner became sports editor in 1942 when Ron Gemmel joined the FBI. Lightner had knocked around the world of pro baseball and done odd jobs and, despite Sprague's skepticism at hiring a former professional athlete, Lightner found a lifetime home with the paper:

> *Gemmel told me, 'All you have to have is an imagination—can you type and do you have a pretty fair knowledge of sports?' Well, I went across the street (Gemmel and Lightner were drinking in the Marion Hotel bar) and talked to Steve Mergler, the managing editor. I said I studied journalism in school—which I didn't—I lied! I got a 30-day trial . . . the trial turned out to be 34 years.*[51]

Clark, Lightner, and many other *Statesman* reporters and employees fit the stereotype of hard-drinking newspapermen, and the Marion Hotel bar was conveniently located across the street from the *Statesman* office. Sprague was more than a casual supporter of Prohibition. But throughout his career, Sprague was able to work with associates who were profoundly different from himself in personality, politics, and lifestyle. Perhaps it began with Sheldon Sackett, so very much his opposite, but it also included subordinates such as Lightner and Clark, who had a totally different outlook toward such things as alcohol and gambling.

Sprague's personal life centered around his family and the paper, and his children recall that they were never far separated. When the family took a trip, Sprague sent travel items back to the *Statesman*, and even a short day trip meant stopping by the office. They took their first cross-country trip in 1927 to visit ancestral haunts in New England, pick up a new Studebaker in Detroit, and visit the Elbert Hubbard shrine at East Aurora, New York; although Sprague never mentioned the eccentric progressive in his writing, he was fascinated by Hubbard's combination of social gospel and simple living, and the trip was interupted to visit the workshops.[52] Sprague loved motoring, and could be quite adventurous in seeking out new territory. In the late twenties he drove a primitive road around Neahkanie Mountain on the Oregon coast, Blanche refusing to accompany him, while the children delighted in the adventure.[53]

Sprague enjoyed hiking, and climbed several of the major mountains in the region, including Rainier, Hood, St. Helens and Jefferson; Blanche accompanied him on some of the less difficult climbs. He joined Chemeketans, an outdoor club, upon his arrival in Salem, and in July was on the club's first ascent of Jefferson:

Ours was the first party this year. The choice lies between steep-lying snow fields and boulder-strewn ridges. Hamilton, the leader, wisely chose the rock ridge. Slow going, careful picking of a path, guarding against starting rocks to roll on those below on the trail. One ridge scaled only to find another jagged point just above . . . muscles feeling the strain . . . blistered feet burning . . . joints working wearily . . . heart going fast . . . quickened breathing. That is about all there is to mountain climbing. It is a test of endurance. The supreme exertion calling for staying power, "moral courage," or whatever you want to call it.[54]

Sprague neither hunted nor fished, although Wallace recalled one abortive fishing trip, probably as a result of Blanche's urging her husband to spend more time with his teen-aged son. The trip, Wallace recalled, was to Alsea and the recollection was of "hard ground for camping, cold breakfast, he wasn't very good at fishing . . . it was a disaster—we never tried it again!"[55]

Blanche enjoyed entertaining, and the Spragues' handsome brick home at 14th and Center, just minutes from the Capitol, was well suited for dinners. The Spragues played bridge, and were founding members of the Capital Card Club, a Salem establishment dating from 1938 and for at least fifty years maintaining a rule of formal dress for its monthly gatherings. Jeryme English recalled, in a paper for the club's fiftieth anniversary, that Sprague had a strict rule against any publicity: the Capital Card Club never appeared in the *Statesman's* society columns while Sprague was alive.[56]

There was little time for recreation during this period, however, as the paper's precarious finances and then the decision to become a political candidate took an enormous amount of time. But in 1938, after receiving the nomination in the May primary, Sprague and his wife and daughter took the train to Oberlin, Ohio for Wallace's graduation. Typically, the trip resulted in a series of "Editorial Correspondence" letters, commenting on politics, farm crops, and life along the way. Sprague's travel columns were invariably interesting, peppered with comments on farming and politics, style and trends spotted along the way. The 1938 trip was no exception, Sprague commenting on public health, floods in the corn belt, college students selling cookware, Gerald L. K. Smith's speech in Akron, and observations in a smoking car: "Many women were traveling. Some were certainly school teachers off for a vacation trip to the Northwest (they handled their cigarettes like a crayon). . . The commercial travel was light; not many drummers fogging up the smoking compartment."[57]

Wallace Sprague recalls the family "lived sparingly" during the thirties, but sufficient revenue was on hand to take short annual vacations, often to the Oregon coast, to buy a new car every three or four years, and to put Wallace through Oberlin College and Martha through Stanford. The family may have had some financial help from Blanche's mother, who came to live with the family in Corvallis. Sprague and his brother Wyatt shared some of the living costs of their only sister, Mazie, a widow who was eking out a living with a small needlework and mending shop in Portland. [58]

Although the Spragues were regulars in the Presbyterian Church, their daughter Martha does not remember much religion in the home. Her father said grace at meals, but in his absence grace was ignored; there were no evening prayers or Bible readings. Sprague read the Bible, but primarily as literature, and it was not required reading for the children. Father was the disciplinarian, and the children occasionally had to select a piece of kindling for a paddling when they misbehaved. Their memories are of kind and caring parents, who were later supportive of their career choices and happy in the company of grandchildren.[59]

In 1931, the Spragues built a large new home at the corner of 14th and Center streets. A formal, Tudor-style house, it served them well for entertaining and had a comfortable library with a big leather chair for Sprague's nightly reading. They were living well above the standard of most Depression-era families; in 1936, Sprague reported a gross income of $16,168 from the *Statesman* and his share in the Corvallis newspaper.[60] But the Sprague children recalled many Sundays with "circulation chicken" picked up in exchange for subscriptions in the rural areas.

Advertising at times limited the paper to eight pages on weekdays, and even Friday grocery advertisements at times might push it only to ten pages. The business team's challenge was even more critical than the hard-pressed reporting team; more than just competition to get the news first, they had to keep the doors open.

Neither Salem newspaper resorted to issuing scrip to employees, as did several publishers in 1932 and 1933. *The Dalles Chronicle, Astorian-Budget,* Woodburn *Independent,* Eugene *Morning News* and Bend *Bulletin* all used scrip, which in most cases was redeemable at advertisers, who in turn traded it for space in the newspaper. *Astorian-Budget* employees received half their pay in "*Budget* beaver pelts," named for the city's fur trading history. Other newspapers cut pay and staff to make ends meet: "Our office girl is reporter, bookkeeper, press feeder, and ad setter if necessary," commented one small weekly. Another noted the receipt of trade for circulation: "Last week we received two cords of wood, eleven chickens and twelve jars of honey."[61]

The new publishers of the *Statesman* had plenty on their plates; not only was the newspaper a poor second in circulation and prestige in Salem, it was also a failing business with an ailing plant.

The rickety old building, occupied by the *Statesman* since 1918, dated to 1859 and at various times in its history had housed the offices of Oregon's governor and Supreme Court, the Salem Post Office and even, briefly, the *Capital-Journal*. It was two-story brick construction, and badly in need of replacement by 1929.[62]

The largest advertisers were groceries and furniture stores, the latter frequently promoting radios. A good-quality Atwater Kent, Philco, or Wards radio sold for about $150, and by 1929 most homes had at least one. You could buy a car in 1929 for under $700 (a Durant 666 sold for $685 and a Model A Ford Tudor for $525), and "high test" gasoline retailed for 20 cents a gallon. Automobiles were the rage. Salem tore up its streetcar tracks in 1927, and the city's auto dealers were doing fine, among them, Douglas McKay, the future governor and U. S. Secretary of the Interior, and Paul Wallace, a close friend of Sprague's. The *Statesman* took advantage of the craze to print a Sunday "Out of Doors" page, a thinly disguised motoring promotion.

It wasn't long, however, before the lavish advertising for cars and fancy radios declined, then stopped altogether; as the Depression worsened, it affected even relatively stable communities like Salem, with its secure base of governmental salaries. And unlike most cities, Salem had two dailies to split the advertising and circulation dollar; the *Statesman* began the Depression era running second in both categories.

The *Statesman's* major problem during the Depression was loss of advertising. Advertising sales in 1929 brought in about $115,000; by 1930 sales were down to $101,000 and they hit bottom in 1933, at $70,348.[63] The situation at the *Statesman* was reflected nationwide; all newspapers lost advertising during this period, and some ceased publication.

Advertising relied heavily on a few active Salem retailers, in particular Bishop's and Miller's clothing stores, Busick's grocery, and later Fred Meyer. The latter two could be counted upon for full-page ads on Fridays, and Bishop's typically put out a multi-page insert each January. In 1935, with the arrival of Bob Sprague, the staff became more aggressive and with an improving economy began to increase volume in the next year. A new Montgomery Wards store in 1937 also boosted advertising by Sears and J. C. Penney.

In 1938, Ralph Kletzing purchased a weekly in Independence and Bob Sprague became advertising manager. He launched an aggressive effort to promote "Oregon's Second Market," producing a marketing sheet showing Salem's attractiveness to national advertisers when compared to other communities of like size. Using 1935 Department of Commerce figures, Bob Sprague pointed out that Salem had relatively fewer retail facilities than like communities, but considerably higher retail sales volume. Average sales per store in ten classifications showed Salem well above the average in most classifications, including such important areas as automobiles, groceries, furniture and apparel.[64] The push was beginning to pay off by the time Charles Sprague went to the Capitol; in 1939, the *Statesman* passed the *Capital-Journal* in advertising volume, according to figures compiled by Bob Sprague.[65]

The shortage of advertising and a relative stagnation in circulation meant the paper was limited in its ability to improve its content and appearance. The *Statesman* did make an effort to improve its typography, however, in 1935 adopting a more readable type face for its headlines, bringing the paper a prize in a typography contest sponsored by the Ayer newspaper directory.[66]

Sprague and Sackett promoted Valley coverage as they worked to make the paper more attractive to a wider audience. Their front pages took on a cleaner format and local news was given greater play. They quickly dropped "*New*" from the masthead, returning to *The Oregon Statesman*. Sprague also placed on the mast the quote, "No Favor Sways Us: No Fear Shall Awe," from the first *Statesman* of March 28, 1851, harkening to the paper's place in Oregon history.

Photographs began appearing with greater regularity; the paper used International Illustrated News photos and increasingly Kennell-Ellis studio pictures on the society page, but local pictures were limited to posed shots of brides, society events, athletic teams, and mug shots taken by local studios, because the *Statesman* lacked a photographer. When the Capitol burned in 1935 the *Statesman* had to rely on prints from the *Oregon Journal* and local photo studios. Floods of the winter of 1937-38 brought a layout of "Statesman Photos" on page one, but the pictures were well below professional quality.

The *Statesman*, like most small dailies of the time, was edited on the "names make news" basis, and filled with short items of less-than-monumental importance. Sprague and Sackett cultivated a crew of Valley correspondents, primarily housewives, who were paid by the column inch and strove to place as many names as possible in the newspaper. Society pages were crammed with names as well. Jeryme English recalled, "In the thirties, when two people went to Portland, that was a scoop. One morning Mr. Sprague came in furious, two of his best friends were engaged . . . and the C-J got it first!"[67]

No one loved the competition more than Hunt Clark, *Statesman* circulation manager from the mid-thirties until after Sprague's death.

Clark was a garrulous, hard-drinking Irishman who also operated one of the city's small movie houses. His specialty was boosting rural circulation, and it was his drummer who brought in the infamous "circulation chicken" consumed by the Spragues on many Depression Sundays.

Subscription income was steady, at about $20,000 a year as the paper grew from 6,000 subscribers in 1929 to 7,000 by 1935. But the *Statesman* had to cut prices to hold its readers; annual subscription prices of $6 in 1929 dropped to $5.40 in 1933 and then to $5 for two years, moving back up to $5.40 in 1936 and then to $7.20 from 1938 to 1943.[68]

Aggressive promotion by Clark and his crew nearly closed the substantial gap between the two Salem papers; by 1939 the gap was only 1,059, at 9,910 to 8,851. The *Statesman* did not gain supremacy, however, until television elevated morning newspapers in general over their evening rivals.

Depression-era dailies tried varieties of gimmicks and promotional schemes to expand readership. The *Statesman* was one of many small papers selling travel insurance policies for a dollar a year, and in 1929 the paper announced that the unfortunate Carl E. Burns was the first fatality covered by the newspaper policy, his heirs collecting the maximum of $1,000. The insurance policies continued through the Depression.[69] Fall 1937 brought a double-barreled effort, as the *Statesman* offered "48 Magnificent works of art . . . forty-eight famous paintings . . . Old Masters and Moderns . . . from the old World and the New," for a few cents per reproduction, along with a free course in art appreciation.[70] The art promotion followed on the heels of a ten-volume encyclopedia, offered through coupons carried in the newspaper. In 1938 the *Statesman* began a popular cooking school, directed by Maxine Buren, which drew 1,200 women on its first day.[71]

The paper's editorial page, however, maintained a familiar but unappealing gray appearance; only a syndicated cartoon broke the columns of type. Serialized fiction still appeared with regularity, as did the long historical tomes of R. J. Hendricks and the disjointed ramblings of D. H. Talmadge, the "Sage of Salem," a printer who simply and inexplicably wrote whatever came to his mind, usually far short of profound. Don Upjohn's frequent jibes at "Charley" and other *Statesman* personnel were certainly not matched by the maundering of Hendricks and Talmadge.

Despite its problems, the *Statesman* had promise and, from the start of their stormy partnership, Sprague had tried to buy Sackett's one-third interest. He worried that his mercurial partner would embarrass the *Statesman*: "I am disturbed because of the rumors which have somewhat involved The Statesman in your political and financial set-up; and fear it will react against us in case you go through with your venture," Sprague wrote in 1930, extending a cash offer of $24,000 for Sackett's one-third interest. "I recognize your talents fully, I think; but I am yet not sure of the success of our working relationship."[72]

In 1930 Sackett bought a small weekly in Marshfield, on the Southern Oregon coast, and he was in the process of turning it into the daily *Coos Bay Times*, serving the communities of Marshfield (later renamed Coos Bay) and North Bend. It was a full-time job and, although Sackett was still one-third owner of the *Statesman*, his major efforts were increasingly directed into his own growing business. In January 1937—after Sackett moved to Marshfield—Sprague took Sackett's name off the masthead, where he had been listed as managing editor. Sackett replied with a letter combining indignation, surprise, and conciliation. While his stock was not for sale, it might be at the right price, Sackett observed, adding that he was not getting his monthly stockholder reports. He was quite upset at being removed from the paper's masthead:

> *I am insistent that I not be ignored on the paper anymore than you are ignored at Corvallis. After all I have spent the bulk of eight years in Salem, still retain my interest and have a selfish interest in being thus connected . . . I do not wish to be disputatious or argumentative but I cannot forget that I have made a sizable investment in time and money in The Statesman, that I went through the most trying period of firing old personnel, getting new people, rearranging office practices, securing a $30,000 loan which the corporation rather quickly paid in good times, and that I know, as a verity, that I have not been a detriment—perhaps an asset at times—in the steady growth of the paper.*[73]

Sackett in his letter agreed to a $100 weekly salary for Sprague, and asked that he (Sackett) should be paid $25 weekly "as a consultant on news and other problems." His name remained off the masthead.

There the matter rested until 1938, when, during Sprague's campaign for governor, Sackett indicated an interest in opening talks, apparently because he was in need of capital to invest in a radio station he owned in Marshfield. Sackett, now an outspoken supporter of President Roosevelt, nevertheless offered campaign advice and support to Republican Sprague, adding, "I do not want to be embarrassing in my requests at a time when you have so much to attend to."[74]

Replying after his November election, Sprague took up the matter of *Statesman* management while he was in the governor's chair, noting that while "from a purely personal viewpoint" he would be happy to have Sackett take over management of the *Statesman*, his advisors counseled against such an arrangement. He then reiterated his interest in purchasing Sackett's interest. Nothing came of the negotiations, and on December 7 Sprague suggested that Sackett's wife, Beatrice, be brought into the organization to assist on the business side while Sprague was in office. Sprague noted that "her name would help overcome possible criticism from some who might be unfriendly to you."[75]

Sackett's flamboyant lifestyle and his outspoken support for New Deal politics made him somewhat of a pariah in Salem's conservative business community; his wife, however, was the sister of a prominent Salem banker and a member of the State Board of Higher Education, and was highly regarded in the city. Additionally, Sackett was fully committed to his Coos Bay operation and could have only limited time to help in Salem; his wife would have had more flexibility to spend time with the *Statesman*.

When Sprague took office, Sackett served as acting publisher during most of 1939, until Sprague purchased his one-third interest; the amount is unknown, but Sackett told colleagues and family that he had been poorly treated by his partner, who caught him when he needed capital.[76] Sprague had purchased some City of Astoria bonds when they were selling at 30 to 40 cents on the dollar early in the Depression, and he cashed them in at par. The remainder of the money needed to complete his ownership came from loans and from sale of Sprague's one-third interest in the Corvallis *Gazette-Times*.[77]

As partners, Sprague and Sackett had taken a failing publication and, during a time of great economic stress, brought it to a position of respectability and even leadership in its community. A solid news staff was in place, advertising and circulation were in competent hands and the newspaper was promoting itself to readers. The *Statesman* was more attractive to read, with cleaner type and layout, its editorial page reflected an effort to bring more than one point of view to readers, and it was competing in the important areas of sports and society.

Sprague's editorials were becoming a force to reckon with as he weighed in on local and state issues, taking a conservative but moderate tack on most local issues and hewing to a straight Republican ticket in partisan politics. Newspaper historian George Turnbull, writing at the time of Sprague's election, noted that "the Statesman has taken a place of exceptional influence in the public affairs of Oregon."[78] The influence was greatest in Republican circles, however; Sprague often wrote as if there were only one party in the state and, practically speaking, that often seemed to be the case. In fact the thirties was Sprague's most consistent decade in political terms; the former Bull Moose Republican had increasingly turned to the party's center and could be counted upon to support Republican nominees, even if at times he swallowed hard to take in the party line.

When Sprague emerged as a surprise candidate for governor in 1938, he was already well known to Republican stalwarts, for he was one of them, and his editorials could be counted upon to praise regulars and damn renegades. Nowhere was this more obvious than in the strange elections of 1930 and 1934, when the office of governor produced some of the most unusual races and candidates in the state's history. Sprague's positioning on those contests would make him acceptable to party regulars in 1938.

3

◆◆◆

The Editor as Politician

The entry of Charles Sprague into Oregon's 1938 gubernatorial race was greeted with surprise by the state's politicians and editors, for the reserved and intellectual Salem editor had never held political office and seemed oddly cast for the role of practicing politician.

Sprague was well known and respected in Oregon's tight-knit editorial community, but his acquaintances among Oregon political leaders, particularly in Portland, were limited, and he had no personal organization behind him to muster to battle.

Yet the political venture, rationalized as a lifelong Republican's duty to give the party a respectable candidate, should not have come as a total surprise to those who knew Sprague. His editorials staunchly supported his party during the Democratic surge brought on by the election of Franklin D. Roosevelt, he spoke on several occasions to GOP audiences, and all through the thirties he eagerly enrolled in public endeavors.

Sprague was a man of ambition as well as service. He always meant to be somebody, and he regarded politics as a high calling. It is doubtful that his editorial positions and actions in the thirties were aimed at elected office, but it is also naive to think that Sprague had never looked in his shaving mirror and seen a future governor or senator.

The setting is also important, for newspapers in the thirties were vital parts of the community fabric, the only real purveyor of news and opinion. Editors were known as men of substance in business as well as journalism; they were consulted by political leaders and expected to be taken into consideration when decisions were made. In the period before World War II, politics and journalism were more closely intertwined than they would become in later years, when journalistic ethics dictated at least lip service to objectivity and balance. "Political reporting in the first decades of the century was considerably different from what it is at present (1968)," Sprague later recalled. "The papers were more ardently commited to causes, and their reporters let their prejudices, or their publishers' prejudices show through."[1]

Candidate for governor in 1938, Charles A. Sprague posed for an official campaign portrait (Oregon Historical Society 98550).

The stars of this generation of reporters were Henry Hanzen of the *Telegram*, Ralph Watson of the *Journal* and John Kelly of *The Oregonian*. These men went beyond reporting; they also plotted and directed, planted stories and rumors, and were often more politician than journalist. "I was as much a lobbyist as a newspaperman," Hanzen recalled later in his life.[2] Hanzen worked in several major campaigns, including that of Senator Charles McNary. Although he may have been the most overtly political of the trio, Hanzen was only a step ahead of Watson and Kelly, both of whom took partisan shots in their daily reporting.

The Portland political reporters were in their element in a wild and raucous 1930 campaign for governor, the first of the electoral dramas of the thirties that would lead Sprague to the governor's office. It began in 1930 with a maverick Republican, a vengeful Supreme Court and an untimely death.

The maverick Republican was George W. Joseph, a descendant of Basque sheepherders, a brilliant lawyer and orator, a Progressive who did not return happily to the Republican fold. Joseph was a crusader for public power, but in 1930 he had two crusades, and the second was more personal. Joseph was about to be disbarred by the Oregon Supreme Court and, even more than he wanted electric power to belong to the people, he wanted personal vindication. Thus opened one of the strangest chapters in Oregon political history.

Joseph served in the Legislature from 1911 and, in the words of his friend and political partner, Henry Hanzen, he was an orator in a class by himself, whose speeches had "a strange mingling of scorn, mirth and the sublime. In attack his eyes blazed, his ridicule was biting, his invective withering. Time and again I saw him lampoon a bill to death."[3]

Joseph's invective got him into serious trouble with the Oregon Supreme Court in 1928, when Chief Justice John L. Rand campaigned for re-election. Joseph had lost a hotly contested case in which Rand wrote for the winning side despite having a serious conflict of interest. Joseph took to the campaign trail and in a memorable appearance got into a shouting match with Rand. The justice called Joseph a liar, and Joseph responded that Rand "is the biggest liar and lousiest skunk." Matters went downhill from there, and in 1930 a Bar committee recommended that Joseph be disbarred for life. Egged on by Hanzen, Joseph decided to run for governor, in large part to vindicate his reputation.[4]

Joseph and Hanzen were two-thirds of a team, the third partner being Julius Meier, Joseph's former law partner and subsequently president of the family department store, Meier & Frank, Oregon's most prominent retail establishment. Meier shared Joseph's view that electric power should be a public enterprise, rather than controlled by the private holding companies that then dominated the field. All three men were Republicans, as were many of Oregon's public power advocates of the day.

Hanzen, described by a contemporary as "hard-punching and relentless, shrewd in analysis or appraisal of men and issues," was political editor of the Portland *Telegram*, which had been founded by Henry Pittock of *The Oregonian* in 1877 to keep a hand in the evening field.[5] The paper was Republican, and Hanzen and editor Lester Adams were Republicans, but in backing Joseph they encountered the party's orthodox wing, with *The Oregonian* as chief spokesman.

The campaign was nasty from the start. With Hanzen running the campaign and Adams writing page-one editorials, Joseph captured the imagination of Oregonians already into the Depression and looking for someone to blame. Republican stalwarts worried about Joseph's appeal and his radical streak.

The Republican establishment backed incumbent Governor Al Norblad of Astoria or patrician state Senator Henry Ladd Corbett of Portland. The *Statesman* lined up behind Corbett; Sprague had written Norblad off after the governor was discovered to have lobbyists for a controversial paving company in his campaign, a Ralph Watson revelation in the *Journal*.[6]

Only two dailies, both Democratic in their leaning—the *Oregon Journal* and the Pendleton *East Oregonian*—joined the *Telegram* to support Joseph. George M. Joseph, a future Oregon appellate judge and distantly related to George W. Joseph, as a Reed College senior in 1952 analyzed news coverage of the race and cited fourteen of the state's dailies as carrying out a "concentrated editorial campaign against George W. Joseph." Both Salem dailies were on the list.[7]

Shock rolled over the Oregon editorial community when Joseph handily defeated his Republican rivals, although in the field of six he did not win a majority. The *Oregon Voter*, a consistent voice for the Republican old guard, advised readers to vote for the Democratic nominee, Senator Ed Bailey of Eugene, advice seldom seen in the *Voter*.[8]

Bailey had won a lackluster Democratic primary, with all the attention focused on the bitter Republican battle and the dueling Portland newspapers. His views on public power, or anything else for that matter, were of little account in an election that was sure to go Republican. Suddenly Bailey became important, when George W. Joseph toppled over as he prepared to review Oregon National Guard troops. The heart attack that killed Joseph on June 16 threw the state's political community into uproar. Republicans were still looking for reasons to crawl back off their collective limb and endorse Joseph for the fall campaign when suddenly, he was gone.

The death of Joseph brought forth a host of hopefuls, and Sprague and others feared the GOP old guard would control the convention to name a replacement. Only one man stepped forward to claim Joseph's public power platform: Julius Meier. The *Telegram* quickly took up his cause and Hanzen moved into high gear to mount a campaign. Meier was never seriously considered by the Republican nominating convention, which named Phil Metscham, Portland hotelier and state party chairman. Although Sprague attempted to defend the process as open and regular, it had the odor of "deal" and Hanzen in a series of articles exposed what he said was the backroom maneuvering.

Ten days later, a whooping, cheering crowd of four thousand nominated Meier as an independent candidate for governor. The only candidate to strongly back public power, Meier poured thousands of dollars of his own money into the campaign and had the backing of all three Portland afternoon papers, as the *News* joined the *Journal* and *Telegram* in Meier's camp.

A battle royal broke out between the *Telegram* and the *Oregonian*, with the former featuring front-page editorials on behalf of Meier and accusing *The Oregonian* and downstate dailies of catering to the private power lobby. For their part, the downstate papers, including both the *Statesman* and the *Capital-Journal*, accused the Portland afternoon papers of bowing to their largest advertiser. As in the primary, there was more steam in the daily press than in the candidates themselves.

The race became intensely personal, and comments at times verged on anti-semitism. Meier was constantly termed "the Merchant Prince," and the *Oregon Voter* at one point early in the campaign felt it necessary to warn against prejudice, noting that not all Jews supported Meier, which the *Voter* felt revealed their civic virtue. The *Voter* soon abandoned Democrat Bailey and eagerly supported Republican Metscham: "Phil . . . a regular guy."[9]

Putnam in the *Capital-Journal* referred to Meier as "merely a sublimated counter-jumper," and Sprague termed him, "A bristling business man dressed up in a clown suit."[10] Putnam, his populism boiling over into viciousness at times, deplored the wealth represented by Meier even more than he opposed Meier's power platform. Sprague deplored the party-bolting of Meier, and his pleading to Republicans to stay with their nominee reached a new level with an editorial imploring Salem merchants to resist voting for Meier because his Portland store would get four years of free publicity.[11]

Despite the efforts of the Republican press, Meier carried an amazing 54.6 percent of the vote in November, with Democrat Bailey second at 28.7 and Republican Metscham a poor third with only 18.7 percent. Sprague criticized "the fatal blunder of the state central commitee in selecting as candidate one who was identified with party organization . . . The party abdicated en masse for Julius Meier." Sprague saw the

Julius Meier, elected on a public-power platform in 1930, was criticized by Sprague, who played the role of Republican partisan in the Depression era (Oregon Historical Society CN009505).

election as "a revolt of the people" against the "old line" GOP organization, which he had backed editorially.[12]

Elected in one of the most stunning years in Oregon political history, Meier could not achieve the voters' mandate. Although he remained a Republican, Meier was checked by Republican legislatures and the deepening Depression, which simply made large-scale state projects impossible. He served a single term and returned to the store, producing a workmanlike and clean administration under constant and intense scrutiny of Republican editors, including Sprague. Sprague never warmed to Meier, and only grudgingly gave him due at the end of his term; he was convinced, at least in his editorials, that Meier would set up a political barony with Henry Hanzen as prime minister, and in every appointment he saw evidence of the plot. Years later, Sprague cited Meier as one of the two best governors during his life in Oregon.[13]

The candle which had burned so brightly in 1930 was crushed by political infighting and economic decline; Oregon did not pick up the challenge of public power as did Washington, where progressives joined under the Democratic banner and won repeated victories on the issue. In Oregon the private power lobby was too strong and the Democrats too weak to cash in on a natural issue.[14] There were many reasons for Democratic weakness, including the role of spoiler played by former Gov. Oswald West, who lobbied for private power interests, and the perpetual fight between "wets" and "dries" on the issue of Prohibition, but the fact that there were so few Democratic editorial voices was also a factor. The *Journal* was the only large-circulation newspaper generally supporting Democrats. The *Capital-Journal* under George Putnam began the decade as a Democratic paper but grew disenchanted with President Roosevelt and the New Deal and wound up backing Republicans. Bob Ruhl in Medford was a strong backer of Roosevelt, with whom he had worked on the Harvard *Crimson* as an undergraduate, but Ruhl was truly independent in his views, and no booster of public power. Only the Pendleton *East Oregonian* and, later in the decade, Sheldon Sackett's *Coos Bay Times* could be counted on for steady Democratic support.

Meanwhile Sprague was a loyal spear-carrier for the Republicans. He backed the hopeless Metscham cause in 1930, endorsed President Herbert Hoover for another term in 1932, and supported the lackluster Joe Dunne for governor in 1934. Few editorial offices were as firmly in the GOP camp as the *Statesman's* in the thirties. Salem was the center of Oregon's Republican heartland, with Marion County registering and voting GOP year after year. But the party was also Sprague's natural home during this era of revolutionary change in government at the national level, changes that simply went beyond his background, upbringing and experience. He was not alone among Progressives; the troops of 1912 had scattered in every direction from isolationism to socialism, but most were to be found back in the party of their birth, wary of Democratic extremes that ranged from Southern racism to big-city "wets" (anti-Prohibitionists) such as 1928 presidential nominee Al Smith of New York.

Sprague was very much a product of small farm towns, of conservative Main Street thinking. His progressive instincts resurfaced from time to time in areas such as conservation and a fear of bigness in government, labor or business; but in 1938 he was still an editor lacking a worldview.

In league with many Republican editorialists, Sprague at first viewed Franklin D. Roosevelt as a lightweight, a child of riches who had either lost his way or was merely an opportunist. Roosevelt was "Frankie" to Sprague during the 1932 campaign, a pale shadow of his illustrious cousin: "Where Teddy was decisive, firm and courageous, Frankie is indefinite, voluble, given to weasel words. He was about the weakest man of those the democrats had under consideration."[15]

The *Statesman* gave F.D.R.'s Oregon campaign trip top billing, acknowledging a crowd of "six to eight thousand" at a brief Roosevelt campaign train stop in Salem, and outlining in detail the candidate's important public power talk in Portland. Sackett, however, in a page-one article three days after the visit, found less enthusiasm than the crowd size indicated, and quoted Governor Meier as firmly in Hoover's re-election camp.[16]

Voters saw more in the New York governor than did Oregon's editors, and Oregon went soundly for Roosevelt in November, giving F.D.R. 58 percent of the vote while electing another Republican legislature and returning Republican Frederick Steiwer to the Senate. Alone among the West Coast states, Oregon remained a GOP outpost during the New Deal, preserving private utilities and rejecting the liberal wing of the Democratic party.[17]

Liberals tried without success to rally around the public power issue that had successfully united Democrats in Washington. Richard L. Neuberger, one of the insurgents, believed that "The ultimate determining factor in a majority of the political contests in the Pacific Northwest is how forthrightly a candidate approaches, or how expertly he straddles, the question of hydroelectric development."[18] Unfortunately for Neuberger and his cohorts, Democrats failed to unite and Republicans either sidestepped or embraced public power. Senator Charles McNary, the state's leading political figure during the decade, was a public power advocate and a Republican; George Joseph and Julius Meier were Republicans. Progressives favored a public role in the utilities field, but they ranged in viewpoint from advocates of complete state control to those who were more cautious about intruding on private ownership.

Sprague took a consistent but cautious progressive view, which had been forged when he entered the struggle to build a municipal water system in Salem. He thought private ownership was preferable, if the service was good and regulation rigorous; barring that, public ownership was acceptable if voted by the people. He was most opposed to public-private competition in what was a natural monopoly field. The public should purchase the facilities of the private company, he felt, rather than enter into competition. Sprague had no objection to public ownership, on his fiscal terms.[19]

From the early twenties there had been agitation for a public water system and a better source than the polluted Willamette, from which the Oregon Washington Water Service Company drew Salem's water. With Mayor T. A. Livesley opposing purchase of the water system, the 1930 City Council was evenly divided, and in April rejected popular agitation to call a referendum on purchase of the water system. Sprague backed an initiative to issue bonds for purchase, and allowed petitions to be placed in his office. The measure passed 2-to-1, despite opposition from the water company.[20]

A series of conflicts followed over the next five years, at times bordering on the comic, as the City Council had two funding measures thrown out because of legal flaws. Both Sprague and the *Capital-Journal's* George Putnam alternately blasted the water company while trying to propose new ideas and shoot down what they feared were extravagant funding proposals.[21] The voters in 1931 finally passed a $2.5 million bond measure, 2264 to 1661, at the same time voting overwhelmingly for the North Santiam River as a water source.[22] But it wasn't until 1935 that exhausted negotiators finally closed the deal to bring North Santiam water to Salem.

The long and often-difficult battle revealed Sprague at his best but also revealed the limitations of his progressive agenda. He was tenacious in pushing city ownership, and returned to the battle after defeat by both the council and the voters, still seeking answers. He held to the principle of public ownership of a critical natural resource, a basic progressive viewpoint. But his caution toward public debt brought him up short on the need to vote bonds large enough to build an adequate system for the future.

In his editorials, Sprague did not hesitate to draw up detailed public programs, outlining legal arguments and charting the various financial aspects of his plan. These editorials were clearly directed at the decision-makers in the case rather than the average farmer or homemaker who read the *Statesman*. Sprague considered himself a player at the table of public policy, and he did not hesitate to place his bets. Although inherently cautious on public (or private) spending, Sprague explored new areas of public policy long before he himself held elective office.

Sprague took a pragmatic view of the larger power issue and, while he opposed huge public debt to construct plants and transmission lines, he was perfectly willing for the public to take over the business of the private utilities. In 1933, after it became apparent that the Roosevelt Administration saw a new role for the federal government in the field of power, Sprague wrote:

> *For ourselves it seems to us that if the people will not agree to let existing companies distribute the juice (from federal dams, at prices set by the federal agency), or if the companies will not make a fair deal in the matter, then the better course would be the third; take over the present plants rather than have uneconomical competition in a field which is a natural monopoly.*[23]

Sprague stayed with this view throughout the decade, opposing the more grandiose plans of the Oregon State Grange to have the state enter the power business. Grange plans passed in 1930 in the Julius Meier floodtide, and again in 1932, but without funding. Voters rejected a $60 million bond issue in 1934 and a similar measure in 1936. Sprague opposed state bonding to build power plants and lines, opting instead for a public-private partnership in distribution of Bonneville power.[24]

The power issue was a high-stakes game in the Pacific Northwest, as Washington moved rapidly toward public ownership and Oregon remained primarily a private-utility state. In Oregon the power issue dominated the campaigns of 1930 and 1934, leaving both major parties in disarray and clearing the way for a little-known editor from Salem. Sprague, who had been an Oregon resident only fourteen years when he took the oath for governor, was elected as a result of political events dating to Oregon's statehood period and culminating in the public power battles of the Depression.

Oregon's pioneers came from the lower Midwest and the border states, funneling through Missouri and onto the Oregon Trail. Later immigrants, responding to tales of a state with plenty of land and opportunity, tended to be from the same areas. Historian Dorothy Johansen wrote that respectability was a big factor in the lure of the Oregon Country over California at mid-century: Oregon stood for law and order, Protestant over Catholic, Puritan morality with an emphasis upon sobriety and thrift—all the trappings of Oregon's future conservative personality.[25]

Democrats controlled Oregon politics through the 19th century, but shifting immigration patterns brought Republican control in the 1900s and, despite the election of Democratic governors Oswald West, George Chamberlain, and Walter Pierce, Republicans held most state and Congressional offices. Power emanated from Portland, where the private utilities and banks were headquartered and conservative gentlemen lunched at the Arlington Club. Portland was as Republican in 1930 as it was to become Democratic half a century later. Democratic strength, laced with Grange populism, was primarily found in rural areas.

Liberal Democrats were shut out of the party's power structure, and had no counterpart to the Republican business establishment. That began to change in the thirties, with the New Deal. Suddenly there were political jobs for liberals, organization and some money from labor, and a host of causes around which to rally, including public power. Franklin D. Roosevelt gave Oregon liberals the first chance in their lifetime to mold a modern Democratic Party. But Democrats made only temporary gains in the critical elections of the thirties, and it was not until World War II, which brought new people and new leaders to the state, that the party asserted itself as a viable player in Oregon politics.

The key Democratic races were the gubernatorial contests of 1934 and 1938, and in both the dominant figure was Charles H. Martin. In 1934, the ever-active Oswald West, with active support from the *Oregon Journal*, recruited Congressman Charles H. Martin of Portland to run for governor on the Democratic ticket. Martin, a retired general already past seventy, was a veteran of the Boxer Rebellion. He was colorful, crusty, profane, and direct—great copy for reporters, and a fine drinking companion for politicians.

Martin's opinions suited conservative Republicans and many newspaper editors. He had the staunch support of George Putnam at the *Capital-Journal*, who saw in him a proper Jeffersonian Democrat. Donald Sterling, managing editor of the *Oregon Journal*, was a confidant who urged Martin to run in 1934. Other editors liked Martin's blunt style and his conservative views; even in the midst of the New Deal, it was hard to find a liberal challenger who could attract editorial backing.

The Democratic party in Oregon was so weak and the press so Republican that it was hard to convince solid citizens that they would be taken seriously on the Democratic ticket. This weakness, combined with Oregon's wide-open primary, frequently resulted in ballots filled with self-starters, opportunists and charlatans. In 1934, the best the liberal wing of the party could do to oppose Martin was Willis Mahoney, the "boy mayor of Klamath Falls," an aggressive self-promoter who latched onto causes and ideas with abandon and was ridiculed by both Republican and Democratic editors.[26] The old Congressman-general easily defeated his liberal challenger, with cheers from the Republican and Democratic right.

Sprague made no endorsement in the Democratic primary—at that time he normally endorsed only in the Republican primary and in the general election—but he remained more skeptical of Martin than his colleagues, citing Martin's age, brief residence in Oregon, and lack of civilian governmental experience or knowledge.[27] Martin had lived only four years in Oregon before leaving for Congress, and had virtually no knowledge or contacts outside Portland.

Liberals were forced to repeat 1930; both Martin and Republican Joe Dunne were conservatives unacceptable to either New Deal supporters or the public-power movement. But in 1934 there was no Julius Meier to draft, and liberals turned to Peter Zimmerman, a Republican state legislator from Yamhill County, a fiery and dedicated public power advocate, a Progressive who had turned left after 1912. He had appeal in rural areas—his campaign staff included the entire executive committee of the Grange—but his ideas smacked too much of socialism to gain a broad appeal, and he absolutely frightened conservative editors.[28]

There was reason for their concern. Described by campaign staffer Richard L. Neuberger as "the most extreme left-winger ever to be within hearkening of a Pacific Northwest gubernatorial chair," Zimmerman collected considerable support from the old Joseph-Meier following of 1930.[29] He won 95,519 votes, finishing at 31.6 percent, well ahead of Dunne. Martin, with 38.6 percent of the vote, became a minority governor. Had Zimmerman presented a broader program to blunt his radical image, he might well have been elected as Oregon's second Republican-cum-Independent governor. For the second consecutive election, the dominant Republican Party had finished a poor third in the state's most important race. Clearly, both major parties were out of step with the people during the Depression, and nowhere was it more obvious than the power issue.

Zimmerman forced Martin to deliver at least lip service to progressive programs. Sterling and others advised Martin to run as an advocate of public power and the New Deal, and in the last weeks of the campaign Martin appeared to be a born-again New Dealer.[30] It was not to last.

Part of the problem was not Martin's doing: the president moved leftward in 1935 and 1936, responding to pressures for more direct action to stem the Depression. The period some called the "Second New Deal" was much more radical than Roosevelt's first two years, particularly in relationships with business. Martin was not the only conservative Democrat to jump ship as a result.[31] But the old general was simply not suited to New Deal programs or players, and as his term progressed he drew farther away from the national party.

The other reason for Martin's shift was labor strife, as the young Congress of Industrial Organizations (CIO) battled for dominance with the entrenched and more conservative American Federation of Labor (AFL). Oregon's huge lumber workforce was a natural target for the organizers, and as the CIO began to show its strength the AFL increased its pressure against recognition of the rival union. Picketing and violence followed.[32]

The AFL picketed CIO mills and many were shut down; "goons" were employed, notably by the Teamsters, one of the strongest AFL affiliates. Martin sent state police to break up some of the picketing, and roundly damned all union leadership. A professional soldier, Martin understood the use of force and would have been comfortable personally leading the charge.

Martin put a special prosecutor, Ralph Moody, on the "goon" cases, and in his most celebrated victory Moody convicted five Teamsters, including Al Rosser, the state Teamster chief, in the burning of a West Salem box factory. When Martin reviewed his term he listed his firm hand in the labor disputes as his major accomplishment. Some 120 people had been arrested in numerous incidents of violence or property damage, and at least 75 were convicted or entered guilty pleas.[33]

Union organizers were working a fertile field; in 1929, Oregon sawmills were paying an average of 41.7 cents per hour, near the bottom of industrial pay scales, and wages dropped steadily for the next four years. In 1930 nearly a third of the state's lumber workers were unemployed; the Unemployed Citizens League enrolled 6,237 members in Portland alone in 1932, and many were lumber workers.[34] Sprague termed the pay scale "a lousy wage under present costs of living," and urged employers to raise wages. He also defended the CIO against charges of communism, a charge that came easily to the lips of the governor and his supporters.[35] Among the state's editors, Sprague was one of the few to side generally with the CIO in its battle to gain a foothold in Oregon, and he consistently refused to call the CIO "Red" despite the presence of communists in labor ranks.

Calling "Red" was a tactic increasingly employed by Martin, however, and it soured him even further with both organized labor and liberals within the Democratic Party. Martin got regular briefings from the Portland Police Bureau's "red squad," headed by W. B. Odale, and the reports tarred any moving target to the left of center, including unions, the American Civil Liberties Union and in particular the Oregon Commonwealth Federation.

The Federation was organized as an anti-Martin force in 1937, and Odale filed lengthy reports on April 16 and 30 as the OCF organized its first convention. Odale alleged 44 Communist Party members among the 348 delegates, and estimated that "fully 80 percent of those attending the convention are engaged in some form of communist activities . . ." Odale's report got wilder as it progressed, finally concluding that "The platform and all resolutions adopted by the convention were prepared by the Communist Party in advance."[36]

Odale's paranoia was shared by Martin, who termed the initial OCF gathering "a convention of 250 nuts," and generally treated his antagonists as enemy agents. More seriously, Martin involved the state police in his attempts to purge leftists, and had officers investigate OCF founders. Martin also pressured party leaders to "check out" OCF activists who applied for state jobs.[37]

The Federation did have its share of communists, but they were outmaneuvered and outvoted and never gained the influence they enjoyed in neighboring Washington state. Monroe Sweetland, a democratic socialist who had cut his teeth in radical politics while a student at the University of Wisconsin, was elected executive secretary at that first convention, in a direct confrontation with communist delegates, who backed Dave Epps. "The big difference between the Washington and Oregon Commonwealth Federations was that theirs never departed from the Communist Party line and we broke, let them know at the first convention that they weren't going to run the show," Sweetland asserted.[38]

The Federation was based on a foundation of organized labor, the CIO in particular; remnants of the Peter Zimmerman public power effort in 1934 and other Grange activists, and New Deal Democrats. Small in size, a "ragtag, bobtail bunch" in Sweetland's words, the OCF was vocal and well-organized in Portland and several key lumber areas downstate. From 1937 until it drifted apart during World War II, the Federation served as the Oregon branch of the New Deal wing of the Democratic Party, and was also in effect the ACLU in Oregon. In 1939, Roosevelt awarded to OCF vice president Byron Carney a major patronage job, that of directing the 1940 federal census in Oregon; with the Depression still raging, census jobs were much prized, and old-guard Democrats were bitter when the position went to an OCF officer.[39]

The Oregon Commonwealth Federation was brought together by hatred of Martin. He had abandoned any pretense of supporting the New Deal, and in particular its public power policies. His dismissal and red-labeling of the OCF added fuel to the fire burning in the young activists, and they set his defeat as their first task, preferably in the Democratic primary of 1938. Martin proved to be a remarkably easy target, a man who had set himself up for defeat with his own words.

Martin was, in Sprague's eyes, "a man of parts; but occasionally some of the parts appear to be missing."[40] One of those missing parts was discretion; the general's blunt and insensitive utterances led many to conclude that another missing part was compassion. Governor Martin called his fellow veterans who could not make payments on home loans in the depth of the Depression "skunks", he excoriated men forced to take relief or federal jobs as lazy and shiftless, told the elderly they could do just fine on $10-a-month relief payments, and called for euthanasia for the mentally retarded, suggesting that the state could save a great deal of money by chloroforming most of the nearly one thousand patients at Fairview Home.[41]

Martin, in short, had a big mouth backed by a lot of opinions. Political reporters loved to quote the governor, and he indulged Capitol regulars with stories of storming the gates of Peking and other military exploits. Reporters dubbed Martin "Iron Pants" for his military demeanor, and the old general wore the name as a badge.[42] Martin also had a sense of humor, which was at times self-deprecating. Replying to the protest of *Oregonian* editor Paul Kelty after he had decided—in the face of a delegation of three hundred farmers—not to veto a farm bill *The Oregonian* opposed, Martin confided: "I must confess I have always been fearful of 'embattled farmers' . . . My friend I have faced bullets but never so many fighting farmers!"[43]

Most Oregonians, however, did not see the old general in his tent; they saw Martin as a fighter and an opponent of change, at a time when thousands of Oregonians were desperate to change their lives.

The election was held in the shadow of the Great Depression, in a state dotted with CCC camps and federal work projects, where support for Franklin D. Roosevelt was strong despite Republican voting patterns for local office. In 1938 Oregon had yet to gain the economic boost of war preparations; there were no shipyards, no giant lumber orders. The Depression ruled.

Oregon had some advantages during the Depression. The Willamette Valley in particular retained its ability to grow food—no Dust Bowl here—and there were few reports of serious malnutrition. Perhaps most important for Salem, state employment remained steady during the Depression, although salaries were reduced. The bulk of state work in the Salem area had to do with state institutions, and prisoners had to be guarded and hospital patients cared for, even in the depths of the Depression. The State gave Salem a buffer enjoyed by no other Oregon community, and as a result there were relatively few business failures in the capital.

Oregon editors, including Sprague, tried to put an optimistic spin on the Depression, particularly while Herbert Hoover was in the White House. The *Statesman* on January 1, 1930 found "a bright outlook for the coming year, despite a tendency elsewhere toward a brief pause in business during readjustments necessitated by the stock market crash."[44] Sprague worried about what was happening nationwide, but believed Oregon was better off than most of the country. He warned that demonstrations by the unemployed had to be taken seriously, but in 1930 was still hoping that the Depression was only a downturn in the normal business cycle. Later in the year he noted that with the exception of a lumber mill, local industries were operating with full crews, and Salem seemed to be avoiding serious trouble. Yet he found it necessary by year's end to urge that married women justify their jobs if men or single women were in need of work.[45]

Relief was never adequate, even after federal funds began to supplement local spending. In the twelve months ending in September 1933, Marion County spent $200,000 on relief, half of which was federal funds. The largest items were for road work.[46] Portland legislators were calling for larger appropriations—which would have required a tax increase—but were checkmated by the more conservative rural counties and, in the case of highway funds, by a conservative Highway Commission, presided over by men such as Leslie Scott, one-third owner of *The Oregonian*, who once told a delegation of the unemployed that if voters didn't approve a sales tax for relief, their alternative was to starve.[47]

Parts of Oregon were harder hit than the Willamette Valley, although even Salem had its hunger pickets, who occupied the Courthouse lawn for a week in 1933. Southern Oregon had a genuine populist revolt, culminating in a 1933 shooting that sent the owner of the *Medford News*, L. L. Banks, to prison. Banks was the leader of a growing movement to install a radical populist government in Jackson County, and as the group grew the danger of violence increased. Banks was being served a grand jury summons in a case involving ballot theft when he shot and killed the server, Constable George Prescott. The killing sobered the community, but feelings continued to run high for years. Robert Ruhl won a Pulitzer Prize for the Medford *Mail Tribune* for his coverage and editorials opposing Banks.[48]

Federal efforts to reverse the Depression by pump-priming and governmental involvement in the economy were not applauded by Oregon's Republican editors, and Sprague was no exception. He was more concerned about government loans and aid to business than he was about massive job programs; the president was over-reacting, he believed, and there was a danger that the programs would get out of control.[49] A year

Medford publisher Robert Ruhl, shown about 1960, was a Sprague backer in 1938 and 1942, and won a Pulitzer Prize for his coverage of Depression-era violence in southern Oregon (Medford *Mail Tribune*).

into the New Deal, however, he moderated his views, giving Roosevelt credit for giving the nation a psychological boost; Sprague found the infusion of "brain trust" ideas and men was helpful. He was drawing back from a firm verdict on the New Deal's "alphabet soup" agencies and programs. After initial rejection, Sprague was taking a second look at F.D.R.[50]

As Roosevelt moved left in his "Second New Deal," and closer to the 1936 election, Sprague began moving away from his "wait and see" attitude of 1934 and into active opposition. In the Republican nominee of 1936, Kansas Gov. Alf Landon, Sprague saw a former Progressive who could be a moderating force without turning the country to the right. Sprague quoted Walter Lippmann with approval when the nation's most celebrated columnist abandoned Roosevelt to support Landon, and suggested that he himself was supporting Landon on the issue of individual liberty versus centralization of power.[51]

Sprague's views on the New Deal were consistent with his outlook on other political issues of the time. He strongly opposed the Townsend Plan for pensions for the elderly, which had thousands of supporters in Oregon. He preferred federal work programs to outright relief, but maintained a conservative outlook on the issuance of government bonds to prime the economic pump. He avoided personal attacks on the president or his wife, a favorite target of many Republicans; and he admired many of the young men around the president, while maintaining skepticism about their work. Certainly no New Dealer, he was a constructive and dispassionate critic, with none of the bile that tainted so many Republican opponents of Roosevelt.

In addition to his yeoman service to the Republican Party, Sprague had spent the decade engaged in state and local issues, including the Salem water struggle, construction of a replacement for the Capitol building after it burned in 1935, support for a unified system of higher education, and one of the remnants of the great Progressive effort—Prohibition.

Prohibition had become something between a joke and a tragedy by the time of its repeal, but in the Progressive Era it was part of the good-government movement, typical of the zeal of the time to reform social ills through legislation. Progressives were often closely aligned with prohibitionists and women's suffragists, and in many states, including Oregon, Prohibition followed women's right to vote. As Sprague recalled, the prewar saloon was a tough place where more than one husband lost a week's pay or staggered home drunk and abusive. By 1933 the law was honored mainly in its breach and clearly repeal was justified, but for many like Sprague it was hard to give up an ideal that society could be improved through law.

Sprague went down with the ship, supporting the 18th Amendment to the bitter end. A teetotaler himself, he accepted the argument that the saloon was the root of many of the problems of the new century. He was particularly disdainful of those who patronized bootleggers while endorsing a "dry" status for others. As late as 1932, Sprague defended Prohibition, "simply because we are convinced that this country as a whole is immeasurably better off than before prohibition . . . In other words we are personally and politically dry."[52]

Although Oregon had been dry since 1914, the issue was controversial in Marion County, one of the nation's largest hop-growing regions, and a few days after Sprague's editorial appeared the county's Republicans passed a motion asking Congress to send a repeal to the states for ratification.[53]

When Oregon voters overwhelmingly voted to repeal Prohibition in 1933, Sprague immediately and typically turned to finding a political method to deal with the liquor traffic. In a detailed five-part editorial study of the various methods of state control, he endorsed the suggestions of a committee appointed by Governor Meier and headed by Dr. William Knox of Portland. The so-called Knox Plan evolved into the state's present system of state liquor stores and licensed premises.[54]

Sprague's other major campaigns of the era were less personal and more pragmatic, as he labored to produce a modern governing system for the state's warring colleges and to build a suitable Capitol to replace the iron-domed building burned in 1935.

Higher education was a lifelong passion for Sprague, and he served both public and private institutions in a variety of roles. In the thirties one role was that of referee, as Oregon State College in Corvallis and the University of Oregon in Eugene engaged in a bitter battle for control and survival, centered on a radical 1932 initiative to reconstruct the state's system and in effect subordinate the University of Oregon to its arch-rival, Oregon State College.

For the newly merged Eugene *Register-Guard* and its editor, William Tugman, it was a battle for the city's future. Tugman came to Eugene in 1927 to edit the Eugene *Guard* for Alton S. Baker; in 1932 Baker purchased the *Register,* and the *Register-Guard* emerged as the largest afternoon newspaper outside Portland. Tugman, a graduate of Harvard and a hard-boiled police reporter at the Cleveland *Plain Dealer*, was five years Sprague's junior and he died eight years before Sprague. For 25 years, their interests and careers frequently overlapped, almost always in agreement.[55] Tugman was as outgoing and rambunctious as Sprague was private and retiring, but the two men shared loyalty to two key institutions, the Republican Party and higher education.

The 1932 effort to subordinate the University of Oregon to its arch-rival was dubbed the Zorn-MacPherson bill after its sponsors, Marion County farmer Henry Zorn and Albany farmer-legislator Hector MacPherson. In the Depression the bill looked promising. It would save money by combining the two major institutions, with headquarters on the Corvallis campus, reducing the U of O to a "normal school" and sending its law school to the private Willamette University in Salem. Eugene, already reeling from declines in lumber, felt not only an economic threat but a cultural threat as well; the university was the heart of the city.

Sprague opposed Zorn-MacPherson, as did nearly all of the state's editors except Claude Ingalls in Corvallis (Benton County was the only county supporting the measure when it was buried in a negative vote of 6 to 1 in the fall).[56]

Sprague, perhaps realizing Zorn-MacPherson was already doomed to failure, occupied himself primarily in opposition to the new state board's plan to build a highly centralized system and to limit the role of both major institutions. In a long and painstaking editorial opening on the front page of August 8 and taking the entire editorial page, he portrayed the plan as a "Frankenstein System," and published a set of charts which he said illustrated its overlapping jurisdictions and bureaucracy. For readers hardy enough to plow through the entire editorial and examine the webbing of the charts, the exposition clearly damned the concept.[57] It was a massive undertaking, and it produced favorable reactions from other editors, including both Tugman and Ingalls. As in other cases in his career, Sprague was writing here for an audience beyond Marion County—he was seeking to project his ideas into the public arena of politicians, editors and educators.

Sprague's exhaustive study of the state system, along with his analysis of state liquor control the same year, revealed a man who truly understood government. He was willing to work at the less-glamorous tasks of making the machinery work, and it was less of a jump than might have been expected when he traded his editor's desk for the Capitol's myrtlewood-paneled office.

His role in building a modern Capitol was more intimate, and he worked both through his editorial page and personally with Bend *Bulletin* publisher Robert Sawyer, who was a member of the State Capitol Reconstruction Commission appointed by Governor Martin. Sawyer and Sprague were close, and corresponded over the years as Sawyer took an active role in state highways, parks and timber.

The Capitol was a grand old structure, completed in 1876 except for its dome, which was finished in 1893. Polk's directory for 1930-31 boasted that "It is fireproof, being constructed of brick and iron, with stone foundation and roof of tin."[58] The boast was disproved in 1935 when the Capitol burned to the ground in the most spectacular fire in Salem's history. The small *Statesman* staff rose to the occasion, in the process

Bend publisher Robert Sawyer, shown about 1950, was a Sprague ally on several fronts, including the new Capitol and forestry legislation (Bend *Bulletin* photo).

helping build the legend of Sheldon Sackett, who headed a team that turned out two pages of copy with pictures from several sources. "Sackett sure could make the keys fly," Bob Sprague recalled, and on the night of the big fire, "He was really, well he was just unbelievable, typing away there, the phones were ringing . . ."[59] It was the best of Sackett's manic side, and the *Statesman* did an excellent job of deadline reporting; the fire broke out about 6 p.m., and the *Statesman* had its full package in the morning edition.

Planning a Capitol replacement immediately produced a dispute over location. Sprague's first instinct was to rebuild the structure on the same site; it was centrally located, which would entail less community disruption than other suggested sites.[60] But architects objected to the old site as too narrow, and attention focused for several weeks on the Willamette University campus, across State Street from the burned shell. Willamette trustees finally offered to sell the campus to the state for $750,000 and a new campus site on adjacent Bush's Pasture. Sprague liked the idea—it kept the Capitol in a central location, provided a larger building site and better future expansion opportunity. He urged Salem to unite behind the plan.[61]

A fractious special legislative session, with the Senate meeting in the Marion Hotel and the House in the Armory, brought forth a plan that pleased few, including Sprague. Governor Martin insisted on a Candalaria Heights site in South Salem, but was rejected; bids to buy the Willamette campus were torpedoed by key senators; and the state's appropriation was limited to $2.5 million, which even with a federal grant was a bare minimum. The new capitol was built on the ashes of the lost structure. Sprague salvaged the best face he could, but regretted that the state would never again have an opportunity to acquire a site equal to the Willamette campus; he concluded that the only good thing about the session was that it could have been worse.[62]

When Capitol architects were chosen, Sprague in a front-page story termed their plan "modern in its design, yet one which shows the restraint and the balance of classical Grecian architecture."[63] He began a thirty-year correspondence with principal architect Francis Keally of New York, which continued through the building of the Capitol Mall complex and into later remodeling of the Capitol.

On behalf of a Salem committee, Sprague also negotiated with heirs of the Willson family, donors of Willson Park, adjacent to the Capitol. Rebuilding the Capitol required acquisition of part of the park, and Sprague secured the approval of the far-flung heirs.[64]

Sprague followed the planning closely, even suggesting changes in the second floor design to add extra seating in the House and Senate galleries, an idea approved by the commission and architect Keally.[65] His involvement with the project was so intense that commission member George R. Lewis of Pendleton wrote, "I think no man in Oregon outside the members of the (commission) has at all times been in closer touch with the developments of the Capitol program than have you. . . ."[66]

The new Capitol was still under construction when Sprague turned his editorial attention to the next projects—a general office building and a library, the beginning of what became the Capitol Mall. The library in particular interested him, and throughout his life he was a regular visitor to its reading and reference room. In editorials beginning in 1936, Sprague pressed for the library, urging haste while federal WPA funds were available. The library's 360,000 volumes were jammed into nooks and crannies in the Supreme Court. When Martin proposed to save money by putting the library on the top floor of a new general office building, Sprague quickly and firmly denounced the plan, presenting detailed architectural and logistical reasons for a separate building.[67]

Through his involvement in the Capitol reconstruction, higher education, liquor control, and other state issues, Sprague was attracting statewide attention by the mid-thirties. Active in the Oregon Newspaper Publishers Association, he had forged personal relationships with the state's leading editors. Sufficiently conservative for hardliners Claude Ingalls and Robert Sawyer, he was also thoughtful and intellectually attractive to such men as Robert Ruhl and Bill Tugman. He had drawn the enmity only of George Putnam, who sensed not only a rival but a personality quite different from his own.

The last thing on Sprague's mind, or that of his peers, however, was a political career in the midst of the Depression. The Republican establishment was perfectly content with Charles Martin in the governor's chair. Republicans still controlled the Legislature, at times with support of right-wing Democrats, and Republican business and utility executives called the state's economic tune. It was a time for the GOP to batten down and let the Democratic tide pass, content with a conservative Democrat in the governorship.

Yet Governor Martin was an old man; he would be 78 years old by the end of a second term. He won in 1934 with only 38.6 percent of the vote and, despite his appeal to conservative Republican business leaders, he had managed to provoke the wrath of sizeable segments of the voting population. He attracted the organized opposition of the zealous young Oregon Commonwealth Federation, and the absolute hatred of organized labor. By any token, Martin was vulnerable; only the GOP old guard seemed not to recognize his vulnerability. It was a vulnerability based as

Gov. Charles H. Martin speaks at the cornerstone-laying ceremony for the new Capitol building in December 1936. He was the first governor to occupy the new building. At Martin's right is Archbishop Edward Howard; partially hidden by a microphone at Martin's left is Secretary of State Earl Snell (*Statesman-Journal* photo files).

much on the general's attitude and comments as on his programs and actions. Martin was talking himself out of office.

But there was no apparent challenger, as prominent Republicans talked themselves out of the race, convinced that the aging general was unbeatable. That was the circumstance in March 1938, as two young men crowded into the cubicle that served as office for the publisher and editor of *The Oregon Statesman*. Ad salesmen and circulation promoters walked by the door; overhead, linotypes clattered and the Associated Press wire spit out the world's headlines. The editor's desk was piled with a jumble of news clippings, reports, magazines and letters in no apparent order. Nearby a battered Royal typewriter was perched on a stand, copy paper in the platen with the beginning of an editorial.

They had come, explained David Eccles and Lowell Paget, to ask Sprague to become a candidate for governor. The Republican party must have a legitimate challenger to Governor Martin. They had heard Sprague speak and read his editorials. The progressive wing of the party could not let the nomination go by default. Would he consider running?

Sprague laughed at the first suggestion, a laugh from the belly. Then he listened, seldom making eye contact, nodding occasionally. Gently, he told them he had a newspaper to run, that he had never run for office and wasn't sure he would be a very good candidate. He enjoyed his independence. They talked a few minutes longer, then Sprague turned rather abruptly to his typewriter and the young men realized it was time to leave.

It had been a long shot, born of desperation to find a respectable candidate. Paget and Eccles were Young Republican leaders, and when they surveyed the list of potential candidates they were dismayed. They had asked the popular Secretary of State, Earl Snell, to enter the race, but he declined. "He patted us on the back in his way of never offending and went his way to re-election," Eccles recalled. Snell, like other potential entries, was convinced that Martin was unbeatable because he had nailed down the conservative vote of both parties.

"Lowell called me one day and said he was down at Amity and went to a Republican meeting and the editor of the Salem *Statesman* was the speaker and he's the greatest thing I ever heard—let's see if we can get him to run for governor," Eccles recalled. Despite their best efforts, Sprague rejected the appeal, and the pair left Salem downhearted. "But by God about a week later he came up to Portland and said he was willing to go. He was a sacrificial lamb, but he agreed with us that the party had an obligation to put up someone respectable."[68]

In the interim, Sprague discussed the idea with Blanche, but not with his adult children. He probably consulted the editors with whom he was closest, Claude Ingalls and Robert Sawyer, and perhaps Palmer Hoyt of *The Oregonian*, who was active in Republican circles. Among his Salem friends, perhaps Paul Wallace and Fred Lamport also were consulted, but the circle would not have been wide. A few key Portland Republicans would have been contacted, certainly Henry L. Corbett, whom Sprague had backed for governor in 1930. But Sprague confided in few people, and always had confidence in his own decisions.

An Oregon resident for only thirteen years, Sprague did not even have the beginning of a political network, but he did know and was respected by the state's major editors, a professional network of some importance. In 1938 editors were community leaders and their words were read; radio news was insignificant at the local and state level, television far in the distance. The closest thing Sprague had to a personal network was Blanche's connection with the PEO sisterhood, a sorority of which she had been state president. Sorority sisters were among the leading women in many communities. Sprague was virtually unknown in Portland; he had been quoted on the editorial pages of the city's dailies, but never in the news columns. He was truly a dark horse, with little hope of victory.

Sprague announced on April 1, which produced the predictable horse laugh from Don Upjohn, the *Capital-Journal* columnist:

> *By making public the announcement on April 1 he played two April Fool jokes also in one maneuver, same being as follows, i.e., viz:*
>
> *(1) One April Fool joke played on Charley Sprague.*
>
> *(2) One April Fool joke played on the republican party.*
>
> *. . . Charley didn't say whether he planned to campaign with a Packard and $40,000 in competition with Sam Brown, his Ford and $40, but it will be an interesting race between the sausage maker of Gervais and the baloney maker of Salem.*[69]

Upjohn was referring to to the populist Republican state senator, Sam Brown of Gervais, a perennial candidate for office, who had run second to Joe Dunne in the 1934 primary. In that campaign, several thousand farmers contributed jugs of gasoline to keep Brown's old Ford running. Brown represented the public power flank of the party, running with Grange support.

Sprague named as campaign manager Portland attorney Bob Boyd, a liberal Republican with good connections. Downstate, Sprague hired Cecil Edwards, an irrepressible young man active in Salem politics, whose father was a *Statesman* printer. The campaign soon discovered that Republican pocketbooks were difficult to touch; conservatives were satisfied with Martin.[70] The action would have to begin in the Democratic primary. And so it did.

The Oregon Commonwealth Federation had Martin in its sights. The question was finding a candidate to carry the flag of the New Deal and public power, which OCF leaders felt were the keys to defeating their nemesis. The 1937 Legislature had a Democratic House for the first time in many years, but many were conservatives and few had a statewide name.

A Bend physician and legislator, J. F. Hosch, stepped forward on January 31 and appeared to fill the bill. One of the most liberal state representatives and a former mayor of both Bend and Redmond, Hosch was president of the Peoples' Power League. Hosch had campaign literature printed and began a speaking tour, but abruptly withdrew from the race on the eve of the filing deadline, citing his medical practice and personal reasons. But it was also apparent that Hosch in his brief tour of the state had found vital constituencies split and lacking financial support. In particular, the public power movement was divided along the lines of personalities, and the more serious division between the AFL and CIO had to be taken into consideration.[71]

Henry Hess, LaGrande legislator and New Deal supporter, upset Gov. Charles Martin in the 1938 Democratic primary, but found himself painted as a leftist in the general election (Henry Hess Jr.)

In Hosch's stead came Henry Hess, a LaGrande lawyer and former state senator (1932-36), filing at the deadline as a surprise entry backed by the Commonwealth Federation and public power advocates. Hess had been supported for a federal judgeship by the OCF in 1937. Monroe Sweetland, OCF executive director, and attorney Gus Solomon called Hess and said many people wanted him to run (perhaps an exaggeration at the time). "Good God, Monroe, do you think there's a chance?" Hess responded and, assured by the relieved Sweetland, the attorney agreed to file.[72]

Martin backers later put forward an elaborate conspiracy regarding the Hosch-Hess switch, which had Teamsters leaders Dave Beck and Daniel J. Tobin dictating the move in order to get favorable treatment for their jailed "goon" colleagues. The *Journal* gave the conspiracy front-page treatment, but named no sources. It was later picked up by other papers in the general election, becoming almost a statement of fact despite a complete lack of proof. Sweetland adamantly rejected the Teamsters link, noting that the Teamsters were not a part of the Federation.[73]

The episode illustrated, however, Hess's vulnerability. The Teamsters were synonymous with labor violence, and that identity, added to the radical reputation of the Commonwealth Federation, left Hess vulnerable to the proper opponent. But unfortunately for Governor Martin, the Democratic primary did not develop into a referendum on the little-known Hess; it turned quickly into a referendum on the outspoken Martin. Hess's turn on the grill would come in the fall.

Monroe Sweetland, executive secretary of the Oregon Commonwealth Federation, master-minded the campaign against conservative Democrat Charles Martin in 1938; Sweetland was a leader in revival of the Democratic Party in the fifties (photo ca 1940, Oregon Historical Society 98548).

Martin had simply made too many enemies, often with his blunt language. On the attack early, former Democratic Congressman Elton Watkins (1923-25, Third District) told a KGW Radio audience that Martin could not win in November, that he had been saved in 1934 by the Independent candidacy of Peter Zimmerman. It was time to "retire this profane old man and his cabinet of lobbyists," declared Watkins.[74]

Martin was already on the ropes when the Roosevelt Administration delivered a final blow, in an effort to purge the Democratic Party of right-wing office-holders. Interior Secretary Harold Ickes, a progressive who was a leader in the public power wing of the administration, sent a "personal" letter to Hess, saying Martin had failed the test of public power. "He is at heart no New Dealer," declared Ickes in the widely circulated letter.[75] The piling-on continued with an endorsement of Hess by Senator George Norris of Nebraska, an icon of the public power movement. "Don't let the old general and the power crowd drive a wedge between the farmer and the industrial worker," he warned. "When Governor Martin was elected I believed as did my friends that he would be a true liberal. He has disappointed all these hopes."[76]

The intervention of Norris and Ickes drew howls of protest from Oregon editors, nearly all of whom were backing Martin. Bob Ruhl in Medford and Ed Aldrich in Pendleton, staunch F.D.R. supporters, fired off telegrams to the president himself, seeking a statement in support of Martin. Aldrich termed the Democratic primary "a clear-cut fight over law enforcement. . . . Secretary Ickes was very badly misled."[77] Their protests were ignored.

The early election count was close and Associated Press and the morning papers had Martin narrowly ahead, due to a slow Portland count. As Multnomah County reported, Hess turned the tables. In four years Martin had failed to attract a following among ordinary voters, and in the ranks of labor and public power he had generated rage. Although the Hess campaign stumbled and was barely into gear when the May primary arrived, Martin's opponents sent him from the battlefield with 52,640 votes to Hess's 59,620. Henry Oleen, another anti-Martin candidate, polled 8,220. The primary was a straight referendum on Old Iron Pants.

The Hess victory brought only brief celebration, for the Democratic Party was badly split and Hess had finished with less than 50 percent of the primary vote. He was still relatively unknown, and there was no reason to think that editors who had supported Martin would choose Hess in November instead of their colleague, Charles Sprague. The Republican establishment, so reluctant to back Sprague weeks earlier in the face of Martin's sure re-election, "all came around," Eccles recalled.[78] Suddenly, the little-known editor from Salem was a force to be reckoned with.

Sprague and his seven Republican rivals had campaigned in obscurity; all the focus was on the Hess-Martin battle, which the *New York Times* branded a New Deal test race. The *Times* ran consecutive front-page stories on the outcome, rare treatment for an Oregon race. Richard L. Neuberger, writing for the *Times*, believed the temporary truce between the AFL and CIO to jointly back Hess was decisive in the Portland area, an assessment seconded by *Times* columnist Arthur Krock two days later.[79] In none of the stories was Sprague acknowledged more than a listing; the national significance of Oregon in 1938 was in the Democratic primary. But for Oregon, the general election just ahead was more important.

Sprague faced a pack of self-starters in the primary, including his own editorial-page colleague, R. J. Hendricks. The old editor, who still wrote a history column for Sprague, filed on a platform stressing prison reform and recognition of Oregon history. Why he chose this time and this race after generations on the sideline was not clear, but he mounted no real campaign and finished dead last. His entry did not seem to damage his relations with Sprague, the latter's son recalled, and Hendricks continued writing his column almost until his death in 1943 at the age of 79.[80]

The other surprise entry was Henry Hanzen, the veteran political reporter and fixer, running on the Joseph-Meier power platform he had done so much to craft. With the entry of Clarence E. Wagoner, a former publisher at Independence, and Charles L. Paine, who cited unspecified "newspaper experience," the primary looked like a journalists' convention. Other entries were J. W. Morton of Hood River and M. S. Schrock, a

Grange leader and dairyman. But Sprague was the only one mounting a serious campaign, and his only real opponent was Sam Brown of "Forty dollars and a Ford" fame. Brown had a legitimate call on the votes of farmers and public power advocates; he had fought their fight in the Legislature for twelve years. "He is not a machine controlled candidate and is free from all entangling alliances with Oregon's political bosses," his literature proclaimed.[81]

Sprague signaled his campaign intentions in a radio speech shortly after he announced his candidacy. It was a standard Republican attack on the New Deal, but couched in the language of a moderate critic. Republicans, said Sprague, have not failed in Oregon despite the party's defeats nationally. He took a cue from the president's "nothing to fear but fear itself" line, challenging Oregon Republicans to not allow the party to "die of fright" or by default.[82]

Sprague accused the national Administration of having run out of ideas, causing the economic downturn of 1937-38. The policies of the Roosevelt Administration, he charged, had "destroyed business confidence" with tax increases and "new-deal-inspired labor unrest." Even in April, Sprague was obviously looking ahead to the possibility that he might need Martin supporters in November, for he did not mention the governor in his speech.

Sprague sketched his personal and business history, then succinctly outlined his views on major issues. He did not avoid the issue of public power, restating his editorial support of strict regulation of private utilities, the right of voters to form public agencies, and opposition to

Sprague found radio a good medium for his 1938 gubernatorial bid and used radio extensively again in 1942 (Oregon Historical Society 98546).

duplication. In similar manner, he supported worker choice on union affiliation while stressing his opposition to violence "by goon squads or by vigilantes."[83]

Sprague repeated versions of his standard speech during travels around the state, always in the shadow of the Democratic slugfest. In April, when he announced his candidacy, he shared his feelings with *Statesman* readers, akin to those of a man on a high diving board: "That is about the state of mind of a political candidate. He blows hot and cold; he gets his nerve up, then feels it ooze away. Then he either does, or he doesn't." Entering the lists for the first time, he professed lack of knowledge about what he would face: "The lady of the house yesterday asked: 'What do you do after you file?' Then, we replied, you start going sort of crazy. Our own sanity will probably be restored by May 21."[84]

On May 21 Sprague was back at his typewriter for a brief time, awaiting the voting results, reflecting that the experience would make him a better editor regardless of its outcome, and expressing some surprise that a politician was treated with such courtesy by the electorate. He was also discovering that campaigning had undergone some major changes, particularly with the use of radio, which he found well suited to his personality and style.[85]

Sprague's campaign poster stands amidst a group of workers in Salem Republican headquarters in 1938 (Oregon Historical Society CN014616).

Sprague had been a college debater and was comfortable in making his argument in a short format. He was never adept at personal campaigning; he was impatient with small talk and idle gestures and uneasy around people he did not know. According to Cecil Edwards, Sprague improved when he had Blanche with him: "she had that effusive motherliness about her, it seemed to kind of keep him warmed up." Although Sprague was a strong speaker, Edwards noted that he "forced himself into an expanded geniality" in order to broaden his voter appeal.[86]

He had the enthusiastic endorsements of every daily newspaper that declared a favorite. The *Capital-Journal* limited its role to the Democratic primary, where George Putnam lay on his shield for Martin. Putnam refused to comment on Sprague, leaving the race to the snide remarks of Don Upjohn's "Sips for Supper;" it was not the C-J's finest hour.

When the votes were counted, the ramifications of the primary were obvious. In the Democratic primary, Henry Hess against two opponents emerged with just under 50 percent; on the Republican side, Charles Sprague against seven opponents emerged with just over 50 percent. Sprague lost only tiny and remote Curry County, which went for Sam Brown. Obviously, Hess had faced stronger opposition in Governor Martin; but equally obvious was the November choice for the 52,640 Democrats who had supported Martin: they would swallow defeat and support the party nominee who had excoriated their man, stay home, or vote for a moderate Republican who seemed reasonable and had refrained from attacking their man. Suddenly April's sacrificial lamb had become the man to beat in November. George Putnam vividly and correctly analyzed his party's position. Democrats, he said, "have walked through the slaughter-house into an open grave."[87]

The politics of 1938 foreshadowed later races in which image was crucial. One of the vital challenges in campaigning is creating the image of relatively unknown candidates. A blank slate can have its message written by the candidate, by his opponent, or by outside forces. That writing can determine the fate of the candidate.

Both Hess and Sprague entered the race at the last minute, without a campaign organization and dependent upon others to form their image. But for Hess, the "others"—organized labor and the Oregon Commonwealth Federation in particular—had their own images to overcome. Labor had been tarred with the "goon" label, and for the past year the OCF had been battered as socialist or worse by the state's editors, Governor Martin, and his friend, Oswald West. Hess, lacking an image of his own, took on the trappings of his supporters, and almost immediately was branded a radical by the state's conservative editors.

There is no solid evidence that Hess held radical views; he was essentially a mainstream New Deal Democrat, a small-town lawyer with some legislative experience. But the radical image may as well have been tattooed on his forehead; it could not be erased. With some skill and press support, a contrary image could have been crafted. Hess had a working-class background; he was a mill hand who had put himself through law school and had a practice defending injured workers and other "little guys." He was also a World War I veteran who worked his way through the ranks to the top enlisted rank in the Army.[88] But these virtues, so important in a small rural state, went virtually unmentioned in the campaign; Hess was linked, instead, to his radical supporters.

Sprague's image, on the other hand, was happily supplied by his colleagues in the Oregon press, and it was one of a reasonable and moderate man, sound in business practice and versed in governmental affairs. Hess was much too busy in the primary, as were his backers, to define another image for Sprague. They had Martin to contend with, and he did not retire gracefully.

In reality, there was probably much less difference between the candidates than the campaign indicated, but the race was branded as that of a moderate versus a radical. In Oregon, and most other states, a moderate will defeat a radical every time. The task for Sprague was to keep his powder dry and stay positive, while leaving for his editorial friends the job of kicking the "radical" can they had tied to Henry Hess.

The Sprague campaign carefully worked the only network it had—Oregon's editorial community. Ralph Moores, who was brought into the campaign as a field worker, had a faithful routine as he moved from community to community. His first visit was with the local editor, who knew the rest of the community first-hand and could provide introductions, insights, and personal support. Excerpts from his field reports to Bob Boyd indicate how heavily he used editors:

> *Then went to McMinnville and found pretty fair situation. Saw first Lars Bladine of Tel Reg. and he's as always staunch. He has list of 10,000 truck drivers and owners and leaders, will write to all of them over their own name. . . . Ken Epley, Ed of Willamina Times is staunch friend of C.A.S. He and Shetterley tried to form C.A.S. club. . . . Merle Chessman (Astorian-Budget) of course my chief counsel. . . . Seaside Signal, editor Max Shafer old friend, and says CAS sure shot. Good talk. . . . Found a red hot supporter and a wise one in the editor, W. Verne McKinney of the Hillsboro Argus.*[89]

Moores found few exceptions to his rule. Even the volatile Sheldon Sackett was in Sprague's camp; Moores reported Sprague's partner was not popular in the Coos Bay business community, "yet the labor people think he's OK."[90] Sackett was supporting his partner against a New Deal candidate, while backing the New Deal on his editorial page.

Moores pinpointed the areas that would give Sprague the most trouble: strong union towns, particularly with sawmills, and the public power wing of the Grange.

In the primary, union leaders had eliminated their chief tormentor, but their support was not locked in for Hess. Sprague had never been a union-basher, and for a Republican he had one great advantage: he employed union labor in a closed-shop contract, and he had never had a strike. But he would have to overcome Hess's natural advantage in labor circles.

Labor put Sprague on the defensive early in the fall with a pamphlet printed by the AFL lumber workers' union, the United Brotherhood of Carpenters and Joiners. Entitled "Charles A. Sprague's Real Views on Labor," the handout lifted excerpts from *Statesman* editorials of the previous three years. Most were critical of New Deal labor measures, primarily the Wagner Act. Sprague had endorsed the Loyal Legion of Loggers and Lumbermen (the 4-Ls), a form of company union, and this endorsement was cited, as was his support of the use of state police in labor disputes. Sprague's comments were then interpreted in the most anti-union analysis possible; it was a rough attack, and pamphlets were in every AFL hall. Labor's efforts were complemented by the Oregon Commonwealth Federation, which circulated a several-page collection of editorial excerpts on issues ranging from public power to housing and relief, all designed to present the Republican candidate as opposed to the needs and desires of working people. Lifted from their context, Sprague's generally moderate views appeared to be those of an angry reactionary.[91]

The strongly worded literature was countered, however, by other actions within the AFL. The state executive board refused to endorse either candidate, stating that either was acceptable to organized labor; the *Oregon Labor Press*, in endorsing Sprague in the Republican primary, issued a strong statement on his behalf; and a supportive letter was circulated to all AFL locals from Herb L. Lange, secretary-treasurer of Capital Typographical Union No. 219, the printing employees of *The Oregon Statesman*.

Sprague had always been more sympathetic toward organized labor than his editorial peers, most of whom were rabidly anti-union. Putnam in particular loathed unions, and gloried in the goon-bashing of his friends, Governor Martin and Ralph Moody. A C-J tear sheet telling "The

Inside Story of Labor Rackets" circulated widely in the primary, glorifying the exploits of Moody.

The C-J was a major player in the effort in 1938 to pass a drastic limit on picketing. Other than the governor's race itself, the initiative was the most divisive issue of the campaign. Neither Hess nor Sprague grasped the nettle until quite late in the race, Hess presuming he had labor support without stressing the issue and Sprague uncertain of the proper approach.

Sprague seized the initiative with an October 23 editorial opposing the measure. He had turned his page over to Ralph Curtis when he declared for office in April, but there was no question that the carefully reasoned and lengthy analysis was that of the candidate. Observing that "a great deal that is being said on both sides is not so," Sprague dissected the measure and found it far too drastic. He agreed with union leaders who concluded that the measure would in fact prevent nearly all picketing, and would not bring an end to Oregon's labor strife.[92]

The editorial forced Hess to stress his opposition as well, but left him "me-tooing" his opponent on an issue where he should have led. There was shocked and angry reaction from Sprague's business backers, as several, including Henry Corbett, were also active backers of the initiative. "Campaign money was waved and then pulled back a little," Eccles recalled, noting that in the end Republicans really had no choice but to back Sprague. "But I think they never fully forgave Sprague."[93]

Editors began to climb off the fence after Sprague's editorial appeared, and finally wound up evenly split, with Sprague's view shared by *The Oregonian, Register-Guard, Astorian-Budget* and Bend *Bulletin;* while the *Capital-Journal, Mail Tribune* and *Gazette-Times* were among those backing the measure. The ubiquitous Neuberger, writing for *The New York Times,* saw Sprague's position as evidence of a leftward movement on the part of Oregon Republicans, Sprague in particular.[94]

Voters, who had been bombarded with anti-union slogans in a campaign that allegedly spent $80,000, voted their fears and adopted the anti-picketing bill by a margin of 197,771 to 148,460. As Sprague predicted, the Oregon Supreme Court later struck down the measure. But the *Oregon Labor Press* had printed Sprague's editorial in full, providing valuable exposure to an important audience.[95]

The final blow on the labor front came from Cecil Edwards, who had been growing nervous about the campaign. He warned Boyd in late September of complacency, "the Hess supporters are getting a tremendous hold in labor groups including employed pension minded groups, and beer tavern people." Boyd apparently took at least some of Edwards's concern to heart; the campaign produced a pension brochure and a labor pamphlet, and put some campaign workers into the pool halls in Portland (probably without consulting the candidate).[96]

Edwards learned that a small sawmill in northeastern Oregon owned by the Hess family was non-union. Edwards began to spread the rumor, and reporters confronted Hess. Yes, the mill was non-union, Hess replied, but his family would have no objections to unionization. The story never took off, but Edwards pressed, and in a "Dear Editor" letter to the state's newspapers, urged them to expose Hess's record: "Obviously the rank and file of labor does not know of the Dr. Jekyll and Mr. Hyde aspect of the Hess personality on labor," he implored. "So it is time the public know that Candidate Hess is affiliated with a lumber mill which operates with 'scab' labor." Deliberately misusing the term "scab" (Hess's mill was not employing strikebreakers; it simply was not organized), Edwards asserted that "repeated attempts" had been made to organize the mill, each time meeting with "rebuff."[97] Proof of the latter charge was not provided. Several last-week editorials endorsing Sprague did mention the non-union mill, and the Sprague campaign focused on it in a radio address directed at union workers. The speech described Hess as two-faced on labor and cited Sprague's use of union labor in his shop.[98]

Problems with unions were only part of Hess's frustration; he was having a difficult time identifying himself in a race where Sprague's editorial friends were painting his portrait in red hues.

Henry Hess advertised himself in the Democratic primary as a "Liberal," but after the primary he tried to pull his image toward the center, terming himself a "Liberal-Progressive." His Voter's Pamphlet statement and all of his early speeches concentrated on his single term in the Oregon Senate, particularly his votes for pensions, public power, labor and agriculture. Hess was no radical, but he was solidly in the New Deal wing of the Democratic Party. He had authored a law to forestall foreclosure of farm properties—a big issue during the Depression, and he had sponsored measures to benefit injured workers.

He needed help from Washington, and got it in the primary, but after Governor Martin was retired to his tent the national party had no further need for Hess, and no additional help was forthcoming. The ever-ready Harold Ickes, Secretary of Interior, undaunted by the wrath he had provoked by meddling in the primary, fired another salvo when he visited the state on October 24. Noting that Sprague had been saying nice things about the New Deal and the president, Ickes accused him of double-talk, prompting Sprague to accuse unnamed politicians of abusing their power.[99] Editors once again rolled out the cannons to blast the Eastern meddler; even George Putnam got into the act, finding Ickes even more to his distaste than Sprague.[100] Hess might have weathered the backlash if Ickes had brought some type of endorsement from Roosevelt, or produced Democratic campaign funds or workers; none of the above arrived to bolster the sagging campaign.

Frustration began to grow in Hess by mid-October, in particular due to his inability to penetrate Sprague's newspaper support. Hess was covered when he spoke, and the reporting was usually straight; but just as often, his appearance in town would provoke an editorial blast. Eugene was a good example. Bill Tugman was a Sprague backer from the outset, and Sprague got kid-gloves treatment when he toured Lane County October 14 and 15. A front-page picture, schedule of appearances, and front-page news coverage were followed by an admiring editorial, concluding, "When Mr. Sprague says: 'I will make no promises I cannot keep'—those words are his highest recommendation!"[101]

Tugman was, in fact, making the most of a series of rather bland statements in Lane County. Sprague, riding a lead, was not making waves in friendly territory. The most controversial statement quoted by the *Guard* was Sprague's praise of Dr. Francis Townsend as "a man who has done more than any other citizen in the United States as an educator in the need of old age pensions."[102] But the candidate made no personal pledges on pensions, certainly not of the type espoused by Townsend. He was leaving no flank exposed; his blandness was virtue.

Blandness was not working for Hess. The campaign that had begun as a race on his Senate record needed spice, and the frustrated Democrat lashed out when he followed Sprague into Lane County a week later, terming Sprague the candidate of private utilities and "the Wall Street bunch." Hess took a shot at "the subsidized press that is dictated to by the private power interests," and went on to accuse Sprague of "losing his head" in Baker, and calling all Democrats "barflies and screwball pinks."[103]

It was good copy, but scarcely the right ticket to win editorial approval. Predictably, Tugman came out swinging, pulling out the record of Teamsters support for Hess when he was seeking the federal judicial appointment in 1937. Tugman returned to the attack two days later, again linking Hess with "goonism" and challenging him to answer the charges when he spoke again in the county the following day. Hess complied, but only to say that "The press says I am supported by the goons. In the primary election I was named by the democrats of this state as their gubernatorial candidate and now they are labeling you goons."[104]

Tugman, of course, was not assuaged. A meeting followed—apparently the first time the editor and candidate had met—and some of Tugman's harsh appraisal was softened, but he was not visibly impressed by the man himself. "The nervous, wiry visitor fails to register as a classic liberal, but he has his points as a politician," was the best Tugman could muster, predicting that Hess would be controlled by "those diverse forces which produced his candidacy."[105]

There was irony in the charge that Hess would bow to the Teamsters, for the union had tried to buy his support, Hess's son recalled a half-century later. "They came to him and said they would support him if he agreed to pardon the goons . . . dad told them he wouldn't do it; he would view every case one-by-one, on its merits," Henry Hess Jr. said. He had been fourteen at the time, and his recently widowed father had taken sons Henry and Raymond on some campaign swings. "He said they were circulating rumors that his sons were in jail, so he thought we should be seen," Henry Jr. recalled.[106]

Similar tableaus were played out in other Oregon communities, perhaps without the flair of Tugman's assessment. But Hess's lack of acquaintance with the state's editors hurt him badly, for it is harder to demonize a man with whom you have shared a cup of coffee. And demonize him they did, in both primary and general election campaigns. The wonder is not that Hess lashed out at the Oregon press, but that he held himself in check as long as he did. In the race to the finish, bitterness would surface in both camps. So Hess lost the Teamster financial support he needed to help in his campaign, but was still labeled in the press as a Teamster agent.

Panic time in a fall election usually comes the last week in October; decisions must be made on how to spend the last dregs of cash in the till and where to schedule the candidate. The dread of last-minute charges and shifting public opinion hangs in the air, cigarettes burn to the butt and black coffee fries on the hot plate. In the primary it was during this final week that the Ickes-Norris duo unloaded on Governor Martin. Would there be a kidney punch this time, and if so from whom?

Hess was moving to the offensive, trying to damage Sprague's personal standing. He formed a "Veterans' Hess-for-Governor Club," using it to imply that Sprague had dodged military service in World War I: "In 1917 when the United States needed actual help and not lip service, Henry Hess proved his Americanism in the same manner *you* proved *your* Americanism (emphasis original). . . . We have no comment to make about the war record or lack of it on the part of the opposing candidate."[107] His election-eve advertising urged, "Save Oregon from 'Hooverism,'" and referred to Sprague as "an enemy of our national administration."

The Sprague campaign released its non-union-mill bomb in late October, and the candidate himself suddenly turned from his bland and conciliatory tone to one of strident attack on Hess's backers, in particular the Oregon Commonwealth Federation. Sprague had always feared political machines—it was his anti-city, progressive streak—and all through the administration of Julius Meier he warned against the establishment of a personal political machine operating outside the main parties. He saw similar dangers with the OCF.

The assault began with an October 24 radio speech, in which he described OCF as "an organization which communists midwifed if they did not actually conceive . . . The Commonwealth Federation is an aggregation of pinks and reds and pseudo intelligentsia." The intemperate attack was clearly for the benefit of the Martin wing of the Democratic party: "The sturdy democrats of this state are democrats. They are not communists; they are not radicals. They resent this invasion of socialists into their party ranks." Perhaps feeling a twinge of conscience, Sprague went on, somewhat disingenuously:

> *I am not a red-baiter. I have fought for civil liberties and political toleration. I am merely relating the facts, facts which are well known to political leaders and deserve to be known by every voting citizen of the state. I want it understood that I am not the candidate of the Oregon Commonwealth Federation or the Workers Alliance. If the voters want a governor who owes his election to the support of those elements, they should not vote for me. Which way, Oregon? Shall we go forward on safe lines of progress, preserving old liberties and true American traditions, or shall we turn the state over to the radicals represented by the Commonwealth Federation and its allies, to whom the new deal program is but a stepping stone in the direction of state socialism?*[108]

It was a demagogic bit of work, of no credit to Sprague, and probably unnecessary in the final reckoning. Its roots may have been in the OCF's use of editorial excerpts to paint Sprague as reactionary, for he referred to "the files of my editorials (which) have been combed and sentences torn from their context to be used to damage me in this campaign." While he claimed not to be disturbed by the tactic, it was obvious that the excerpts had been gnawing at his sense of fairness.

The episode revealed another side of the cool, reserved editor, the man of calm demeanor and reason: When Sprague was under personal attack, he bridled and lashed back. Don Upjohn had penetrated Sprague's cool demeanor several times with his "Sips for Supper" barbs. Now the Commonwealth Federation was painting him as a heartless reactionary.

Sprague's protective shield was breached. He was angry, and his wrath was unleashed in the KOIN broadcast.

Nor did he relent during the campaign's final days. In another KOIN address on November 1, he asked voters: "Shall we put in power in Oregon an administration which owes its election to a combination of radical left-wingers, labor racketeers and political spoilsmen?" Once again, he flailed the OCF as "the camel's nose of state socialism or communism . . . a united front for radicals of various shades of pink and red and of parlor intelligentsia to screen their drive for screwball legislation."[109]

Sprague's editorial friends took up the strain, but instead of zeroing in on the Commonwealth Federation (which they had already thoroughly worked over), most of the last-week editorials concentrated on Hess's labor ties, leaving the clear implication that if Hess were elected Dave Beck and other Teamster leaders would be in the governor's anteroom.

The editors were echoing exactly the themes that were pushed by the Sprague campaign: the Republican was moderate, thoughtful, a man of affairs and an employer of union labor to boot; the Democrat was associated with leftists and, worse than that, the dreaded Teamsters Union and its "goons." By the time the campaigns collapsed into exhaustion, and Sprague delivered an election-eve broadcast from the creaky old *Statesman* news room, voters could have been excused if they asked for a break. The moderate tone of September and early October had degenerated, and Sprague himself bore much of the blame for the kidney punches.

There was no need for a midnight watch on this election return; unlike the primary, no results reversed on the following day. Sprague carried all but three counties (Deschutes, Union and Coos), and rolled up a 12,000-vote margin in critical Multnomah County. In the primary, the hot beds of union opposition to Martin had been Multnomah County and the lumber regions, including Coos, Columbia, and Clatsop counties. In the general election, Sprague lost Coos but had large margins in the others; labor's anger had been vented and effectively countered.

In other results, Republicans cleaned house: Rufus Holman was elected to the U. S. Senate, Earl Snell re-elected Secretary of State, Homer Angell elected to Congress from the Third District; only the durable Congressman Walter Pierce escaped the deluge. Sprague would work with a Legislature overwhelmingly Republican: twenty-two Republicans to eight Democrats in the Senate and forty-seven to thirteen in the House.

The Democratic debacle prompted one student of the period to declare that, "Following the reversals of 1938, the Democratic Party declined rapidly as a political force in Oregon politics," as the party entered another period of fratricide.[110] Losing candidate Hess moved to Portland to practice law and served as U. S. Attorney for Oregon under the Truman Administration.

Oregon Democrats had peaked in 1936, riding the coattails of a popular president to pick up two of the three seats in Congress and elect a majority in the state House. Their registration was climbing, and the parties went into 1938 at parity. What, then, caused the 1938 Democratic disaster in Oregon?

First and foremost, the 1936 gains had only papered-over a deep and serious rift centering on Governor Martin and his relations with the important liberal constituencies of labor and public power. Martin was the last conservative Democrat to govern Oregon, but his departure did not purge that wing of the party; the ever-active Os West remained, and unleashed a savage attack on the Commonwealth Federation, warning that it planned to "Russianize" the Democratic Party. For its part, the Oregon Commonwealth Federation was neither deep enough nor broad enough to serve as a de facto Democratic Party, although the OCF tried to carry out that mission for a short time.

Secondly, the national Administration—after purging Martin—had larger fish to fry; Oregon was beyond the borders of Franklin D. Roosevelt's vision. National columnists Drew Pearson and Robert S. Allen proclaimed the 1938 result "a zero" for the New Deal, adding: "The Result for Oregon—50-50. Oregon got a good Republican governor in Charles A. Sprague, but a crackpot Republican Senator in Rufus Holman."[111]

Thirdly, in Sprague the Republicans had the perfect candidate for the times, a man who hewed to the party line but had no voting record to assail and who seemed to talk common sense and moderation. Oregonians were tired of strife, whether it came from labor picketers or Democratic infighting, and Sprague with his cool demeanor and even speaking voice appeared as a shaft of light. That Sprague was an employer of union labor in a race where that made a difference was pure serendipity.

Fourth, the Sprague campaign better than the Hess campaign seemed to understand the emerging importance of image and the use of radio. Sprague laid out a platform, but he did not dwell on issues or voting records; he labored instead to project himself as a man of reason, a healer and a listener who had made no promises other than to use good common sense. Hess tried to run an issue campaign, complete with every vote he had cast in the Senate and elaborate comparisons of his views with those he attributed to Sprague. Particularly on radio, with its irretrievability and short attention span, issues fade but style endures.

Sprague had headed off the Democrats' best chance to build a modern party, and he had turned the Republican party toward a centrist position.

Whether the same result would have obtained had he held to his initial rebuff of Dave Eccles and Lowell Paget, no one can say. But he rose to deliver his inaugural message with almost universal appreciation from his party.

Ready to move into his Capitol offices, Sprague carried as few encumbrances as any governor in the history of the state. He asked the voters for patience as he learned the new job: "I suppose a governor will make as many mistakes as an editor but I hope the people will be as tolerant of me as governor as they have been of me as editor."[112]

He had not bargained with any man or faction to enter the race; the party had come to him. He made few promises to support or oppose the legislation of special interests, and he owed few men a job. He was not dependent upon political office for income or career, for he remained the owner of a substantial business and enjoyed his editorial role.

With this freedom to maneuver and with the almost-universal appreciation of his party, Sprague faced a new year that seemed to have no clouds on its horizon. He could look forward to at least a brief honeymoon in office before the critics descended.

Perhaps it was an omen, but on election night, while he and his wife celebrated at the *Statesman* office, the Sprague house was burglarized. A month later, in a complex bit of political horsetrading, Senator-elect Rufus Holman left his office as State Treasurer early, allowing Governor Martin to appoint conservative Democrat Walter Pearson as Treasurer, leaving Sprague only a 2-to-1 Republican margin on the important Board of Control and denying Sprague the opportunity of appointing a successor to Holman.[113]

And waiting quietly in a security cell at the Oregon State Prison was a young man named Leroy Herschel McCarthy, with only the new governor between him and an appointment with the state's new gas chamber.

4

◆◆◆

A Progressive Governor Goes to War

Oregon's new governor could best be described as a moderate Progressive firmly returned to the Republican camp. Sprague fit William Allen White's description of Republicans who won in 1938 elections as, "new leaders of Republican liberalism who are the residuary legatees of the old Bull Moosers," representatives of a middle-class revolt against both the New Deal and the right-wing ideologues of the thirties.[1]

Republicans of Sprague's generation could be classified by where they stood in 1912, when Teddy Roosevelt's Bull Moose vanguard took on the old guard and captured the hearts of many young men. Walter Lippmann, among others, confessed that no politician ever captured his heart like T.R. When the progressive movement splintered in the flagwaving of World War I, its cadre moved in many directions. Some turned left to socialism, communism, or the more moderate position of promoting public power. Others went to the right, and were active in the nativist campaigns during and after World War I. Sprague resisted this rightward movement, although through the thirties he maintained a concern over "foreign elements" that might dilute the northern European stock of Oregon.

Sprague held very strong views that the genius of America was in the opportunity it offered: Every man could be successful through hard work and acceptance of the mainstream culture that Sprague himself embodied. Progressives believed in equality of opportunity, rather than a strict notion of equality for all. This belief figured in their view of racial and ethnic minorities, who should have the chance to advance and be properly recognized. Those who failed should not be able to blame their failure on circumstance.

When the Progressive lawyer, Louis Brandeis, was nominated in 1916 to the Supreme Court by President Woodrow Wilson, Ritzville editor Charles A. Sprague wrote one of his rare editorials on a national appointment, observing that although Brandeis "is a Hebrew," that should not disbar him from appointment. Many leading scholars, lawyers, philosophers, financiers and businessmen are Hebrew, he noted, and as their population increases more of them will succeed. "That this is true," he intoned in progressive style, "indicates the realization of the promise of America—equality of opportunity."[2]

If the Brandeis editorial reflected the naiveté of a very young editor, it also revealed a deep-seated belief in the American system as seen through middle-class eyes. As a moderate progressive, Sprague viewed government as a force to combat social evil, but he was skeptical of centralized power. He supported federal power dams and transmission lines, but favored private utilities under strict regulation. He had supported ambitious federal projects to tame the unpredictable Willamette River, control its flooding and improve navigation, but others had taken stronger leadership roles. A typical progressive in his belief that nature should be harnessed for the good of mankind, he was too restrained to engage in the boosterism that characterized Oregon business leaders and editors of the twenties and thirties.[3]

The new governor was a small-town man, champion of the values of Main Street, mainstream Protestant churches, and public education. He neither understood nor appreciated big cities and their amalgam of ethnic cultures and social strains.

His compassion was limited by the size of the public purse, and he did not support deficit finance, regardless of the need. A publisher who employed union labor, he backed the rights of workers to organize and maintain a union shop, but he opposed violence on the picket line and supported the use of state police to maintain order.

His views were all a matter of public record, as he found during the campaign, when opponents searched his editorials for fodder against him, but the man himself was unknown outside his own community and circle of editorial colleagues. Discovering the inner man was not as easy as researching his politics; the quiet, scholarly editor revealed himself to very few people. That he would expose himself to the glare of a statewide political campaign was quite remarkable, explained only by a strong sense of obligation augmented by more than a touch of personal ambition.

As he mounted the Capitol steps for his inauguration in January 1939, Sprague would have passed a citation carved in marble: "The mind of man knows no employment more worthy of its powers than the quest of righteousness in human affairs—no goal of its labors that is superior to the discovery of the good in the guidance of life." It was particularly appropriate for the new governor; few occupants of the office held as strong a view that government could be used for the moral progress of man.

In his efforts to preserve moral virtue and principled governance, Sprague was in the tradition of Oregon politics. Oregon was one of less than a dozen states possessing what political scientist Daniel Elazar termed a "moralistic political culture." In such a setting voters and politicians agreed that government service was public service, and that the moral obligation of the governors should transcend their obligation to a particular political party. This resulted in support for a governmental role in social engineering ranging from Prohibition to wage-and-hour regulation, but it did not always mean a strong federal role. Moralistic cultures often preferred to do their good at the local level, and feared centralization.[4]

This image of a moralistic culture fit Oregon at mid-century, and it fit Sprague's outlook. His own heritage followed the path of migration described by Elazar as carrying the moralistic culture west: from New England to the upper Midwest and finally the Northwest. Moralists were likely to believe in weak political parties, in public-private partnerships, and merit ratings for public servants.[5] All were positions Sprague held throughout his life.

He was the twenty-second governor since Oregon achieved statehood in 1859. Most governors in the 19th century were Democrats, serving single terms and returning to their farms or law practices. Sylvester Pennoyer took on the Populist label for his second term (1891-95) and rode the unruly farmer-labor revolt through those tumultuous years.

Governor Sprague poses in 1942 with former governors (from left) Oswald West, Ben Olcott, Albin Norblad, and Charles Martin (Salem Public Library, Ben Maxwell collection).

Republicans dominated Oregon congressional and legislative politics after the crash of 1897 but it was Democratic governors who left lasting marks on the state's history. George Chamberlain (1903-09) and Oswald West (1911-15) were charismatic personal politicians, reformers who carried direct government into office and succeeded in passing some reforms through Republican legislatures. The third Democratic governor, Walter Pierce (1923-27), was elected with Klan support in the reactionary tide of 1922, but proved to be more progressive than his supporters had anticipated; a blunt and free-spoken man of the soil, he proved particularly durable in Oregon politics, later serving ten years in Congress from eastern Oregon. The other dominant governors of the period were the men immediately preceding Sprague, Julius Meier and Charles Martin.

Reserved and sober, carefully controlling his emotions, the governor-elect on January 9, 1939 stood at the threshold of the most important four years of his life. He was now in control, as he was when the creaking old presses began to roll, the din of their cylinders filling the air and the vibration shaking the aging *Statesman* building four blocks away.

On January 9, 1939, an air of goodwill filled the House chamber; there was warm applause for Governor Martin as he delivered his farewell address. Seated proudly in the audience, the new governor's family anticipated the moment of Sprague's inauguration. Their joy, and that of the audience, was tinctured by the shadow of approaching war and the jackboot of fascism. The approaching storm gave the new governor a theme for his speech:

> *Over the world political and economic pressures have reacted against the idea of democracy. Authority is invoked to take up the slack in loose, popular government. The distinction between the new dictatorships and the old autocracies lies in the present glorification of the state instead of the person in power. This means nonetheless the submergence of the individual. While the aims of the present national administration are far different from those of European dictators the consequences of its centralization of power are apt to be somewhat similar; the submergence of the individual in the institution of government.*
>
> *It is precisely at this point that the greatest danger in modern trends of government lies. For the individual does not exist for the state, but the state for the individual. In the long history of humanity the most precious spark is that of individual freedom. . . .*[6]

Turning from the intellectual to the practical, Sprague called for a program of progressive forestry, expanding and improving public forests and putting burned and cut-over land into state ownership for permanent management. Additionally, he pledged to reduce the state property tax for schools, eliminate the state's budget deficit, and begin reorganization of Oregon's fragmented public school system. He vowed to oppose a tax increase or imposition of a sales tax. Sprague called for reform in several areas of humanitarian concern: expanded parole and honor camps for prisoners, a modest increase in old-age pensions, abolition of the pauper's oath,[7] and stricter enforcement of liquor laws. He envisioned a pension system for public employees. It was a platform along the lines of the Progressive platform of 1912, humanitarian but restrained, granting government a role in social and moral affairs but clearly within the traditional economic and political system.

Turning to the sensitive power issue, Sprague quoted Governor Meier's inaugural message, adding, "I think we need to recapture the vision of George W. Joseph and Governor Meier and utilize these abundant water power resources for town *and* country, for farm *and* factory (emphasis original)." He urged the Legislature to approve revenue bonding for public utility districts and require contributions by public districts in lieu of taxes.

Predictably, newspaper reports picked up his no-tax pledge and his support for revenue bonding. Editorial support was universal, with even George Putnam conceding the speech to be "conservative though constructive, consistent with his pre-election promises, carefully thought-out, clearly worded and refreshing in those phrases in which he definitely commits himself to a fixed policy."[8] Other editors agreed with the tone and substance of the speech, and declared its goals could be accomplished.

The *Oregon Journal* printed a full-page photo layout and personality sketch and Portland and Salem society pages dwelled on the Inaugural reception and ball. "Everything was formal, white tie and tails, the Capitol was just gorgeous," Jeryme English recalled. Formal balls were held at the Armory, Crystal Garden, and Marion Hotel following a reception in the governor's office. Portland radio covered the social scene, interviewing newspaper society reporters. "In those days we described women's dresses. . . . I had to reword when they wore the same dress a second time," English recalled.[9]

The new governor was formal in his bearing and dress, as if to remind himself of his step from the rattle and bang of the grubby old *Statesman* office to the polished marble of the gleaming new Capitol. English, who lived near the Capitol, recalled Sprague passing her house resplendent

Posing for a formal portrait before attending an inaugural ball, the Spragues were joined by daughter Martha (*Oregon Journal*, now Oregon Historical Society CN014446).

in bowler hat, black coat with velvet collar, and a walking cane: "I couldn't believe that was my boss!"[10]

Sprague had been honored in a less formal fashion the Saturday night before his inaugural, at a Portland gathering of nearly seventy-five Oregon editors, with his old partner Claude Ingalls as toastmaster. Notably missing from the published list were two of the men with whom he was closely associated in different ways: George Putnam and Sheldon F. Sackett.[11]

As the band played on, with formal receptions for legislators and a round of dinner parties marking the change of administration, Sprague was facing simultaneously his first really hard decision as governor. Leroy Herschel McCarthy, a boyish-looking 28-year-old from Portland, faced the death penalty for the murder of a Portland service station attendant in a nickel-and-dime holdup. McCarthy's parents came to the Capitol and pleaded with Sprague to spare their son's life. Sprague's daughter Martha, who was home at the time, recalls her father agonizing over the decision, obviously unsure of the right course of action. Cecil Edwards worked on the case with his boss; Edwards had been on a parole commission, and knew the prison system well. Edwards and Sprague stayed up most of one night reviewing the record, "to see if there was anything extenuating that could be found to counter that execution.... He couldn't find a thing." McCarthy had been in trouble all his life, and there was no doubt of his guilt. Sprague told Edwards, "Well, I've got the power but I don't believe I have the right."[12]

Sprague's problem was accentuated by the introduction of a legislative resolution (possibly at Sprague's request) requesting that he commute the sentence to life in prison. When the Senate voted 21 to 9 against the resolution, the die was cast; if he commuted the sentence, the new governor would be defying not only a judge and jury, but also the Legislature. "Governor Sprague, visibly distressed by the difficult choice presented him in his first ten days in office, announced his decision thirty minutes after the vote," the *Statesman* reported. As preparations began for the execution, George Putnam added to the controversy by assigning a woman reporter to cover the execution, hoping to reflect "the reactions of the death drama to the feminine mind." After first granting permission, a nervous prison warden denied the request on the grounds that it had never been done before; Putnam replied that that was exactly his point.[13]

The execution of the young man was soon forgotten in the furor that accompanies any new administration struggling to put its house in order while simultaneously dealing with a legislative session. But Sprague did not forget it. He never mentioned editorially the agony he went through in the McCarthy case, but his once-supportive view of capital punishment changed in later years and he advocated repeal, finally labeling the act a "debasement" of Oregon's citizens.[14]

Before leaving for the Capitol, Sprague put his *Statesman* house in order, calling Sackett to serve as acting publisher, and firmly distanced himself from *Statesman* editorial policy, a move that "didn't do the paper any good," in the view of his son. Both Wallace Sprague and Jeryme English remember Sackett as rarely being in the office during the time he managed the paper for the governor. Occupied with his Coos Bay operations, Sackett left business matters to Wendell Wilmarth and Bob Sprague and editorial decisions to Ralph Curtis. Sprague's son Wallace was getting an apprenticeship, having received his master's degree in history from Harvard in 1939. He joined the *Statesman* staff that summer, feeling ill-prepared but writing news and an occasional editorial to assist Ralph Curtis. Living at home, he seldom discussed *Statesman* issues with his father, who was tied up with state business.[15]

At the Capitol, Sprague built the nucleus of his executive team. Campaigners David Eccles and Cecil Edwards joined Sprague's staff, Eccles as executive secretary and budget director, Edwards as personal secretary. Sprague's frugality, already well established at the *Statesman*, gave Eccles and Edwards a jolt when they learned that they were working for less pay than their counterparts in the Martin administration. Eccles complained; Sprague chuckled and said, "Dave, what you need is a budget director!"[16] After the 1939 legislative session Sigfrid Unander came on as director of a new state planning and research office. He replaced Edwards in 1940 when the latter went on active National Guard duty as a horse buyer; Unander in turn entered the Navy in 1941 and was replaced by George Aiken.

With the exception of secretary Helen Beeler, the entire staff was new to state government and, as Sprague looked for people to fill positions, he went outside the old-line Republican or Capitol ranks, often making enemies of those rejected. When the Parole Board was set up in 1939, Sprague appointed Paul Kelty, recently retired managing editor of *The Oregonian*, and Roy S. Keene, athletic director at Willamette University. When the Salem School Board fired his friend, Superintendent Silas Gaiser, in 1939 after a bitter internal battle, Sprague hired him as unemployment commissioner. C. M. Rynerson, who as editor of the *Oregon Labor Press* had been a key labor ally in 1938, gained a spot on the Industrial Accident Commission. Lloyd Smith was chosen as corporation commissioner, and Portland City Commissioner Ormond

The Board of Control, made up of Oregon's top three elected officers, was the dominant force in state government during Sprague's term as governor. In January 1941, newly elected Treasurer Leslie Scott is congratulated as he joins the Board. From left: Secretary of State Earl Snell, Scott, outgoing Treasurer Walter Pearson, and Sprague (Salem Public Library, Ben Maxwell collection).

Bean as public utility commissioner. Bob Boyd, Sprague's campaign manager, was installed as attorney (and the governor's eyes and ears) at the sensitive Oregon Liquor Control Commission, where Sprague obtained the resignations of all three commissioners, naming in their stead Lloyd Wentworth, Lowell Stockman and J. N. Chambers, who were all sympathetic to his intent to tighten liquor regulations.

Sprague's appointees were often young liberal Republicans, and generally held in high regard. In only two areas did he generate serious controversy. Sprague purged the Board of Aeronautics in October when four of the five members resisted his wish to fire the inspector, Allan D. Greenwood. The latter, Sprague alleged, was running the Young Democrats out of his $350-a-month office. When the Board unilaterally gave Greenwood a month of termination pay, Sprague told them the action "reveals a lack of cooperation with my administration which I will not tolerate," and fired the four. Later in the year, in his role as chairman of the Board of Forestry, he engineered the termination of J. W. Ferguson as state forester, replacing him with Nels Rogers. A far more serious area than the tiny Aeronautics Board, the case involved an audit and subsequent civil actions to recover some $9,000 in funds that had allegedly been misused.[17]

In both cases, Sprague was holding firmly to his view that state jobs be "on the level" and involve neither politicking on the job nor inside deals with friends. He also terminated a cozy deal in which the superintendent of the Oregon State Hospital leased his own farmland to the hospital and in turn was able to use a crew of hospital patients to improve his land.[18]

Legislative leadership, solidly Republican, changed little in Sprague's term, and as a result Sprague's relationships with key players were continuous and several of his most important programs were crafted over two sessions. Sessions were short, typically adjourning in March; the public did not expect and the Legislature did not intend to overhaul the Oregon system in two months in Salem every two years.

Legislating was a job for mature men, preferably men of substance, and those outside this mold—women, eager young men, union workers and liberals—were heard but not heeded. The work was done in smoky committee rooms whose doors were frequently closed when votes were taken, and in the bars and restaurants of Salem. Legislative pay was low ($3 a day in 1939), expenses limited, and more than a few legislators were heavily subsidized by the dinner checks of well-heeled lobbyists. It was an old boys' club, complete with cigars, spittoons and logrolling. Sprague was not an old boy by anyone's definition. The Spragues entertained legislators, but without serving liquor. Blanche enjoyed

Blanche Sprague christens Salem's first direct airmail flight, in 1941 (Salem Public Library, Ben Maxwell collection).

entertaining, but the dinners were likely to be proper and lacked the atmosphere where a key vote might be courted as the evening mellowed.

Sprague told David Eccles, "I don't intend to try to boss the Legislature. That's their job; I'll take care of it after they do it." Harry Boivin, whose legislative career stretched over forty years and included presiding over both houses, recalled Sprague as one who kept his distance from legislators. "I never could figure out who was running things," said newsman Paul Harvey of Sprague's approach to the Legislature.[19]

This attitude forced Sprague to use the veto at times when he might have headed off unwelcome legislation. He established his veto style very early, in a warning to legislative logrollers. The victim was a typical special-interest bill, which would have tightened the already-firm grip on river pilotage held by the Columbia River Pilots' Association and the Bar Pilots' Association; it was engineered by legislators who were either pilots or employed by the pilots. Several days later Sprague vetoed a similar measure aimed at helping optometrists. The vetoes were applauded editorially as signs he would not bow to special interests, and a nonpartisan observer saw them as evidence of "Governor Sprague's determination to eliminate unworkable, poorly drafted, and so-called 'freak' legislation, and second, his opposition to restrictive legislation which he suspects to be designed more for the protection of special interest groups than for the public good."[20]

The intensity of his first legislative session brought on an unspecified illness in early February, and for several days Sprague governed from his home; at one point the Board of Control met there.[21] The Board, consisting of the governor, secretary of state and treasurer, was the state's most powerful agency at the time, responsible for all state institutions, including the prisons and hospitals, and also for appointing several key officials. The same officers constituted another powerful board, the State Land Board, in charge of all state-owned lands.

The new governor was cautious in his first term, coming out strongly primarily on questions of public power, liquor regulation, and an effort to legalize slot machines and pinball. His most lasting effort, reform of forestry laws, took two sessions to enact, spurred by a second major fire in the Tillamook Burn west of Portland. (The forest burned in 1933 and again in 1939.) The vast charred desert was reverting to county ownership as a result of tax foreclosures. Other forest land, cut and abandoned, was also given up for taxes as the Depression continued and the timber industry declined. Very little thought had been given to reforestation or management. Sprague, imbued with the conservation ethic of Teddy Roosevelt and Gifford Pinchot, was appalled and concerned. Oregon's heritage was going to waste and a future timber shortage loomed, he feared. His Inaugural pleaded for action, and his 1941 message presented a detailed program.

The 1941 package came from his Oregon Economic Council, with Portland banker E. B. MacNaughton as chairman and Bend publisher Robert Sawyer heading a committee on forestry. By choosing men with impeccable Establishment credentials, Sprague was able to enlist industry support and his plan went to the 1941 session as "the industry plan."

The plea was, in fact, largely the brainchild of Eccles, who in a December 1938 memo laid out much of the framework. Eccles suggested that the state take over forest lands that had reverted to the counties for taxes, and press for state assessment of timber lands and a larger state role in fire protection—even if it meant the use of general funds. "The presence of large bodies of tax foreclosed logged land, ranging up to 20% of some counties, is a serious threat to the state from every conceivable standpoint. . . . The existence of this land in a kind of economic no man's land will ultimately become a serious burden against every taxpayer in Oregon," Eccles warned. He also suggested that a new state forester was needed.[22]

Sprague viewed the Burn on foot and in the air, the latter a harrowing experience, recalled Eccles, who was in the single-engine plane with Cecil Edwards, State Forester Rogers, Sprague, and the pilot, when the motor stopped. "It's all straight up and down," Eccles recalled. ". . . Cecil turned to me and said, 'How's your family?'" Before the governor and his aides could panic, the pilot re-started the motor—it was a vapor lock, he said—and the flight went on to Portland. But Sprague refused later airplane trips in single-engine craft.[23]

The Tillamook Burn exploded again in 1939, and the disaster focused attention on fire prevention and reforestation. Sprague's forestry proposals would face a receptive audience in the next legislature. The second Tillamook Burn got everyone's attention. As the 1941 session convened, Bob Sawyer explained the plan in a three-part series in the *Oregon Journal*. Sawyer, one of the most conservative of Oregon editors, was backing a plan for a massive public forest, made up by assuming responsibility for burned-over and cut-over lands, whether owned by public or private interests. Only through the establishment of public forests, he argued, could the pressure to liquidate private lands be eased and timber placed on a sustained-yield basis. Sawyer was also supporting a law requiring at least a minimum of reforestation on private lands, based on the progressive conservation agenda of Gifford Pinchot.[24]

Fire-shocked legislators readily accepted the plan in 1941, and at a signing ceremony for the fifteen-bill package, Sprague told reporters, "I hope that future generations of Oregonians will find my monument growing in the forests of this state. . . . I regard these bills as the most important work of the entire session."[25] Regulation of forest practices on private land was the most revolutionary part of a package the prestigious *American Forests* magazine described as "blazing a new trail" in forestry. "Oregon will now prepare its own answer to the charge so often made by proponents of federal legislation that states cannot exercise necessary controls over cutting of private timber," the article concluded.[26]

The most important elements of the legislation were expanding the state's ability to acquire private land, and the nation's first set of logging regulations. These required western Oregon loggers to leave 5 percent of the seed-bearing trees, and eastern Oregon pine loggers to leave all pine under 16 inches in diameter. Viewed a half-century later, the regulations are mild, but at the time they were a breakthrough in one of the most individualistic industries in the nation. It was progressive forestry in the Gifford Pinchot mold, emphasizing wise use and sustained yield, and two decades later Sprague still considered it his major gubernatorial legacy.[27]

After leaving office, Sprague continued to battle for a larger state role in forestry. In 1945 he called for state bonding to acquire burned-over and cut-over lands, and subsequently backed bonding plans by Gov. Earl Snell.[28]

Sprague was able to muster near-unanimous support for his forestry package, but it was harder to gain support for other elements of his program, and he took his share of lumps in both sessions, winning the majority but losing in several key areas as he failed to counter the power of lobby influence and the relaxed style of a one-party legislature with a limited agenda. Most legislators were not as pure as Sprague in the areas of alcohol, gambling and other temptations, and some were susceptible to the siren call of well-financed lobbyists; clashes were inevitable, particularly in the sensitive area of alcohol. Sprague's son recalls the constant pressure from the liquor lobbyists as being particularly bothersome to the governor; it was one of the best-financed and most powerful at legislative sessions of this era.[29]

Sprague was an abstemious man, never seen to drink even wine, utter the Lord's name in vain, or play a card game other than bridge. He did not lecture others, and he put up with his share of the "unsaved" in his newspaper office, but his notion of public morality was close to the views one might have heard from the pulpit of a Scottish Presbyterian church.

States such as Oregon created a conflict of interest when they began selling liquor in state-owned stores and using the profit to finance government. Sprague supported state regulation to promote social morality rather than to increase income for worthy state purposes. He saw the state as protector of public morals, a typical Progressive view.

Although Sprague was able to quickly quash attempts to legalize pinballs and slot machines by threatening a veto, liquor was a much more complex issue. The Knox Law confined the sale of hard liquor to state stores; hard liquor outside the home could be consumed in so-called "clubs" where one brought a bottle or had an identified bottle in a "locker" behind the bar. Liquor interests constantly sought "liquor by the drink," or open bars. Sprague in 1939 vetoed such a bill, and the veto was upheld. He was less successful in efforts to confine to state stores the sale of fortified wine, which was being sold in the Skid Road area of Portland and other places of heavy alcohol abuse. Sprague's efforts to put fortified wine under OLCC control were thwarted in both sessions by the liquor lobby. Liquor bills were important and heavily lobbied—his fortified wine bill in 1941 failed by a single vote in the Legislature's last hour when, during an uproar on the floor of the House, one member switched votes as the final gavel fell.[30]

If he could not tighten the cork on the bottle through legislation, Sprague clearly hoped to enforce existing laws to the hilt. He was particularly concerned about Klamath Falls, where railroad construction and lumbering had boomed in the twenties. The city grew from 4,800 to 20,868 in the decade, and with the flood of workers came dens of iniquity of various shades. In 1939 the state began a crack-down. The OLCC in March suspended a dozen liquor licenses, and in May Sprague ordered State Police detective Lee Bown to investigate reports of wide-open gambling, which had figured in a series of blasts from Circuit Judge Edward Ashurst. When Bown, after spending two weeks in the area, came back criticizing Ashurst and reporting that he could get no one to talk about the alleged abuses, Sprague dashed off an angry note to Deputy Superintendent H. G. Maison. He had not asked for an investigation of the judge, he reminded Maison, but for an aggressive follow-up on his leads. The saber-rattling apparently had at least temporary effect—Ashurst told Sprague in June that "the big gambling houses have taken out their tables"—but Klamath soon resumed its tolerance of illegal activity.[31]

The Klamath situation was further complicated by accusations from Ashurst and others that state Rep. Harry D. Boivin was "the man to see" regarding liquor licenses. Boivin, an attorney, certainly did represent many applicants for licenses before the OLCC, but that was not illegal, although some considered it unethical. Sprague undoubtedly had the wily Klamath Democrat—among others—in mind when he asked the Oregon State Bar to expose "trimmers" who used political pull to obtain clients. Admitting that "there is nothing strictly unprofessional in the practice of the so-called political lawyer," Sprague informed lawyers, "I have instructed the Liquor Commission to keep the counter between them and the people with whom they deal whether salesmen or lawyers or applicants for licenses." The governor also came down hard on lawyers who told the families of prisoners that they (the lawyers) had "pull" with the Parole Board.[32]

Sprague's moral outrage had not yet been extended to the field of civil rights. No mention was made in his 1939 or 1941 legislative messages of proposed measures to outlaw segregation in public places. The legislation had failed in 1937, and in 1939 it passed the Senate, only to die in the House. Sprague did not publicly state a position on measures Capitol reporters insisted on labeling "so-called civil rights bills." He had editorialized in support of the 1937 measure, but only after it had failed. The *Statesman,* like most newspapers of the day, used rampantly racist language that makes a reader cringe half a century later. Illustrating how rare it was to even see a black person in Salem in 1939, the *Statesman* actually put on its front page a minor auto mishap with the lead: "'Ah suah thought I was gonna be kilt,' said William Pinkston, husky negro, who arrived in Salem late yesterday afternoon after a car he was trying to start on backward compression went over an embankment . . . "[33]

Although in Salem he was insulated from much racial contact, Sprague must have been aware of at least some of the worst cases of discrimination.

Kathryn Hall Bogle recalled that when she applied for a job with the Federal Employment Service, four leaders of the NAACP, led by Kenneth Smith, called on Sprague to inform him of the situation so that he could guard against sabotage of her application and so he would be aware that there might be threats or violence against her should she get the job. Bogle was only the second black woman to hold a government office position in Portland.[34]

There was de facto segregation in Portland, with separate recreational facilities, restaurants and hotels that would not serve blacks, and Southern Oregon was reported to have "sundown towns," where blacks could not stay overnight. When the NAACP and Commonwealth Federation co-sponsored a dinner to honor senators who had voted for the 1937 anti-discrimination bill, it was "the first inter-racial dinner to be held in a first-class Portland restaurant," according to Federation executive director Monroe Sweetland. The restaurant was the Bohemian, operated by Richard Neuberger's family.[35]

Sprague was a bit more courageous on civil liberties. Although he signed a measure barring from the Oregon ballot any party advocating overthrow of the government, he vetoed a bill setting up jail terms and fines for broadly-defined acts of sabotage, saying the measure smacked of the excesses of World War I. Both actions were in conformity with Commonwealth Federation views, and Monroe Sweetland told a colleague, "It certainly puts us on the spot with our consciences when Sprague takes such a firm stand on civil liberties and yet embraces such a conservative economic program we can never support him."[36]

The Commonwealth Federation was finding Sprague a bit of an enigma. "Governor-elect Sprague continued to sound the progressive note of his pre-election speeches, which many had assumed to be merely a campaign device," Sweetland told the press the week before Inaugural. "Excepting for an incidental criticism of the Federal Administration, he said little to indicate he was a Republican."[37] But as the session wore on the OCF's patience wore out, and Sweetland concluded on adjournment: "Governor Sprague started his regime with a bang, but before the end of the session his leadership was largely discarded and even some mildly progressive proposals made by him were scuttled. He failed to assert leadership in any direction, and the pledges made to pension and relief and public power groups were apparently forgotten when their enactment would have required that he take issue with his Republican legislature.[38]

Sprague was the last Oregon governor to face the issue of public power as a mandatory agenda item; by the end of World War II the debate was basically over, Oregon remaining primarily a private-utility state in contrast to the public-power orientation of Washington. Sprague forged an unusual alliance with Peter Zimmerman to pass legislation requiring a vote for any substantial sale of securities by public utility districts. He overcame Zimmerman and other public-power advocates on a bill requiring public districts to pay state and local taxes. In the eyes of Sprague and other moderates on the issue, the playing field was now level; but zealots on both sides were not satisfied.[39]

Among the dissatisfied was the Bonneville Power Administration's new director, Paul Raver. BPA attorney Allan Hart prepared a lengthy analysis of Oregon laws which Hart said placed extraordinary obstacles and hazards in the path of a people's utility district. Sprague rejected a total overhaul—"I do not believe the Legislature has any stomach to go through another prolonged battle over utility district legislation"—but agreed to work with BPA.[40] Little came of it; Raver got some very minor revisions, but the 1939 law remained basically intact for many years.

Forestry and utility law were Sprague's most lasting legacy, but he also eliminated the state property tax for local schools, and won approval of a new state office building and a $1.8 million expansion of state institutions. Sprague also brought absolute integrity and honesty into state government, and launched the public careers of some of the finest public servants of the next two decades. He failed, however, to reorganize the state's fragmented public school districts, and he was unable to restore

On the Wendell Willkie campaign train in Oregon (from left): Blanche, Mrs. Rufus Holman, Senator Holman, Sprague, Mrs. Willkie and the candidate (Sprague Family Archives).

voting rights to ex-convicts and to provide pensions and civil service for state workers.

Sprague found time to enter the campaign of Wendell Willkie in 1940, and pushed for the inclusion of Oregon Senator Charles McNary on the Republican ticket. He toured seven states for the ticket, delivered radio addresses and forged a personal friendship with Willkie. But the speaking trip was one of the few times he left Oregon during this period, as the approaching war took more and more of his time.

As early as 1939, Sprague found himself caught up in issues of war and defense preparation, and his final year in office was dominated by Oregon's growing role in the international conflict. As a Pacific Coast state with harbors and hydroelectricity, Oregon was an obvious location for defense industries, but was also an area most vulnerable in case of war with Japan.

A voracious reader, Sprague had long been concerned about Japan, and while most Americans were focused on the war in Europe he was warning of threats in the Pacific. Half a year before Pearl Harbor, he warned fellow governors of the threat from Japan, and urged the strengthening of American bases in the Philippines.[41]

Sprague got a taste of the Asian conflict in 1939, when pickets tied up shipments of scrap iron to Japan for several days in Astoria, Coos Bay, and Portland. The pickets included Chinese children, and adults of varied ethnic backgrounds, and they were supported by longshoremen. The Japanese were buying up scrap iron for their defense plants, and the Northwest with its rusting old lumber machinery was a prime exporter.

Wallace Sprague and his father, about 1940 and perhaps on a campaign swing on behalf of the Willkie-McNary presidential ticket (Sprague Family Archives).

Americans were overwhelmingly pro-China, and many objected to the shipments. "Let's Keep Our Scrap Iron," headlined an *Oregonian* editorial urging the U. S. government to buy and stockpile the material.[42]

The dispute drew West Coast longshore leader Harry Bridges to Astoria, and the Japanese consul in Portland to the Capitol. Kenichi Fujishima told Sprague that continued delay in loading the Norway Maru at Astoria could result in a breakdown of friendly relations with Japan. Sprague said he was powerless to intervene—the state had no legal role in the matter. A mass meeting in Portland drew some 2,500 to protest the shipments, and telegrams of support from Senators McNary and Holman were read.[43]

A federal arbitrator ruled on March 11 that there was no labor violation in the longshore actions, the shipments were legal and the picketing posed no hazard to dock workers; picketing intensified to the point that ship owners threatened to close the entire Port of Portland. For the previously sympathetic *Oregonian*, that was too much, and editors urged pickets to take their pleas to the State Department. A tense meeting followed, at which leaders of the picketers promised Sprague they would withdraw to avert a port closure; Sprague for his part wired Senator McNary asking for a federal investigation to see if any treaties could be invoked against the shipments.[44] Sprague's intervention closed the matter, but it was only the first of several incidents leading up to the war. The incident also illustrated Sprague's lack of practical political skills; knowing the sentiments of his constituency, he still failed to take advantage of the situation with condemnations of Japanese militarism or cruelty, and dealt with the matter strictly on an administrative rather than a political basis. He remained a newspaperman reluctant to generate headlines.

Two years later, Sprague was dealing with American Legion demands for a state militia, helping launch Henry J. Kaiser's massive ship-building efforts in Portland, and feeling the natural anxiety of a father with a son of military age, when Pearl Harbor was bombed.

Blanche Sprague's diary for December 7, 1941 expressed what must have been in the hearts of millions of American mothers that day. "The awful thing has happened. Japan opened fire upon Pearl Harbor," she began an entry that described a day in Portland visiting the Kaiser shipyard, then a radio address by the governor, finally private thoughts on the trip home. "Now at 10:30 p.m. Arthur is in his office working. Wallace called from Seattle and told me he has been ordered into his uniform. Little did I dream this for him."[45]

Serious and studious like his father, young Sprague had left Salem for good, and his mother could only wonder about his fate and that of others who had grown up around the two-story brick home on Court

Pensive and worried, the governor at his typewriter on December 7, 1941 as he prepares official statements on the outbreak of World War II (*Oregonian* photo).

Street. The young men who had tossed footballs in the back yard, courted her daughter, sprouted all gangly and down-whiskered before her very eyes—some would die and all would be changed forever by what was to come. So, too, she mused as she watched her husband work on his task for Monday morning, would her Arthur be changed by what was ahead.

A somber governor called the Capitol press corps to his office early Monday morning. He was declaring a state of emergency. Someone asked what that meant; the governor was not sure, exactly, but it seemed appropriate.[46] Thus did Oregon enter into the war it had been preparing for since at least 1940.

Advice was coming from every side. Worried parents were trying to contact members of the Willamette University football team, which was in Honolulu playing a post-season game. State officials were expecting orders to active service, there were immediate spottings of suspicious characters lurking near vital transportation links, bridges or defense plants.

And, of course, there were the Japanese. So foreign in their appearance, so quiet and mysterious, so clannish. So *un-American* in every way. What had *they* been doing to prepare for this day? What would *they* do now that *their* country was at war with *us*? What could *we* do about it? Fear of the unknown raced through the entire Pacific Coast, doubled by ignorance and even hatred of a race little known or understood by the dominant white stock.

Japanese-American leaders had been worried since Japan intensified its attack on China and it became apparent that most Americans were siding with China. Howard Nomura, past president of the Japanese American Citizens League (JACL), pleaded in the *Oregon Journal*: "We, too, are Americans. . . . We have no ties with Japan and have cast our lot with the other Americans in our America. Our loyalty and faith in the future of our country are firm."[47] Nomura's assertion that Americans of Japanese descent were as loyal as those whose ancestors came across the Atlantic was a view shared by Governor Sprague. Writing for the 1940 annual edition of *Japanese Courier*, he urged: "Americans of European descent need to cultivate virtues of tolerance and consideration. I am sure if these are extended our Japanese-Americans will respond with appreciation and added devotion to what is our common country."[48]

In the wake of Pearl Harbor, Sprague's first reaction was to differentiate between foreign-born Japanese aliens and the second generation, who were American citizens. On December 8, he ordered aliens to remain in their homes awaiting further orders. He apparently hoped, however, that citizens of Japanese ancestry would be undisturbed. In telegrams to Portland Mayor Earl Riley and Multnomah County Sheriff Martin T. Pratt, Sprague noted "some complaints that Japanese-American citizens were being interfered with in employment at lumber mills," and requested

Bracing for all-out war, a sober and stern Oregon Defense Council poses at its meeting on December 7, 1941 in the wake of Pearl Harbor. With Governor Sprague are (from left): Robert H. Baldock, highway engineer; Jerrold Owen, state defense coordinator; Charles P. Pray, state police superintendent; David Eccles, executive secretary to Sprague; Col. Elmer Wooten, adjutant general; Brazier Small, Portland (Salem Public Library, Ben Maxwell collection).

Pre-war Rose Festival guests, a troupe of Japanese dancers poses in 1938 with Sprague and Blanche. A year later, anti-Japanese sentiments began building in Oregon with the Japanese incursion into China, and protesters blocked the loading of ships carrying scrap iron to Japan (Oregon Historical Society)

that deputies protect them from molestation.[49] And in a radio address a week after Pearl Harbor, Sprague tried to set a proper code of conduct:

> *It is proper to observe the conduct of enemy aliens and to report any suspicious action to the authorities. No direct violence should be visited upon them unless they are caught in some overt hostile act. Remember we have some of our own citizens residing in their countries. We do not want to invite reprisals on them.*
>
> *As to those of Japanese, German, or Italian descent who are American citizens, they must be protected in their rights as citizens and should not be molested unless they should be observed in any act of treason.*[50]

The Pacific Coast had a history of hostility and even violence against Asians, who had been encouraged to immigrate to build the railroads and for mining and other labor-intensive occupations. Japanese immigration was not a factor prior to 1890; that year's federal census revealed only 2,039 Japanese immigrants and native-born citizens of

Japanese ancestry. But in the next twenty years, 127,000 Japanese entered the United States.[51] Japanese immigrants were concentrated in California, but significant populations developed in Oregon and Washington. By the 1920 census, California counted 70,196 residents of Japanese ancestry; Oregon had 4,022 and Washington had 17,134. Despite their reputation as superb fruit and vegetable farmers, most Japanese lived in cities. In Oregon, 1,675 or 42 percent lived within the Portland city limits. In Washington, 7,742 or 45 percent lived within the Seattle city limits.[52]

Immigrants established their own communities, with the men often sending for "picture brides" from their native land. The issei, or first generation, were isolated from the mainstream society in large part because of language barriers, compounded by nativism and racial prejudice. In an attempt to limit the Japanese community's ability to expand farming operations, the 1923 Oregon Legislature, heavily influenced by the Ku Klux Klan, passed a measure preventing Japanese aliens from owning land. The measure attracted unanimous support in the Senate, and only one negative vote in the House.

Anti-immigrant legislation created two classes of Japanese Americans. The first generation, the issei, were barred from becoming citizens and could not legally own land; the second generation, the nisei, by virtue of birth in the United States were citizens and could own land. The constitutional standing afforded citizens is considerably greater than that afforded aliens, but little practical distinction was made between the two classes, as all those of Japanese heritage were singled out for suspicion in the aftermath of Pearl Harbor.[53]

World War II found some 4,071 Japanese Americans living in Oregon, of whom 1,680 resided in Portland, the sixth-largest concentration on the Pacific Coast. Other concentrations were the predominantly truck-farming areas in Washington and Clackamas County, 245 and 163 respectively and in the orchards of Hood River County, 462. Marion County had 193 Japanese-American residents, many in the Lake Labish farm area north of Salem. Men outnumbered women almost 2-to-1 and citizens outnumbered the issei 2,454 to 1,617.[54]

Even after Pearl Harbor, some Oregonians were still trying to find a way to protect the rights of Japanese Americans. Only four days after Pearl Harbor, Clarence E. Oliver, a teacher at Jefferson High School in Portland, proposed that Sprague appoint emergency committees of prominent citizens in each county with sizable Japanese American communities, to serve in a "guardianship capacity for the people of Japanese blood residing in our state." Oliver proposed that other Americans post bonds of good conduct for their Japanese American friends, and that only those found guilty of misconduct be interned.[55]

Inexplicably, the December 11 letter from Oliver was misplaced by the governor's staff, and Sprague, with apologies for tardiness, did not reply until January 8. He declined to intervene. Vouching for the sincerity of the second generation, Sprague viewed the matter as one of maintaining public order, which he told Oliver was largely a matter for local authorities.[56]

Another plan came from C. B. Lewis, a Portland nurseryman, who proposed in February that all Japanese be requested by the governor to volunteer for work camps in eastern Oregon, where they would do reforestation, construction and other federal projects.[57] By the time the Lewis plan arrived, however, political events and a rising tide of anti-Japanese sentiment had pushed Sprague to react.

Stories of Japanese victories in the South Pacific were beginning to arouse the population. Sprague's newsroom colleagues added fuel to the flame by the constant use of the word "Japs" in headlines. The word had an ugly, harsh intonation, but quickly became the term applied to anyone with Japanese ancestors; it was an easy headline word and it summed up the view of Americans toward their neighbors. "Japs" it was, and remained through the war.

News coverage seldom included the views of Oregon's Japanese Americans; ordinary citizens were seldom sought out by journalists of the time, and certainly not aliens or non-English speakers. A sympathetic feature article in *The Oregonian's* Sunday magazine by political writer

During a power outage in January 1942, the governor reads his newspaper by lamplight (Salem Public Library, Ben Maxwell collection).

Herbert Lundy drew several emotional and racist replies. Lundy found instances of support for Japanese Americans, tolerance in the public schools on the part of teachers and students, and understanding by others in the community. He concluded, "The Japanese race in Oregon awaits uncomfortably on a munitions dump of public opinion, fully aware that wars engender blind and cruel hatred, yet hopeful that the spark which may ignite the explosive will not be fanned either by their own people or their Caucasian neighbors in this land of democracy."[58]

Some of the "munitions dump of public opinion" exploded on Lundy; readers called for his firing, the imprisonment of all Japanese, and suggested that "cold steel" was the solution to the Japanese situation.[59] It was typical of a rising tide of intolerance as the new year brought more setbacks in Asia.

Sentiment for removal of the Japanese was overwhelming, fed by the patriotic thumping of the American Legion, which took the lead in urging internment. Sprague's own pleas for tolerance in December and Lundy's *Oregonian* article were weak reeds in a mounting storm of anti-Japanese protest. *Oregonian* Editor Palmer Hoyt, the *Journal's* Marshall Dana and Portland Mayor Earl Riley urged evacuation. The Portland City Council refused to renew business licenses of Japanese Americans, and Sprague's own insurance commissioner allowed cancellation of Japanese fire insurance policies. In Oregon no public protest was entered by any of the groups one might have expected to speak—churches, civil libertarians, the Red Cross, the YMCA and YWCA, international peace organizations—none stepped forward. On the Pacific Coast, the only elected official to oppose internment was Harry Cain, the mercurial mayor of Tacoma.[60]

There were individual voices, expressed in a handful of letters to editors, and a few Japanese dared defend themselves in the same manner. Editors of the student newspaper at Hood River High School exercised considerably more compassion than their professional peers, who were increasingly clamoring for evacuation. The student newspaper printed a plea, two weeks after Pearl Harbor:

To those of Hood River—if you please,
These are our friends—these Japanese
Not "japs" or even Japanese—
They are Americans, our schoolmates these.[61]

The student journalists would soon bid farewell to their friends, for the pressure of organized opposition was sweeping aside the few voices of reason.

Politically, Sprague was now forced to look to his right, as Secretary of State Earl Snell entered the Republican gubernatorial primary on February 1. Snell was a veteran of World War I, active in the American Legion, "a war veteran for Oregon's wartime governor," reminding voters that Sprague had not served in uniform.

As early as 1938, when Sprague entered a campaign that others bypassed, it was apparent that his challenger would be the popular auto dealer now working just down the hall in the Capitol. If Sprague failed to pursue his political openings, Snell never missed a beat, building in two terms as secretary of state one of the most formidable political organizations in Oregon history.

Only two weeks after Snell's entry into the race Sprague sided with those who viewed all Japanese as potential enemies. His action came in a brief telegram to Attorney General Nicholas Biddle:

> *I am convinced that our people on this coast demand more thorough action for protection against possible alien activity particularly by Japanese residing on coast. I do not believe measures now being taken are adequate and urge further and prompt action to remove this menace and recommend internment. We want no repetition of Honolulu experience here. Recommend your agents confer with military and police authorities to plan positive protection for Americans, with decent treatment of Japanese.*[62]

A week earlier the Council of State Governments' executive director, Frank Bane, had requested Sprague to issue—jointly with governors Culbert Olson of California and Arthur B. Langlie of Washington—a public statement urging citizens to respect the rights of Japanese Americans and refrain from vigilante action. Bane's draft release concluded: "Persecution of aliens, commercial exploitation of the helpless, discrimination against loyal groups on racial grounds is a betrayal of the principles for which we have gone to war. Alert and vigilant citizens can aid in the defense of the nation against subversion; not by taking the police powers into their own hands, but by transmitting any evidence of subversive activity to the nearest office of the Federal Bureau of Investigation."[63]

The release, which Bane said had been approved by the Justice Department, was part of an internal war going on at the time between Attorney General Nicholas Biddle and military authorities over what action should be taken on the Coast. Biddle resisted internment, but the president acceded to the military's request to proceed with wholesale evacuation of the Pacific slope between the mountains and the sea. Biddle had urged only selective evacuation of strategic areas. Sprague, lacking inside knowledge of the Roosevelt Administration, was likely not aware of the internal struggle, but it is apparent from his correspondence with Bane that they had discussed a press release of some sort.

Sprague consulted Olson and Langlie and, in a reply to Bane, rejected the proposed release, terming it "too soft," and fearing that it would "blow off in our faces." Noting that California was moving Japanese aliens and citizens back from the coast 100 miles, Sprague indicated he was still unsure of Oregon's decision and wanted no statement such as Bane proposed.[64]

Bane had used language quite similar to that used by Sprague in December, and Bane and Sprague apparently spoke on the telephone before the draft was prepared. Sprague knew as early as February 5 that an evacuation might be in the offing. The Army requested a list of facilities that might be used for "evacuated enemy aliens and their families," and Sprague, after sending a list of CCC camps and fairgrounds, might have also requested Bane to write up a statement.[65] Whether Sprague had

Japanese Americans load belongings at Portland's evacuation center in 1942; Sprague defended their rights in the immediate aftermath of Pearl Harbor, but turned against them in February and supported evacuation (*Oregon Journal*, now Oregon Historical Society 49760).

urged the gist of the language in Bane's draft, only to be dissuaded by the more conservative Olson and Langlie, can only be speculated. What is certain is that less than a week later, Sprague sent his telegram to Biddle, and was committed to a policy of internment.

In the following days, he received numerous letters congratulating him on his stand. On February 19, President Roosevelt issued Executive Order 9066, giving the War Department authority to remove Japanese aliens and Japanese-American citizens from designated military areas. On March 3, evacuation was announced.

Within a month, while in the midst of his campaign for re-election, Sprague was already turning his attention to using Japanese evacuees in agricultural work, primarily in the eastern Oregon sugar beet fields. The governor had his hands full, with Earl Snell's challenge on one hand and a constant barrage of war demands on the other. He had been dealing with preparations for over a year. He used radio to report on visits to defense installations and other preparedness matters. KOIN broadcast weekly "Oregon Reports" in 1942, with Sprague and Civil Defense Director Jerrold Owen the first guests.[66]

Veterans' groups had been among those pressing Sprague to set up a state guard as early as 1940, but Sprague resisted the pressure in the

Riding with Oregon soldiers in an early World War II parade, Sprague is shown in 1941. The governor was not a horseman, although he probably learned to ride as a child in Iowa (Statesman-Journal photo files).

1941 legislative session, asking only for authority to form the unit if needed. Sprague's own experience with World War I excesses in Ritzville played a major role in his reluctance to mobilize patriots, and his position was supported by organized labor, which feared such a unit would be employed to break strikes. (There was good reason for their fear; Sprague later revealed that the Legion had suggested to him that the Guard be available for "strike duty.")[67]

Sprague worked more closely with union leaders than any Republican governor of his era, and served as an informal negotiator in at least two major labor disputes. He appointed labor leaders John Brost and Gust Anderson to his prestigious Oregon Economic Council, albeit after Commonwealth Federation protests that labor had been overlooked. He utilized other labor leaders such as C. M. Rynerson, Ralph Peoples and Bill Bowes in advisory work or to represent him.[68]

In 1941 Sprague presented to the AFL convention a plea that labor avoid any strike in defense industries, warning of a severe public backlash. He also urged the AFL to avoid high initiation fees or other actions that would bring forth public censure.[69]

When President Franklin D. Roosevelt visited the Oregon Shipyards in 1942, Sprague was on hand to greet him, along with Edgar Kaiser (on Sprague's left) and son Henry J. Kaiser, operators of the huge defense plant (*Oregon Journal,* now Oregon Historical Society 98545).

Much of the union activity centered on the giant Oregon Shipbuilding yard erected by Henry J. Kaiser; the yard launched its first vessel, the *Star of Oregon*, in September 1941, with Blanche Sprague christening the ship. An excruciating housing shortage forced Kaiser to build Vanport, a thrown-together city of 42,000 along the Columbia River. Vanport was quickly filled, attracting a substantial number of African Americans, for whom other housing was limited.[70]

Portland citizens, already worried about the movement of so many uniformed men through Portland, were even more concerned about the influx of young black men, whether in uniform or on the job. One of the committees Sprague appointed to deal with the war's demands on the home front found, somewhat to their surprise, that some newcomers objected to Portland's segregated public facilities. Walter W. R. May, chairman of the committee, advised in a memorandum to Sprague that a "Negro spokesman . . . proposed that if a recreation center intended for Negroes is set up it should be a recreation center for all though it might be used in the main by Negroes."[71]

The committee estimated that Portland's prewar black population of 2,040 had already swelled to 3,790; by war's end Portland's African American community mushroomed to an estimated 21,000. Many of the key shipyard unions, including the huge boilermakers' union, remained sharply resistant to African Americans, and most could find jobs only as laborers.[72] There is no record that Sprague attempted to use his office to secure greater equality in the workplace, but most of the migration occured after he left office.

Faced with ever-mounting demands, in June 1941 Sprague finally created a Defense Council to assist him. As early as January, *Oregon Journal* editorial writer Tom Humphrey had observed that 35 states had such a council and that there was evidence linking the councils to the creation of defense jobs in those states. Sprague was by nature not a man who relished setting up more government agencies. He delayed on Humphrey's obvious suggestion until summer, then convened a 29-member Defense Council with himself as chair, Ross T. McIntyre as vice-chair and Jerrold Owen as coordinator.[73] Sprague did not take a major hand in attempts to attract more wartime industry to Oregon, apparently leaving leadership to Senator Charles McNary and W. D. B. Dodson, the Portland Chamber of Commerce lobbyist in Washington.

As a Pacific Coast state, Oregon faced special danger as well as opportunities for the defense industry. Rumors swirled after Pearl Harbor, old men volunteered to patrol the sand dunes and harbors with their deer rifles, and children were taught the profiles of airplanes to be spotted. Scrap drives, savings campaigns, and knitting circles were organized, and victory gardens sprouted overnight. The loggers' children of Mapleton won fame in 1942 when, to help Sprague win a challenge to Governor Olson of California, they collected 70 tons of scrap in two days—at that time the best per-capita effort in the nation.[74]

Oregon was not without its self-starters and the youngsters of Mapleton were not the only prolific performers. One of Sprague's problems was finding ways to turn aside counter-productive efforts while keeping enthusiasm high.

Funneling the martial instincts of thousands of Oregon hunters and ex-servicemen into a constructive organization called for a certain amount of diplomacy. Companies of "guerrillas," primarily middle-aged men armed with deer rifles and drilling in their work clothes, sprang up in the woods and farms along the Oregon coast. The Tillamook Guerrillas were particularly zealous, and Sprague issued enrollment cards and armbands. The Army, uncomfortable with the idea of unknown warriors marching around with loaded weapons, asked the state to be sure that at least the leaders of these groups were checked for reliability.[75]

The matter of a state guard was more serious, and an elaborate command structure was set up, headed by Col. Ralph P. Cowgill and with units in all major cities. By mid-1942, Cowgill was reporting the enlistment of over seven thousand men, with the force still growing. Guardsmen provided their own weapons but were given regular military training, and reported to professional soldiers. The guard had an intelligence section, a unit of engineers and later a special "timber unit." By the end of 1942 the guard had 464 officers and 8,486 men.[76]

Oregon's National Guard, the 41st or "Sunset Division," had been ordered to federal service on September 26, 1940, and earned numerous battle stars in the Pacific. While the young Oregonians were overseas, the state itself played host to several training camps, hospitals and even a German prisoner-of-war camp.

With the advent of war came the predictable maze of new regulations, and for the fedaphobic Sprague a host of headaches as he tried to comply with directions that at times bordered on the ludicrous. The governor's office was besieged on the one hand by an avalanche of federal orders and on the other by Oregonians upset by the regimentation, which at times went beyond common sense.

A pitched battle grew up between the military bureaucracy and retailers of cap pistols and finally the federal Office of Civil Defense sent a terse telegram clarifying that "prohibition against all fireworks includes cap pistols and all kinds of fireworks." Midnight clam diggers were another target, the Ninth Corps commander restricting clam digging to daylight hours.[77]

Of more serious concern were internal battles over allocation of federal defense funds, and a federal order to cut the highway speed to 35 miles-per-hour. In the latter case, Sprague penned a protest to the Office of Defense Transportation, in which he noted that it would take workers more than four hours a day to commute from Salem to the defense plants in Portland. Buses in eastern Oregon, he added, could not operate in high gear at 35 m.p.h., and the lower speed limit would simply mean a demand for more buses and trucks. The limit remained but was honored more in breach than in observance. The state's fire departments were pitted against each other in bids to get pumpers authorized for civil defense work, bringing angry letters from downstate districts who felt passed over in favor of rivals.[78]

The work of mobilization involved an enormous number of citizens. Observation posts were staffed and an air raid system established, which had actually been tested prior to the war, on October 31, 1941, with 562 posts manned for a test blackout in which most of western Oregon was dark for fifteen minutes. By the end of Sprague's term some 110,690 persons were enrolled in civilian defense work, with over half assigned to duty of some sort; of the 800 official observation posts, 550 in western Oregon were staffed around the clock, and on the coast a beach patrol of American Legion members mounted a 24-hour watch.[79]

By the time he was ready to go to the voters for re-election Sprague could present a long list of wartime accomplishments, including uninterrupted labor peace, the mobilization of both paramilitary and civilian forces in the tens of thousands, and an effective state defense organization. Sprague also claimed to be, in 1941, the first governor to conduct a census of labor skills for the defense industry, and to follow it with a similar inventory of women workers.

Despite his solid if not spectacular record, Sprague had failed to attract headlines during his three years in office. The headlines were dominated by the war in Europe, and after Pearl Harbor the war in Asia. News rooms were depleted, newspapers reduced in size due to newsprint rationing, and reporting from Oregon's capitol was light. A skillful politician might have turned this to his advantage with a blitz of press releases, but Sprague consciously spurned publicity-seeking proposals from his staff and advisors. His efforts as 1942 opened were dominated by the war.

Sprague's 1938 slogan, "Progressive in Ideas, Conservative in Finances" actually summed up the man and his legacy as governor. Yet, as he prepared to seek a second term, Sprague did not have a vivid image with Oregon voters nor had he made a substantial effort to create an image.

Sprague had avoided or finessed major confrontations; he always disliked confrontation, in business or in politics. His rare flashes of anger—directed at the Aeronautics Board, Klamath Falls vice, attempts to legalize gambling—created a brief flurry of comment, but they were exceedingly rare, and the governor bore the reputation of a cool and somewhat puritanical individual. He did not try to avoid publicity; it simply was not a primary objective.

Perhaps Dave Eccles expressed it best in a letter directed to a woman who wanted "a brief outline of the outstanding achievements of this administration," in November 1939. Eccles cited progress in several areas, but concluded: "I confess that this has not been a particularly spectacular recital, but the governor has, by design, rather avoided the spectacular. He conceives of the job as governor as being essentially a business job and requiring a business-like approach."[80]

Ironically, considering his initial reactions to the man, Sprague probably had more in common with Julius Meier than with most of his predecessors. Like Meier, Sprague had no political network and was viewed with skepticism by Republican stalwarts. As the Depression foiled Meier's hopes to build a public power system and other progressive reforms, so did the advent of World War II divert Sprague from reforms in state government and natural resources. Sprague did not prove to be as combative as Meier, but he shared Meier's zeal for fiscal restraint and good administration—both men brought new blood into state government and made enemies in so doing. Both men were aloof in personal relations. Meier had a razor-sharp wit that could leave marks, while Sprague's dry humor was easier to weather, but neither was a backslapper or a joiner.

Sprague's product *was* business-like, deliberately so, but there were no serious efforts to package the product or the man. His door was always open, as it was for forty years at the *Statesman*, and passers-by at the Capitol could gawk into the inner office and perhaps see the governor himself in shirt sleeves at his typewriter. But Sprague was not really approachable. There was much in his demeanor to suggest that he had better things to do than to talk with strangers, and the open door did not produce an influx of visitors.

Press access was good, reporters commenting that Sprague was more accessible than Governor Martin had been, but Sprague, for better or worse, could never generate headlines the way the old general could, and he absolutely resisted "stunts" or what would come in later years to be termed "photo opportunities." Ill at ease with most people, Sprague was perhaps most comfortable with the men who covered him. But even then, one reporter recalled: "He was smarter than hell, but he didn't seem to act like a newspaperman—more of a teacher, a moralist."[81]

Perhaps of greater importance, Sprague often didn't act like a politician, either. Legislation is sometimes compared to the art of making sausage—the process can get messy before the final product is ready for the public—and Sprague was reluctant to enter the butcher shop. He operated at arm's-length and didn't have a staff person designated as legislative liaison.

Sprague was also limited by his own deeply felt concerns over deficit finance and federal intervention. Even when added funds rolled in as the economy improved in 1940, he preferred a solid bank balance to increased public works or more staffing in the overcrowded state institutions. His fear of centralization caused him to resist federal programs that might have produced useful partnerships. After three years he had a cash balance in the state treasury but few friends created by new or improved programs.

His vetoes, while generally sound and logically presented, left little hope of favors from the ever-present special interests which could have been helpful in his campaign; and at times he forgot his friends. In 1941 he vetoed a marketing bill urged on him by most of the state's dairy farmers, turning his back for no really strong reason on a large group of people who had been with him in 1938.[82]

His style in dealing with appointees and colleagues also failed to produce the loyalty he might have expected. "I heard many important men come down and talk to him, and come in my office and call him names—they got what they wanted but they just didn't like the way he did it," Eccles recalled. "Charlie Sprague was a very loyal person and his staff and the people close to him felt very close to him personally, but he was not one to make friends with other people. People reacted to him that he was kind of cold and unresponsive, and he had no small talk whatever." Robert Notson, who covered Sprague as a reporter, found him "too conscientious to be a good politician; he didn't like to compromise his ideals. Sometimes he would give people an appointment but then make them believe they were not really his first choice—the result was a loss of their support."[83]

Blanche projected more humanity, but in this era a first lady was to be seen and not heard. Cecil Edwards accompanied her on visits to prison inmates, where she talked with the younger convicts about family, home and jobs. This was all low-key and never publicized. The governor would call before touring the prison, assuring a stiff and formal reception, asking few questions, never making eye contact.[84]

Sprague's habits of seldom meeting the eye of a visitor and of ending a discussion abruptly by standing up or even turning to his typewriter were the stuff of legend at the *Statesman*, but for outsiders it was the antithesis of proper political behavior. The mannerism was often attributed to shyness, but Sprague's nephew, who worked with him for thirty years, felt it was in reality a form of aloofness or preoccupation: "I always had the feeling that as you were talking to him, he was thinking about something . . . something worthwhile!"[85]

The combination of his personal style and the preoccupation of the media and citizens with the war stripped Sprague of the advantages of incumbency in the Republican primary of 1942. Incumbency was not an automatic advantage in Oregon in any event—when Mark O. Hatfield was re-elected in 1962 he was the first governor since Sylvester Pennoyer in 1890 to gain a second term. There was no reason why, based on his record, Sprague should have had trouble in his own party's primary. But his record was not enough in the face of a challenger who was almost the mirror opposite of Sprague, the governor who ignored or could not master personal politics. Failure to pay proper attention to politics or people was a charge that was never made against Earl Snell. In his 1942 challenge to Sprague the polished secretary of state drew from a pool of personal contacts seldom matched in Oregon political affairs.

5

◆◆◆

The Voters Speak—Twice

"I think sometimes I am running against a signature, which is featured on all my opponent's campaign signs and literature, a signature made familiar by the thousands of birthday and congratulatory letters turned out annually by his staff in Salem (Charles A. Sprague, KGW address, May 13 1942).[1]

"With all the sincerity I possess, I urge him to write letters to the citizens. If there ever was a time when the people of our state should feel a warmth and a closeness to our government and to our public officials, it is NOW. I make this solemn pledge—If I am chosen as your governor, I shall write to the good citizens of my native state more letters than have ever been written heretofore (Earl Snell radio address, May 14 1942).[2]

Essentially, the campaign of 1942 was summed up in that last-minute exchange of gibes between the incumbent governor and his challenger, the secretary of state. Sprague's frustration had been building during the four-month primary campaign, which was conducted as he faced the difficult Japanese American issue and other pressures of the war. He loosed his frustrations in his May 13 broadcast, setting Earl Snell up for the perfect riposte on election eve.

By that time, it was over. In reality, it was probably over on February 1, the day Snell declared for the nomination. He had been working toward the office for seven years, and in the process created one of the most impressive political organizations the state had ever seen. Even after his sudden death in a 1947 airplane crash, the organization lived on and for years men would be described as part of "the Snell organization."

As secretary of state, Snell headed the divisions of motor vehicles and elections, with which nearly every Oregonian of voting age had some contact; thousands of papers dealing with voting, driving or automobiles carried his signature, as did billboards urging safe driving. Snell cultivated

Earl Snell, popular secretary of state and heir apparent to the governorship, easily defeated Sprague in the 1942 Republican primary (Oregon Historical Society).

a large, sweeping signature that was easily recognizable. David Eccles, who had no use for Snell, recalled that there were "five or six people in Snell's office who could sign his name so you couldn't tell the difference. He had one man . . . in an office down in the basement; he went through newspapers from all over the state and clipped weddings, graduations, 50th anniversaries, all that stuff and they got a letter from Earl Snell—all those people. The State of Oregon paid thousands of dollars for it."[3] Sprague, watching this from his nearby office, may have been reminded of Josephine Preston, his nemesis of thirty years before, and her relentless pursuit of votes for school office in Olympia.

Because Snell was banned from seeking a third term, he would be out of office in 1943 unless he ran for governor or Congress; Sprague was aware of that, and relations between the men were correct but cool. In Board of Control and Land Board business no serious disagreements surfaced, but underneath each man kept an eye on his rival.

As a politician, however, Snell was in a league of his own. Sprague later recalled a Board of Control trip to central Oregon: "Snell heard of an old friend who was working nearby. We stopped the car and went to a sheep-shearing shed where his friend was at work and the two had a brief visit."[4] Affairs of state—and Oregon's governor and treasurer—waited amidst the bleating of the flock and clutter of the clip as Snell cemented another vote.

To the extent that Earl Snell had a known philosophy of government, it was to go along with Republican ideas and Republican businessmen. He made his way not by proposing programs or policies but by dint of the natural friendliness of a car dealer, which he had been in the small Columbia River town of Arlington. Snell rose to become Speaker of the

House in the 1933 Legislature, and was subsequently elected twice as secretary of state. To the people of Oregon, he was a nice man who remembered their names and took time to visit. He was a joiner; he belonged to the American Legion, Elks, and a host of other organizations, in all of which he had loyal friends.

By contrast, Sprague had his own ideas and was considered somewhat unreliable by the Portland business establishment that ran the Republican party. Voters saw a governor, but not the man inside the office. He had no political machine, and never tried to cultivate one. He belonged to no fraternal orders, practiced his religion without public announcement, and had among his small circle of friends very few politicians. Sprague had to run on his record—and he did—for the other characteristics of a winning candidate were missing.

Sprague had paid his party dues, most auspiciously in 1938, when his entry saved Republicans from embarrassment or worse. In 1940 he had led the effort to draft Oregon Senator Charles McNary for president, then fell in behind the Wendell Willke-McNary ticket and campaigned in several states. He had supported the party editorially for ten years before entering office. Naively, he expected the party and its leaders to return his loyalty in 1942.

Oregon Voter editor C. C. Chapman, who understood Republican politics as well as anyone during this period, summed up the men six months before Snell announced:

> *Earl Snell has the genial personality of a country stove in the back of the hall; folks get up close and visit. Governor Sprague has the platform personality which radiates illumination but no warmth. Snell by courtesy and manner has acquired a multitude of friends and knows them; Sprague by composure and reticence has acquired a host of enemies and doesn't know them or his friends. Snell, the politician, has a following. Sprague, the statesman, has prestige. . .* [5]

Chapman's analysis was prescient, and in it there was little place for party loyalty. The discerning old editor was not part of the Snell machine; he was much closer to Portland's inner Republican circle, the Arlington Club crowd that made key decisions for Oregon's economy and often for the Republican Party as well. Sprague's 1938 decision to oppose the anti-picketing initiative did not go down well with the Arlington Club, and Sprague in three years as governor had failed to penetrate the group, although he called on such luminaries as Henry Cabell, E. B. MacNaughton and Henry Corbett for service. Sprague was always Salemoriented; he saw big cities as less desirable than the Main Street culture of small and medium-sized towns, and he had little interest in what cities had to offer. Neither his ego nor his intellect seemed to demand an outlet in the city.

He also refused to acknowledge the enormous political power of the private utilities based in Portland. Ormond Bean, Sprague's Public Utility Commissioner, proved to be a champion of the consumer, and forced a $1.7 million PGE rate reduction during his term in office. Bean's action was totally in line with Sprague's progressive philosophy of strictly regulated private utilities, but it was not in line with the power structure of the Arlington Club. In 1942 the utilities backed Snell with their considerable financial muscle, and Bean was out of a job when Snell took office.[6]

But Sprague took no credit for Bean's actions, and the mass of Oregon consumers may have accepted the utility's claims that it had voluntarily lowered rates. Despite his years as a newspaperman, Sprague was loathe to sound his own horn, and the understaffed news rooms of the war period did little probing. As a result, the big Portland papers seldom carried stories about the governor unless they were war-related, and the huge mass of Portland voters, many of whom were new to the state to take defense jobs, knew the governor less than the persistent Snell, whose signature was omnipresent and whose face beamed down on them from billboards. Sprague appointed a good number of Multnomah County residents to state positions, but he was not acquainted with Portland's neighborhoods and local politics. It was a serious flaw, for the city dominated the 1942 voting rolls.

The governor's advisors knew of this weakness, but persuading Sprague to get on the campaign trail was no easy task. "If he just could have worked harder at his public relations, (created a) warmer impression with people at large," Eccles later reflected. "In a group, if half a dozen people were there, they all loved him, loved his intellect. But in a crowd, he was just tongue-tied, unless he had a speech . . . he was uncomfortable in a group of strangers."[7]

Friends, realizing that Sprague could not handshake and smile his way to re-election, urged upon him other political maneuvers. Phil Brandt in Corvallis had prepared an analysis of vulnerabilities in the summer of 1941, ranging from Sprague's veto of a dairy marketing bill to his appearance on the same stage as the controversial longshore leader Harry Bridges at a CIO convention. He urged Sprague to apologize to the dairymen—which apparently he did in January—but he saw no antidote to the Bridges incident, chalking it off to reactionary forces. Then, in an interesting insight, Brandt wrote:

Circumstances: He knows too much.

Areas or groups affected: Difficult to estimate.

Significance: Probably none. This criticism came from a discussion in which the remark was made that in his public addresses the governor had rarely if ever failed to make a sound contribution to the thinking of the group addressed. The comment was, "That is true, but a lot of people are beginning to wonder how anyone can be so well informed. He just knows too much."

Suggested corrections: Keep on telling them.[8]

Sprague's intellectuality, when coupled with his distant manner, could be off-putting and was clearly a campaign problem. A poll done for Sprague early in the campaign, which found a 50 to 36 percent edge for Sprague with 14 percent undecided, discovered a key item. Fourteen percent of those who planned to vote for Snell termed him "a personal friend," remarkable even in a small state. By contrast, only one percent deemed Sprague a "personal friend."[9]

Staff workers found Snell's friends everywhere: hunting buddies in eastern Oregon, Legionnaires, and Elks around the state. William Walsh wrote from Marshfield that a man Sprague had appointed to a major state commission was planning to vote for Snell because they had been school friends. And Snell's letter-writing was legendary. A campaigner reported to Sprague that an old-timer in Baker "seemed to have the idea that you were hard to approach, believe he had met you sometime at Salem and probably you hadn't time to visit with him as he expects folks to do. It seems that Mr. Snell had been remembering him with Christmas cards and etc." Nor was there a lot of good news; petty griping about liquor stores and local taxes was not balanced by positive comments. "The taxpayers in this county are sore and they want to take it out on some one. A lot of them are going to take it out on you," was a typical campaign report.[10]

Sprague's problem was compounded by his obvious awkwardness when he did attempt to do "the political thing," and when he appeared Snell was often there as well, always upstaging him. Travis Cross, just graduated from Salem High and working part-time in *Statesman* sports, took pictures of Sprague and Snell at a Salem Senators' groundbreaking; later, when the field was opened, the Capitol duo showed up as pitcher and catcher. Paul Hauser, Jr. wrote in the *Statesman*: "The governor had plenty of swift and a good curve, but his control was a bit erratic. His first pitch was ten feet to the right, his second ten feet to the left, and his third hit the dust ten feet in front of the plate."[11]

Pitching was not the only area in which Sprague simply couldn't exercise the common touch. In still another joint appearance with Snell, they are pictured in the *Statesman*, with Sprague looking out of place holding a shotgun at the opening of a trapshoot meet. The caption noted that "despite expert coaching from Secretary of State Earl Snell the clay birds went sailing blithely on, unshattered. Snell, a fair country trapgunner himself, later posted a very creditable score of 92 kills out of 100." Snell would wave his sombrero at rodeo parades, while Sprague looked uncomfortable. A 1939 picture shows him at the San Francisco Exposition "Oregon day," riding a stagecoach with a much-more-relaxed Pendleton Round-up queen; Sprague is clad in western garb, and looks like a man searching for the exit.[12]

Sprague's political style had changed little from 1938, but in that election he had faced a man with no more charisma than his own; Henry Hess was nervous, lacking in humor, and uneasy on the campaign trail. In comparison with Hess, Sprague actually seemed friendly in what Cecil Edwards termed "forced geniality." But Earl Snell was no Henry Hess; voters called him by his first name, remembered greeting cards from his office, felt free to take up his time with idle chatter. In 1938, Hess was forced by his lack of personal appeal to run on his record. In 1942, Sprague had no choice but to adopt the same tactic.

Trying his best to do "the political thing," Sprague is astride in the 1939 Pendleton Round-up parade (*Oregon Journal,* now Oregon Historical Society 014466).

Snell, whose World War I career was limited to several months in an Army band at nearby Fort Lewis, played his "war record" to the hilt. "The ONLY CANDIDATE for Governor Who Served in the First World War," was the advertisement headline over a long list of "ex-service friends of Earl Snell."[13] The candidate was a former state commander of the American Legion, and a regular visitor at posts across the state; during World War II the Legion was one of the strongest political forces in Oregon.

"During World War I, I was privileged to serve my country," the former bandsman told a radio audience. "As a veteran of the last war, I know their concern over the day of their return when they must repair the broken chain of their families and businesses and social ties. . . ."[14] The implication, of course, was that Sprague had avoided service. There was no effective reply; Sprague could point to his record of war preparedness, which was substantial, but in this emotional time there was enormous support for veterans, even if they had never left the Pacific Northwest.

Having donned his American Legion cap to conquer the issue of keeping the war-time governor on the job, Snell turned to two other obstacles: Sprague's experience as incumbent for three years, and the issue of party loyalty to the man who had pulled the GOP's chestnuts out of the fire in 1938.

Snell had advanced from city councilman to four terms in the House, the last as speaker, and served eight years as secretary of state, an office that was as busy as it was visible. He had three times the governmental experience of Sprague, and it was not negligible.

Regarding 1938, Snell asserted that he had served the party by avoiding the race: "Four years ago he wished personally to run for governor, but acceded to the pleas of party leaders and friends that he delay his candidacy until 1942," read a letter to party workers. No "party leader" stepped forward to claim the honors, but insiders knew that if the pressure had been applied it would likely have been behind the closed doors of the Arlington Club.[15]

Sprague could not refute Snell, but he hoped that the party faithful would pay attention to his record. Opening his formal campaign on April 15—only a month before the voting and ten weeks after Snell declared—Sprague called upon Republicans to keep faith with him: "In 1938 when our party stood in prospect of defeat I did not desert my party. I do not believe that my party will desert me as its leader now that it rides the flood tide of victory." He added that he had kept his promises and his independence. If that meant he was "a poor politician," Sprague noted, so be it: "I do not believe that the people of Oregon want as governor of the state 'just another politician.' I believe the people want performance, not politics."[16]

Never mentioning his opponent by name, Sprague went on to catalogue his four-year record, stressing fiscal responsibility, preparedness for the war, and his forestry program. He took credit for eliminating the state property tax levy, and said the state economy would now allow a reduction of 20 percent in the income tax. It was an attractive platform for an incumbent governor, and Snell chose to avoid a direct challenge.

Instead, Snell hitched his wagon to an incipient property tax revolt in Multnomah County, the roots of which could as logically be laid at his door as at Sprague's, and which in reality was a product of local politics and had little to do with the governorship. Put simply, the Multnomah County Assessor for a period of years had been playing politics with the assessment roll, applying one rate to commercial and industrial property and a much lower one to residential property. Multnomah County homes had been assessed at an average of 38 percent of their true cash value, unimproved land at 86 percent, and business and industrial property at 73 percent of value. The Oregon Constitution requires equal treatment of property within a taxing district, and a group of business owners finally took the case to the State Tax Commission, which ruled in their favor. The Oregon Supreme Court agreed, and a homeowners' tax revolt was unleashed. The Legislature had adjourned, and the issue was thrown into the 1942 political campaigns. Sprague was urged to call a special session, but he could see no legislative solution to the Multnomah County problem.

Oregon Business and Tax Research convened a special meeting to consider "The Tax Tangle in Oregon," and Ralph Watson churned out a series of editorial-page pieces in the *Oregon Journal* in the month before the primary election. Earl Snell grabbed the brass ring, and made as his major campaign issue replacing the three-person State Tax Commission with a single commissioner.[17]

It was a disingenuous attack, for it was the assessor in Multnomah County—who had been warned repeatedly of the problem—who was at fault. The Tax Commission was simply carrying out a 1929 law, for which Snell had voted, that gave the state limited supervisory authority over assessors.

It fell to Commissioner Charles V. Galloway to try to defend the imbroglio, but the elderly commissioner was not up to the task. He wrote a long, detailed explanation, but then made a very bad decision to release it on a radio broadcast. Galloway droned on for what must have been over an hour, surely talking to empty air for all but the opening minutes.

Decipherable only as a written text, and difficult to decipher even then, Galloway's defense only helped Snell as he castigated the commission.[18]

Estimates varied on the pocketbook impact of moving all assessments to 60 percent. Galloway estimated the average homeowner would pay an additional $4.73 per year, or 7.58 percent; the *Journal* used a more inflammatory figure, citing a $62 million shift from commercial to residential property. Talk was in the air about a "homestead exemption" to hold down residential taxes. It was an explosive issue with no easy solution, and it offered a very tempting target. Snell was not one to miss the hint.[19]

The Multnomah County tax tangle was intensified statewide by several changes in tax collection dates approved by the 1941 Legislature, and the effect in 1942 was that some tax bills carried an 18-month levy instead of a year's levy. As expected, this brought complaints, which were difficult to handle because the law was so complex. By laying the blame at the feet of the hapless commissioners, Snell was blaming the servants rather than the masters. All the laws had been passed by the Oregon Legislature, some of them while he was a member, and none had drawn a protest from Snell—or from Sprague for that matter.[20]

Sprague, insensitive to political nuances and poorly connected in Portland, had not seen the freight train when it began moving, and he could not prevent the wreck. His pledge of a future 20 percent tax cut was pie-in-the-sky bye-and-bye; the tax tangle of 1942 was here-and-now. In frustration, he lashed out in a radio address, accusing Snell of offering no proposals of his own and raising no criticisms of his (Sprague's) record: "In fact, judging from his addresses to date, it would appear that he is running for office against the tax commission. . . . Beheading the tax commission may satisfy local vengeance but it reduces no one's taxes. Does Mr. Snell propose also to abolish the supreme court which sustained the tax commission in its rulings?"[21]

But Snell continued to lay the entire tax situation at Sprague's door, while reminding voters that he was the only war veteran in the race. Finally, he accused Sprague of damaging Republican unity with his attack. "It is an obvious confession of weakness," Snell apprised his radio audience. "The governor has made it perfectly clear that he doesn't intend to do anything about it. I say something should be done." Then Snell promised, "it *will* be done."[22]

The last-minute exchange of blows enlivened what had been a gentlemanly contest, attracting little newspaper attention. With the war raging and gasoline rationed, neither man travelled extensively, relying on radio and friends to carry the message. In the case of Sprague, the editorial fraternity rallied once more to their comrade, if without the crusading spirit in which they had demonized the "radical" Hess.

Sprague won the endorsement of every major daily except Coos Bay, where his old partner had turned against him. Sheldon Sackett felt he had been badly treated in the sale of his *Statesman* stock, and as he grew older he grew more bitter toward Sprague. His editorial was well-reasoned and fair, however, citing Snell's considerable governmental experience and noting that interpersonal skills were often needed to get things done in Salem.[23]

Typically, the Republican editors reminded readers of Sprague's role in 1938, trying to bring forth a loyalty vote. Admitting Sprague was "no ball player" politically, they countered that Oregonians deserved an independent governor who would not accept the dictates of others. Merle Chessman at Astoria and Bob Sawyer at Bend stressed the theme that Sprague had made good on his pledges; Republicans should feel an obligation. Similar support came from Eugene, Corvallis, Klamath Falls and Medford. C. C. Chapman in the *Oregon Voter* provided a firm endorsement.

The Democratic papers—the *Oregon Journal, Capital-Journal* and *East Oregonian*—did not endorse in the Republican primary. *The Oregonian*, the state's largest Republican voice, followed its usual practice of not endorsing in the Republican primary, apparently to remain free in November to praise whoever the party had nominated in May.

Sprague also won three endorsements of limited value in a Republican primary: the Oregon Commonwealth Federation and both the AFL and CIO, although the AFL also endorsed Snell.

The handsome brick house on 14th Street was the Spragues' home for three decades (Sprague Family Archives).

Snell amassed 79,696 votes to Sprague's 56,245, en route to an even bigger win over Democrat Lew Wallace in the fall. Particularly disappointing for Sprague was the margin. Snell captured 58 percent of the vote in the two-man race, and overwhelmed Sprague in the tri-county area of Multnomah, Clackamas, and Washington counties. Sprague carried the university counties of Lane and Benton, and remote Wallowa. He lost his home base, although Marion County essentially was Snell's home as well; he had lived in Salem only five years less than Sprague.

The day after the votes were counted, the ubiquitous Don Upjohn wrote in the *Capital-Journal's* "Sips for Supper:"

> *This a.m. we find a note on the desk . . . Governor Charley Sprague called at 8:55 a.m. with this message: "Ask Sips if he knows where Os West's dog is."*
>
> *Lest this goes over the heads of members of the younger generation let us recall that way back when Walt Pierce was elected governor, Os West advised him to go get himself a dog. "It'll be the only friend who follows you out of the statehouse when you are through as governor," West told him.*[24]

Despite his attempt at self-deprecation, Sprague took the defeat hard. "It hurt, particularly some of the business about not being in the war, implying that he hadn't done his duty and Earl Snell was a war veteran," Eccles recalled. And Blanche wrote in her diary, "Arthur has been deeply hurt by the vote of the people—I am not grieving too deeply for I think it may be a blessing in disguise. He should not work so hard as he has had to and the *Statesman* needs him."[25]

A generation later Sprague told Forest Amsden: "Earl was a remarkable man, immensely popular. He thought the office was his by right, and I guess it was." But at the time Sprague felt overwhelmed, writing to Bob Sawyer, "I was up against the strongest personal political machine that has been organized in this state for a great many years."[26]

Editorials and letters assured Sprague that he had simply come up against a master politician. Merle Chessman quoted a Snell supporter as saying, "Two good men were running and one was a politician." From the unlikely pen of the Commonwealth Federation's Monroe Sweetland came regrets: "If we have to have conservative governors—and I suppose we do for a while yet—I want them to have the character, principle and fairness which you exemplify."[27]

Oregonian editors, having sat on the sidelines, determined that "the voters have decided, in effect, that the governorship requires more than efficiency, and that Mr. Snell's human touch casts the balance."[28]

Following his defeat in the 1942 Republican primary, Sprague dedicated the majority of his time to the war effort, including the ever-complex question of Oregon's Japanese Americans, some four thousand of whom were in concentration camps in sparsely populated areas of the West. The federal government was under enormous pressure to increase sugar production for beverage alcohol and for use in munitions. Amalgamated Sugar Co., the major producer in eastern Oregon, convinced farmers in Malheur County to convert other crops to sugar beets, and the conversion began as early as March 1942. But the county's labor supply was off to war or more lucrative defense jobs, and there was no one to harvest the expanding sugar acreage. Sugar producers appealed to the president, and the result was a frantic effort to get the Japanese internees into the fields.

Sprague, working through his new secretary, George Aiken, led the effort on the West Coast. Sig Unander was now in the Navy—the Spragues were taking him to a Portland train on December 7 when Pearl Harbor was announced—and Aiken was serving in his place. Aiken was publisher of the weekly *Ontario Argus*, in the heart of sugar beet country along the Oregon-Idaho border.

An Oregon plan was unveiled in Salt Lake City on April 7, as representatives of Western states met with Milton Eisenhower, director of the War Relocation Authority (WRA). Aiken cobbled together a plan to house Oregon Japanese Americans in abandoned CCC camps in Malheur and Harney counties, and engage them in the sugar beet harvest and in road building the rest of the year. The workers would be paid prevailing rates, and supervised by federal authorities. Oregon was the only state to present a real work program at Salt Lake City, and Aiken was told by Eisenhower that the plan would get serious consideration. Returning to Oregon, Aiken found a number of public works projects suitable for the internees, but federal officials rejected the Oregon plan.[29]

Rebuffed by federal authorities on the public works plan, Sprague and Aiken concentrated on the beet harvest. Farmers were growing desperate, their pleas for help flooding into the governor's office. Plans flew back and forth, foundering on the question of who would guard the workers, which was primarily to protect them from local zealots. Finally Sprague signed an agreement with Malheur County and Amalgamated Sugar Co. officials, under which they guaranteed that state and county forces would be used to protect some four hundred evacuees whom the sugar company could recruit in the camps. The final step was Sprague's call to the White House, in which he informed Roosevelt's secretary, Grace Tully, of the critical nature of the situation; by return telegram he was given authority to recruit workers. In accepting Sprague's plan, WRA

Director Eisenhower made it clear that he expected the state to protect the workers, warning Sprague that they would be removed if any disorder occurred.[30]

With the beets needing spring thinning, Sprague intensified his efforts, but was frustrated by governmental divisions of authority. On the very day he received WRA approval to recruit workers, the Army sent more than five hundred Japanese farmers from Hood River and Wasco counties to California, before they could be recruited to help in the fields. Never a fan of federal efficiency, Sprague was beside himself, his anger compounded by the frustration of simultaneously trying to campaign and thin beets.[31]

His frustrations increased after the primary, as recruiters failed to find sufficient volunteers at the Portland Assembly Center; the internees were alarmed by the breast-beating of patriots all around them, including several from Malheur County. Sprague, stunned by his primary defeat, was inactive the last half of May, as some 1,100 acres of beets were plowed under and Ontario merchants and families went into the fields to try and save the remaining 13,000 acres. A similar situation prevailed at Nyssa.[32]

The situation was finally saved, not by the governor or any public official, but by 43 young nisei who had gone to Nyssa to thin beets. They agreed to wire and telephone other internees, urging them to come to Malheur County. By June 11, the target of four hundred workers was reached, and the crop saved. "Had it not been for these Japanese in Malheur County, I do not know how in the world we could have taken care of the crops," a sugar company executive wrote Aiken.[33]

The result of the May-June thinning was a bumper beet crop in the fall, but even more labor would have to be imported to bring in the crop. The recruiting machinery was cranked up, and Sprague once more threw himself into the effort. The result was both embarrassing and sobering.

Amalgamated Sugar tried to recruit in the huge (fifteen thousand people) camp at Tule Lake, California, but found few takers. Only eight hundred workers volunteered, despite assurances from Japanese American workers in Malheur County that they were being well-treated. The Tule Lake camp contained evacuees from Oregon, but a majority were urban Californians with no agricultural experience and no desire to spend the bitterly cold late fall and early winter in the back-breaking work.

Sprague fired off an appeal to the Tule Lake project director, who published it in the camp bulletin. Noting a need for five hundred workers to harvest beets, Sprague stated: "In view of all that this office has done on behalf of the Japanese citizens of Oregon to protect them in their rights, it appears to me that an appreciation of that fact would be manifest by them and that they would now answer the call to work."[34] Perhaps wondering just what it was that the governor had been doing for them, most of the Tule Lake internees sat on their hands. Sprague was furious; he lost his temper, and in a departure from his usual regard for factual information, fired off an angry and intemperate telegram to President Roosevelt:

> *. . . the greatest pool of idle labor in all the west exists within a day's ride of the fields where labor is needed. This labor is to be found in the WRA camps for Japanese evacuees from which efforts to obtain voluntary recruitment have been a dismal failure. . . . According to information given me today only 6,000 of the 15,000 in camp pretend to do any work, nine thousand live in absolute idleness and grouse about the food and treatment accorded by the government. . . . If voluntary recruitment fails, then Japanese evacuees should be compelled to work, or told that they will be deported after the war. Will you not instruct WRA officials to give positive assistance in recruitment programs?*[35]

The telegram ignited a firestorm when it became public. Sprague asked Hugh Ball, Japanese-speaking editor of the *Hood River News*, to make a hurried visit to Tule Lake to personally assess the situation. Ball carried with him Sprague's telegram to Roosevelt, and gave it to the *Tulean Dispatch*, the camp newspaper. Editor Howard Imazeki refused to publish it, and wrote Sprague, terming the telegram "shocking to say the least," adding, "I believe your whole mental attitude is warped regarding the Japanese-American and alien Japanese people in the camp." Imazeki challenged Sprague's figures on the Tule Lake population. He noted that it took many people just to run the camp, which he concluded was not as easy "as you may be able to think in your magnificent and well-heated Salem gubernatorial office." He added a postscript: he was off to Idaho to work in the beet fields.[36]

Hugh Ball filed a report to Sprague, blaming a paternalistic WRA policy for the troubles. Ball had interviewed over one hundred internees, and found the young men bitter and cynical. He quoted some: "Why should I work for people who hate me because I am an American born of Japanese parents? . . . We are not good enough to be accepted as American citizens, so why should we help Americans? . . . They have branded us as traitors—well, if that is the way they want to think about us, let it be that way." Ball told Sprague that if nothing else worked, the young men should be drafted. In a conciliatory letter to editor Imazeki, Sprague shared Ball's concern about postwar backlash: "It is my opinion that the readiness of

Japanese now in centers such as that at Tule Lake to respond to these calls for work will contribute greatly to the favor in which they will be received by communities after the war is over.[37]

If Imazeki's letter was critical, a subsequent letter from three Oregon evacuees absolutely peeled Sprague's hide. They presented a statistical rundown on Tule Lake, rebutting point-by-point his telegram to the president, and sent a copy of their letter to F.D.R. After deducting women, children, and the aged, they concluded that only four thousand men between the ages of 18 and 60 resided at Tule Lake. They then detailed the tasks required of this able-bodied work force: eight hundred farm workers to harvest camp crops, five hundred construction workers building barracks, three hundred and fifty cooks and helpers, one hundred hospital workers, and so on for three full pages. Having refuted Sprague's facts, they proceeded to his threat of forced labor or deportation:

> *Since when has it become the policy of these United States to FORCE any person or group of persons to work? We understand that forced labor is an AXIS principle, not a DEMOCRATIC principle.*
>
> *Prior to evacuation, it was stressed that it was the duty of Americans of Japanese Ancestry to be evacuated. We have been told that to do so was our share in the war effort. Now that we have been completely evacuated and before we are barely settled in our new community, your good office comes forth with the statement that it is NOW our duty to assist in the war effort through participation as beet workers in the same state which only a few months previous was clamoring for our evacuation. . . .*
>
> *Your statement, "Japanese evacuees should be compelled to work or be told that they will be deported after the war," is duress in the most vicious sense. It is an Axis technique, the very principle against which the United Nations are now fighting. Such a coercive statement from a high office tends only to defeat the united efforts of all majority and minority groups.*[38]

The letters were sobering; in his concern for the war effort Sprague had been a party to massive injustice, and his plans to help the sugar beet harvest were undertaken without consultation with Japanese Americans and in utter disregard of essential facts. He had refused to wave the bloody shirt in the manner of colleagues from neighboring states (Idaho Governor Chase Clark was quoted saying "Japanese act like rats, breed like rats," and the nation should "send them all back to Japan and then sink the island.").[39] But his sugar beet program operated as if the Japanese were akin to prisoners of war instead of citizens, which about two-thirds of the internees were. If it was not an Axis principle, it was certainly below Sprague's stated standards for public office.

He began the road back shortly after this exchange of letters with the angry young men at Tule Lake. Responding to a suggestion from Mildred Bartholomew of the Portland YWCA, who had undertaken a survey of the Minadoka Camp, Sprague sent a letter to the Japanese American Citizens League for publication in its newsletter, expressing "gratitude to the Japanese in the various relocation centers who have responded to appeals and gone out to assist agriculturalists in the harvesting of their crops." Sprague may have been the only public official in the West Coast states to ever thank the Japanese Americans for their work, although Amalgamated Sugar had admitted they had saved the 1942 crop in Malheur County.[40]

Sprague's letter of appreciation was sent in late November; six weeks later he left office. Relieved of the burden of office and chastened by his exchanges with the young nisei at Tule Lake, Sprague had two years to ponder his response to the next big challenge—the return of the Japanese Americans to their Oregon homes.

It was not until much later that Sprague was able to discuss his role in the Japanese American internment, regretting that he had not spoken against the plan. At the time, he was less driven by any philosophical pointer than by the feeling that he had to go along with federal directives concerning the war, and he was pressed by the political challenge of Earl Snell.

In his replies to Clarence Oliver, to Gresham missionary Azalia E. Peet, and in correspondence with Japanese American Citizens League leaders, Sprague had consistently expressed support for Japanese Americans' professions of loyalty, and sympathy for their plight. He helped Newton K. Uyesugi, JACL state president, obtain entry to medical school in Indiana. In February, Congressman John Tolan of California held a series of well-publicized hearings on the West Coast, examining the question of Japanese Americans, and many political leaders appeared to issue anti-Japanese statements. Coming as it did in the midst of his challenge from Snell, it would have been an excellent time to wave the flag, but Sprague was absent from the February 26 Portland hearings and did not send a representative.[41]

With the exception of Clarence Oliver and C. B. Lewis, neither of whom were personally known to Sprague, there was no cry for state action to help the Japanese Americans. The JACL itself adopted a posture of accepting internship and the loss of civil liberties; after some early pleas for moderation editors joined the clamor for evacuation, and there was no organized civil liberties opposition.

Later in his life, Sprague confided his regrets. Charles Davis, Oregon ACLU chairman, who presented Sprague the first E. B. MacNaughton Civil Liberties Award in 1962, recalled that Sprague told him of his great regret at acquiescing to internment. Forest Amsden, who worked with Sprague on the Oregon Constitutional Revision Commission, recalls Sprague commenting that he was powerless to change the internment order: "They'd have sent troops and removed me from office." [42]

Despite his later regrets, it is difficult to imagine Sprague acting differently. He had, after all, taken a similar tack in World War I, when his editorial page became more militantly patriotic and less tolerant of German Americans as the war progressed. In 1918, patriotic fervor was orchestrated from the White House and governors' mansions on down to local leagues. But World War II on the Pacific Coast was much more a time of peril, and in its opening months the limitations of the Japanese military machine were not yet understood. When compared to other editors or politicians of the day, Sprague's words and acts were remarkably moderate, and he rejected opportunities such as the Tolan hearings to use the occasion to his advantage. In 1942, opposition to internment would have been an act of political courage unmatched by any other major politician in the state; it very likely would have produced a recall petition.

As in World War I, Sprague's position was heavily influenced by his personal situation at the time. Instead of the need to establish himself in a community where he was young and unproven, he faced an aggressive political challenge and the obligation of speaking for an electorate that had decidedly made up its mind on the issue of the Japanese Americans. A February 12 *Oregonian* poll showed that 80 percent favored the evacuation of all aliens and 36 percent also favored evacuating citizens of Japanese ancestry.[43] Sprague took his evacuation position five days later.

It is inconceivable that Sprague would have resisted Executive Order 9066; the war was only three months old, its outcome far from certain, and the necessity for discipline was paramount. He might have issued a protest to the president, and perhaps the Frank Bane statement began as an effort to influence the debate. If that was his intent, he would have been the only prominent political figure on the West Coast to enter even a mild protest and he would immediately have become an object of national attention. But it is unlikely that was his intent, and certainly that was not the outcome.

Fully occupied with the war, Sprague still had time for introspection in 1942; it was a long half-year, sitting on boards and commissions with Snell and feeling, in small ways that could not be revealed, the hurt of rejection. And yet, was it really rejection or was Snell the only man who could have beaten him in 1942? Was there still a political future?

At the time of his 1942 defeat, *The Oregonian* had suggested that Sprague should consider running for the Senate in 1944, when Rufus Holman's term expired. "That rather stern aloofness which has militated against Mr. Sprague in the intimacy of our own state might be considered a virtue in one going to the United States Senate," advised *The Oregonian*.[44] Sprague was unsure as to his plans, he told his Coos County chairman shortly after the defeat, but he leaned toward returning to the newspaper. Soundings were made in 1943 by Bob Boyd and Bob Sawyer. To the latter, Sprague replied that he was "out of it," commenting, "I have always thought the spectacle of a man defeated for public office attempting to make a comeback rather pathetic."[45]

On the Spragues' first day back in private life, Blanche wrote: "Off the display shelf! Now I can do as I wish." On the day of Snell's inaugural she

Back at his Statesman desk after his stint at the Capitol, Sprague began his column, It Seems To Me, on May 16, 1943 and continued for 25 years (Statesman-Journal photo files).

had written, "Arthur and I had dinner at home alone afterward—quite a contrast to four years ago."[46] The couple regained their privacy, but Sprague brooded over the public repudiation even as he resumed his *Statesman* duties.

To his readers he began with "Good Morning, Everybody!" and concluded the first editorial of his post-gubernatorial life, "We shall seek to use the knowledge and experience gained in doing a political swing shift, in the important and scarcely less arduous task of editing and publishing a daily newspaper in a state capital."

For the citizens of Oregon, and for Sprague personally, perhaps the greatest benefit of the term was not what was done *by* Sprague, but what the experience did *for* him. Ahead was a quarter-century career as the state's leading editorial writer and, increasingly, its elder statesman and public conscience. It simply could not have happened without the broadening Sprague received in the myrtlewood office.

On May 16, 1943, without fanfare or introduction, a column signed by Sprague appeared in the left front-page column of *The Oregon Statesman*. "It Seems To Me" was born; it would be Sprague's most important contribution to the political and civic life of Oregon for a quarter-century.

The column may have been suggested by Hunt Clark, who was attempting to pull the *Statesman* out of a circulation slump that occurred while Sprague was at the Capitol. Sprague's first year back provided little breathing space; Ralph Curtis and Steve Mergler were tired from carrying the small news staff during Sprague's absence. In May Mergler bought a weekly in Mt. Vernon, Washington and Curtis was in the process of buying a weekly at St. Helens.

Sprague was negotiating with a young war correspondent for the position being vacated by Curtis. Asahel Bush carried the name of his grandfather, founder of *The Oregon Statesman*; he was filing Associated Press copy from the South Pacific when Sprague offered him the position at $65 a week (considerably less than Bush's AP check, with combat bonus). Bush hoped to return to Salem, where his wife and children waited, but he told Sprague he felt an obligation to AP to finish the war. It was a fateful decision; nine months later, the young reporter was killed by bomb fragments at Tacloban in the Philippines. He was one of two Salem natives who died reporting World War II.[47]

In June the Oregon Newspaper Publishers Association presented Sprague with its highest honor, the Amos E. Voorhies award for editorial leadership, and elected him vice-president of the association. But he was leading a very shallow team, hanging on until the war could end and veterans return. Perhaps fortunately, wartime controls on newsprint were tight and the *Statesman* could not have printed larger papers even if it had had the staff.[48]

Struggling with personnel shortages, his son and his nephew both still in the service, Sprague had plenty on his hands in 1943. He had little to say about his successor, who had made a half-hearted and unsuccessful effort to carry out his campaign pledges of a single-person Tax Commission and a solution to the problem of Multnomah County's variable tax ratio. When the House defeated Snell's single-commissioner concept, Sprague allowed himself a moment of satisfaction: "The results are not surprising. The issue was a phony, even if worked as a political ruse. . . . The writer draws considerable satisfaction in having steadfastly defended the tax administration in Oregon against unjust and sometimes malicious onslaught."[49]

Sprague's major activity as 1944 opened was announcing for a delegate position at the Republican National Convention, where he planned to promote the candidacy of Wendell Willkie.[50] Willkie's outspoken liberalism appealed to Sprague in much the same way Theodore Roosevelt had drawn him, and the men maintained a correspondence. Sprague's plan to attend his first national political convention was abruptly shattered, however, on February 25, when Senator Charles McNary died in Florida, where he had gone to recuperate after the removal of a brain tumor. Suddenly and tragically, Oregon had both U. S. Senate seats on the 1944 ballot.[51] McNary's successor would be forced to go to the electorate in three short months.

The state's other Republican Senator, Rufus Holman, was already facing a stiff challenge from University of Oregon law dean Wayne L. Morse. Holman was vulnerable; always a maverick, he had in his later years turned isolationist and reactionary, and become an embarassment to the Republican Party. Sprague had rejected the race in 1943, after showing some initial interest. Less than a year later, a sharp-profiled young man with intense eyes beneath imposing black eyebrows sat in Sprague's editorial office and again raised the question. The men knew and admired each other—as governor, Sprague had defended the younger man against conservative lumbermen who objected to the law professor's views on labor matters.[52] No, the editor told Wayne L. Morse, he would not be a candidate against Senator Holman; the field was open for Morse to run in the Republican primary.

Now there was a second Senate opening. Many expected Governor Snell to resign to receive the appointment, or to be a candidate in the primary. Snell instead named Roseburg attorney and veteran timber lobbyist Guy Cordon. Sprague immediately let it be known that he was thinking about the Senate, and days later he was in the race. Unlike his previous campaigns, he retained his editorial responsibilities, although he did not comment on the primary election.[53]

Sprague had no real bone to pick with Guy Cordon, who had drafted some of Sprague's forestry plan and was perhaps the state's leading expert on timber taxation. Cordon lobbied in Washington for a group of Oregon counties, looking after their interests in federal management of the forests. A pleasant but private man, Cordon was uncomfortable with public appearances or encounters with the press. He was part of the Snell organization, and a former state commander of the American Legion.

Announcing his candidacy, Cordon said he would run on a four-pronged platform: support the war, assure veterans of assistance in returning, support international cooperation for peace, and "an end to governmental control 'approaching absolute dictatorship' at conclusion of the war."[54]

Cordon chose an elegantly simple campaign strategy and it was effective: he stayed in Washington and sent out press releases reminding voters that he was "on the job." More loquacious friends of Cordon and Snell made appearances on the senator's behalf. "Senator Cordon has put duty before everything else," declared state Senator Marshall Cornett in a radio broadcast. "Accordingly, he has been on the job in Washington and has left his campaign in the hands of his friends because he honestly felt he'd best be able to help Oregon during these wartime days when so much is at stake."[55]

Cordon's friends in timber, the American Legion, and Southern Oregon financed a campaign costing some $23,785, about $6,000 more than

Sprague's comeback attempt in 1944 was thwarted—again in the Republican primary—by Sen. Guy Cordon, newly appointed to the position by Governor Snell (Oregon Historical Society CN001522).

Sprague spent. Most went for radio and newspaper advertising; Cordon did not set foot in the state during at least the last two weeks of the campaign (perhaps not even during the last month; no coverage appeared in major papers), and he broadcast from his Washington office on election eve.[56]

By contrast, Sprague rushed around the state in an intensive two-month schedule of personal appearances, using the extra gas stamps allocated to political candidates. But, lacking a confrontation with Cordon, he was overshadowed by the Morse-Holman bombast, which reached high-decibel levels as Morse accused Holman of being an isolationist out of touch with current affairs. Morse in turn was lambasted by the GOP right, which linked him to Harry Bridges and other left-wing labor leaders and tarred him for being a college professor. Rex Ellis, miner-cum-legislator, wrote from Sumpter that, "We must stop sending college professors, Lawyers and theoists (sic) to Washington." Ellis would vote for Holman and Sprague, although he scolded the latter for vetoing one of his (Ellis's) bills five years earlier.[57]

Cordon won a narrow victory, 68,666 to 63,944, and he won it in two areas: Portland and Douglas County. Cordon's home-town friends gave him an astounding margin of 2,870 votes to 639 for Sprague (by contrast, Sprague's home county gave him a margin of only 5,697 to 4,874). A 2,600-vote margin in Multnomah County, where neither man had a network but Cordon had old Legion and Snell friends, completed the win. Each man carried exactly half of Oregon's 36 counties, Sprague's strength coming in the university counties and eastern Oregon.

Across the ballot, Wayne L. Morse scored a decisive win over Rufus Holman and both Morse and Cordon went on to easy general election victories. Replying to a letter from Wendell Willkie, Sprague confessed: "I guess I am too much like you; more concerned about principles and issues than about the finesse of politics." He professed satisfaction with other results, however, terming Morse's defeat of Holman "an occasion for national rejoicing. It really was more important to have Morse win than myself."[58]

Sprague's deceptively cheerful reply to Willkie masked a bitter disappointment. This was not a race against a political master like Snell; it was against a man almost unknown in most parts of the state, who had not even mounted a personal campaign. Sprague could only take it as a personal rebuff, a final signal from the voters that he did not have the temperament for high public office. His son recalled that the election caused a period of depression, furthered by a nasty skin rash (eventually traced to his breakfast cereal); later in the summer, Sprague made a long, rambling train trip from Salem to Chicago to Washington to visit

Wallace, who was awaiting overseas orders. Returning home, he hired a managing editor and forever turned his back on political campaigns.[59]

Why had he returned to politics, after telling friends he would devote his energies to reviving the flagging *Statesman*? It is likely there was a search for personal redemption in the decision—and he assumed too much from his editorial colleagues. They had almost unanimously backed him in 1942 against a popular man whom many considered a friend; surely they would come to his support in 1944. Cordon was no giant in public affairs, limited in his professional interests, and lacking in campaign style.

Nothing worked quite as it might have, beginning with the editorial club. Bob Ruhl defected to Cordon, largely on the basis of their Southern Oregon connection; Merle Chessman and Bob Sawyer sat on their hands and made no endorsement; neither Portland paper made a recommendation. Cordon also picked up the *Capital-Journal*, leaving Sprague with a hard core of Bill Tugman, Claude Ingalls, Frank Jenkins at Klamath Falls and C. C. Chapman at the *Oregon Voter*.

It is interesting to speculate on the type of senator Sprague might have become, particularly in his relationship to the volatile Morse. What is most likely is that he would have been a one-termer, neglecting visits to county fairs and drafty Grange halls while he labored on the great issues of the day. What is certain is that the 1944 race killed any remaining political ambition; at age 56 Sprague was already heading into what might be for other men a last decade of active service. His was to last, instead, for a quarter-century, at a pace and with effects that could not be foreseen in the bitter defeat of May 1944.

Searching for a retreat and a break from the intensity of the past six years, Sprague turned to the Little North Fork of the North Santiam, a crystal-clear stream emptying into the main river only 20 miles east of Salem. Healing from his election wounds in 1944, he began discussions with architect Pietro Belluschi, and in 1947 plans were completed. The cabin—really a river lodge—was completed in 1948 and was an important part of his life for the next fifteen years.[60]

While the river home gave Sprague a private place to retreat to and heal the wounds of political defeat, there was no retreat from the pressures facing him at the postwar *Statesman*. With Ralph Curtis and Steve Mergler leaving to publish weeklies, the paper was in serious trouble and needed a jump-start. Sprague found it in a stubbly little Iowan whom he knew only slightly but who had first applied for a job in 1940 while he was reporting for the Associated Press from San Francisco.

6

◆◆◆

Transforming The Oregon Statesman

Charles A. Sprague and Wendell Webb knew each other mainly by reputation and through common acquaintances when Sprague hired Webb as managing editor in mid-1944. Webb was given a free hand in the newsroom except, as he soon learned, with the purse strings.

Thus began an odd-couple relationship that lasted until Sprague's death: the rumpled, friendly little managing editor, cigarette ashes on his spotted vest, moving at rapid shuffle around the news desks while downstairs the immaculate, reserved, and aloof publisher worked in his office. Each in his own way was loyal to the other and yet neither was ever able to fully understand their differences.

Together they rebuilt the newspaper from the tired remnants of a publication that had survived Depression, war, and the absence of its publisher while he followed the siren song of politics. But it was a fine time to build; postwar euphoria and demands for consumer goods fueled an increase in advertising dollars, and there was an influx of young men anxious to establish themselves in reporting jobs after years on overseas battlefields. Webb was barely in command before they began to arrive, and with a handful of prewar holdovers he built a new and aggressive news room to challenge the dominant *Capital-Journal*.

The new managing editor loved the flare of newspaper combat; Wendell Webb had seen the other side of combat in the Battle of Midway and other South Pacific assignments he had shared with the late Asahel Bush and other AP correspondents. Webb was formed in the old school of reporting—a real newspaperman got the story, never mind what it took—and it had carried him on a roller-coaster ride though Des Moines, Omaha, San Francisco, and the South Pacific, with calmer and ultimately more fateful times in two Oregon towns. In McMinnville, he worked for the Bladine family and married Lillian Paul; in Coos Bay, he wrote for Sheldon Sackett. As the war wound down, it was Lillian who urged him to pursue the *Oregon Statesman* job that he had first applied for in a letter to Sprague in 1940. Correspondence had been renewed when Asahel Bush cast his lot with the AP. Webb was hired as Sprague wound up his losing senatorial campaign. There was much to be done.[1]

As he looked around his new quarters, the scene that greeted Webb could not have been encouraging. The newsroom floor dropped nearly a foot from the back wall to the front and desks were shimmed to compensate; the desks themselves appeared to have seen a previous century. He stubbed out a cigarette, fumbled in a vest pocket for another, sized up the clutter of wire copy and discarded newspapers strewn about the room. A reporter was beginning the calls to police and hospitals—the overnight business of a daily newspaper. Others would soon begin their daily routine, for a morning newspaper never really sleeps.

But the physical plant was the least of Webb's worries. Among the small staff he found many people with titles, but few to report the news. Everyone was an editor of some sort, but in total there were only seven people on staff. Webb described Sprague as "one of Oregon's better governors, a leader in the Republican party . . . he was also an abstemious, non-smoking pillar of the Presbyterian church," whose editorials were "splendid—and ponderous. The Statesman's cheering section of friends and the intelligentsia was not enough in a highly competitive field." The *Statesman*, Webb found, "carried no spark, no rapport with the general public," and was losing the race with the *Capital-Journal*.[2]

The afternoon paper had a veteran staff, and the acerbic Upjohn's column was rivaled only by the tartness of Putnam's editorials. The C-J had a bite and, if you didn't happen to be on the receiving end, it made for lively reading. The *Statesman's* Depression-era columnists were ponderous or worse, and while Curtis and Mergler were acceptable journeymen they did not have the writing flair to attract readers away from the C-J. When Webb arrived, the *Capital-Journal* was clearly the circulation leader, with some 12,699 readers to 9,613 for the *Statesman*.[3]

Hunt Clark had been hustling circulation, but Webb's assessment of the product was accurate. It did lack spark. In Webb, Clark found a willing partner and a lifelong friend as well; the men enjoyed a drink and a yarn together, and no two people took as much glee in scoring a scoop of any kind on a rival.

Webb and Clark immediately arranged with the Southern Pacific to put 200 papers on its northbound train each morning, and got the Army to let the *Statesman* leave two thousand or more papers on a nickel-in-the-cup honor system in mess halls at nearby Camp Adair. The temporary circulation boost was enough to get several extra tons of newsprint—then strictly rationed—but it was a temporary fix, and they realized new ideas were needed.[4]

They toyed with a number of circulation boosters, but it was Webb who came up with the winner, an annual grade-school spelling bee that delighted Webb's joy in the company of children and also focused attention for several weeks each year on the *Statesman*, with its list of contest words. The spelling bee, co-sponsored with KSLM, began in 1951 and ran for ten years, and was credited by many with pulling the *Statesman* up to the C-J's circulation level, then surpassing it finally in 1955.[5] That is an exaggeration, for many other forces were at work—not least of them the staff Webb was hiring—but the spelling bee became a *Statesman* icon.

Fortunately for Webb's plans, the *Statesman* had finally begun earning money as the war ended. The end of the war and the subsequent growth of Salem brought a new prosperity to the Statesman Publishing Co., and by 1948 the company had registered four consecutive years with a profit margin above 15 percent. From 1939 to 1944, the company's profit margin ran around 3 percent, but it actually lost money in 1942.[6]

Sprague was not taking a large salary for himself. His federal tax statements show his Statesman salary moving from $9,600 in 1943 and

Wendell Webb's brainchild, the annual Statesman Spelling Bee, was the inspiration for the misspelled signs held by news staffers in this 1959 photo. Seated, left to right, are Lillie Madsen, Maxine Buren, Webb, Jeryme English, Tom Wright; standing, left to right, are Wes Sullivan, Russ Bieraugal, Jerry Stone, Conrad Prange, Garth Fanning, Tom Marshall, Bob Gangware, Mervin Jenkins, Don Scarborough, Dan Davies (*Statesman-Journal* photo files).

Robert Sprague, nephew of the publisher, served in business and advertising roles at the Statesman from 1935 until the newspaper was sold in 1973 (Author's collection).

1944 to $14,000 in 1945, scarcely a large amount for the owner of a substantial business. He did his own taxes until 1948, when he finally turned the business over to an accountant, doubtless influenced by a three-year running battle with the Internal Revenue Service over the amount of taxes due on his 1945 return; the affair finally wound up with the IRS providing him with a $900 credit for over-assessment.[7]

Advertising was driving the new profits, as Salem businesses began to recover from the Depression and at war's end looked to new consumer spending habits. Net advertising sales increased 133 percent in only four years (1943-47), surpassing a 58 percent increase in circulation revenues. Salem was on the verge of the postwar boom, and it was easy to predict more growth.[8]

During the Depression and war the *Statesman* had attracted a handful of reporters and editors who had moved on by the time Webb arrived. Webb's core in 1944 consisted of City Editor Isabel Childs, Sports Editor Al Lightner, the women's page duo of Jeryme English and Maxine Buren, Valley Editor Marguerite (Peggy) Gleason, Lillie Madsen, farm and garden editor; and Lightner's new sports reporter, Jerry Stone.

Webb's first job was to hire someone to run the news desk, replacing Ralph Curtis. He found a tall, slender B-17 pilot with a long, lean face and a shock of vivid red hair. J. Wesley Sullivan had done his required bombing missions and, with his "ruptured duck" discharge pin firmly in place, he set out in July 1945 to select a job; he was ahead of other veterans and he had his pick. On advice from George Turnbull, journalism professor at the University of Oregon, Sullivan called Webb and was hired at $45 a week, which was $10 a week more than either Portland paper had offered and twice what he had been offered in Grants Pass, the hometown of his wife, Elsie. For his $45 Sullivan was to put out the newspaper. He was the only desk man, essentially in charge after Webb went home, and he worked from 5:30 p.m. to nearly 2 a.m. Casting an envious eye on the nearly new *Capital-Journal* printing plant, Sullivan began work in what he was certain was "the oldest, most decrepit newspaper plant in the state":

> *I sat at a rickety table on one end of the newsroom. At my left was a cubby hole in which a single Associated Press teletype sat churning out copy at 53 words per minute, our only contact with the outside world.*
>
> *All the world, national, and regional news, sports and markets came in on that lone wire. What's more, it stopped at any time anyone wanted to send a message. I also had to punch out Salem area news for the AP wire on that same machine. . . .*
>
> *To get some idea of the financial constrictions under which we operated, I had to buy a lamp for my table. I would have gone blind trying to read copy from the light of a bare bulb hanging from the middle of the newsroom. I bought my own dictionary.*
>
> *None of this hampered in the slightest my enthusiasm for my work. Wendell didn't interfere, but he did critique my work the following morning. He had the greatest "nose for news" I've ever seen. He was one of the finest copy editors. And, most importantly, he was a man of the people. He knew what people, the readers, wanted. "What have we done new this week," was his persistent question.*[9]

The core of the Statesman newsroom in the post-war period was made up of (left to right): Wendell Webb, managing editor; J. Wesley Sullivan, news editor; and Robert E. Gangware, city editor. Webb was a World War II correspondent; Sullivan and Gangware were among the first returning veterans to take jobs at the paper (Statesman-Journal photo files).

Almost immediately, war veterans began arriving, most with no more genuine newspaper experience than Sullivan; Webb was running a training school in addition to a newspaper. But his new hires were mature men, some with families, and they became a cohesive social unit as well as a newsroom. Soon they had the *Capital-Journal* veterans puffing to stay even. With Webb putting out his trademark half-sheet memos and little notes tucked in an envelope, morale was high. Sprague suddenly had a newspaper to go with his editorial page.

Bob Gangware had been in the infantry in Europe and Conrad Prange in a medical unit in the Pacific when they arrived in early 1946. Gangware had done a little basic reporting in Ohio, Prange was a pixieish little man from the German-Catholic Mount Angel community, with an endearing personal manner and rollicking humor. Gangware, neat and dark-browed, with eyesight so bad it was a wonder the Army had allowed him to carry a weapon, was hired to understudy Isabel Childs. Webb promised his new man that he could be city editor if Childs ever quit; jokingly, he told Gangware to hope for a wedding. Childs was a single woman past forty, so that prospect seemed unlikely, but she surprised everyone by marrying Harold Rosebraugh and resigning. Gangware moved to the city desk and Isabel Rosebraugh later returned as a writer in the women's section.

The immediate postwar period brought a rush of returning veterans, some passing through and others remaining at the *Statesman* to anchor the newsroom in the next three decades. Russ Bieraugal, a quiet Army veteran, gradually took over the night city desk and remained after Sprague's death. Van Eisenhut, a ruggedly handsome fighter pilot, enrolled as Sullivan's assistant, had his career interrupted for a stint in Korea, but returned to eventually become managing editor after Sprague's death.[10]

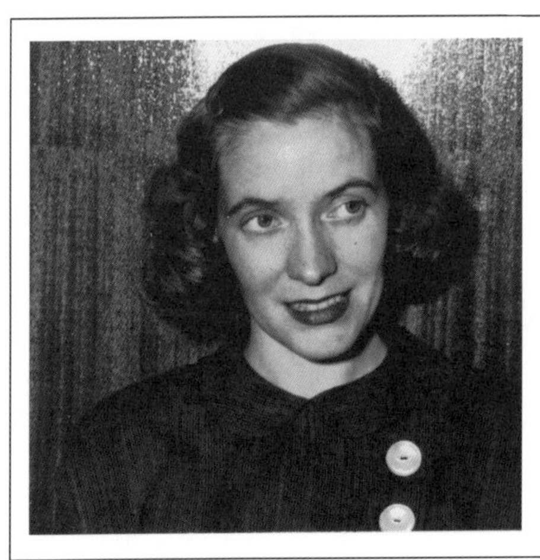

Hired fresh out of the University of Oregon, where she had been a controversial student editor, Marguerite Wright served as Sprague's researcher and assistant for nearly two decades (Tom Wright).

Tom Wright, political writer and later state editor of the Statesman, found himself in political controversy during the administration of Gov. Mark Hatfield (Tom Wright).

Like most newsrooms of the period, which had been dominated by women during the war, the postwar period saw only rare hiring of women outside the traditional women's pages. The exception at the *Statesman* was the talented and energetic Marguerite Wright, hired in 1947 upon graduation from the University of Oregon, where she had edited the *Daily Emerald*. Although she was intermittently a reporter, Wright was primarily a researcher and writer for Sprague, and often worked part-time while raising four daughters. Sprague, living with a highly intelligent wife and raising a daughter with the same qualities, was willing to take a chance on the outspoken young graduate, who had a U of O reputation as a radical. Wright's path to full-time reporting was always hindered by Webb, who didn't take to uppity women, but in Sprague's office Wright was treated as a professional. Working side-by-side in the cramped office, the unlikely duo became close friends, although Sprague saw himself as a father figure. Once, when Wright was nursing one of her four children, she was mortified to find her blouse dripping wet; without hesitating, the former governor doffed his suit coat, wrapped it around his lactating assistant, and suggested she take the afternoon off.[11]

Wright's husband, Tom, joined the staff in 1948, out of the University of Oregon on the GI bill; he had worked briefly at the *Register-Guard* while attending school. With Gangware, Sullivan, and Prange, he became one of the cornerstones of the newsroom.

The incomers worked and played together; poker games were organized, Gangware providing a well-used Army blanket on someone's kitchen table, Webb complaining every time a "wild card" version was suggested, Prange working on a cigar, Bieraugal betting too much, and the competitive but quiet Wright taking home the pot. There were rivalries; once when Sullivan wanted to run for the school board, Wright threatened to run against him. But most were patched over in the common need to produce a better *Statesman*.

There were also larger gatherings. At annual office picnics, Sprague was known to cheat in the sack races, leaving one leg outside the sack. No one complained; his employees enjoyed the spirit in which the publisher, now in his sixties, participated.

The state's second-oldest newspaper celebrated its Centennial in 1951, featuring a giant commemorative edition produced by Marguerite Wright. A program featured a panel of speakers including author and future U. S. Senator Richard L. Neuberger, Reed College historian Dorothy Johansen, and *New York Times* West Coast bureau chief Lawrence E. Davies. *TIME* magazine was already calling Sprague an "elder statesman" in its coverage of the anniversary.[12] Poised for a second century, the morning paper was now staffed for a real run at its afternoon rival. Sprague and his managing editor made an unusual team. The tall publisher stood nearly a foot above his associate, who stooped from a spinal injury received in a car accident. Webb was stocky, Sprague trim; Webb rumpled and careless about his dress, Sprague tailored and neat despite the mess of the printing plant. But their physical differences were less than their places in the culture of the news room, and even in the community.

On the 100th birthday of The Oregon Statesman, in 1951, Blanche cuts a cake as Sprague looks on. To Blanche's right is Wendell Webb. Wallace Sprague is at far right, back row (Statesman-Journal photo files).

The staff understood and appreciated the roles of Webb and Sprague. Tom Wright believed that Webb filled a role for Sprague that others filled for political leaders who wanted to be above the fray, yet keep contacts. "Sprague wasn't about to go to the Elks Club, where local policy was being made, so-to-speak," Wright observed, nor was Sprague likely to show up at the bar of the Marion Hotel, popular watering-hole for legislators, lobbyists, and other movers and shakers—and for much of the *Statesman* staff as well. Webb could and did; he was a genuinely warm and unpretentious person who made hundreds of friends for his boss over the years.[13]

Sprague's office was on the ground floor of the old building; the newsroom and presses were above. Marguerite Wright inherited the half of the office once occupied by Sheldon Sackett, and worked back-to-back with Sprague until they moved to a new building in 1953. Sprague would already be at work when she arrived at 8:30 each morning, unless he stopped at the State Library to read periodicals or ask for material. Wright's job was to do research, again using the State Library, seeking out national material that *Statesman* readers would not have seen for short editorial fillers as well as some full-length editorials. Sprague wrote

Still in the days of hot lead, the composing room crew poses for a 1951 Statesman centennial picture. The crew included a husband-wife team, Foreman Hugh McCain (far left) and his wife, Lillian (third from right) (*Statesman-Journal* photo files).

the controversial pieces, and reviewed her editorials. It was his page, but Wright's prolific research and strong work ethic freed him from some of the digging and routine writing chores.

As Sprague moved back into public life, as a member of numerous boards and commissions and in 1952 as an alternate delegate to the United Nations, he relied increasingly on Webb. The U.N. assignment came as the *Statesman* was beginning construction of a new office and printing plant on Church Street. With Sprague in New York, Webb was essentially in charge of the construction as well as the newsroom, an extraordinarily heavy assignment, with the publisher sending instructions and comments almost daily from across the country.

Sprague had built printing plants at Ritzville and Corvallis, and he had an extraordinary mind for detail, quizzing Webb on everything from electric outlet placement and wall paint color to the details of the press the *Statesman* had purchased from *The Oregonian*. Sprague hired Pietro Belluschi, the influential Portland architect who was now dean of the M. I. T. School of Architecture, and stayed in contact with him while in New York. Memos flew back and forth, Sprague suggesting a hauling firm for the new press, rejecting a color change in the mortar, even worrying about the exact shade of green for the bindery. A letter typical of his bent for detail instructed Webb on wiring the plant's remelt pot, which recycled the lead type; another letter went into great detail about the design of a basement door. In addition, Webb was negotiating a new contract with the pressman's union, normally a job for the publisher. Again, letters and telegrams of advice flew back and forth across the country.

Despite their close working relationship, the two men were never personally close, and did not socialize. Reporters believed it was in part a class thing. Webb was not intellectual and did not move in Salem society; he was most comfortable with a glass of bourbon and a cigarette, his feet propped up, to talk with a good friend. He had little interest in politics, and his idea of news leaned toward short pieces on local affairs rather than weighty international reports.

He always called his boss "Mr. Sprague," and was in return called "Webb," in the manner of men of Sprague's generation, who often began correspondence with the recipient's last name. But Sprague called his younger news staffers by their first names, and over the years this grated on Webb almost to the point of obsession. It became a sign of rejection; he never seemed to realize that it was simply the way many of Sprague's generation addressed colleagues. The misunderstanding was typical of the way the two men seemed to be trains in the night, proceeding to a common destination on parallel tracks.

Sprague had hoped for a role for his son, Wallace, who had spent two years on staff in 1939-41, following his graduate work at Harvard. But the younger Sprague, reacting to a natural desire to be his own man and also to the Eastern orientation of his new wife, began his career elsewhere. In 1946 he joined *Parade* magazine as an assistant editor, subsequently moving through a series of positions there, then with the New York *Herald-Tribune* organization and Bowater Paper Co. In 1952, while at the United Nations, Sprague was able to spend time with his son and family, and it became apparent that transplanting them to Salem was unlikely.

In 1940 Sprague had arranged for his two children and his nephew to each purchase 10 percent of Statesman Publishing Co. stock. Over the years, Bob Sprague had fallen behind in making payments on the stock, and as a result of this and other developments, Sprague had lost confidence that he could be counted upon to play a larger corporate role than his position as advertising director. With Martha living in California with her physician husband, Wallace apparently entrenched in the East, and Bob not a viable candidate for leadership, Sprague as he passed his 65th birthday in 1952 was beginning to be concerned about the future of the family newspaper.

Partnership with the acerbic and aging Putnam was not an option, although Sprague had briefly considered it in 1939, to the extent of discussing it with an Alfred G. Hill, who proposed himself as an

A proud grandfather with Wallace and his two sons, Charles and John, about 1952 (Sprague Family Archives).

On their fiftieth wedding anniversary in 1962, the Spragues pose with Dr. Melvin Hurley and Martha, and Wallace and Mary Lou Sprague (Sprague Family Archives).

intermediary with Putnam.[14] By 1952 Putnam was moving slowly, shuffling in and out of the C-J newsroom, wearing his old-fashioned editor's green eyeshade, chewing a pipe, retiring after his work day to the state liquor store and nursing his drinks at the home he shared with his sister in one of the city's fine old neighborhoods. He must have considered sale to Sprague, for his rival was the logical purchaser, but if any consideration was given by either party it was damaged and perhaps destroyed by "the fat and naked Venus" of 1953, Putnam's final populist shot at Sprague.

It all began innocently enough. An elevator operator at the Supreme Court named Carroll Moore, a bachelor, by living frugally and saving his modest state earnings, left $25,000 for a memorial to the pioneers. Pioneer Trust Company, as trustee, had sole authority to commit the funds, but the bequest languished from Carroll Moores's death in 1937 until 1950, when a city advisory group was appointed. The advisory group and Sprague saw the grant (now grown to $34,000) as a way to enhance the rather austere lines of Pietro Belluschi's new Marion County Courthouse.

Sprague was on the Courthouse commission, and he wanted to use the grant for a fountain. He confided to Bob Sawyer in January 1953 that he had persuaded the Moores trustees to purchase a fountain; Belluschi had a New York sculptress in mind. When yet another advisory commission was set up to guide the trustees in selecting the memorial, Sprague was appointed, with Salem banker Chandler Brown and Belluschi. They consulted Thomas C. Colt, Jr., director of the Portland Art Museum.[15]

Colt and Belluschi were cosmopolitan men and not likely to be in tune with Salem's conservative tastes. In New York Colt discovered a bronze casting of Auguste Renoir's "Venus Victorieuse," a nude sculpted about 1900, available for $18,000. He and Belluschi recommended its purchase, terming it a work of genius. Salem newspapers revealed the choice when Sprague and Brown asked the County Court for approval to install the Venus near the entrance to the new building. "Sprague said that the Renoir work is not voluptuous," the *Capital-Journal* reported, adding a comment from Brown: "'Only the ignorant of matters pertaining to art' could be critical of the Renoir piece." The *Statesman*, perhaps anticipating the reaction, carefully pointed out that the statue was "feminine without being sensuous . . . She is not a 'glamour girl' but one symbolical of maternity."[16]

Venus Victorieuse was, in the words of Charles Sprague, "feminine without being sensuous . . . She is not a 'glamour girl' but one symbolical of maternity." But rival editor George Putnam labeled the Renoir statue, "Fat and naked Venus, pagan goddess of love," and in a long-running and at times comic battle, Putnam and Salem's puritans won—Venus was unveiled, not in Salem as Sprague had desired, but at the Portland Art Museum, where it remains to this day (Portland Art Museum).

Putnam accepted the challenge with alacrity and customary bluntness. "Fat and naked Venus, pagan goddess of love is a surprising emblem for a palace of justice and a strange memorial for its donor, who will probably turn over in his grave and also probably be a shock to sedate Salem," he huffed. "If the committee wanted a Venus in the altogether, why not give the American gals a chance? If it had consulted the veterans, they would have chosen Marilyn Monroe, their favorite pin-up girl in the nude the world around, in standing or reclining pose. . ."[17]

Putnam was just getting started, and he was quickly augmented by shocked Salemites, with the C-J bannering one letter to the editor: "Pagan Goddess Statue Arouses Writer's Ire." Putnam was refused a photograph of the statue, and excoriated the commission for denying to his readers a look at "the vulgar French Venus." A friend of Moores's declared, "A statue of Buddha would have been just as appropriate. Selection of the chosen figure was a travesty on intent of the donor."[18]

Putnam had stampeded the crowd, and early backers began a retreat. Mayor Al Loucks, a congenial fuel oil dealer, polled his Kiwanis Club and found only three supporting votes; he dropped his support for the statue. Belluschi, in a hurried trip to Salem, defended the choice; but he left the next day and Loucks, Putnam, and others remained. The feisty old ex-governor, Oswald West, turned out to be a schoolmate of Carroll Moores. If Moores could somehow be called back for the unveiling, West gleefully observed, he would respond: "My God, Butch! That's old Dickey Woods. How her prices must have risen. She belongs down on Peppermint Flat."[19]

Sprague soldiered on, but the battle was increasingly going to Putnam. Sprague chalked criticisms off to the normal controversy that accompanied a great work of art.[20] But the affair was beyond his control, and becoming somewhat of a joke as well as a serious affront to Salem puritans. The *Capital-Journal* printed letters of protest from the Stayton Church of Christ, the Salem Garden Club, and assorted groups and individuals rallied to the cause when the C-J finally published a photo of the controversial statue. Pioneer Trust bowed to the protests and withdrew the Venus on June 20.[21]

Sprague accepted the verdict with as much good humor as he could muster, protested when Putnam suggested a statue of Asahel Bush, and urged a cooling-down period: "We still hope we shall not get for the memorial what Belluschi called 'a little man in a raccoon cap,' and a beard, and a woman beside him in Mother Hubbard and sunbonnet, the conventionalized pioneer figure."[22]

Unfortunately, that was exactly what Salem got, after a period of nearly five years, in which committee suggestions ranged from a log cabin to a series of modernistic sculptures; predictably, Putnam objected to the

Crusading editor George Putnam wore an editor's eyeshade and kept a pipe clamped in his mouth as he directed the Capital-Journal from 1919 until he sold the paper in 1953 (*Statesman-Journal* photo files).

modernistic works, Sprague to the log cabin. Finally, perhaps in exhaustion, officials nominated an Avard Fairbanks grouping of a pioneer family. Looking remarkably like the grouping Sprague and Belluschi had feared, it was placed in an obscure corner of Bush's Pasture, where the persistent may find it today, the pioneers peering over Willamette University's playing fields.

Eventually, thanks to several tongue-in-cheek articles in national magazines, Venus Victorieuse found a home in the Portland Art Museum. Los Angeles collector Victor M. Carter saw an article in *Time*, bought the Venus and loaned it to the Portland museum, which later purchased it for the permanent collection. It was unveiled in October 1953 before a crowd of four hundred Portland guests and a small Salem contingent. *The Oregonian* inexplicably sent its aviation writer to the ceremony, resulting in a failed attempt at humor and renewal of complaints that Venus was too hefty, "built for posterity, not for beauty," the reviewer concluded. The statue convinced Chandler Brown, however, that he and Sprague had been correct in backing its acquisition.[23] Venus later became part of an outdoor sculpture mall at the museum.

Putnam gloried in the battle and the opportunity to take his rival down a notch after his well-publicized United Nations stint. As the "fat and naked" Venus worked her way up-river to Portland, Putnam began his passage from the scene, selling the *Capital-Journal* later in 1953 to Bernard Mainwaring. Putnam became editor emeritus, writing for the C-J until his 1961 death in a fire at his home.

Mainwaring owned all or part of newspapers in Baker, Ontario, and Nampa on the Oregon-Idaho border, and lived in Nampa with his family. He and Sprague had known each other over the years, and Sprague stayed in the Mainwaring home once while he was governor. Salem had been a

Mainwaring goal for at least thirty years, since graduation from Oregon State College, his son recalled.[24] A large, robust man eleven years Sprague's junior, he had bought a property that was losing the competition.

The *Statesman* had a pair of advantages: as a morning newspaper, it could move into surrounding Willamette Valley towns without challenging the local afternoon dailies and, even more important, television was on the horizon with its intense competition for the attention of afternoon news readers. The tide was clearly with Sprague, and *Statesman* staffers were celebrating their overtaking of C-J circulation when the news was released that the papers were merging on a 50-50 basis.

A terse announcement in editions of November 29, 1953 stated that, "In making this move the publishers are conforming to a pattern of newspaper operation which has become well-nigh universal in all cities of the United States outside the largest cities, a pattern made necessary by rising costs of newspaper publishing." News and editorials would be separate under their existing personnel, other operations would be combined in the new *Statesman* plant, effective December 31. Sprague sold his new building to the newly formed Statesman-Journal Corporation for $400,000.[25]

Newsroom competition remained fierce, but for the old-timers it was never quite the same. Their spacious new plant, finally replacing the disheveled old building on Commercial Street, would be shared by their deadly rivals and, after finally catching up, they would be locked into partnership. There was grousing and bitterness in the dim and smoky Stagecoach Lounge, which had replaced the Marion Hotel as the watering spot for reporters working a late story.

The Sprague and Mainwaring families split the stock of the new company equally, and placed all but the news and editorial operations under a single budget. The newsrooms of the two papers had been quite different. Much of the C-J budget was tied up in the relatively high wages of people who had been with the paper since before World War II, while the *Statesman* was growing rapidly with a young staff, trying to expand into the Willamette Valley, desperate for more reporters and editors.

By 1957 the operation had drifted into a pattern in which the *Statesman* was given 7/13ths of the news budget and the *Capital-Journal* 6/13ths, based on the fact that only the *Statesman* published seven days a week. From the beginning the split was controversial; Webb argued strenuously that a morning newspaper had to be staffed about eighteen hours a day, much more than an afternoon paper. For their part, C-J executives felt the split was in part recompense for giving up their plans for a Sunday paper, and the money was necessary to build up the lagging afternoon paper. The split was formalized in 1959.[26]

There were some comparative data backing Webb's position. In 1957, Sprague surveyed eleven joint operations in which there was a seven-day paper and a six-day partner. The 1956 average of the four with comparable accounting systems was 55.6 percent for the seven-day newspaper; the *Statesman* was running at 53.1 percent in 1956, and 7/13ths would amount to only 53.9 percent. But the arrangement was apparently the price of corporate peace, and Webb could only fume and yield.[27]

Bernard Mainwaring and Sprague got along well, with Mainwaring picking up much of the business side of the joint operation, giving Sprague more time for his column. But Mainwaring died from a heart attack in 1957, less than four years into the new arrangement, and threw into the breech his widow, who was hopelessly unprepared, and his 27-year-old son, who was just making his way through the chairs of the C-J newsroom. The relationship was bound to be uneven: "It was kind of a strange relationship . . . so much difference in our ages. He was very kind, but the whole organizational side was very difficult," Bill Mainwaring recalled.[28]

Circulation had been combined under Hunt Clark but, as the *Statesman* continued to pull away from the C-J, the Mainwarings increasingly charged that Clark had allowed his old competitive juices to overwhelm the new team arrangement. Angry memos followed, the Mainwarings accusing Clark of immoral as well as unprofessional behavior. Sprague sided with his old compatriot and refused to fire him. The result was that the circulation departments were separated, "to keep peace in the family," according to Bill Mainwaring.[29] The circulation trend continued, however; at the time of Sprague's death in 1969, the *Statesman* circulation of 32,619 was more than 10,000 ahead of the C-J.

To add to the uneasiness of the situation, the new combination was not making the 5 percent profit on gross income that Sprague and Mainwaring had hoped for in 1953. Reporting to the board shortly after Bernard Mainwaring's death, Sprague cited a profit on gross of 1.2 percent, 5.0 percent and 2.6 percent during the first three years of joint operation. Some debts had been retired but no dividend had been paid.[30]

Amazingly, Sprague then asked the Mainwarings to consider combining the newspapers into a single *Statesman-Journal*, with only one edition a day but with a "big package" Sunday edition. Economies would be primarily a reduction in news and production staffs. It was a staggering proposal for one who had placed so much of his identity in *The Oregon Statesman*, and it was undoubtedly prompted by Bernard

Mainwaring's death. But Sprague's report indicated considerable thought behind his proposal. Conditions which encouraged competing newspapers had changed, he said, including the loss of political party affiliations and the rise of objective reporting. Under these conditions, "duplicate reporting becomes superfluous." Sprague also noted that radio and television were erasing the time differences between morning and afternoon publication.[31]

Sprague then reverted to his customary caution, and recommended that for the present no change be made, but efforts should be initiated to reach the 5 percent goal. One price of the drive to deliver a respectable profit was the 7/13ths news budget arrangement, and the infamous $2.50 weekly raises Webb was forced to deliver in the face of inflation in the sixties.[32]

The meager pay raises built a *Statesman* legend that Sprague was insensitive to the financial needs of his employees. Certainly he did not always seem to understand the need for adequate pay, in a day when the double-income family was the exception rather than the rule. In reality, Sprague was paying competitive wages; the real problem was that the entire industry was operating on the cheap. In 1959, *Statesman* pay was competitive with *The Oregonian* and *Register-Guard;* the top *Statesman* reporter salary of $125 weekly compared with six-year basic pay of $131.50 in Portland and $117.75 in Eugene; first-year reporters at the *Statesman* were earning $82.50 compared to $78 in Eugene and $73 in Portland.

A study of eighteen of Oregon's twenty-two non-Portland dailies in 1964 showed *Statesman* average pay of $124 weekly for up to five years' experience, and $138 for over eleven years compared favorably to a state average of $97 and $130, respectively. (A subset of the 1964 study showed that four dailies with circulation over 10,000 paid $104 and $142 respectively.) In 1969, the year of Sprague's death, a national survey of 373 dailies served by A. P. indicated an average beginning scale of $111 for newspapers of the *Statesman's* circulation size, compared to $141 at the *Statesman*; and an average of $162 after five years for the surveyed dailies, compared to $172 at the *Statesman*. Additionally, in most of the years listed, *Statesman* news staffers were granted a week's pay as a Christmas bonus.[33]

At the time of the 1954 merger, Salem was the only city outside Portland with competing papers. The Depression had taken its toll of two evening papers in Portland, the *Telegram* and the *News*; in Astoria and Klamath Falls, competing papers had merged to form a single newspaper. Other combinations, in Eugene and Medford, dated back much further. There was no special reason why individual newspapers hung on as long as they did in Salem—other than the individualism of George Putnam and Charles A. Sprague.

Sprague's decision to enter into a 50-50 deal with the Mainwaring family was apparently based on several considerations, according to his son. They included the fact that Wallace had embarked on a publishing and business career in New York and seemed unlikely to assume the publisher's role in Salem, a need to ease the burden of carrying both business and editorial responsibilities, and a desire to assure continuation of the *Statesman* as an independent voice.[34]

Sprague himself, in a thirteen-page report on the first three years of the joint operation, gave the decision a more financial cast, saying it was to counter mounting publication costs and avoid duplication in advertising solicitation and composition. Another reason, he added, was "mutual protection against advertiser pressure for costly rate favors."[35]

The latter reason was directly tied to the entry into Salem of the Meier & Frank Company, Portland's largest retailer. The giant store drove a hard bargain, and Sprague worried that Aaron Frank would try to work the two Salem papers against each other to get a special advertising rate.[36] Purchase of a store site was announced by M & F on March 8, 1953, and nine months later the Statesman-Journal merger took place.

Sprague had never been comfortable with Portland business leaders, although he worked with those who were active in Republican politics. He came to respect Julius Meier, but had no real contact with Meier or his nephew, Aaron Frank. In 1950, Sprague attacked Frank in a column, for allegedly pressuring *The Oregonian* to give the store favorable coverage of a federal labor hearing on a dispute at M & F. The column was picked up by several downstate papers, where every community had a core of advertisers who feared shoppers driving to Portland, and became a cause celebre for a week, forcing *The Oregonian* to assert its independence from advertiser pressure and the *Oregon Journal* to deny that it had yielded to M & F threats. (Frank had, in fact, pressured *The Oregonian*, his son admitted many years later; the elder Frank believed that a newspaper's largest advertiser deserved better treatment in the labor story, and several pages of advertising were pulled.)[37]

When Meier & Frank announced its plans to open a store in Salem, Sprague provided Aaron Frank with a list of people to contact in Salem, and Frank and his son Gerry paid him a courtesy visit. The visit did not go well; Sprague was obviously ill at ease, perhaps recalling his assault on Frank in 1950. His old failure to meet the eye of a visitor served to put the two men off, and his habit of abruptly ending a conversation added to the discomfort. "Dad couldn't believe it," the younger Frank recalled, "it was just not common courtesy."[38]

Gerald W. Frank was well chosen to head the Salem store; he was already an expert retailer and he had the energy and personal style to make the Portland firm seem as if it had been in Salem for years. In reality it had; the store had over ten thousand account-holders in the Salem area, and those regulars were the core of the estimated 75,000 people who jammed the store on opening day.[39]

Salem's business community had been changing since 1947 when the Capitol Shopping Center was built on the edge of the Capitol Mall, with a large new Sears store as its anchor. But Meier & Frank was something else. To the predominantly rural and small-town clientele it brought a touch of a "real city," with an in-store restaurant and a policy—new to Salem at the time—that the customer was always right.

Its new manager threw himself into the civic life of Salem, in an aggressive effort to counter the "outsider" image, but he found Salem "a very introspective city," in which "somebody had the men's business and somebody had the jewelry business and somebody had the women's business and somebody had the furniture business and nobody stepped on anybody's toes. It was a very ingrown community and had been for some time."[40]

Meier & Frank changed the economic picture of the two Salem newspapers, quickly becoming the largest single advertiser and forcing other major stores to boost their advertising as well. Almost immediately, pressure built for the *Statesman* to expand into nearby communities in order to bring more advertising contacts for Meier & Frank.

As their paper grew and expanded, *Statesman* staffers were becoming recognized in the community. Al Lightner and Hunt Clark supplemented their *Statesman* salaries by officiating at football and basketball games, and Lightner became a nationally known referee. In 1956 he attracted national headlines when he forfeited a basketball game to USC when fans in Berkeley pelted him with hot pennies from the stands. Another time he posed as a doctor's assistant at the 1954 "Miracle Mile" race between Roger Bannister and John Landy, and was in the room when a doctor sewed up a nasty cut in Landy's heel just before the race, which Landy lost. Lightner's "scoop" was denied at first, then Landy admitted that he had cut his foot on a broken light bulb and did in fact have the stitches. On another occasion a friend got Lightner into the 1955 World Series and he found himself in a box seat near the newlyweds Eddie Fisher and Debbie Reynolds. Lightner's Walter Mitty experiences made for great columns and built a loyal following.[41]

Sprague engaged in a number of civic projects, playing a major role in the 1944-45 drive that saved the last half of the 100-acre Bush estate as a city park, and taking a leading role in the successful effort to bring West Salem into the City of Salem. The end of the war brought new types of issues, and with it a new image for Sprague.

Sports Editor Al Lightner was well known as a sports official, and refereed major college basketball games on the West Coast (Al Lightner).

In 1952, retiring President Harry S. Truman named him an alternate delegate to the United Nations. In the postwar era Sprague had defended Truman and his embattled secretary of state from the rage of the Republican right, and he editorialized vigorously against Senator Joseph McCarthy and the "ism" that bore his name. Sprague provided a nice balance in the U.N. delegation, by party, by region, by experience, and by temperament. The U.N. stint contributed to his growing reputation as Oregon's leading editorial voice.

As governor and during the Depression, Sprague's fiscal caution and fear of centralized power had put forward his conservative side. The war ended the Depression; the booming economy of the ensuing era meant that issues of government finance were less pressing.

As hot war ended and the Cold War began a new form of conservatism arose, the red-baiting of Senator Joseph McCarthy and his friends in state legislatures as well as the nation's capital. Sprague did not like what he saw as the nastiness of the Cold War took its toll. Beginning in Oregon with the return of the Japanese Americans in 1945 and extending through most of the fifties, issues of fundamental human rights were at issue.

Domestic red scares were linked to the spread of international communism. Americans watched in alarm and horror as communism spread in Europe and Asia. The search for local complicity became intense, even in remote Oregon. As he increasingly spoke out against the Red hunts and in support of a balanced foreign policy, Sprague emerged as a Republican liberal at a time when that breed was becoming scarce.

7

Civil Liberties under Siege

When the American Civil Liberties Union initiated an Oregon award for contributions to civil liberties in 1962, the board of directors convened to select a recipient for the honor, dedicated to E. B. MacNaughton, the multi-faceted banker, newspaper executive, college president and civil libertarian.

"Sprague's name came up and that was it . . . no other names were even suggested," recalled Charles Davis, state chairman at the time. The liberal Portland Democrats who dominated the organization considered only the Republican editor from Salem. Davis recalled Sprague's brief acceptance speech, delivered "with really very great emotion . . . he said we should know that he had a major failing, that he had failed to do what he should have done with what he thought was one of the most tragic violations of civil liberties of citizens in the United States, in 1942, when he acquiesced in evacuating and interning Japanese Americans, and although he was not the first to join the clamor, he had joined in the clamor."[1]

Portland banker, publisher and Reed College president, E. B. MacNaughton served as an important advisor to Sprague's administration and later joined forces with Sprague to support returning Japanese Americans (*Oregon Journal*, now Oregon Historical Society 012709).

The first recipient of the E. B. MacNaughton award of the Oregon chapter of the American Civil Liberties Union, Sprague receives the 1962 honor from President Charles Davis as Blanche looks on (Oregon Journal, now Oregon Historical Society CN014614).

Davis and his colleagues were aware of Sprague's position, of course, but they also had benefited from what became a quarter-century attempt at atonement, as the wartime governor became Oregon's leading editorial voice for civil liberties. The transformation actually began with the return of the Japanese Americans in 1945, as Sprague editorialized for their safe return and also spoke at an emotional meeting in the heart of anti-Japanese country.

There was a highly personal element in Sprague's adoption of civil libertarian values. Because of his controlled and even stern demeanor, Sprague was perceived as someone who acted entirely from intellectual impulses. While that was often the case, he was also very much a man of personal experience, of loyalty to people and causes, and in each of the major civil libertarian causes for which he is best remembered there is a highly personal element as well as an intellectual dislike of cheap demagoguery.

In the case of the Japanese Americans, Sprague felt a need for personal atonement. Later, he threw himself into the effort to defeat a loyalty oath for teachers, who were a special circle of which he and Blanche had once been members. Finally, his persistent and strong condemnation of Senator Joseph R. McCarthy owed a great deal to his fear that the

Republican Party, in which he was active for most of his life, would be transformed by witch-hunting into a right-wing party of intolerance and hatred.

Sprague had not always placed such a high value on civil liberties. In both world wars he had "joined the clamor" against those whose foreign ancestry placed them in a vulnerable position. This was typical of progressives; at their extreme, some were active in the Ku Klux Klan both North and South, but more simply had little exposure to other cultures or races, and were protective of the white Protestant class they represented. Sprague was of this latter group, and he brought that background to the Capitol in 1939. His record as governor was moderate, but not distinguished, in the protection of human rights. Until the postwar era Sprague saw civil liberties as an issue primarily for state and local protection. His position had been made clear during his first year in office. "In case the state is flagrantly derelict in protecting the rights of its citizens then the federal government is justified in taking steps to preserve such rights. But the federal government is justified in interfering under no other conditions," Governor Sprague asserted in a statement to a 1939 Congressional hearing.[2]

The seeds of a broader philosophy came from Sprague's religious beliefs and liberal arts education. His brand of Presbyterianism was ecumenical; he served as president of the Oregon Council of Churches (1943-47). Never deeply involved in church dogma, Sprague served First Presbyterian in practical roles, chairing its building committee and serving as trustee; he was founder and for twelve years a director of *Presbyterian Life*, the denomination's monthly magazine, making two trips a year to national meetings. From 1941 to 1947 Blanche served on the General Council, the national governing board of the denomination, also making twice-yearly trips across the country.[3]

But Sprague's view of the religious life was much broader than any denomination. He came of age in a time when an evangelical social gospel was particularly active in the rural Midwest, and the idea of using the political process to advance moral causes was common among progressives. Once convinced of the moral values of civil liberties or civil rights, Sprague would not be reticent to employ political means to implement change. As a much younger man, he had embraced Prohibition for just that purpose.

But Sprague's values had to transcend a woeful lack of exposure to other ethnic groups. He had been raised in an Iowa county where the major ethnic outsiders were Welsh and Bohemian immigrant farmers. He had lived in all-white towns lacking sufficient numbers of Jews to support a synagogue and hostile to "foreign" elements of any sort. He lived in a time when racially and ethnically insensitive terms were used freely, and found their way into his newspapers upon occasion. But World War II and later the United Nations exposed Sprague to ideas and people that allowed him to push beyond his own limited background.

Sprague's efforts to relocate Oregon's internees from the camps into the sugar beet fields of eastern Oregon had been motivated more by concern for the war effort than for his Japanese American constituents. The letter (see Chapter 5) from three young Oregonians interned at Tule Lake, accusing him of fascist tactics, brought him up short. He began to examine the other side of the issue—the effect of his own words on people who had pursued the American dream and been utterly and forcefully rejected.

His views began to change in 1943 and 1944. The Oregon Senate in 1943 passed a memorial to Congress urging that all Japanese be deported; Sprague compared the memorial's suggestions to those of the Nazis, ironically echoing the charge made against him by the Tule Lake internees.[4]

His very first "It Seems To Me" column challenged former Congressman Walter Pierce's rampant racism, terming it "blind prejudice and unwarranted hatred." Pierce had employed the worst of the racial stereotypes against Japanese: "It is not only the yellow skin and the slant eyes, but it is the ruthless nature, the cruel heart, their traditions which take the place of religion, their methods of living, dual citizenship, and their aggressive nation . . ." Sprague quoted at length from the letter of a young Japanese American girl writing to Salem friends, in which she made a moving statement of her American patriotism (she had a brother in the U.S. Army), and her fear of deportation. Sprague said that the Japanese should be permitted to resume residence in Oregon, and concluded his column: "We got along all right with them before, and can again—if the passions of race prejudice are not fanned to flame."[5]

As the war wound down, efforts intensified to prevent the return of Japanese Americans, whether citizen or alien. The most extreme voices in the American Legion, the Grange, and other organizations actually called for the foreign-born to be sent back to Japan. Newspaper headlines, invariably using the pejorative "Jap," screamed of atrocities committed by the Japanese army. Public opinion was at the boiling point, and political leaders in Oregon were silent if they did not actually join in the intolerance.

Sprague urged his successor, Gov. Earl Snell, to join California's Gov. Earl Warren in recognizing the rights of the returnees and ordering law officers to prevent "intemperate action," and he accurately predicted that claims would eventually be filed against the Federal government.[6] Snell not only refused to extend a welcoming hand, but in the ensuing legislative session he sponsored and signed one of the harshest anti-Japanese laws of the postwar era. At the federal level, both Walter Pierce and retiring Senator Rufus Holman were among the most rabid of the anti-Japanese voices.[7]

On December 19, 1944 the Army ended the exclusion of Japanese from the Pacific Coast. On December 22 Sprague appealed to citizens to "absorb into community life those who do return." But in many cases, although the threat of Japanese invasion was gone and the bravery of Japanese American troops had been widely heralded, the returnees were facing bitter opposition.

The heart of the opposition was the lower Columbia River Gorge, with the Hood River Valley at its eastern end and the Gresham area at its western end. In this narrow corridor less than 50 miles wide most of the farm-based Japanese American internees lived. Their land had been hurriedly leased at forced rates well below market, and many lease-holders were not anxious to relinquish this profitable arrangement.

As World War II opened Hood River County had one of the largest concentrations of Japanese in Oregon, 462 people or 4 percent of all residents. The Japanese lived primarily within their own community, conscious of racial barriers. Only half returned to Hood River County after the war, and they faced bitter threats, both economic and physical.[8]

Even before the Japanese began returning, Hood River achieved national notoriety when the American Legion post removed the names of sixteen nisei from a public honor roll of local servicemen. The Legion urged "total elimination of all alien Japanese and their sons and daughters of American citizenship from the Hood River area and . . . 'fair disposal' of property held by these people."[9]

The Hood River Legion was not without supporters in the Oregon press. The Albany *Democrat-Herald* discounted the heroism of nisei combat veterans by noting that they had not served against Japanese troops. The *Democrat-Herald* and the Pendleton *East Oregonian* charged that the Japanese would "out-breed" whites, their alleged fertility part of a Japanese plot. The fear of "fast-breeding" immigrants has always been an element in nativism and was widely used by those who opposed the return of the Japanese.[10]

Albany and Pendleton editorials were in the minority, however, as most Oregon editors, including Sprague, criticized the Legion's removal of names. Typical was Robert Ruhl's statement at Medford: "the Hood River action is not right, is not American, is opposed to every principle of fair play and tolerance for which the democracies of the world stand and are now fighting."[11] National pressure intensified and the national

American Legion, despite its usual policy of local autonomy, first requested and then ordered Hood River to restore the names.

In Gresham, founders of an anti-Japanese group wanted to move swiftly in the 1945 Legislature to strengthen existing laws against aliens owning land. "We want to get this job done before the boys come back (from the war), because if we don't do it the returning service men will," said one farmer.[12]

Opposition soon appeared, however. *The Oregonian* labeled the group's purpose economic, not patriotic; the Portland Council of Churches and the American Civil Liberties Union immediately protested the move, and Council President H. J. Maulbetsch became the victim of personal threats. This prompted George Putnam in the *Capital-Journal*, a veteran of the battle against the Ku Klux Klan, to compare the threats to Klan tactics.[13]

Once again, the Albany *Democrat-Herald* joined the mob, accusing the Japanese of "colonization" and of teaching their children that "Japan has the first claim on their allegiance. . . . Those who refuse to become assimilated should be rejected." The *Oregon Journal* urged the government to delay allowing the Japanese to return, citing a fear for their safety.[14]

Although he supported evacuation of Japanese Americans in 1942, Sprague later regretted the action and helped the evacuees return to their homes. In 1953 he was honored by Japanese Consul Masayuki Harigai, at a Portland dinner celebrating the Emperor's birthday (*Oregon Journal*, now Oregon Historical Society CN010868).

There was reason for the concern. A mass meeting February 9 in the Gresham high school, featuring the 85-year-old Walter Pierce, drew about one thousand people. A professional organizer from Seattle was hired and, at a March 8 mass meeting, memberships were solicited to push the effort beyond the Gresham area. Speakers called for the removal of all Japanese from the country.[15]

Church leaders and others began organizing a counter-campaign, which peaked at a meeting in Gresham March 16, attended by about one thousand people. The principal speakers were Sprague and E. B. MacNaughton, the Portland banker and civil libertarian. Sprague said he had assented to the evacuation order only because the Army ordered it: "Up to that time and since then, I know of not one single act of sabotage or traitorism committed or on record as having been committed by any person of Japanese extraction in the state of Oregon, and to the best of my knowledge I know of none on the entire Pacific Coast." Sprague quoted U. S. Census figures to rebut Pierce's claim of Japanese "breeding"; Oregon's Japanese population had actually dropped from 1930 to 1940. MacNaughton expressed fear of appeals to prejudice and compared it to the fascist regimes in Europe.[16]

Sprague's statement that he had only reluctantly agreed to internment went against the record; he had called for internment before the presidential order, when he might have protested or at least kept silent. But he was sincere in regretting his action, and his speech was to encourage those supporting the return of the internees. Gradually, opposition to the Japanese receded as evacuees returned to homes and farms. But lingering racism and ethnocentrism played a final act, as legislators approved a measure directly linked to the Gresham campaign.

Governor Snell had failed to urge reconciliation with the returning Japanese, and in the 1945 legislative session his office wrote and lobbied a measure which passed the Senate unanimously and the House 53-2, all in two hectic days as the Legislature rushed to adjourn in mid-March. The loosely-worded law, subsequently declared unconstitutional, subjected anyone leasing or selling land to Japanese aliens to severe penalties.

Oregon editors, perhaps surprised by the sudden emergence and passage of the bill, remained silent. Even upon adjournment only Sprague spoke out, in a March 29 column. Noting that there were only 1,617 Japanese aliens in Oregon in 1940, Sprague said the measure was less important for its impact on these aging aliens than for what it said about "almost insensate prejudice within the white mind. . . . (the bill) is so studied in its malevolence, so vicious in its effort to freeze animosity into law that one is startled at the mental psychosis which produced such legislation." The producer, of course, was Governor Snell, the man who had defeated Sprague in 1942.[17]

The record of Oregon editors in meeting the challenge of the internment did not reveal great editorial courage. The fact that so few spoke out in 1942 is not surprising, because there was virtually no opposition to the evacuation. The only visible organization representing Japanese Americans, the Japanese-American Citizens League, had acquiesced in the internment and advised cooperation.[18] Also it must be remembered that the entire Pacific Coast genuinely feared imminent invasion or at least sabotage during the early months of the war. That editors did not react to protect the rights of the Japanese in 1942 was not surprising, although it was certainly not commendable.

By late 1944, however, any danger of invasion or defeat was over, and nisei combat units had distinguished themselves in American uniforms. The 1944 case *for* the returning Japanese was more clear-cut than was the 1942 case *against* evacuation. In 1942, evacuation could be rationalized as a method of protecting the Japanese—and in some cases that may have been the case—but in 1944 that was no longer a serviceable rationale.

Only Sprague and *The Oregonian* spoke on multiple occasions for the returning Japanese. Sprague wrote seven editorials or columns from Thanksgiving 1944 through March 1945, all supportive of the rights of the returning Japanese. No other Oregon daily had more than three editorials on the topic during this period, which included the Hood River American Legion affair, the Gresham citizens' movement, and the Legislature. Oregon editors simply did not give the rights of the returnees priority on their editorial pages, and when editors did speak they generally followed changes in public mood, for instance after the Council of Churches and ACLU had condemned the action. Editors were clearly not willing to get out ahead on an issue so volatile, sensing the parameters of their community. Sprague was beginning to emerge as an editor who would speak out on a volatile issue; his next opportunities came with the rising tide of anti-communist agitation beginning to sweep the nation.

Red-baiting did not begin with the February 1950 emergence of McCarthy and his infamous list of subversives in the federal government; similar tactics had been taking place in state legislatures since before World War II. Some of the most serious incursions on personal liberty took place at the state level and were provoked by newspapers of the Hearst chain. Both Washington and California were deeply involved, and to an alarming degree the targets were institutions of higher education.

In California the Tenney Committee and in Washington the Canwell Committee—legislative bodies carrying the names of their chairmen,

Jack Tenney and Albert Canwell—were on a mission to purge state universities of communists or their sympathizers. The methods involved hearings, loyalty oaths, and other forms of pressure, with appointed governing boards and university administrators joining in. By 1950 the state universities in Seattle and Berkeley had been torn asunder by the strife; Oregon academicians hunkered down in hopes the wind would blow over the state.

Oregon faculty had a minor scare in 1949, when Oregon State College President A. L. Strand summarily fired two non-tenured professors, Ralph Spitzer and L. R. LaVallee. No reasons were given at first and, when the professors cried political persecution, Sprague and Bill Tugman in Eugene raised a tentative civil liberties defense of political speech.[19] But the issue faded rapidly as Strand roasted Spitzer for his support of a discredited Soviet theory of genetics, and the OSC faculty failed to support their colleagues. Later examinations of the issue indicate that Sprague and Tugman had been correct in their concerns, and that they apparently had been cashiered for their political beliefs, but at the time the incident passed quietly and without legislative involvement. Sprague and Tugman did not pursue their initial concerns, and other editors sided with Strand.[20]

Sprague and Tugman appeared willing to draw a line between a communist speaker and a communist professor. Tugman explained: "Communism needs to be discussed and studied freely on every campus. If Mr. Molotov would accept an invitation to speak in McArthur Court and expound Communist doctrine we would welcome it, but if he were employed as a permanent member of the staff we would object."[21]

Other editors were less subtle in their reasoning, and most gave full support to authorities. The *Oregon Journal* called for "a showdown at

Bill Tugman, editor of the Eugene Register-Guard, joined Sprague in 1951 to defeat a teachers' loyalty oath, one of several civil liberties' issues in which the men formed a united front (Register-Guard).

the University of Washington, at Oregon State College and the University of Oregon, and in every other college and university in the United States where Communist propagandists may have infiltrated as teachers." George Putnam lumped his enemies together, asserting, "The infiltration of radicals in faculty is the bane of universities as it is of labor unions."[22]

The crucial question, Sprague and Tugman stated, was membership in the Communist Party. The two editors believed that CP membership went beyond the limits of academic freedom, reasoning that the CP enforced loyalty to party doctrine, which was not compatible with academic freedom. It was a position widely held by academic administrators of the time, including President Raymond Allen of the University of Washington.[23]

In the University of Washington case, Oregon editors, relying on information carried by the news wires, concluded that the professors had been fired on the basis of communist affiliations, and no sympathy was shown. At Oregon State, when it appeared early in the incident that the professors were being dismissed for radical political views, Sprague and Tugman came to their defense; but as the OSC administration shifted its case to that of taking the "communist line," support for the professors disappeared.

Oregon had avoided the excesses of the Tenney and Canwell committees, but when Joe McCarthy cranked up his publicity machine in 1950, it became increasingly obvious that the political benefits of bagging a few commies were too rich to be resisted. Predictably, the first shot was fired by the same man who had called for deporting Japanese Americans in 1943, Senator Tom Mahoney, a conservative Democrat from Portland.

Mahoney announced plans to introduce a measure creating a committee similar to the Canwell Committee in Washington state, but it would focus on private colleges. The real target was not difficult to discern; Portland's Young Democrats had just voted to censure Mahoney and the deciding vote was cast by a Reed College student.[24] Mahoney approached politics in a very personal manner and his zeal in punishing opponents was legendary.

Mahoney was a serious force within the Legislature, he was close to the Republican leadership, and he enjoyed pulling the tail of liberal Democrats, in particular Senator Richard L. Neuberger. The latter took his threat at face value, and immediately mounted a counterattack. Neuberger visited Sprague, who responded with a warning the next day that, "A Mahoney-led witch-hunt would be in the McCarthy tradition, complete with sound effects."[25]

Neuberger also fired off a "heads-up" to E. B. MacNaughton, then serving as Reed's president. Neuberger enclosed a copy of the Sprague editorial, adding, "I have talked to him twice about Mahoney's proposed witch-hunt, and I am sure you can count on him as a vigorous opponent of the project."[26]

By the time MacNaughton replied to Neuberger, Mahoney had dropped his investigation, but a teachers' loyalty oath had quietly taken its place. Introduced on March 15, 1951, SB 323 was similar to loyalty oaths adopted in several states, requiring public school teachers to swear that they had not been a member of the Communist Party "or any other organization that believes in, advocates or teaches the overthrow of the United States government or the government of the State of Oregon by force or by unlawful means." Additionally, the bill required disclosure of "Whether the applicant has contributed time or money to the support of, or has subscribed to, taught or advocated the principles of such party or organization."

The loyalty oath attracted virtually no attention from Capitol reporters, however; they were preoccupied with inside politics and tax issues. It remained for two editors, Tugman and J.W. Forrester of the *East Oregonian*, to bring the issue out into the open. The two men were close to the major campuses—Tugman's newspaper was staffed by University of Oregon journalism graduates, and Forrester had been the sports information officer at Oregon State.

In a ringing editorial terming the measure "little better than an instrument for terrorism," Tugman warned that SB 323 would create a climate in which it would be impossible to teach about communism or Marxism. He contrasted it with the affirmative oath administered to most public employees, pledging to support the nation's laws; this loyalty oath

Pendleton East Oregonian editor J. W. Forrester was a key Sprague ally on civil liberties and civil rights, and also a close friend of the older editor (Tom Wright).

was a negative oath and singled out teachers as more suspect than other public employees. Forrester saw the oath as an attempt at thought control.[27]

Despite the strongly worded editorials, the measure passed the Senate 25-5 and appeared to be on a fast track in the House. Neuberger had succeeded in diluting the measure somewhat by amendment in the Senate Education Committee with the help of Tugman, who was now joined by Sprague. Tugman recalled "one very violent hearing at Salem at which both Charlie and I spoke. Of course being a vet and the father of such I could say some things Charlie could not. Besides I am just Shanty Irish and Charlie is always a gent. . . . Anyhow it was a rough house and after it was over we realized we had won a battle but not the war."[28]

Sprague continued to work behind the scenes, but he did not speak editorially until it appeared that the House might pass the measure. When he weighed in on May 3, he termed the bill "a product of fear," repeated his argument that teachers should not be singled out, and warned that passage of the bill would lead to additional incursions on civil liberties.[29]

Passage of any anti-teacher measure without strong opposition from the education lobby would later be unthinkable, but in the fifties the climate was very different. Maurine Neuberger, wife of the senator and now a House member herself, had been active in the teachers' union, and recalled that "teachers were afraid to speak out . . . afraid to participate in politics."[30] Fearing budget reprisals, the State System of Higher Education had a policy preventing a faculty member from directly contacting a legislator during session. University of Oregon professors communicated with Tugman, and it is likely that other contacts were made. Three faculty members from the private Willamette University walked across State Street to testify against the measure, but the state system maintained neutrality.[31]

Tugman's and Sprague's editorials of May 1 and May 3 produced no echoes from other editorial writers; except for Forrester's early editorial, other papers remained silent during the entire debate. Eugene Rep. Earl Hill tipped Tugman that the measure was about to emerge from its House committee with a favorable recommendation; Tugman alerted Sprague.

Politicians normally came to Sprague, sitting in the hard chairs of his unobtrusive office on Commercial Street, waiting for an audience along with any reader who happened to drop by. But in the case of the loyalty oath, it was Sprague who walked the few blocks to the Capitol to seek out key players in the closing days of the session.

Sprague roamed the marble halls, pulling friends aside and urging them to shelve the bill. When it emerged from committee, he appealed personally to Speaker John Steelhammer to send it back for one more hearing. With the Legislature driving for adjournment, such a concession was exceedingly unusual and would not have been granted to others. The resultant hurry-up hearing gave Sprague another chance to make a personal appeal, but the short notice and caution kept educators away. Once more the bill emerged from committee, and once more Sprague returned to the Capitol corridors he knew so well.

Among those he focused on was a young Salem college professor, Mark Hatfield, who was serving his first session and who had signed on the bill as a co-sponsor. Sprague button-holed Hatfield three times, the latter recalled, in a manner "very gentle but very tenacious." Sprague clearly felt strongly about the bill, and Hatfield said he was prepared to drop his support, although he had spoken for the bill in committee and was one of three designated to carry the bill on the floor of the House. But Hatfield and other House members never had a chance to cast a final vote on the loyalty oath, because of Sprague's backdoor maneuvering as the bill headed for the floor and almost certain passage on the session's final night.[32]

Sprague fell back on a political tactic he had seldom employed as a practicing politician—the backroom deal. Discussing Sprague's subsequent role in killing the oath, *Oregonian* reporter Malcolm Bauer used a baseball metaphor:

> *He went to Speaker John Steelhammer, Majority Floor Leader Earl Hill and Judiciary Committee Chairman Carl Francis, all friends, and arranged for a Tinker-to-Evers-to-Chance play that recommitted the bill to the committee and to Francis' pocket, from which it never emerged. . . . Excusing his maneuver, Sprague told this writer: "I figured this was a time when 'children of light' might learn something from the 'children of darkness.'"*[33]

Sprague and Steelhammer were not personally close, although both were part of the Salem civic leadership. Steelhammer was a traditional backroom operator with cigar and whiskey near to hand, who later became a lobbyist. Steelhammer may have called Sprague "old square ass" in the House lounge, but he knew Sprague's power in Salem, editorially and also in a personal sense, and he must have understood the urgency in the former governor's manner.[34]

Maurine Neuberger watched the maneuver unfold from her seat in the House. A freshman Democrat in a Republican chamber, she was not part of the action, but she recalled Sprague appearing outside the House rail, where invited guests are allowed into the Chamber: "As I remember looking around over the floor that day, everyone looked a bit ashamed if they were going to vote for it, and there was Governor Sprague facing them. I don't know, he must have talked to some of them individually. He would have had to."[35]

The House Journal for the day simply records that Hill moved the bill be taken from the calendar and referred to Judiciary, where it died with the end of the session later that same night.

University of Oregon Faculty Secretary George N. Belknap wrote a letter of appreciation to Tugman. In his reply, Tugman thanked Belknap, but added, "Charley Sprague, of Salem, did more than anyone else to stop Senate Bill 323 in the closing hours."[36]

The loyalty oath was an example of the multi-faceted approach that was unique to Sprague among Oregon's journalists and politicians. He worked with Democratic liberal Richard Neuberger when the bill was in Senate committee, then he joined Tugman and Forrester to speak editorially against the measure, and finally he pulled political experience and Republican contacts out of his pocket to divert the measure before it came to a House vote. Alone among Oregon editors, Sprague had the stature to use both his pen and his political background in such a course of action.

Charles Davis experienced the value of Sprague's support, as he worked the state in an attempt to build the tiny ACLU chapter. Davis scheduled a session at Salem's First Presbyterian Church to discuss obscenity, and Sprague introduced him and made supportive remarks. The crowd was large but never heated. "You can't imagine what a supportive situation you get into when Charlie Sprague's involved," Davis recalled.[37]

Davis regularly called on Sprague, finding him receptive and open to conversing for an hour or more on some topic of concern. Sprague would not always agree, Davis said, recalling advice that a legal challenge to a Nativity scene on the Capitol Mall was simply not worth the trouble to contest; "But you could always count on a very friendly, thoughtful audience." Davis counted on a small core of editors to support him on difficult issues: Bob Frazier in Eugene (following Tugman), Eric Allen Jr. in Medford, Bud Forrester in Pendleton, and Bob Chandler in Bend. All of them were, in turn, influenced heavily by Sprague.[38]

What Davis discovered was that this elder statesman was also a bridge in an Oregon editorial community in transition. His influence in editorial circles—and it was beyond dispute now that his voice was the most powerful—was in part because he was the only one among the editors of the fifties and sixties who was anchored in the pre-World War II past, yet constantly looking ahead to the last third of the century.

Sprague led the almost-universal Oregon newspaper opposition to Senator Joseph McCarthy. Like the teachers' oath, McCarthyism cut very close to Sprague's heart. A man not given to suffering fools lightly, Sprague was affronted by McCarthy—as an American, as a Republican, and as someone who believed deeply in civility and proper form in society and government. McCarthy met none of Sprague's tests of propriety, and was seen by Sprague as a dangerous demagogue capable of bringing out the worst in people. At the heart of his opposition was his fear that McCarthy would destroy the Republican Party, or at least make it over into something totally unacceptable to Sprague's progressive views.

Sprague became a crusader against McCarthy and went after him with a zeal unmatched by any of his Oregon colleagues. Sprague was an editor to be reckoned with, and no Oregon editor of his generation was as frequently quoted. This was particularly true of his editorials and columns on McCarthy, which regularly showed up on other editorial pages. Before 1950 was out, the state's fifteen largest dailies printed 34 editorials on McCarthy and McCarthyism, and 27 were critical. Another five were neutral, and only two, in the Oregon City *Enterprise-Courier,* favored McCarthy. Twenty-one of the critical editorials came from Sprague's well-used Royal typewriter.

When Republicans made gains in the 1950 general election, Walter May in the *Enterprise-Courier* suggested that Republican wins in the November election were largely due to McCarthy, despite the "Salem and Portland editors" who had failed to support McCarthy.[39] Sprague's response was blunt:

> *To the extent that republican victories in the late election were the result of McCarthy's charges and campaigning, it should be an occasion for republican shame and humiliation. For McCarthy failed miserably to prove his charges. . . . As far as the political effect is concerned, months ago The Statesman said the McCarthy charges in the surheated atmosphere over communism would have effect and probably win votes for the republican party. The technique of propaganda is well recognized. Hitler put it very simply: repeating the Big Lie often enough finally becomes convincing. If the E-C relishes victory by employment of that technique it is quite welcome. The Statesman regrets it . . . . The Statesman assures the Enterprise-Courier that it is not opportunistic, that it still regards McCarthy as a purveyor of falsehood and the method he employed as a menace to democratic government.*[40]

In cutting Walter May down to size, Sprague used another editorial as a foil for his opposing views. He seldom quoted other editors simply to buttress his own comments; he preferred a debate, and could be quite vigorous in criticizing a colleague. One result was that other Oregon editors, with the singular exception of George Putnam, appeared reluctant to take Sprague on; he was quoted often in support but very rarely did peers challenge his views, because they knew that he would respond. His seniority, experience and countenance added weight to his written words and, in the case of McCarthy, Sprague set the standard for the state's editors.

Sprague had labored his entire life in the Republican Party, and was not about to abandon the field to McCarthy and his ilk. His opposition reached its peak in 1951 when the Multnomah Republican Club invited the senator to address its annual picnic. Here, in the swarthy and scowling flesh, was the man who wanted to steal the party from Sprague and his cohorts, and the ex-governor was not about to let him enter the state quietly:

> *We believe in free speech in Oregon, so let this adept at the technique of the Big Lie have his say, and let who will attend. But if the republican party is to endorse McCarthyism it deserves to be laid in a grave both wide and deep. And to win the presidency by condoning McCarthy's tactics would be to obtain office under false pretenses.*[41]

Sprague's August 13 column was quoted by the *East Oregonian* and *Mail Tribune*.

Sprague returned to the issue on August 24, the eve of McCarthy's visit, quoting extensively from material printed in the Madison, Wisconsin, *Capital-Times* by editor Bill Evjue, and concluding, "Because The Statesman regards him as a mendacious demagogue it protests his appearance in Oregon as a guest of an organization identified with the republican party."[42]

Editorial opposition also appeared in the *Register-Guard, Mail Tribune, Gazette-Times*, *East Oregonian,* and *Oregon Journal*. Several echoed Sprague's concern about Republican divisions over McCarthy, and Tugman quoted with obvious approval a Young Republican leader protesting the senator's appearance at the GOP picnic. *The Oregonian* pointed out that McCarthy's host, the Multnomah Republican Club, "is not, by the way, an official party organization."[43] *The Oregonian* also used the occasion to print a four-part series written by Robert Fleming of the Milwaukee *Journal*, a leading McCarthy critic. Fleming's articles appeared at about the same time as the Evjue article in the *Statesman*, giving readers of the state's two morning newspapers a thorough dose of criticism. The net result of this onslaught was that nearly every newspaper reader in Oregon had been exposed to McCarthy's darker side, and should have known that neither the senator nor his Portland hosts were "official representatives" of the Republican Party. The message could hardly have been clearer: McCarthy is a dangerous demagogue and a rogue Republican not worthy of the party label he bears.

This loud editorial voice appeared to be lost, however, on the GOP leadership. Appearing at the McCarthy rally were Gov. Douglas McKay and much of the state's Republican Party leadership, including National Committeeman Ralph Cake and Committeewoman Olive Cornett. But only a few elected officials were on hand, as was a small band of hecklers.[44] The McCarthy road show proved to be of modest success; he got a relatively small crowd for a man who was then dominating the nation's headlines. In a column the following morning, Sprague noted the poor turnout defined a "wide cleft" between McCarthy and his critics within the GOP.[45]

McCarthy made no further Oregon appearances and the 1952 election of Dwight D. Eisenhower raised hopes by GOP editors that Ike would clean the party's stables of McCarthy and his associates. Sprague in particular never let up on McCarthy, always hopeful that the Republican Party would discipline its errant senator. In 1953, when McCarthy went after Charles E. (Chip) Bohlen, who had been named ambassador to the Soviet Union, Sprague called for Eisenhower to lead the counterattack. "McCarthy has humiliated the administration enough," he wrote. "Eisenhower should make this a showdown fight. McCarthy has asked for it." Again, the column was reprinted, the same day by the *Mail Tribune* and later by the Bend *Bulletin*. Less than two weeks later, Sprague was again urging Eisenhower to move against McCarthy.[46]

Sprague was less decisive when the House UnAmerican Activities Committee came to Portland in 1954 and unleashed an attack on Reed College which resulted in the firing of Professor Stanley Moore and the temporary suspensions of two others who refused to testify before the Congressional panel. He drew a line between public and privately supported institutions: "We think Communists shouldn't be allowed to teach in schools under public support; but a private institution should be free to determine its own policies." Beyond that statement, he offered no advice to Reed trustees or officials, and failed to provide support for Moore, who was strongly supported by Reed faculty on the grounds of academic freedom.[47] When Moore was fired for refusing to tell the trustees whether he was or had been a communist, neither Sprague nor any other

Oregon editor came to his defense. Sprague may have seen it as a Portland issue; more likely, anti-communism simply prevailed and he supported the attack on an individual (Moore), after defending the institution (Reed) from unfair criticism.[48]

Sprague believed the Cold War was real and communism a genuine threat, while deploring the tactics used by McCarthy and his minions. Sprague was identified as one of Oregon's leading liberal Republicans, an editor who supported many of the causes of the Truman Administration while continuing to cast his vote with most Republican candidates.

On his 65th birthday in 1952, Charles A. Sprague was a vigorous man with no thought of retiring. He was about to open another period of his life, beginning with service at the United Nations.

Sprague had been turning increasingly to national and international issues, and strongly supported President Harry S. Truman in the most difficult issues of his second term, the firing of General Douglas McArthur and the persistent red-baiting of Senator McCarthy. Sprague had been leery of Truman initially; Truman was the product of one of the enemies of Sprague's old Progressive days, the big-city political machine. But as Truman grew into the office, Sprague found himself admiring Truman's courage and his judgment on foreign policy. Consistently in the postwar period, Sprague opposed his own party on domestic communism and support for Chiang Kai-shek and Taiwan; and he backed Truman on the United Nations, the Marshall Plan, Korea, and several controversial appointments.

Sprague had backed Thomas E. Dewey with little enthusiasm in 1948, and in 1952 faced a choice between Robert E. Taft, whose views were far too conservative for his tastes, and Dwight D. Eisenhower, who he saw as lacking the background for the White House. He turned in the Oregon primary to Governor Earl Warren of California, the most liberal of the GOP contenders.

Sprague and Warren were acquainted from the days when Warren was attorney general of California, and Sprague governor of Oregon. Warren called on Sprague in the cramped old *Statesman* office, one of many political leaders who squeezed into the cubicle with Sprague and Marguerite Wright (who usually remained during these visits, although occasionally sent on a "research errand" when the talk turned overtly partisan).[49]

Sprague introduced Warren at a West Salem rally, citing his broad experience as preferable to Eisenhower's military background.[50] Eisenhower easily defeated Warren in the Oregon primary, and Sprague fell into line behind Ike in the general election, but he confided to Richard L. Neuberger that he was doing so more out of party loyalty than personal instincts. The Republican campaign, he observed, had left him depressed, and "the Nixon business adds to my despair. . . . His nomination left me cold, because I never liked his campaign tactics against Mrs. Douglas." Sprague told Neuberger he intended to vote and stay within the GOP, lest it become "only a shell of reaction. . . while I have a lot of sympathy for Steve Anderson (Oregon Young Republican leader) in his shift to support Stevenson, who is to me more appealing than Eisenhower, I intend to vote for Eisenhower. I am more interested in the long war than in the single campaign."[51]

Sprague's candid confession to Neuberger was in response to a letter from the latter, urging Sprague to break from solid GOP support of candidates, particularly in the case of Senator Guy Cordon, who would be running in 1954; Neuberger was already considering the race.[52] In the 1952 general election, Sprague did break ranks to support two Democrats seeking office: Robert Y. Thornton for attorney general and Edith Green for secretary of state.

Sprague changed the political identification of his newspaper in 1953 from "Republican" to "Independent Republican," reflecting his increased concern about the reactionary tendencies within his party.[53] His concern embraced both the Taft wing of traditional Midwest conservatives and the radical right represented by Joe McCarthy. Communism, domestic or foreign, was becoming the defining issue in American politics, and increasingly the lightning rod for the issue was the aristocratic mandarin, Dean Acheson, Truman's second secretary of state.

Sprague shared little with Acheson other than a dedication to reasoned discourse, but as the foreign policy debate became increasingly shrill after Truman's upset win over Dewey in the 1948 election, Sprague began siding with Acheson against the Taft and McCarthy wings of the Republican Party. In 1950, an editor disgusted with his own party's machinations called on the secretary of state because "I wanted to assure him of one citizen's confidence in him and his work."[54] Charles Sprague was no ordinary citizen of course, and Dean Acheson was no ordinary secretary of state.

Having delivered his message of "one citizen's confidence in him and his work," Sprague proceeded to analyze for his readers Acheson and his task, terming him "eminently qualified by training, native intelligence and character to guide our international affairs. It is a shame to have him sniped at by the McCarthys and the Wherrys, for cheap political capital."[55]

The next time the two men talked was September 10, 1952, when President Truman approved Acheson's suggestion that Sprague serve as an alternate delegate at the United Nations. Sprague was in regular contact with a Salem man, Carlton Savage, a career diplomat serving as executive secretary to Acheson's policy steering committee. It was Savage who arranged Sprague's 1950 visit to Acheson, and there is little doubt that he played a role in Sprague's 1952 appointment to the United Nations. Acheson called Sprague to offer the appointment, and a State Department memo indicates that Sprague was quick to accept: "Mr. Sprague said that he was flattered by the Secretary's request and that although he hardly felt competent to serve such a responsible office, he thought perhaps to have a representative from the Northwest and West Coast would be a good thing, and he would arrange to do it."[56]

Sprague was in the East for the September 13 announcement; the Associated Press identified him as only the second westerner to serve as an alternate, the first being Helen Gahagan Douglas, the Californian defeated by Richard Nixon. Typically, Sprague used the occasion to educate his readers on the duties (and limitations) of serving in the delegation, then turned to other aspects of his trip home: blue morning glories and goldenrod over the backyard fences of Midwest towns, a huge new fertilizer plant in Pocatello, and a $50 million parking garage in Chicago.[57]

Despite the nonchalance of his column, Sprague was excited about the prospect of mingling with international diplomats, making new contacts and re-entering the heady world of politics without the personal responsibility of setting policy. Less than a month later, he was flying into New York's LaGuardia airport en route to the gleaming new U.N. headquarters; the 1952 session was the first in the permanent building on the East River.

Typically, Sprague saw the United Nations as a learning experience as well as a chance for service, and he approached the task with relish. He and Blanche, living in a hotel suite, would be free of the daily tasks of home and office. He expected to meet new people and engage new cultures; perhaps he did not expect that it would affect his editorial priorities as well, but the lessons of that New York winter played a role in what became in his later years a growing commitment to justice for people of other cultures and races.

8

◆◆◆

A World of Many Cultures

In 1952, only seven years after its charter had been approved, the United Nations was engaged in struggles focusing on the conflict in Korea and the Cold War in general. In the gleaming new headquarters on the East River leading journalists as well as political leaders prowled the polished halls, brushing shoulders with diplomats in colorful national dress.

Sprague was more than a country editor; his travels as governor and in other capacities had taken him to New York on several occasions, as well as to Chicago and Washington. He was on a first-name basis with leading American politicians. But men more sophisticated than he were in awe of the array of world leaders gathered for the annual U.N. sessions, and he approached his assignment with the eagerness of a young diplomat. In the early days of the U.N., alternate delegates had higher profiles than in later years, when the body took on many new members and the bureaucracy swelled. Sprague did not expect to be a wallflower at the dance of diplomacy; as always, he expected to be a full participant.

The new alternate lunched with Secretary of State Dean Acheson and Senators Theodore Green and Alexander Wiley, Senate representatives on the five-person delegation (the others were Warren Austin, Eleanor Roosevelt and Acheson). He learned that the delegation was to strongly oppose admission of China, but to take special efforts not to offend the small nations that were making up a "third bloc" along with some the neutral giants, India in particular.[1]

Sprague felt at ease with the delegation and immediately formed a friendship with Mrs. Roosevelt, with whom he worked on Committee Three, which was assigned most of the human rights issues. He was given major responsibility for handling the delicate Freedom of Information issue, as Mrs. Roosevelt concentrated on other areas. Blanche and he dined alone with Mrs. Roosevelt and also with Acheson, and permanent bonds were established. The Spragues saw Mrs. Roosevelt in 1961 when she came through Portland on a speaking tour and, when the former first lady died, Sprague's warm tribute recalled her work for humanitarian concerns at the 1952 session.[2]

Eleanor Roosevelt, shown here with Uruguay Delegate Darwin Branco, played a key role in the 1952 United States delegation to the United Nations, with Sprague as her alternate on the Human Rights Committee (Franklin D. Roosevelt Library).

The bipartisan nature of the U.N. delegation—its head, Warren Austin, was a former Republican governor of Vermont—and the need for a united stand in the face of vigorous Soviet positions helped deepen Sprague's independence within the Republican Party. At delegation sessions, Sprague entered into vigorous debate on policy issues, although there was really only one vote that counted: that of Acheson, voting for the president. The delegation was an extension of the White House, and while delegates were free to argue policy, and clearly they did, once policy was set, they fell into line.

Awaiting his major assignments, Sprague observed the major debates (Korea dominated), and the major players, noting their maneuvers and mannerisms:

> *Vishinsky is of medium height, rather slender in frame, his face sharp featured, somewhat ruddy of countenance. His hair is white and he has a small white mustache. He is by no means the typical Slav, broad of form and face. In speaking his face is mobile, not grim and dour like Gromyko's and expressive. His eyes are bright and sharp in their gaze. He speaks rapidly, punctuating his address with choppy gestures of his right forearm. He appears to*

> *revel in scorn both in language and elocution. His style was developed in Russia where he made his fame as prosecutor in the famous purge trials of 1937.*
>
> *For all his vituperation he professes eagerness to preserve peace—on the Soviet model.*[3]

Awaiting the call-up of the Freedom of Information debate, Sprague was able to make a brief trip to Rhode Island to give speeches on the U.N., visit with son Wallace and his family in nearby Short Hills, New Jersey, and take in a Helen Hayes play and a concert by pianist Theodore Uhlman.

Keeping abreast of November elections, *Statesman* labor negotiations and building plans, Sprague was also preparing for his assigned role in the Freedom of Information debate, which began October 24, while Mrs. Roosevelt was away on a trip to India. Sprague carried the American position.

The Freedom of Information debate was long-standing and complex, of less importance in practical terms (there was no method by which the U.N. could police any agreement) than it was in defining the nature of the post-colonial debate. Emerging nations were still dominated by Western media, not only in terms of the information that was presented *to* the former colonial states, but in terms of the information presented *about* them. In many ways, the latter sparked more contention. The new nations were desperately trying to project favorable images of their nation-building, but the Western media, particularly the big news services, Associated Press and Reuters, had an inescapable tendency to focus on what went *wrong* rather than what went *right*.

The developing nations saw the issue in terms of sovereignty; the West saw it in terms of freedom of information. The Soviet bloc, which completely controlled its own media, saw it as a wedge to split the West and the former colonies. The debate had flared in previous sessions, and was a major topic of discussion at the 1952 convention of the American Society of Newspaper Editors.

At the ASNE convention, Edwin Canham, *Christian Science Monitor* editor and a 1949 delegate to the U.N., warned that freedom of information was becoming a serious U.N. issue. Canham had participated in U.N. approval of two "conventions," or preliminary agreements by which freedom of movement and access to information was guaranteed, along with a balancing "right of correction," the latter to satisfy the former colonial nations. The conventions had not been opened for signature of governments, however; they remained essentially statements of ideals.[4]

As the 1952 session opened, a group of nations not aligned with the United States or the Soviet Union moved to open for ratification only that part of the 1949 convention that dealt with the right of correction. This controversial provision would have required foreign news agencies to "correct" statements that were found improper by officials of the nation involved; although there was no effective way to enforce the edict, it would have served as a constant source of friction between Western news agencies and nations recently emerging from colonial status. The United States opposed the correction policy and had agreed to the 1949 freedom of information policy only as a package in which correction was one element. In 1951, the United Nations had assigned a rapporteur to examine the entire area of freedom of information; the U.S. policy was to avoid action on any element—correction in particular—until the rapporteur could complete his work, which was not expected in 1952.

Sprague opened debate on October 24 by urging that ratification be delayed. Egypt and India immediately pressed for approval of the convention, opening a debate that required twenty-two meetings of Committee Three. As the debate proceeded, Sprague was face-to-face with the Soviets, and his remarks attracted considerable national attention.

"(Arkady A.) Sobolev, delegate from U.S.S.R made a propaganda speech attacking U.S. press as monopolistic and war-mongering. I reserved the right of reply at end of debate," Sprague noted in his diary for October 27. The following day, Sprague offered himself as "Exhibit A" to counter Soviet charges, an editor who wrote his own editorials with no control from government "or from anyone else." The editorials, he noted, consistently supported the U.N. and the settlement of international disputes through negotiation.[5]

It was one of four major speeches Sprague made on the topic as it wound its way through Committee Three and the General Assembly. He was gaining support among the unaligned nations, particularly with several journalists who served on Committee Three. The State Department's confidential post-session assessment of the delegation noted that the U.S. had enjoyed higher standing in Committee Three than in previous sessions, adding:

> *Governor Sprague, who was our spokesman on freedom of information, made an outstanding contribution and helped to maintain our prestige on the committee. As a newspaper publisher and editor, he was able to refer frequently to his personal experience and to speak directly to other newspapermen in the*

> *commiittee. His tact, parliamentary skill, and ability to extemporize all proved valuable assets during the course of a difficult debate.*[6]

Sprague picked up strong support from Yugoslavian delegate Vladimir Dedijer, a journalist of "huge physique, keen intelligence and vigorous personality." Dedijer, biographer of Tito, blasted Soviet domination of the media in Eastern European satellites, in a speech Sprague termed "moving and eloquent."[7]

The State Department gave Committee Three delegates a larger degree of autonomy than in past sessions, and Sprague was able to suggest plans to mitigate the American position on freedom of information. He advanced a proposal for technical assistance to journalists through the United Nations, and called for international seminars to bring journalists with opposing views to the same table. His proposal was adopted by the General Assembly, and became one of the foundations for future U.N. work in the field of media training and information technology.[8]

The U.S. was outvoted 25-22-10 in the General Assembly on the right to corrections, with Sprague presenting the U.S. position to the plenary session. The United States would refuse to sign the corrections policy, Sprague announced, citing it as a "hazardous step" that could lead to a barrage of propaganda in the guise of "corrections" to truthful news reports that did not enjoy the favor of a host nation. Sprague noted that the resolution was without effect: if a newspaper was responsible, it would print a correction without being urged to by an official agency; if it was not, the U.N. could not force it to issue a correction. One reporter noted the psychological problem for the U.S.: "The Assembly's decision puts this government at the moral disadvantage of not adhering to a U.N. convention to correct false news reports. There could be some embarrassing repercussions, say some observers."[9]

Although Sprague's work was highly praised by State Department professionals, he came away from the session with mixed feelings about the views of his country and his own newspaper colleagues. He began examining U.S. policy as he met with the Nieman Fellows, a group of journalists selected for a year's study at Harvard. Bob Frazier of the *Register-Guard* was among the group, and Sprague held a lengthy question-and-answer session. Upon adjournment of the U.N. session, Sprague filed a report which was quoted extensively in the publishers' trade journal.

The report was described as "a hard slap at the policy of the U.S. Mission to the U.N., which had been shaped in consultation with spokesmen for various segments of information media." Sprague described a wide cleavage between the West and the smaller nations. He listed two primary reasons: distrust of international news media because of poor and sometimes unfair reporting of Third World national interests and culture; and deficiencies in Third World media due to economic limitations and lack of press freedom. Sprague called for greater care in selection of foreign correspondents, and American offers of technical assistance to developing nations.[10]

Following his return to Oregon, Sprague made a hurried trip to New York for a session of American media leaders concerned with the Freedom of Information issue. They met with the U.N. rapporteur, Salvador Lopez of the Philippines; Sprague told Eleanor Roosevelt that Lopez was "groping to find a way out of the impasse."[11] Others would struggle for years with the same difficult issue. Sprague was taking part in one of the opening rounds of a debate that would occupy the United Nations for the next thirty years, under the mantle of "cultural imperialism." The debate spawned an entire discipline of studies, called "development journalism," in which the news media was urged to be a partner in nationalism by consciously balancing news reports in order to stress positive as well as negative news, to help build national cultures.

Sprague's performance on Freedom of Information led to another delicate assignment, representing the U.S. in the debate over South Africa's apartheid policies. Even more than the Freedom of Information debate, the apartheid question found him torn between his own views and his duty to represent administration policy.

The delegation was badly split on policy toward South Africa, and when Sprague was asked to take on the issue, he urged a policy under which the U.S. delegation would be free to side with India or with a group of eighteen nations to put greater pressure on South Africa. In 1952 the pressure-point was the "colored" population of South Africa, primarily Indians and Pakistanis; no consideration was given to rights for the black population. But even the "colored" proposal was highly controversial.

Sprague lunched with Madame Vijawa Pandit, the influential Indian delegate, and also met with Pakistan's delegates; he was moved by their concerns. In two intense discussions within the delegation, Sprague urged a stronger position; the U.S. was simply backing a general scolding of South Africa, and he felt the U.S. could not in conscience support legalized racial discrimination. "The Secretary said he disagreed . . . that we needed to stand by our friends (such as South Africa), who are helping out in Korea. Also he cited our dependence on South Africa for uranium. However he did not defend South Africa's policies," Sprague wrote in his diary.[12] The progressive Republican on the delegation was finding himself more liberal on the issue than the Democratic administration.

Two days later, Sprague presented the U.S. position, despite his personal misgivings ("there can't be 'two secretaries of state,' and here I am under instructions and must cooperate"). His speech draft had been heavily edited, it was "too balanced, too much like carrying water on both shoulders . . . (I was) particularly unhappy that it was so mild with respect to the disgraceful race policy of South Africa." While he carried out his role with favorable notice and good press coverage, he was not happy with the situation. Sprague met with a delegation from the NAACP, again playing the role of loyal spokesman for the policy, but feeling betrayed.[13] Forced to vote an abstention as the eighteen-nation compromise plan was approved 35-2-22, setting up a three-member investigation into South African racial policies, Sprague felt the U.S. had yielded the high moral ground to others, and should have joined in the eighteen-nation resolution.[14]

Sprague's United Nations service was generally free of partisan politics, but he did find himself confronting the outspoken Wisconsin Republican, Senator Alexander Wiley, who was using his position to harass the president on allegations that some American citizens employed by the U.N. were communists or sympathizers.

In a closed meeting of the delegation, Wiley exploded; he wanted to change the U.N. rules to give the secretary general the power to oust all American communists from U.N. employment. Secretary General Trygve Lie had already axed one employee and disciplined eleven others under pressure from the U.S., but Wiley wanted to go much further and essentially allow the U.S. government to determine qualifications for any American citizen employed by the U.N.

The debate became heated, with Acheson urging caution. The gist of it was leaked to A. M. Rosenthal of the *New York Times*. Sprague protested being "driven by panic into appeasement of Congress." The U.S., he wrote in his diary, must understand it does not run the United Nations, and he urged the delegation not to be draw into "the hysteria of the campaign." Afterwards, he noted, State Department representatives were grateful for his comments, but on the way back to his hotel he shared a ride with Wiley, who "said I should join in closing doors to employment of Reds who are out to destroy this country."[15]

Sprague had a long conversation with Deputy Secretary Richard Winslow, who was seeking advice; Sprague insisted that the rights of Americans employed at the U.N. must be protected. About the same time, he accompanied Mrs. Roosevelt to the U.N. personnel chief to try to reverse the firing of an American who had been dismissed without notice when he was called before a grand jury investigating Reds in the U.N.[16]

With Truman a lame duck, the issue proved to be a wild card for the remainder of the session, the secretary general trying to pacify both sides of the American political equation without causing a rebellion in his own ranks. Following the Republican victory in the general election, Secretary General Lie submitted his resignation. Sprague had a meeting with John Foster Dulles, the secretary of state-designate, just before Christmas; again he urged respect for the civil liberties of U.N. employees, but Dulles made no commitment.[17]

The entire affair strengthened Sprague's independent streak. New York also made Sprague a much more cosmopolitan man; he and Blanche not only attended Broadway plays and concerts, they dined with international diplomats. In three months Sprague acquired an education that would be disseminated in his editorials and columns over the next sixteen years.

For the first time in his 65 years, Sprague was thrown daily into close working relationships with equals of color; their votes and voices were equal to his, their arguments lucid and appealing, their conversation at lunch or informal meetings educated and stimulating. It was an experience that would deepen what had been a modest commitment to civil rights. Prior to 1952, he could be counted upon to "do the right thing," but after 1952 he could be counted upon to lead on civil rights. It was part of the continuing education of Sprague and, by extension, the citizens of Oregon. His daily column became a liberal arts education for its regular readers. Increasingly in this period, particularly after his U.N. service, Sprague was turning to the task of educating insular Oregonians about the importance of human rights.

In the fifties, Sprague moved beyond his early views that civil rights and civil liberties were primarily a state responsibility, to be enforced by

Blanche Sprague, ca 1955 (Sprague Family Archives).

Sprague was a longtime supporter of the Salem YMCA, and a room is named for him; in 1950 he and Blanche were joined by YMCA Secretary M. E. (Gus) Moore and his wife at an event honoring Sprague as Salem's First Citizen (Al Jones photo).

federal order only if a state would not or could not protect the rights of its citizens. He was seeing more of the dark side of his own state and city, the historic racism that lurked just beneath the state's respectable demeanor.

Oregon had had its share of atrocities as the frontier was "cleansed" of native Americans, and the state had passed laws in the 19th century barring free Negroes and prohibiting "Chinamen" from owning land. In the twenties the state followed California in prohibiting Asian immigrants from owning land. Japanese Americans returning from the indignity of concentration camps met the hostility described in the previous chapter. Indians still faced overt hostility, and people of color were advised to move on before dark in several cities in southern Oregon.

During the fifties, Oregon's small non-white population grew faster than the white population, although it remained less than 2 percent of the state. Blacks were the largest minority, at 18,133 in the 1960 census. Native Americans counted 8,026; Japanese 5,016 (a 20 percent increase from 1940, although many of the internees moved elsewhere); Chinese 2,995. As Oregon's total population increased by 16.3 percent in the fifties, the non-white population increased by 51.4 percent.[18]

Although the non-white population was heavily concentrated in the Portland area, the city's daily newspapers virtually ignored citizens of color, and reported on their activities primarily when they involved encounters with the law; it was a stereotypical approach taken by many American newspapers of the time. Sprague was not immune to this failing; in 1951 he had argued for the retention of "Little Black Sambo" as a grade school story, when it was attacked by the NAACP.[19]

Sprague supported the Legislature's fair employment practices act in 1949, and he argued for tolerance of mixed-race marriages, which were banned in Oregon until 1951. But the limited civil rights legislation that had been passed prior to 1953 did not enjoy general editorial support; in most cases the newspapers were simply silent.

The Portland newspapers had dipped their toes in the civil rights stream in 1950 and found it chilling. Initially supportive of a city ordinance barring discrimination in public accommodation, both *The Oregonian* and *Journal* retreated when citizens circulated referendum petitions, and stood mute as the measure was beaten. What is most remarkable is not that the measure failed, for the city's leaders were obviously far ahead of their constituents, but that the Portland dailies had nothing to say after the issue was placed on the ballot. Despite their early backing of the proposal, they simply abandoned the field.

Most of the downstate newspapers had so few minority readers that race could be ignored as a "Portland problem." The silence was broken in 1953, but not entirely to the liking of civil rights groups, for those who spoke were clearly of two minds. With the editorial division, Sprague's views became important, for his was a voice to be cited in debate.

It was Sprague's first major effort following his return in January from the United Nations. Sprague probably had met more people of color in three months at the United Nations than he had during his entire lifetime. He returned to share his new insights with readers, and to press for greater equality of races, once again going beyond his editorial page to place his personal prestige on the line.

Phil Hitchcock, a liberal Republican who was becoming somewhat of a Sprague protégé, introduced a measure barring discrimination in public facilities such as hotels, bars and restaurants. With a host of co-sponsors, SB 169 carried the Senate Judiciary Committee on a 5-2 vote. But the state's powerful hotel, restaurant and beverage industries weighed in against the bill, using an old Oregon political tactic: referral to the voters of a measure legislators wished to dodge.

As the Senate debate neared, a Sprague column observed that arguments against the bill were based on "freedom of association," and responded, "there are many crimes committed in the name of freedom; and discrimination is one of them." Sprague urged passage, concluding, "In good conscience we cannot do other than respect fundamental rights."[20]

Sprague's position prevailed in the Senate, which voted down three minority reports before finally passing the public accommodations bill 21-9 on March 16. The real battle was yet to come, and Oregon's editors were split on a proper course of action. Perhaps the most unusual, and unfortunate, element of the editorial debate was that the Portland dailies, which served most of the state's minority population, remained silent throughout the entire affair.

Sprague's cross-town rival opened the campaign to defeat the civil rights bill with an editorial the day after Senate passage. Asserting that discrimination against religious and racial minorities was on the wane in Oregon, the *Capital-Journal* proclaimed the measure "no more a part of democracy than the compulsory regimentation practiced against racial and religious minorities by the nazis and communists." The C-J's editorial was the base for ensuing editorials against the measure in Grants Pass and Albany.[21]

News coverage of the measure intensified with the likelihood of a difficult House struggle, as opponents began calling for referral to the voters. The measure went to the State and Federal Affairs Committee, traditionally dubbed the "Speaker's Committee," because it was expected to follow his wishes. Mark Hatfield, who was only in his second session but already making moves toward statewide prominence, chaired the committee, and supported the civil rights bill. He had six Republicans on his committee and only one Democrat, Maurine Neuberger. But Republicans were split and referral sentiment was building.

Bill Tugman in Eugene took on the issue of referendum, urging the Legislature to not duck its responsibility. The measure now counted three newspapers in favor (*Register-Guard, Oregon Statesman* and *East Oregonian*), and three opposed (*Capital-Journal, Democrat-Herald* and *Daily Courier*). Portland's big dailies remained silent. Once again it was left to downstate editors Sprague, Tugman and Forrester to carry the cause of personal liberty. And once again Sprague went beyond his editorial page.

Repeating his role in the 1951 teachers' oath controversy, Sprague made the walk from his Commercial Street office to the Capitol to testify at an April 7 hearing in Hatfield's committee. This was the critical point for the measure; it had support in the full House, but four votes could kill it in committee. Several African-American leaders testified with Sprague and the bill squeezed out of committee on a 4-to-3 vote. House approval was then relatively easy. The critical vote came as predicted, on a motion to send the measure to voters via referendum. The House rejected that tactic, 39-18 and then passed the public accommodations bill, 46 to 11.

Hatfield recalled that in committee the most effective advocacy came from a delegation of Portland minority leaders, but Sprague's editorials were helpful in House debate, particularly to rebut Salem Rep. W. W. Chadwick, a hotel owner and leader of the opposition. "I'm sure I quoted him, especially when Chadwick made a strong pitch against it [the bill], as representing Salem business. . . I'm sure as part of the rebuttal I was able to quote Charles Sprague," Hatfield recalled.[22]

Sprague apparently did not involve himself in the intense personal lobbying he used to defeat the 1951 loyalty oath, but he was in the gallery when the vote was taken in the House.[23] In a follow-up column, Sprague said the action set "standards for treating human beings as individuals and not as a race."[24]

Sprague continued his support as attempts began to refer the measure to a vote of the people; in two editorials he urged citizens not to sign the petitions, which were being circulated in hotels, restaurants and bars. The petition drive failed to reach the ballot.

A year later he weighed in behind the U.S. Supreme Court's landmark *Brown v. Board of Education* ruling, crafted by his old colleague, Chief Justice Earl Warren. As the decade brought more defiance of court rulings, Sprague backed the use of troops in Little Rock, and stood firmly against Southern governors attempting to defy school integration. Closer to home, in 1959 he urged the Legislature to pass a pair of bills to ban discrimination in real estate practices.[25] Sprague was well acquainted with the problem, for by the time the 1959 session convened he had begun work as chairman of the Oregon Advisory Committee to the newly created U.S. Civil Rights Commission.

As Sprague convened the first meeting of the Oregon advisory commission in November 1958, he faced around the table his old adversary Monroe Sweetland, now publishing a weekly in Milwaukie and serving in the state Senate, and three people new to his acquaintance: Mrs. Ulysses V. Plummer, Jr., a social worker and wife of one of Portland's leading black realtors; David Robinson, a lawyer active in the Anti-Defamation League of B'nai B'rith; and Dr. Joel V. Berreman, a University of Oregon sociologist.[26]

No formal hearings were held by Sprague's advisory body; the group responded primarily to information from civil rights leaders, churches and local contacts. Members brought to the work their own considerable backgrounds, and reports of racial problems were not hard to come by.[27] Oregon had a lingering reputation for racism, and Sprague's committee found that of six downstate cities surveyed, four "reported policies of exclusion and a fifth seemed to discourage Negro residents." Excerpts were attached from correspondents, without identifying communities:

We have virtually a monolithic Nordic white social group in the entire valley. There is an unwritten law that no Negroes may reside in the area. . . . Orientals are tolerated but Negroes not at all. Some 2 years ago a Negro family with a young child who was critically injured in a highway accident and received a lengthy period of hospitalization found housing—a rental unit—and were just taking occupancy when the owner received an ominous phone call to the effect that the "nigger" must be gotten out of here or your house will be burned. (This report was later identified as coming from Medford)

* * *

When we came to (the) county in 1952, we were assured not once but several times by agents that all of the county was "such a nice place to live, because there are no colored people here.

A back country native told us of 20 acres of good soil he was sure he could buy at a reasonable figure since it was owned by a Negro war veteran in Los Angeles who would never be permitted to live on it.

* * *

. . . according to old-timers, there is a time-honored tradition extending back at least two generations that "this is a sundown town." . . . On frequent occasions they quite boastfully relate skillful manipulations engaged in to prevent invasions of colored peoples into the vicinity.

* * *

Two or more years ago a Filipino war veteran and his family who had purchased real estate in the county was fired upon by unknown assailants.[28]

The findings were sobering, and they were augmented by a pattern of racial segregation in Portland, home to most of the state's African-American population. A Portland City Club study in 1957 found almost complete segregation. Sprague's committee added that, both in the suburbs and inside the city, new housing appeared to be closed to blacks, and 46 percent of Portland whites in a recent poll believed blacks should be segregated. Realtors were identified by the advisory group as contributing to the segregation, and laws passed to remedy the imbalance were doing little good.[29]

The grim assessment was presented by Sprague and Mrs. Plummer at the national conference of advisory boards in June 1959. Oregon looked no more progressive than other northern states, despite its small minority population. Sprague professed to be encouraged by the commitment of his peers, but he also saw the racism in the nation's capital as evidence of the job ahead.[30]

One of the accomplishments of the advisory body was to link together previously isolated civil rights advocates, who had been serving as lonely outposts in non-metropolitan areas. The advisory body gave them hope, and contacts with other like-minded people; human rights councils were formed in several communities, including Salem. Among the contacts the group relied upon were newspaper editors. One of the most courageous was Eric Allen, Jr. in Medford. Allen waded into the middle of an effort in 1960 to find housing for a black meteorologist, who had been transferred to Jackson County by the U.S. Weather Bureau. Rebuffed in attempts to find housing in Ashland, he got help from a newly formed Medford human rights council and found housing without the help of realtors.[31] The meteorologist and his family stayed less than two years, never feeling comfortable in the community, but Allen continued to battle for tolerance over the next two decades.

By the time of the commission's final report, Oregon had passed its 1959 legislation, and Sprague was able to report progress in "the opening of *regular* channels to minority groups (emphasis original). Access to housing is now a right rather than a privilege." The law required realtors to show any listed property to anyone who inquired, and to accept earnest money and offer it to the owner. Prior to 1959, blacks were often forced to use informal intermediaries because realtors would not show most properties to minorities. Despite improvements in the law, Sprague quoted a 1961 report of the Portland Urban League: "As yet the Urban League knows of no nonwhite family which has been able to purchase a home in a newly built subdivision developed for open occupancy."[32]

Substantial progress was reported in employment, although a practice of exclusion was charged to longshoremen. A problem in the 1959 report—discrimination in services such as barbershops and retail stores—was addressed in a 1961 state law. (Sprague scolded Salem barbers who would not cut a black man's hair, forcing him to drive 45 miles to Portland; "how absurd" he commented.) A year later, reporting to a statewide conference in Eugene, Sprague concluded: "Oregon's laws against discrimination are now quite adequate. The people need to 'grow up' to the principles embodied in the laws. In all communities persons should be ready to exert leadership so that conflicts which may arise may be handled with speed and equity."[33]

Sprague was taking just such a position of leadership in Salem, which continued to lag in its acceptance of blacks. A 1962 Oregon Civil Rights

Honored by Salemites on his 75th birthday, Sprague was introduced by attorney and friend Roy Harland, as Blanche looks on (Sprague Family Archives).

Division study found that of 12,000 state civil servants working in Salem, only four were black. Three of the four had had very bad experiences trying to find housing for their families; all eventually located, but the report identified Salem as a continuing problem. A human rights commission was formed in Salem, with Marguerite Wright as one of the prime movers along with Jim Welch of the *Capital-Journal*. Wright worked with Sprague in forming the commission, and obtained editorial support. "If you wanted to succeed in Salem, if you could get Sprague's support before you went public with it, the chances of success would be vastly improved," she observed.[34]

Sprague never had a large contingent of minority contacts; Marguerite Wright could not recall seeing a Native American, Asian, or African American in Sprague's office in the years she worked closely with him. But as he learned more about problems of discrimination, he waded deeper into the current of change.

With the complex issue of Native Americans, he was less successful in determining a proper course. Perhaps reflecting the nation at large, Sprague grappled with and ultimately rejected personal guilt in the plight of Native Americans, but he had trouble deciding where to go from there.

It was a critical time in the nation's long and stormy relationship with the continent's original inhabitants, for the federal government was trying to carry out a policy known by the ominous title of "termination." While the term itself could have been applied to U.S. policy toward Native Americans in the 19th century, when thousands of natives were killed, in the 1950s it referred to a policy of terminating the existing relationship between the federal government and the tribes, which was largely based on maintenance of reservations. A Republican Congress and president supported termination, but it also had bipartisan support in national circles and even in some Indian councils. Essentially, the goal was to cut the ties of dependency, break up the reservations, and force Indians into the white world.

The whole idea of a separate and dependent nation within a nation did not suit Sprague, and in 1952 he supported efforts to sever the relationships of four small Oregon coast tribes.[35] In 1954 he leaned toward the Congressional termination legislation, but worried whether Indians were ready for the step, warning that "the prime test should be, what is in the best interests of the Indians themselves?"[36] He was not ready to answer the question himself.

Most reservations were on land non-native people did not want, but one of the few exceptions was in Oregon. The million-acre Klamath Reservation contained some 720,000 acres of prime pine forest and, as Oregon's timber industry cut deeper and deeper into their own reserves and then began clear-cutting the national forests, the Klamath trove loomed large on the horizon. In the case of the Klamaths, termination involved not only the future of the Indians themselves but—of greater interest to many Oregonians—the future of their valuable timber.

The Klamaths were a major focus of attention in a three-year study financed by the Fund for the Republic: The Commission on the Rights, Liberties and Responsibilities of the American Indian. Sprague was one of five commissioners, who worked for more than three years (1957-60) and spent $182,782 to produce a report published as *The Indian: America's Unfinished Business.*[37]

The commission was weighted toward the dominant culture; its one Native member, W. W. Keeler, was principal chief of the Cherokee Nation, but he was also a vice president of Phillips Petroleum Company. Other members were from academe: former University of Oregon President O. Meredith Wilson, now at the University of Minnesota, was chair, and recruited Sprague; historian Arthur Schlesinger, recently retired from Harvard; and Karl N. Llewellyn, law professor at the University of Chicago. The commission retained as executives William D. Brophy and his wife, physician Sophie Aberle, both long involved with Indian work.

Keeler, who would in 1961 head a Kennedy Administration study of Indian affairs, argued articulately for recognition of the special qualities of Native culture. In a particularly intense session, Keeler tried to explain differences in thought patterns:

> *I am an engineer and can compete with the trained white man in that field. I can reason logically, beginning with premises or use a formula and judgment, and solve engineering problems. Even though I know the basis of the white man's thinking, I am satisfied that the best work I have done in my life has been a result of intuitive thinking.*
>
> *Intuitive thinking is natural with the Indian, and feeling is a determinative factor in the Indian's decision. I see the Indian as a person whose mainspring is wound up by feeling and his mind operates intuitively. . . .*
>
> *This analysis also applies to education where Indian children in the schools are taught to reason. The child tries to reason with his parents. The parent cannot weigh reasons but there is something in the core of his being, deep inside, that feels what his child is saying is wrong. But he cannot argue with his child using white man's logic. . . . Their children are being lost in a world so different from their own—a world which they cannot enter.*[38]

Keeler was moving into an area uncomfortable for the logic-dictated Sprague, who steered the discussion to the commission's task of finding ways to help Indians assume a role in the wider society. "We should not go too far into the theory of psychology in trying to determine Indian values," he cautioned.[39]

The commission later returned to the dilemma raised by Keeler: how to assimilate without destroying the values Keeler articulated? "If we become skillful in communicating to Indians," wondered Sprague, "will we not destroy their Indian-ness?"[40] He would return to the issue later in his columns, never clearly seeing an answer. What was clear to him, based in large part on his own struggles with the social problems of Klamath County, was that there had already been a cultural mingling, perhaps to no good end. During another long discussion of Indian values, Sprague observed that "whatever scale of values Indians may have had, in the instance of the Klamaths, they have been completely uprooted."[41]

By the time of Sprague's comments, commission specialists were confirming a sobering and comprehensive five-part series in the Eugene *Register-Guard*. On all sides there was agreement that the Klamath termination had been hastily done and was in danger of becoming a social disaster. Congress ordered termination of the Klamaths in 1954, to be completed by August 1958, but the *Register-Guard's* investigation led reporter William Dean to suggest: "Today the contrasts between the visible intent of the law and conditions on the reservation lead one to wonder whether PL 567 was designed for the Klamath Indians or some other group."[42]

"Some other group" hardly required definition; the Ponderosa pine on the Klamath Reservation was worth millions. Sprague found himself, while sitting on the commission, also involved in a complex web of negotiations and strategy that ultimately involved his old editorial colleague, Bob Sawyer; the American Forestry Association and National Lumber Manufacturers' Association; U.S. Senator Richard L. Neuberger, and a host of state legislators and private interests. At stake was the immense Klamath forest, some four billion board feet of timber, worth at least $100 million.

The 2,133 Indians listed on the final tribal roll of the Klamath tribe in 1957 lived on one of the most valuable reservations in the nation, surpassed only by oil-laden Indian territory in Oklahoma. Some of the riches could be realized over time, as the huge pine forest was harvested; the 23,826-acre Klamath Marsh was valuable only if left alone for wildlife preservation. There was little immediate income.

The average Klamath family's income was well below that of other rural families in Oregon; most Klamaths were still living in poverty. Housing, sanitation, and health were poor and many Indian children did not remain in school to graduate. Tribal income came almost exclusively from harvest of the Klamath forest, which was producing about $2.5 million a year at the time of termination. The Klamaths were poor people living in a rich and verdant land, surrounded by a sea of hostile white faces in one of the toughest counties in the state.[43]

Three "management specialists" (T. G. Watters, Eugene Flavel and William Phillips), appointed in 1955 to plan the termination process, came to the conclusion that Congress had been misled in 1954 by a Department of Interior statement that Klamaths were integrated into the larger society and were ready for termination. A 1957 Oregon Legislature interim committee agreed.[44]

Sprague had followed the Klamath issue since it surfaced in 1954, and had been aware from his gubernatorial days of the social problems of Klamath County. He began to work with Watters, an increasingly outspoken advocate for Indian interests. Watters and Flavel (Phillips resigned in 1956) were adamant that the Klamath forest not be sold in a way that would "dump" valuable timber on the private market at a depressed price, favoring the lumber industry at the expense of the Klamaths.[45] The management specialists were in an uncomfortable position; they had been appointed by Secretary of the Interior Douglas McKay, but they had become increasingly disenchanted with the termination policy McKay had backed. When the commission met in

Oregon in May 1957, Watters and Flavel arranged through Sprague to meet privately with commissioners "and give them the works" regarding the Klamath situation.[46]

The management specialists openly pushed for federal purchase of the Klamath forest. Sprague agreed with Watters and Flavel, as did Bob Sawyer, now out of the Bend *Bulletin* (sold in 1953 to Bob Chandler) and very active in the American Forestry Association, a respected organization of private foresters and conservationists. The AFA was up against a strong lobbying effort by the National Lumber Manufacturers' Association, which wanted the timber sold at once, preferably at a low price.

The task of Sprague, Sawyer, and others was to rally support for legislation sponsored by Senator Richard Neuberger and Representative Al Ullman, to delay the designated 1958 sale date at least a year, and to authorize the U.S. Forest Service to purchase the timber. The Eisenhower Administration had abruptly reversed its Indian policies in 1956, when Douglas McKay was succeeded by Fred Seaton, and the latter was working closely with Neuberger. Their main enemy, aside from the timber industry, was time; if no law was adopted in the 1957 Congress, the timber would be "dumped" to make Klamath termination payments compensating tribal members for the loss of the reservation.

Sawyer, concerned that Congress would not approve the estimated $100 million to purchase the Klamath forest, suggested to Sprague bonds issued by a public trust which would then sell the forest to private owners over a period of years. In his response, Sprague urged governmental ownership, but he also pulled E. B. MacNaughton into the discussion; among MacNaughton's many roles was that of a trustee of Resources for the Future. Two small private mills moved into the Chiloquin area, preparing to bid for Klamath timber, but in September 1957 Neuberger was able to pass an extension of the sale date to the following summer.[47]

Turning in his column to the issue, Sprague consistently supported governmental purchase, preferring federal to state ownership, a reversal of the view he once held as governor. In 1958 he swung behind a Neuberger-Seaton compromise that provided for both private and federal ownership.[48] Ultimately, 1,660 of the 2,133 enrolled Klamaths decided to withdraw from the tribe and accept payment; a trusteeship was set up for the remaining members. The withdrawing members were paid $44,000 each, loosing a "gold rush" of some consequence within the Klamath Falls business community. One tract of timber, consisting of 92,000 acres, was sold to a private company (Crown Zellerbach); the remaining forest went into the Fremont and Winema national forests.[49]

The Klamath affair was sobering to termination advocates; studies increasingly showed serious problems with the policy, and both the

Oregon legislative interim committee and the commission urged the government to slow the process. The commission issued a lengthy list of conditions that should precede any termination, including several to avoid the near-disaster of the Klamath timber sale. The Klamath termination process served as a school of hard knocks for all involved and was a major factor in the ultimate abandonment of termination.[50]

Sprague and his colleagues were also influenced by a mountain of reports, meetings with tribal leaders, and travel to some remote reservations. In his 70th year, Sprague took a six-day raft trip on the Colorado River, followed by a 14-mile muleback ride out of the canyon, joining a trip organized by his son-in-law, Dr. Melvin Hurley. The Colorado trip was preceded by an inspection of Navajo country. He took a particular interest in education, and observed that "the reservation system has broken down as an island of Indian culture and of Indian economy. What whites call civilization in its forms good and bad is reaching the hogans."[51]

Sprague and Arthur Schlesinger, joined by their wives, also toured an Apache reservation in 1958 and met with tribal leaders and talked with Apaches. Many Apaches continued their traditional dress and practices and Apache was the common language in most homes. The report, punched out on Sprague's typewriter, commented favorably on tribal leadership but found serious problems with housing, medical care, and education. Termination, they noted, was seen as inevitable but "discussion of it contributes to their insecurity."[52] The idea was also becoming increasingly unsavory to the commission.

The commission issued a preliminary report in 1961, coincidental with the appointment of a Kennedy Administration task force chaired by W. W. Keeler. Reporting the commission study, the *New York Times* found Keeler's overlapping role significant, then concentrated on the commission's recommendation that the government slow down its termination policies. At a news conference, Keeler predicted the presidential group would also call for a slowdown on termination.[53]

Considering the effort that had gone into the report, news coverage was disappointing and sometimes misleading. Joseph Lyford, public information officer of the Fund for the Republic, wrote a scathing note to United Press International, criticizing what he called "ham and tripe" coverage, including the use of stereotypical language. He had a point; the lead of the UPI dispatch was the following: "Once upon a time the Indian had little to worry about but bears and buffalo and bows and arrows. The slender, keen-eyed warrior subsisted on a simple diet and his steely nerves were legendary. But today, according to the Ford Foundation's Fund for the Republic, warriors are going to fat, suffering from overdoses of firewater and sugar and their nerves are shot."[54]

The commission's recommendations went far beyond a finding that Indians had diet and alcohol problems; the most serious findings and recommendations dealt with the relationship of the tribes to the federal government in health, education, and legal matters. The 56-page report and the work of commission specialists provided fodder for later studies of Indian affairs. Some 24,000 copies were sent out and another 7,284 were requested.[55]

In its report, the commission said termination should await economic, health, and educational progress among the tribes, and even then should proceed only if Indians were involved in the planning. The government should not hold out offers of special payments (such as the Klamath timber) to induce Indians to support termination, and should restructure the Bureau of Indian Affairs to "counsel and assist the Indian, not control or regiment him."[56]

In the end, Sprague was unable to reconcile his deeply felt progressive belief in assimilation of all Americans into the dominant white middle-class culture with the need to maintain a separate Indian culture. Returning from a 1957 trip into Navajo country, Sprague told commissioners: "I am impressed with the fact that Indians are in a critical period of transition. Their survival as a race or as worthy individuals depends quite as much on them as on the Government and non-Indians." Eighteen months later he told an Oregon conference that "they (Indians) must learn to assert themselves less as a separate race, but more and more as citizens equal under the law with other citizens, and not superior simply because they got to this continent a few millennia before the palefaces."[57]

As the commission began work on its final report, Sprague reviewed drafts, writing to Executive Director Sophie Aberle:

> *I think we must try to banish two points of view: First, the guilt complex of Americans of this generation over the sins of their ancestors; and Second the persecution complex of the Indians of this generation. The controlling attitude now should be, not recompense or propitiation, but how to fuse this substantial and resistant minority bloc into the prevailing economy and culture so they will be self-reliant, independent, free citizens, participating in the general community life without necessarily being extinguished as a race or a culture.*[58]

Sprague could not free himself from his Progressive past; he believed the salvation of Native people was to accommodate to white society. He was willing to provide help in the adjustment, but the idea of a separate society within the country was not acceptable. He believed Indians could have both their unique culture and the benefits of the majority culture; or perhaps he simply could see no way out of the conundrum.

As late as 1967, Sprague was drawing on the commission's work as the Kennedy and Johnson administrations attempted to find a balance in federal relations with the tribes. He found common ground from his work with both Black and Indian populations, and that common ground was the need for the white majority to be involved in efforts to raise the quality of life for minorities. The *Statesman* increasingly became a forum for issues dealing with discrimination, and those who boasted of the city's lily-white heritage could count on a scolding from Sprague.

The physical demands of a Grand Canyon float and muleback ride or a trek through an Apache village were taken in stride as Sprague passed seventy years without slowing his pace. At an age when most men were well into retirement, Sprague climbed Grizzly Peak, the south flank of Mt. Jefferson, in company with his son, and he continued his activities with the Chemeketans hiking group.[59]

Sprague owed a great deal to his physical vitality. He came from a long-lived family; his older brother lived into his nineties, and one grandmother lived beyond one hundred. He did not live a spartan life, but he enjoyed exercise and walked almost daily from his home to his office, then downtown for lunch; companions had to stride rapidly to keep pace. He used neither tobacco nor alcohol, and his home life was seemingly free from domestic stress.

He needed the vitality, for he was simultaneously engaged in Salem church and civic work and expanding his interest in national affairs. His United Nations service provided the contacts that brought him an invitation in 1954 to serve on the Board of Trustees of the Carnegie Foundation for International Peace. Richard Winslow, with whom he had worked at the U.N., joined the foundation as an executive and was instrumental in naming Sprague to the board as well as two other 1952 alternate delegates, Ernest Gross and Philip Jessup. The board was a combination of liberal blue-bloods, academics, and two journalists, Sprague and Edward R. Murrow. As was always the case, meetings of the prestigious board produced material for "It Seems To Me" upon Sprague's return to Oregon.

While at the U.N., Sprague had had two long meetings with Winslow to discuss a committee of leading citizens to evaluate the U.N. At the Carnegie Foundation, they were involved in an effort to form a "World Affairs Service Bureau," but it failed to obtain funding. In 1958, however, Sprague participated in an abbreviated version of the inquiry, a 24-person panel discussion and seminar sponsored by the Brookings Institution.[60]

He also found time to accept presidential appointments to a panel studying labor-management relations in the atomic energy field, and to serve on an emergency board investigating a dispute between railroads and their conductors and brakemen. This sometimes frenetic activity came at a time of great change in Oregon politics and in Sprague's professional life at the *Statesman*. Republican domination of state and national office was challenged for the first time since Sprague had recaptured the governorship for the party in 1938. Within the GOP, deep and sometimes bitter divisions appeared. Sprague and his expanding newspaper were caught up in the cataclysm, and the central figure was Sprague's ticket mate from 1944, Senator Wayne L. Morse.

9

◆◆◆

Turbulent Politics of the Fifties

Oregonians have an independent streak in terms of politics, often marching to quite a different drummer than the nation as a whole. Oregon was staunchly Republican while Franklin D. Roosevelt was in the White House and the New Deal swept neighboring states. The fifties were quiescent at the national level; Americans liked Ike, put up with incursions on their civil liberties through fear of a Red menace, and prospered in the postwar economy with its emphasis on material consumption. In Oregon, however, the fifties marked the emergence of a true two-party political system. The Republican lock on Oregon was broken, and as the decade ended Democrats held both U. S. Senate seats and all four House seats and had a majority in both houses of the Oregon Legislature.

When Sprague was elected governor in 1938, the New Deal flood of Democratic registration was at its peak, 48 percent of the Oregon electorate registered as Democratic, but these Democrats insisted upon splitting their ballot between the popular president and a succession of cautious Republicans at the state level. The major catalyst for change in Oregon was the war, which brought new industries with their accompanying labor force and labor unions. Although lumber and agriculture remained the top two employers, Oregon was expanding its industrial base and population was migrating into the growing tri-county area around Portland. Oregon grew by some 40 percent during the forties, the vast majority of the growth coming from immigration. The newcomers were urban dwellers with shallow political loyalties; they were ripe for organization, but the moribund Democratic Party took a decade to do the job.[1]

The job was complete by 1960, however; behind the scenes the veteran organizer Monroe Sweetland and the state chairman, Howard Morgan, led party organization while a coterie of unusually attractive candidates finally attached a respectable image to the party so long dominated by tired conservatives whose politics were often to the right of the Republicans.

Oregon newspapers, always closely associated with Republican politics, lost much of their partisan flavor during the decade, as new men took the reins from editors who had come to their positions before World War II. By 1960 only two of the powerful editors and politicians who were influential before 1950 remained in power, and both had experienced substantial life changes. The two men were Senator Wayne L. Morse and Charles A. Sprague.

While Sprague was at the United Nations in 1952, Morse was beginning his metamorphosis from Republican to Democrat. In 1953, Morse adopted the label "Independent" and left the Republican caucus in the Senate. The same year, Sprague changed the Republican designation the *Statesman* had carried since 1929, and adopted an Independent Republican label.

No direct relationship should be assumed between these actions, but the state's dominant politician and leading editor were reacting to the tenor of the times, and to changes in their own lives. Sprague had expanded his horizons at the U.N., moving in new circles and facing new issues. Morse was coming to grips with a party alignment that was never comfortable and had become a liability. Sprague had been rejected by Republicans in 1942 and again in 1944; Morse was humiliated in 1952 by Oregon's old-line GOP leadership.

Morse and Sprague began political life as progressive Republicans, but Morse was always to the left of Sprague, which was perhaps inevitable considering their backgrounds. Sprague was rural Iowan, coming of age under Theodore Roosevelt; Morse was leftish Madison, Wisconsin and was deeply influenced by Bob LaFollette. By the time LaFollette raised his ill-fated Progressive Party banner for the presidency in 1924, Sprague had returned to the Republican camp; Morse took part in LaFollette's campaign. From LaFollette came Morse's lifelong concerns for working people and his ties to organized labor. Morse and Sprague held progressive views on conservation, they championed the virtues of hard work and small towns, and Morse could be as puritanical and moralistic as Sprague. Both men were indelibly marked by their progressive years.[2]

During the time that Sprague identified the *Statesman* as Republican in newspaper directories, he took the label seriously; he viewed his paper as a spokesman for his party, particularly in endorsing candidates. The style was rooted in the 19th century, and by the fifties most newspapers had dropped party affiliation, although in Oregon many carrying Independent labels were more predictably Republican than Sprague.

Sprague had grown increasingly disenchanted with the plodding and predictable governors who followed him, and the domination of Oregon Republican politics by business and financial leaders in Portland. The

Republican Party, one observer noted, "has come dangerously close in late years to control by a few men. . . . Sometimes known as the 'Arlington Club Crowd,' less than a dozen of them have succeeded with some regularity in dictating party policy and hand-picking the party's candidates for major office."[3] The task of faithfully supporting Republican candidates was growing more difficult. Sprague's candidates for president were spurned by the GOP national conventions in 1944, 1948, and 1952. And Oregon Democrats were finally beginning to produce attractive candidates.

Wayne Morse was also working his way across the political landscape, although with much more clatter and bang. Morse's passage to the Democratic Party was perhaps inevitable, given his views, but Morse was given a firm push in 1950, a heavier shove in 1952, and by 1953 the break was irrevocable.

The 1952 election, with its Eisenhower landslide and the election of Republicans to all top state offices except attorney general, was the last GOP sweep of the Oregon ballot. Democratic insurgents, led by Sweetland and Morgan, were still engaged in trench warfare to purge the right wing of the party. They were not close to victory in 1952, and one obstacle was the uniform front of Republican editors. Political scientist Maure Goldschmidt noted the importance of newspaper editors in the last pre-TV election, when Democrats registered nearly as many voters as Republicans, but could not produce results. Voters drawn to the party by the charismatic figure of Franklin D. Roosevelt were not as consistent in their choices as the Republicans, he stated, adding, "They are therefore easily swayed by the Republican-controlled press and by the greater name familiarity and prestige of the Republican candidates for state and local office."[4]

One of the candidates who had benefited from the Republican press was Morse, who launched his political career in the same 1944 election that ended Sprague's political ambitions. The two men shared many views and had known each other since the thirties; Sprague became a consistent backer of Oregon's junior senator.

Sprague boosted Morse's growing national standing, proud of the Oregon senator when he was mentioned as a national leader, and ever ready to defend him against his critics. The pattern had begun in the 1944 general election, when Sprague defended Morse against a particularly vicious attack from George Putnam. The latter, supporting right-wing Democrat Willis Smith, accused Morse of being supported "by all the socialistic and communistic interests in Oregon," and went on to print without attribution a statement from "a prominent Republican" accusing Morse of teaching communism at the University of Oregon. Sprague, labeling the charge "twaddle and bunk," excoriated Putnam for the anonymous charge and praised Morse's independence. Sprague's attack flushed to the surface the "prominent Republican," who turned out to be Governor Martin's old goon-buster, Ralph Moody.[5]

Sprague was not alone among Oregon editors in supporting Morse. Bill Tugman was a personal friend from the days when they fought together to save the University of Oregon, and Bob Ruhl was a lifelong backer. But Sprague had a unique connection with Morse because of their parallel 1944 campaigns. He had seen, even in that campaign, both the platform eloquence and the righteous wrath of his colleague. The contrast between those two sides of Morse—the one cuttingly logical and lawyer-like, the other acerbic and relentless—consistently bothered the moderate Sprague.

The men corresponded; they were "Charley" and "Wayne" in their letters. But Sprague worried about Morse's low boiling point and the intemperance of his attacks, particularly on fellow Republicans. "He can run a temperature on political questions faster than most any man in political life," Sprague observed in 1946, adding a year later, "I can't help wishing our junior senator would conserve his vocal grenades for really important matters."[6]

Yet, in the same year, Sprague responded to a *Collier's* magazine request by naming Morse as one of the top three senators of 1946, primarily for Morse's insistence that the U. S. adhere to the new International Court of Justice and for his efforts against racial discrimination and filibustering.[7]

Senator Wayne Morse at the Oregon State Fair, a favorite place for him to show livestock and race his trotting horses. Morse and Sprague were friends, then rivals but never personal enemies, for over 30 years (Oregon Historical Society, Tom Wright collection).

The dichotomy continued for the next five years, Sprague praising Morse's stands on major public issues, and scolding him, publicly and privately, for his intemperate outbursts. "May I, in all kindness, offer you a suggestion?" Sprague wrote as Morse engaged in a bitter dispute with the *Register-Guard* over the senator's defense of President Truman's steel mill seizure. "Treat yourself once in a while to the luxury of being wrong!" Morse replied with a detailed and legalistic three-page defense of his position.[8]

Sprague, whose columns were terse and to the point, abhorred windy prose and once counseled Morse: "From the standpoint of prolixity may I say it is one of your worst. You take 37 columns to say in substance what (pardon me) I said in five paragraphs. You were never an editor or you would have learned how to compress your words. Just a friendly criticism. Cordially yours, Charley." Replying that he "totally agreed," Morse inserted Sprague's five paragraphs in the *Congressional Record*.[9]

When Morse was injured in 1949 while racing his trotting horse at the State Fair, Sprague paid a hospital visit and the men discussed possible challengers to Morse in the upcoming Republican primary. Morse and Sprague discussed the possibility that William Walsh of Coos Bay would be a candidate, which would have been difficult for Sprague because Walsh had been a faithful county chairman for Sprague in 1942 and 1944. But Walsh declined, after getting from Morse a statement of opposition to the controversial Columbia Valley Authority then under consideration by the Truman Administration.[10] Morse's only opponent was a right-wing farmer from the small town of Deadwood in Lane County. Deadwood Dave Hoover served no purpose other than to let Morse know how angry Republicans were over his independence. The message was sobering; Hoover and another unknown, John McBride of Medford, combined to get 40 percent of the GOP vote. In the process, Morse lost one of his Republican newspaper allies, the conservative Bob Sawyer of Bend. Sprague strongly endorsed Morse, urging Republicans to "swallow their qualms about party regularity," and support Morse "with pride as well as purpose." Morse was renominated, but the first step in his political passage had been taken.[11]

Sprague and Morse had much in common in their relationship to the Oregon Republican party. Sprague had taken the path of party loyalty and then been rewarded in 1942 with rejection; Morse had tried early in his Senate career to support his party, campaigning for its candidates and supporting the leadership on most key votes. But it was clear in 1950 that he too would face rejection at some future point. He increased his liberal positions almost immediately, siding with President Truman on closing the steel mills, and voting with him on other important issues while also trying to become a force in the liberal wing of the GOP. When Congressional reporters voted Morse the best Republican senator in 1951, Sprague printed the accolades with pride, and he appeared to bless an incipient effort by Salem attorney Steve Anderson, a national Young Republican leader, to draft Morse as a 1952 candidate for president.[12]

But Morse's national stature only widened the gulf between him and the conservative GOP leadership in Oregon, epitomized by the Salem car dealer, Douglas McKay, an American Legion stalwart serving as governor. McKay and the party's conservative wing clipped the senator's wings in May, and by the end of 1952 Morse was well on the road to the Democratic caucus.

At the May primary Oregon elects its delegates to the national political conventions, and traditionally those with the most votes were given positions on key convention committees. (Reforms in party rules changed this in the seventies.) In 1952, only Governor McKay out-polled Morse for a position in the GOP delegation. Morse accordingly ceded to McKay the delegation chairmanship, while asking for a spot on the platform committee. Busy in Washington, he asked alternate Clay Myers to represent him at the delegation's organizational meeting. It was a fateful decision, for while Morse was a formidable foe in personal combat he was less so by proxy.

Party regulars used the occasion to discipline the increasingly independent Morse. Prior to the voting, they agreed on their challenger, 29-year-old Mark Hatfield, a one-term legislator from Salem. In a resounding 13-5 vote, Hatfield was elected to the national platform committee, and Morse was given no convention role. Delegate Gordon Orput told his colleagues: "It would do more harm than good to put Morse on any committee. He's a controversial hot potato because of his New Dealish attitude."[13] Morse knew that the vote went far beyond the clutch of delegates in a Salem hotel room. The Republican establishment was sending him a message he could not ignore: If you stay in the party and maintain your present political views, we will fight you every step of the way.

The action, reflected Sprague, showed "too much peevishness on the part of the delegation. After all, Morse is a national figure of consequence, and stood second in the popular poll just concluded. While his would be rather a lone voice on the party platform committee, still it is one that should be heard if the party is to embrace broad elements and present an appeal which will meet with popular response."[14]

Even when Morse bolted the Republican ticket after the GOP nominated Richard Nixon as Dwight D. Eisenhower's running mate, Sprague did not participate in the wrath that consumed most Republican editors. The split between Morse and Tugman was the most bitter, because the two had shared causes in the past. Tugman's son said the final break came when Tugman challenged Morse sharply on the issue of Truman's seizure of the steel mills. Tugman locked himself away in the university library for several days, exhaustively researched Morse's record, and wrote a long critique. Morse reportedly read the editorial, crumpled the paper into a ball, threw it at the couch in his office, and ordered Tugman cut from his mailing list. Across the state, Republican editors indulged in a form of Morse-bashing that revealed the depth of their party allegiance.[15]

Sprague, at the United Nations when Morse announced his shift, commented in a letter to his nephew: "I see that Morse 'resigned' from the party last night. . . . He is where he belongs. He has pretty well demonstrated he can't work in any team. He may survive in politics but he sacrifices a great deal of influence."[16]

Commenting editorially upon his return to Salem, Sprague noted Republican eagerness to purge Morse in 1956: "Morse, they say, committed the unforgivable sin when he quit the party. Morse, they say, no longer belongs to us. No, he now belongs to the nation." Sprague publicly cautioned Morse against his rising militancy and strident tone: "It's all very well to function as a public conscience, but it can easily be overdone. Morse can add to his unpopularity for party defection . . . or conceivably he might regain public favor by some brilliant display of conscience and independency (sic) on vital issues. He will not do it by just being a political irritant."[17]

In his detailed study of editorial treatment of Morse's party switch, University of Oregon graduate student Blaine Whipple (later a Democratic national committeeman) found that Sprague's treatment of Morse became more critical after 1952, but there was no hint of a personal feud in the writing, as appeared to be the case with other editors. Sprague's criticism was delivered in "reasonable and tolerant tones," although increasingly it focused on "deficient" personal characteristics. Whipple studied the daily newspapers in Portland, Salem, and Eugene through 1956, and found the *Statesman* and *Oregon Journal* to be more balanced and fair in editorials on Morse than *The Oregonian, Capital-Journal* or *Register-Guard*. But in every case, he asserted, it was clear that membership in the Republican Party "is of primary importance to an Oregonian seeking major political office if he is interested in the editorial support of the five papers studied here."[18]

Politics was a personal thing with editors of the time, perhaps more so with Morse because of his maverick streak, but personal also because editors were very much a part of their community and expected to have a personal relationship with their elected leaders. Oregon in the fifties still had a small-town feel; political leaders were called by their first names and freely mixed with the editors and reporters who covered them. When Warren C. Price wrote his history of the Eugene *Register-Guard,* the subtitle, "A Citizen of Its Community," could as easily have been applied to the *Statesman,* or several other Oregon papers.

In Oregon, and particularly among the downstate dailies, there was what might be called "a community of editors," for the men who edited, and in many cases owned, the newspapers were in frequent contact, looked to each other for ideas and guidance, and carried on what one observer termed "an editorial talk show," on their pages. A. Robert Smith, whose Washington D.C. column was carried by several, described an eminence about the senior editors, with Sprague clearly the leader. "He was above the emotional attachment . . . he seemed to speak from Mt. Olympus."[19]

"It was a period when individuals did count for something," observed Robert Notson, who was moving through executive positions at *The Oregonian* in the fifties. Describing Bob Ruhl at Medford, Notson observed that Ruhl was a frequent traveler, but "back he would come right in the middle of things and the first thing you knew he would sort of dominate the thinking of the community."[20]

The editors themselves prized the interaction. When Bob Sawyer had been retired for a year, he wrote Bill Tugman: "My present status has many advantages, but, also, a lot that I once enjoyed is gone. One of those pleasures was in some degree keeping in touch with you and Charley Sprague in editorial conversation." Whether it was an editorial conversation or an editorial talk show, the interaction was very real and it affected affairs of the state. It also magnified the voice of an individual editor, for if his views were considered important they were reflected in other papers. Bob Frazier described Sprague's influence as "like casting a stone into a still pond"; the ripples gradually spread across the state's editorial pages.[21]

Downstate editors saw themselves as separate from the large Portland dailies, with their corporate ownership and multi-person editorial boards. *The Oregonian* and the *Oregon Journal* were big business and the journalists who wrote the stories and editorials were hired hands who knew little about the business side of their papers. They were quite removed from the world of community journalism as practiced by Oregon's downstate newspapers.

In downstate Oregon, the essential structure of the newspaper industry had remained unchanged for fifty years. Oregon newspapers in 1950 were still home-owned, often by the same families that had guided them through the Depression. No complex chain-of-command led from newsroom to regional office and finally to national headquarters. Reporters could walk a few feet to the publisher's modest office, where the buck always stopped. Oregon editors identified with the personal leadership of the state; indeed, they were part of that leadership. Most editors of the period considered themselves to be community editors, responsible for and responsive to local needs and interests. But communities were changing, Oregon was more a part of the outside world, and the influx of newcomers during and after the war was forcing the state's editors to broaden their coverage and their views.

Although wartime growth in the Portland area gained the most attention, after the war growth spread into the Willamette Valley and the small timber towns of Southern Oregon. The university communities of Corvallis and Eugene swelled with returning veterans on the GI Bill; Lane County grew by 82 percent and Benton by 69.5 percent in the forties.

Newspapers changed as well. Consumer demand was frustrated during the war, with rationing and limited supplies of goods. As newsprint became more available and advertisements poured in from department stores, car dealers and others taking advantage of the postwar consumption frenzy, the state's daily newspapers grew fatter. Staffs were expanded as veterans returned, and the press took on a much larger role in coverage of community affairs.

While the Portland dailies' combined circulation increased 53 percent (from 265,116 in 1940 to 405,756 in 1950), circulation of downstate papers increased even more dramatically. The Medford *Mail Tribune* jumped from 5,769 to 12,727, an increase of 121 percent; in Roseburg the *News-Review* went from 3,520 to 7,512, up 113 percent. The lumber industry was the major factor in these increases. In Eugene, lumber and education pushed the *Register-Guard* from 14,726 to 27,360, an increase of 86 percent.[22]

Oregon journalism in the World War II era was dominated by men who began in journalism at the time of World War I, often at weekly newspapers. Nearly all were also publishers, and ownership gave them added standing in a civic leadership that was still dominated by Main Street businessmen.

The postwar period was the twilight of many of their careers. Among the leading editorialists whose careers pre-dated the war, few were still active into the sixties. George Putnam had sold the *Capital-Journal*, but he was still writing editorials at the time of his death in a 1961 house fire. Sprague in his column noted that the two old foes had been closer in recent years, and labeled Putnam "a scourge of wrongdoers, a foe of sham and hypocrisy, a defender of personal liberty."[23] Sheldon Sackett still owned the Coos Bay *World* (originally the *Times*), but spent most of his time outside the state, working up new deals.

Others among the prewar generation were retired or dead. Bill Tugman left Eugene in 1955 to buy a weekly on the Oregon coast. Robert Ruhl by the mid-fifties had turned most editorial writing over to Eric Allen, Jr. Merle Chessman of the *Astorian-Budget* died in 1947; Claude Ingalls of the Corvallis *Gazette-Times* retired in 1950; Edwin O. Aldrich of the Pendleton *East Oregonian* died in 1950; and Robert Sawyer of the Bend *Bulletin* sold his paper in 1953. Of these, only Sackett and Aldrich were Democrats; Aldrich had introduced President Truman when he campaigned in Pendleton in 1948.[24]

Portland editorial boards did not exert influence proportionate to their large circulations. *The Oregonian* had lost the editorial edge that caused journalism historian Frank Mott to write, "It was not the *Oregonian's* circulation, its undeniable prosperity, or its good news coverage that gave it its reputation: it was Harvey W. Scott's editorial page."[25] Scott edited the paper from 1860 to 1910, carving a wide swath across the state's politics. His successors half a century later maintained a firm defense of all that was Republican, but had a predilection to discuss such safe topics as gardening, fishing and obscure foreign leaders.

In much the same manner, the *Oregon Journal* had lost the luster of founder C. S. Jackson, a Democrat personally close to President Woodrow Wilson; and Jackson's legendary blind editor, B. F. Irvine, who wrote editorials from 1919 to 1937.[26] Successor Marshall Dana was a leonine presence who as a young man had been a zealous crusader for public works, particularly the development of water power and irrigation. But, in the view of some contemporaries, in later years Dana was given to utterances with little meaning.[27]

The absence of strong editorial leadership from the big Portland dailies encouraged downstate editors to look within their own ranks for direction when the issues went beyond their immediate communities, and editorials were often quoted by other editors. A survey of the state's fifteen largest newspapers in 1950 revealed some 44 editorials reprinted by peers; exactly half were from Sprague's editorial page or column.[28] The pattern was little changed a decade later: the same papers for a two-month period in 1963 used 33 reprints or direct quotes, and 14 were from Sprague.

By 1960, a postwar generation had established themselves as leaders in the field: Bob Chandler at Bend, J. W. (Bud) Forrester at Pendleton, Eric Allen, Jr. at Medford, Bob Frazier at Eugene, Bob Ingalls at Corvallis, Fred Andrus at Astoria, Jim Welch at the *Capital-Journal*. But, in sharp contrast to the prior generation, only Chandler, Forrester, and Ingalls also owned their newspapers.

Chandler and Forrester recalled that the downstaters saw themselves as separate from the large Portland staffs. The downstaters were one-man shops; there were no editorial board meetings, and when they walked down Main Street the townspeople they encountered knew who had written that day's editorial.

Chandler and Forrester were very different—Chandler was solidly Republican, Forrester a dependable Democrat. Chandler was blustery, immovable in his opinions, scathing in opposition; Forrester was soft-spoken, and opposed without alienating. But they were alike in their admiration and emulation of Sprague, who may have been the only man in Oregon that Chandler held in awe.

A brash young Californian, Chandler bought the Bend *Bulletin* in 1953. Shortly thereafter he wrote an editorial unfavorably comparing BLM forest management with that of the Forest Service. "I got a note the next day: 'Dear Chandler: Don't make invidious comparisons. Sprague.' I tried to avoid it in the future!" Chandler recalled. Chandler liked to tell the story about a phone call from Sprague in December 1964. Sprague asked him to visit the next time he was in Salem. "A summons from Sprague was not to be ignored. . . I made plans to go there the next day and left home about 6 a.m.," Chandler later wrote, describing a nightmarish trip in which he narrowly averted being swept away by a swollen North Santiam river, and had to hole up in a rural cafe for four days before he could walk to safety. "It was another couple of weeks before I could get to Salem," Chandler noted, "to agree to undertake another now-forgotten chore, simply because Charles A. Sprague asked me to do it."[29]

One of the younger editors who came on the Oregon news scene in the fifties, Robert Chandler of Bend admired Sprague and shared his willingness to serve in public positions (Bend *Bulletin*).

Of all the younger men, Forrester was closest to Sprague, despite their political difference, and Sprague encouraged him to engage in public service. "He had more influence on me than anyone else in getting myself into public affairs. I concluded after watching what he had done that I had something of a responsibility in getting myself involved in public affairs and I concluded that there was not a clash there, that I would not be serving two masters. Believe me, not all my colleagues agreed on this," Forrester said, adding, "Jim Welch told me, 'I don't think an editor should even belong to a church.'"[30]

The difference between Forrester and Welch, who was a warm and humorous man and wrote most of the C-J editorials after the death of George Putnam, was simple: one man owned the newspaper and the other was an employee. Forrester and Chandler were in the mold of Sprague and others of his generation, Welch was in the mold of newspapering's future.

In an age before television and the domination of newspaper chains, this circle of editors could exert an influence across the state, particularly if they were in concert on matters of principle, and even more so if they were willing to take additional action for their cause. Bob Frazier, after his return from a Nieman Fellowship in 1953, put together informal gatherings of postwar editors, with the conspicuous addition of Sprague, who did not always attend but was always invited.[31] Sprague seldom joined the social gatherings; he was a generation older, did not smoke or drink, and was never an easy conversationalist. But when the others were in Salem, they invariably visited Sprague at the *Statesman*. Notes and telephone calls were exchanged, but the key to Sprague's influence with the others was his front-page column and his editorials.

Robert Notson and Forest Amsden, coming at politics from opposite ends of the ideological spectrum, with Notson a conservative Republican and Amsden a liberal Democrat, agreed that Sprague's influence could be attributed to a combination of the governorship and his column "It Seems To Me." "Legislators would read that column to find out what they thought about public issues," said Notson. "I have a feeling that Sprague had more influence through his column on state government after he was governor, than he ever had as governor." Amsden found Sprague's daily column was "must reading" for every politician and editor in the state; he saw it as a powerful agenda-setting tool: "If those in power have to react to you, right or wrong, you have power, and he had it in spades from about 1950 on. By setting an agenda for public discussion, he had become an institution."[32]

Sprague was able to devote more time to his column after 1954; his U.N. service was over, the new building was occupied and the merger with the *Capital-Journal* did relieve him of some aspects of the day-to-day duties of running a significant business. The column reflected Sprague's wider exposure from the United Nations and other national service, and his disenchantment with Joseph McCarthy, Richard Nixon and the right wing of the Republican Party, both nationally and in Oregon, where the Snell Machine produced candidates and the Arlington Club crowd dictated policy.

In 1952, writing from the U.N., Sprague bucked the Snell organization's candidate for secretary of state, terming Earl Newbry "stupid rather than venal" in a letter to Webb, and endorsing Democrat Edith Green on his editorial page.[33] Green lost, but a second Democrat endorsed by Sprague, Robert Y. Thornton, won the race for attorney general, ushering in the Democratic tide of the fifties.

Endorsements of Green and Thornton did not signal defection from Republican ranks, however, and Sprague backed newscaster Tom McCall against Green for Congress in 1954. He knew McCall from the lanky Portlander's days as executive for Gov. Douglas McKay, and saw a maverick streak that could be healthy for the GOP. His most difficult decision, however, was not the Green-McCall race in Portland, but the 1954 contest between two men he knew well. One had defeated him in 1944 and the other was a man with whom he shared causes, personal visits, and the respect of one leading journalist for another. Richard L. Neuberger's challenge to Senator Guy Cordon was one of the nation's most important campaigns in 1954, and it was a difficult one for Sprague.

Newspaper people liked Neuberger and his wife Maurine. They were good copy, always a criteria for reporters; Dick was quotable, always willing to help a reporter on deadline. Underpaid news scriveners held Neuberger somewhat in awe, for he actually made a good living by free-lancing, a feat that was possible in the age of the big magazines, but exceedingly difficult. Neuberger always credited his wife with his political success, and there was much truth in that, for she had a warm and easy manner that helped mediate Dick's intensity. Also, Maurine was photogenic in an age when newsrooms assessed women more for their physical attributes than their intellects. The slim and leggy former gym teacher was photographed in a Jantzen swim suit, managing in one photo to boost a local product and please the boys in the newsroom. Elected to the Oregon House in 1948, she became an equal partner in every respect. (This led Neuberger to quip, in those days of Democratic torpor, that the situation had improved vastly from the time when the Democratic legislative caucus could meet in a phone booth; now, he cracked, it could meet in bed!).[34]

Oregon's husband-and-wife legislative team, Richard and Maurine Neuberger, strike a campaign pose on the Capitol steps. Sprague and Neuberger supported opposite political parties, but maintained a close relationship for many years (Oregon Historical Society CN021262).

Dick Neuberger was the voice of Northwest liberals in the national media, particularly outspoken as a supporter of public power. His 1938 book, *Our Promised Land,* is one of the best literary expositions of the politics of electric power during the Depression.[35] He had been a frequent contributor and briefly a staff writer for *The Oregonian*, whose editors loved his writing as much as they hated his liberal politics. His failure to gain what he thought was fair treatment editorially brought him into sharp conflict with both Portland papers in the period before he launched his 1954 drive to unseat Senator Cordon.

Neuberger had personal ties with Malcolm Bauer, *Oregonian* city editor, but even Bauer was not able to convince him that the newspaper was not deliberately slanted against his political career. Neuberger was particularly critical of *The Oregonian* for taking moderate or liberal positions on issues and then endorsing Republicans like Guy Cordon and Doug McKay, who voted in exactly the opposite way. "Integrity calls for the rising above partisanship and above personal malice," Neuberger lectured editorial writer Herb Lundy. "Do you believe the *Oregonian* editorial page does so? . . . One might ask if a blacklist exists on the *Oregonian* editorial page, a device I doubt if is (sic) used on almost any other page in America which claims for itself high ideals."[36]

With the *Oregon Journal*, there was never a large comfort zone; the Neubergers believed that *Journal* political writers, in particular Ralph Watson and Larry Smythe, actively worked against Neuberger. In a 1948 letter to Donald J. Sterling, *Journal* managing editor, Neuberger claimed there was a *Journal* policy "to mention me in print only 'when absolutely necessary,' and not favorably if possible." He claimed he had confirmed the policy with *Journal* reporters. Neuberger threatened to write an article for a journalism magazine, entitled, "I am on a newspaper's black list." The article was never written, or at least never printed, but relations were strained with the *Journal*.[37]

With Sprague, Neuberger's relationship was more complex. For nearly twenty years, the two men had talked freely about politics, and had shared the burden in several battles for civil liberties or civil rights. Neuberger had been an overnight guest of the Spragues in the thirties, and the Neubergers were acquainted with the Sprague children as well as the elder Spragues. Neuberger had profiled Sprague twice, for *The Oregonian* and for *The Nation*, both in flattering terms. Neuberger was not above flattery and Sprague, despite his seeming diffidence, was not without ego; but Neuberger had a deep and genuine admiration for the older man.[38]

Neuberger never complained about Sprague's treatment of him personally, but he did entreat him to break from his pattern of backing Republicans, and endorse candidates more in line with his views on issues. Writing between Democratic defeat in 1952 and victories in 1954, he implored Sprague:

> *I am quite discouraged to think that a person of your views can support Republicans like Cordon, Ellsworth, etc. It seems to me that partisanship should not erase issues, which lie at the root of political decisions. Your attitude on international affairs—and on most domestic questions—is so divergent from these men that your backing of them cannot really make sense. Perhaps I am wrong. You know that I yield to no one in my respect for your sincerity and honesty, and thus I know you will understand this letter. . . .*
>
> *You and I have been friends for a long time, and I believe you will give me your honest views on the situation. Have we reached the stage in Oregon where it is impossible for a Democrat to win a major policy-making office?*[39]

Neuberger talked to Sprague before entering the campaign against Cordon, and was encouraged to run; among the issues discussed was

Neuberger's Jewish origin. Sprague predicted it would be used against him, but would react in his favor. When the attack came, Sprague immediately rose to Neuberger's defense.[40]

With the newly converted Democrat Wayne Morse campaigning vigorously on his behalf, Neuberger embarked on a barnstorming campaign of personal appearances, a blizzard of press releases and letters to the editor, and made a display of energy that the shy and aging Cordon could not match. Cordon did not even campaign during the primary, and when he arrived in the state in September, he was forced to be on the defensive. Neuberger attacked Republican "giveaways" of natural resources, including timber sales, tidelands oil leases, and a private power company's plan for dams in Hells Canyon. Cordon, never a strong campaigner and a stranger to the news media, was perhaps less known in his home state than any senator. The party desperately called in Republican big-leaguers, but this tactic didn't always redound to Cordon's benefit, as when Speaker Joe Martin referred to "my friend, Si Gordon."[41]

Sprague reluctantly supported Cordon; the U.S. Senate was on a razor-edge of control, and his endorsement was one of party control. He liked Neuberger and supported him on many issues, but he didn't want the Senate in Democratic hands. His editorial assessments of the two candidates made it very clear that his was a vote on party, not personal, grounds. Before declaring his stand, he had helped Neuberger's cause on two major areas of debate, Hells Canyon and Cordon's failure to join Morse and a handful of Republican liberals in purging Joe McCarthy. Sprague sided with Democrats and against McKay and Eisenhower on the Hells Canyon project, favoring a high federal dam instead of private dams. Bud Forrester, a Neuberger partisan, felt that Sprague's stand on Hells Canyon was critical, because it stripped the issue of some of its partisan overtones.[42]

The race was so close that early newspaper editions had Cordon in the lead. From Pendleton the Neubergers had an early-morning call from Forrester: "Don't give up yet, they haven't counted the votes from Hells Canyon!"[43] The final count gave the new Democratic senator a margin of less than one vote per precinct. In Multnomah County, Edith Green defeated Tom McCall (who had retired Homer Angell in the primary) to wrest the Third Congressional District from Republican hands.

Sprague was personally pleased to have his friend in the Senate, and the two men resumed their relationship immediately, only to have it ended by Neuberger's untimely death in 1960. But Sprague was correct in worrying about the impact of Neuberger's win on the Republican majority in the Senate. With Wayne Morse voting with Democrats to organize the 1955 Senate, Lyndon B. Johnson was elected majority leader by a single vote. Oregon had provided the margin of Democratic control; LBJ awarded Morse with a coveted seat on the Foreign Relations Committee, the podium from which Morse later assaulted Johnson on Vietnam. On February 17, Morse and state Democratic chairman Howard Morgan drove to Eugene, where the senator filed as a Democrat and vowed to take the fight to his former party in 1956.[44]

Republicans were gunning for Morse; for many, it was a personal grudge as well as a matter of political control of the Senate. The designated candidate was Gov. Paul Patterson, a pleasant lawyer from Hillsboro who had assumed the governorship when Gov. Douglas McKay was tapped by Eisenhower to be Secretary of the Interior. Patterson had few enemies, made a good public appearance and enjoyed support across the Republican spectrum. But on January 31, 1956, in the midst of a strategy session in Portland's Arlington Club, he collapsed and died from a heart attack. The situation was reminiscent of 1930 and the death of George W. Joseph; and 1930 repeated itself as the GOP establishment picked a candidate who was not Sprague's choice for the office. In 1956 it was Doug McKay, another product of the Snell organization, pulled into the race just before the filing deadline by the national GOP hierarchy.

Sprague had always supported McKay as he moved through a succession of offices from Salem City Hall to the governorship, but privately he questioned his neighbor's qualifications. He feared McKay was in over his head as Secretary of the Interior, and was not pleased when President Eisenhower pressured the Salemite to run in 1956.

Doug McKay was a common man, and he liked to remind his audiences of that fact. He had become wealthy selling cars at his Salem Chevrolet dealership and had risen to the Eisenhower Cabinet, but he was most comfortable in small-town gatherings with old friends from the Snell organization, telling stories from the Great War and exchanging easy banter and small-talk. Conservative to the bone, he almost worshipped Dwight D. Eisenhower, his wartime commander. (McKay served in both wars.) When Eisenhower drafted him to go to Oregon in 1956 as the party's designee to put Wayne Morse away, McKay obeyed.[45]

Sprague was disappointed. He already had a candidate in the race: Phil Hitchcock, formerly a liberal Republican state senator from Klamath Falls. Hitchcock was now handling public relations for Lewis and Clark College. Sprague complained twice in his column about the White House's intrusion, then dumped on the Party: "We think Hitchcock should stay in the race, both because of his splendid qualifications and to repudiate the notion that Oregon is a province of the GOP GHQ. . . . The *Statesman* feels that the Republican Party should draw on fresh material, especially where there is available a man of Hitchcock's character and ability."[46]

Sprague's reasons for resisting the McKay candidacy were confirmed in the ensuing primary. McKay carried all the baggage of his own decisions as interior secretary, plus those of the Eisenhower Administration. His late entry angered Hitchcock backers, who rallied to give him 99,296 votes to 123,281 for McKay (who finished under 50 percent, as two unknowns picked up an additional 25,991 votes). Although Hitchcock later endorsed McKay, many of his backers stayed away. Democrats nominated a strong statewide slate, and the newly elected Senator Neuberger was on the hustings for Morse.

The gloves were off, in the roughest Senate race since Morse had sent Rufus Holman packing. His face thrust forward as he pushed home a point, Morse went immediately for the jugular, accusing McKay of "give-away" of natural resources and involvement in a reactionary administration. A master of debate and declamation, Morse reached oratorical heights he would not climb again until the Vietnam War. He had, one reporter observed, "an inexhaustible supply of indignation," and plenty of the self-righteous rectitude that increasingly bothered Sprague.[47]

Editorial support favored McKay, with the exception of strong pro-Morse editorials from Medford, Pendleton, and Coos Bay. But the strongest anti-Morse blast came from a very unlikely source, the *Denver Post,* edited by Morse's former confidant, Palmer Hoyt. While editor of *The Oregonian*, Hoyt had himself passed up the 1944 Senate race to support Morse, and he was furious when Morse changed parties. In an editorial presumably written by his editorial page editor, Robert Lucas, once of the *Astorian-Budget*, Hoyt's *Post* peeled the hide from Morse. Titled "The Apostasy of Senator Wayne Morse," the editorial described him as "the one senator who has deliberately treated two-party government with contempt." The P*ost* charged that "The tragedy of Wayne Morse is the witless corruption of his own great intelligence and the embrace of cynical political behavior to serve his own ends, rather than those of the people—Republicans and Democrats—whom he represents."[48] The *Statesman* was one of several Oregon papers reprinting the editorial; Hoyt and Lucas were respected by Oregon editors, and their scathing attack served well to punish the maverick.

Sprague in his own editorials and columns was not as harsh, but by reprinting the *Post* editorial he bought into the charges. He backed McKay, but it was not a focus of his fall editorial page; he devoted considerably less energy to McKay's race than he had invested in Phil Hitchcock's losing primary battle.[49]

The Republican rout was complete with Democrat Robert D. Holmes elected governor, and Charles O. Porter and Al Ullman joining Edith

Green in Congress. Sprague lost more than his candidates; he lost one of his strongest reporters when Tom Wright joined Holmes as press secretary. Both Wrights had become increasingly active in Democratic circles, Marguerite changing her registration from Republican at the time of Morse's party switch.

Writing in the election aftermath, Sprague observed: "Oregon has become a two-party state. This will mean that political interest will become more acute, party rivalry more intense. Whether that will mean better government for Oregon remains to be seen."[50] He shed no tears for McKay, and did not irrevocably split with Morse, although their relationship entered a new phase.

Replying to a Sprague congratulatory note, Morse admitted that "your opposition to me in the campaign saddened me very much . . . I was hurt by some of the things you wrote." He invited Sprague to visit him in Washington, adding: "I would like to think that the personal friendship that once existed between us is not beyond revival."[51] It was not beyond revival, but it never flourished again; conciliatory messages were exchanged when Morse was named to the United Nations delegation in 1960, and occasionally after that, but other circumstances intruded into the relationship in the late fifties and made the renewal of old bonds difficult.

The man elected governor in the Democratic tide was no stranger to Sprague. As a young newcomer to Astoria in 1942, Bob Holmes had chaired Sprague's re-election campaign in Clatsop County, and Sprague held him in high personal regard. Holmes defeated Republican Elmo Smith, a newspaper publisher and president of the Senate, who had succeeded to the office in January upon the death of Paul Patterson. Accordingly, Holmes won only two years; he would have to run again in 1958.

Sprague must have empathized with Holmes, for his situation with newly elected Secretary of State Mark Hatfield was much like Sprague's with Earl Snell. Every time the Board of Control or Land Board met, there was the personable challenger, exploiting a very visible but noncontroversial office. Hatfield was no Snell; he was much deeper intellectually, a better public speaker, more liberal in his views, and he was not an "old boy" in the Snell fashion. But he had a nose for publicity, and his handsome face seemed to be everywhere. Mark Hatfield had about him in 1958 the same air of inevitability that Earl Snell had had in 1942.

The beleaguered Holmes had his hands full from the very beginning; decades of Republicans in the office had built up a solidly Republican civil service, and he ran into Hatfield around every corner. There were so few highly visible Democrats in Oregon, even in 1956, that at times filling positions was difficult. Inevitably, every Republican displaced for a Democrat brought the charge of "spoils." Although Democrats held a strong majority in the House, the Senate was ruled for the first time by a coalition of fifteen Republicans and two Democrats, a pattern that continued well into the Seventies.

Sprague supported most of Holmes's program, and was pleased that Holmes was able to pass some of the school reorganization Sprague had begun in 1941. Sprague liked Holmes personally, and the governor sought out Sprague for advice, recalled Tom Wright.[52]

Blocking Holmes's path to a full term were his Board of Control colleagues; in early 1958 Hatfield, State Treasurer Sig Unander, and state Senator Warren Gill of Lebanon began efforts in the Republican primary. It was a campaign particularly devoid of major issues, and the more it centered on personality the more inevitable Hatfield's victory became; he carried the field with 50 percent of the GOP vote while Holmes was besting two weaker opponents. Sprague termed the Republican contest "mostly a personality race," adding: "Hatfield, young and glamorous, outpaced the more reserved but well equipped Unander. Hatfield's nomination appears to confirm the conclusions of the legislative junta that pushed him into the race on the ground that he would make a candidate with more voter appeal."[53]

Rivals for the governorship in 1958, Mark Hatfield (center) and Robert Holmes looked to Sprague for his endorsement, but until the final week of the campaign the former governor was "on the bleachers." Sprague came off the bleachers when Sen. Wayne Morse unleashed a personal attack on Hatfield. This photograph was taken in 1960 as Sprague and Holmes served as co-chairs of an executive reorganization commission appointed by Hatfield (Statesman-Journal files).

Sprague had committed early and strongly for Unander, agreeing to serve as state chairman for his former assistant; his endorsement was in the minority. Unander had served in a variety of party offices while Hatfield was building a personal organization largely independent of the party. The treasurer had a resumé that would appear to qualify him for office, as Sprague observed in his endorsement.[54] But Unander lacked any sense of the personal touch—a wealthy man, he campaigned in a Bentley automobile—and Sprague's high assessment of his skills was not shared by many others. Among political reporters he had a reputation as a man who was both cheap and inept; Paul Harvey recalled Unander reading *The Oregonian* in the Capitol press room to avoid paying for a subscription, and other tales abounded. Probably no person outside his own family elicited as much personal loyalty from Sprague, who again backed him against Wayne Morse in 1962, and when Unander was dying in the state mental hospital Sprague was a frequent visitor.[55]

Hatfield was closer to Sprague's political views than was Unander, but had never developed a personal relationship with Sprague. As a college student at Willamette, Hatfield had worked part-time in the office of Secretary of State Earl Snell, and learned from the master the art of creating a statewide image through use of the office. Hatfield campaigned for Snell against Sprague in 1942, then as a Navy officer was one of the first Americans to enter Hiroshima after the atomic blast. It had a great impact on the young man, and was an element in what became a lifelong commitment to the cause of international peace. Hatfield's staunch anti-Vietnam War position in the sixties was rooted in his experience among the Japanese survivors of World War II.[56]

While at Stanford University getting his Master's degree in political science, Hatfield formed a close relationship with Travis Cross, the high school reporter and athlete who had haunted the *Statesman* sports department in the early forties, serving what amounted to an apprenticeship under Al Lightner and acquiring a lifetime admiration of Sprague. Cross became Hatfield's image man, working closely with the media and serving as his co-strategist.

Because of his youth (he was 28 when elected to the House) and his academic career, Hatfield was viewed with some suspicion among Republican old-timers, and immediately branded a "liberal." He recalled being forced in his first campaign to defend himself in rural areas because he required students in his political science classes to read Marx and Lenin. A Willamette student riding a bus was spotted by one of the county's rural residents reading a copy of "Red literature" and, when queried, he replied that it was for Professor Hatfield's class.

"There went the rumor that I was a commie—one of those pink professors—and I spent a great deal of time in that '50 campaign denying that I was a communist or a communist sympathizer," Hatfield recalled. "As a consequence, I got the sort of reaction that 'I'm not afraid to take an oath' . . . I sort of had that kind of background," he added, explaining how he came to be a co-sponsor of the teachers' loyalty oath Sprague had been so instrumental in killing in 1951. "I suppose he was kind of disappointed that I was on that side," Hatfield said of Sprague's attempts to lobby him against the oath.[57] More probable is that Sprague chalked the stand up to Hatfield's youth and his obvious political ambition.

Sprague was nearly two generations older than Hatfield and, Hatfield said, "He wasn't one of the people you felt a warm relationship with, because he just wasn't that sort, but you had this deep, abiding respect for him." Hatfield, a student of the life of Herbert Hoover, compared Sprague to Hoover in his mannerisms—shy, reticent, making personal contacts only with difficulty, and avoiding eye contact.[58]

As Hatfield made his way quickly through the Legislature, drawing increasingly heavy votes in conservative Marion County, Sprague supported his candidacy; and when Hatfield ran for secretary of state in 1956, Sprague "cordially" recommended him.

The Hatfield gubernatorial campaign was a virtuoso performance, with Travis Cross wielding the baton; the centerpiece was an elaborate wedding in July. Hatfield was Oregon's most visible bachelor until his highly publicized marriage that summer to Antoinette Kuzmanich, a striking college counselor from Portland. Some 1,200 attended the ceremony, and the *Statesman* played it with a front-page article and photograph.[59]

Hatfield went into the fall race as odds-on favorite. But both campaigns were hoping for key editorial endorsements, the most important being Sprague's personal backing and *The Oregonian*. The latter took its usual Republican position, but Sprague agonized and finally told his readers he would "hold to a seat in the bleachers" in this campaign.[60]

Sprague had endorsed Holmes in the Democratic primary, which was no surprise since Holmes faced two aging right-wingers. But the Holmes camp, which included the Wrights, whom Sprague respected and who also knew that he regarded Hatfield as something of an upstart, dared to hope for an endorsement in the fall as well. As a former governor, Sprague identified with the problems Holmes faced, particularly the personality challenge. But Holmes was a Democrat, and in Hatfield the Republicans clearly had a rising star. Sprague's "in the bleachers" editorial ranked as a win for Holmes; it was laced with praise for the governor, and clearly stopped short of endorsement only because of party affiliation. Hatfield, noted Sprague, "needs seasoning."[61]

Sprague's editorial appeared on October 30, a small ray of good news for a campaign that knew it was trailing and didn't know how to gain the initiative. Issues had been negligible, sometimes downright silly, and it was apparent that Hatfield's clean-cut image was prevailing. Polls had been taken, and both sides knew Hatfield was comfortably ahead as campaigners readied for the final week.

The week was dominated by a single event: on October 31, in a Medford speech, Senator Wayne L. Morse unleashed a savage personal attack on Hatfield, bringing up a 1940 accident in which the 17-year-old Hatfield had been driving a car that struck and killed a 7-year-old girl near Salem. Hatfield had never been charged, but his family ultimately paid a $5,000 civil judgment. Morse said that the civil case, which revolved around Hatfield's description of the accident, showed that Hatfield "cannot be believed under oath as a witness."[62]

The attack backfired on Morse—and by implication on Holmes—and it immediately brought Sprague off the bleachers. He walked into the secretary of state's office obviously agitated, Hatfield later recalled, describing Morse's attack as "the most unconscionable attack I have witnessed in public life." Hatfield described the encounter as "the warmest personal experience I ever had with the man."[63]

It was Morse who drew Sprague's wrath, but he observed that "some of Holmes' over-zealous supporters must have put the material in his hands."[64] Other editors rushed to their typewriters with similar disgust, although Sprague appears to have been the only editor who actually changed position because of the attack; Holmes maintained the endorsements of the Medford *Mail Tribune*, the *East Oregonian* and *Coos Bay Times*. The others were already in Hatfield's camp, the Morse bomb serving only to intensify their support. Students at Willamette and Oregon State hung Morse in effigy, and the Salem Chamber of Commerce canceled a Morse speech scheduled for the day before election. Feelings were running at fever pitch.[65]

The major loser in the case was Morse. Holmes had already lost the race, and Hatfield suffered no ill will as a result. For many editors, including Sprague, the sudden blow strengthened their feeling that Morse was a man dangerously out of control on a personal level.

The 1940 accident was a matter of public record; the $5,000 judgment had been appealed to the Oregon Supreme Court and it was known to Hatfield's advisers (Travis Cross had a response statement locked in his desk for the day when someone would raise the issue) and to his political foes. One report of the affair has Holmes aide Harry Hogan giving the material to Morse aide Charlie Brooks, with the admonition that the Holmes campaign had decided against using the material. Morse advocates take a different view; Ken Johnson, who worked for Morse in a later campaign, said the senator insisted in conversation that Holmes was aware of his (Morse's) plans and he would not have carried them out without the approval of Holmes. Morse biographer Mason Drukman is uncertain, but places ultimate responsibility on the senator. Neither Wright knew of the Morse statement before it was made. The polls were bad, Tom Wright recalled, and "Someone thought they could turn it around. Whether Holmes okayed, I could never be sure; there were people who said yes, and people who said no."[66]

Sprague laid the majority of the blame at Morse's feet; he had been increasingly upset about Morse's personal attacks on opponents, and he remembered the 1952 incident in which Hatfield took the seat Morse wanted at the Republican National Convention. Morse had reason to retaliate, Sprague reasoned, and he did.

Morse's attack added to Hatfield's margin of victory, most observers agreed, and furthered Morse's image as a live grenade that could go off at any time. Universally, Oregon Democrats piled on the senator, who took public responsibility for the statement. The chasm that was developing between Morse and Dick Neuberger was widened by the incident. By 1958 the two men were communicating by letter and leaked press reports; their split was a tragic irony, for they were two of most promising men ever elected to office in the state.[67]

A year later, after Morse announced that he would campaign against Neuberger in 1960, the junior senator was diagnosed with cancer. Dick Neuberger suddenly died of a cerebral hemorrhage on March 9, 1960, barely two months before the Democratic primary. Governor Hatfield appointed a conservative Democrat, Supreme Court Justice Hall Lusk, to fill the remainder of the term. In the ensuing campaign, Neuberger's widow recaptured the seat, with Sprague abandoning his party to endorse Maurine over Republican Elmo Smith.[68]

The decade had witnessed a major change in Oregon's political landscape: the state had become a genuine two-party state; its senior senator had switched political parties and won re-election under the new affiliation; one of the men who fought hardest for a liberal Democratic Party was cut down in his prime; and the Republican Party had a new leader capable of national prominence. As the script unfolded, Sprague softened his party-line affiliation and no longer saw the *Statesman* as strictly a Republican organ, although candidates of that party always had an advantage on his page.

The change of editorial label had many causes, not the least of which was Oregon's changing political climate; suddenly the other party had candidates attractive to a progressive editor. Sprague's service at the

United Nations, where he worked closely with national Democrats, including Dean Acheson and Eleanor Roosevelt, helped to moderate his views. And the looming ascendancy of the Republican right, beginning with the Taft wing's influence over President Eisenhower and the rise of Richard Nixon, was of increasing concern to an editor who had endorsed Wendell Willkie and Earl Warren.

The decade saw the *Statesman* news side beginning to play a role equal to that of the editorial page, as Sprague finally realized his hopes of having a full-time political reporter and a correspondent in Washington, D. C. The *Statesman* was moving to the forefront of Oregon dailies, with Wendell Webb's news staff matching Sprague's editorial excellence.

It had long galled Sprague that he could not support a regular desk at the Capitol between legislative sessions. Even during the Depression, both the *Journal* and *Oregonian* had a "Man in Salem" but the *Statesman,* along with every other downstate daily, had to depend on the wire services. In the case of the *Statesman,* it was Associated Press, and from 1936 until his retirement in 1975, AP meant Paul W. Harvey, Jr.

Harvey was a quiet, pleasant journeyman but he was not an aggressive reporter. The Associated Press role was to handle major state stories and make sure the Capitol was staffed in case a big story occurred; it was not to do investigative reporting. For that, Harvey had neither time nor inclination.

Legislative sessions after the war meant detaching someone to cover the session, with others filling his regular duties. Wendell Webb covered the 1947 and 1949 sessions himself; others included Les Cour and Bob Gangware. But as soon as the final gavel dropped, the *Statesman* returned coverage of state politics and government to the AP or reporters assigned to individual stories by the city desk. With the Capitol only three blocks away and much of the *Statesman* readership directly or indirectly involved in state government, it was not an acceptable situation, and as long as it existed the *Statesman* could not really call itself a complete daily newspaper.

Sprague would probably have made the investment in 1957, but for Tom Wright's acceptance of a job with Governor Holmes. Wright had begun to cover politics in the 1956 election, and it soon became apparent that he had a strong sense for the job, and the aggressiveness that some others lacked.

When Governor Holmes lost in November 1958, Wright was without a job, and he began the process of making inquiries. As spokesman for a liberal Democrat, and as a Democrat himself, he would have faced some closed doors at Oregon's Republican dailies, and he wasn't sure what reception he would receive at his old newspaper. He had not applied at the *Statesman* when he was asked to meet with Sprague, Webb, and Gangware. It was Sprague who called the tune, Wright recalled, "He went at it head-on and there were a lot of people dismayed at that move, including Wendell and Gangware and some of the people at the paper, who thought that, gee-whiz, here was a guy who had left here and he was welcomed back with a better job than he left."[69]

From the very beginning, both Sprague's assessment of Wright's abilities and Webb, and Gangware's concerns about his liabilities proved true. Wright was a seasoned reporter, the most versatile in the newsroom; he had worked both city and news desks, most of the beats and was a good photographer as well. And he had a talent for cultivating sources. His work with Holmes had given him insight and contacts in both parties. But his association with Holmes was, from the start, a liability with the newly elected Republican governor. Wright used his contacts to "scoop" several of Hatfield's major appointments; the new governor went so far as to have his office checked for "bugs."[70]

Wright's ability to almost daily beat the *Capital-Journal* on State stories was grist for *Statesman* morale, and the newsroom at the end of the decade had a palpable feel of confidence. Wes Sullivan spent the 1957-58 year at Harvard on a prestigious Nieman Fellowship, the paper's first. The *Statesman* news crew was much younger than the C-J staff, and was pulling away in circulation. "We were the gung-ho outfit, we were young and had a helluva esprit-de-corps," remarked Conrad Prange, whose "Comes the Dawn" humor column was another reason for the paper's popularity. "We had just a great time, and basically I think it was that you were shooting for something other than just your own paper—if you could scoop the *Journal*." Despite the merger, or perhaps because of it, the juice of competition flowed, and was shared by both the veterans and the younger reporters.[71]

Prange's lively column was matched photographically in the late fifties when John Ericksen, a young Salem native, became the staff photographer, replacing Don Dill. Ericksen had a wonderful eye for human-interest shots, and Webb soon initiated a "Brighter Side" photo, daily on page one. The Prange and Ericksen features helped lighten the normal diet of tragedies and disasters that are a staple of morning newspapers. Sprague finally had the sort of human-interest commentary that had plagued him for so long from the C-J's "Sips for Supper." Prange never engaged in the nasty little digs that Upjohn had used to taunt Sprague, however; his forté was dry humor and puns that he wove into stories he heard as he went about the city.

Wes Sullivan won a coveted Nieman Fellowship at Harvard University and spent the 1957-58 academic year at Cambridge. Sprague spoke to Niemans that year, and is pictured with John Armstrong of The Oregonian, also a Nieman; Sullivan, and Nieman Curator Louis Lyons (*Statesman-Journal* photo files).

Many of the *Statesman* staff were active in the community; Prange worked for the Catholic Church and its charities, while Gangware, Wright, and Sullivan were all active in First Presbyterian Church. Gangware also was involved in the YMCA and Chamber of Commerce and Sullivan in school governance, and Wright was an Army Reserve officer.

It was a style of journalism Sprague had practiced from his days in Ritzville—personal, close to the community's established powers, interested in and defensive of community progress—and he gave his staff free rein in outside activities. Sprague simply did not see the journalist's day ending when he or she walked out of the newsroom door; journalism was a calling, whether that meant writing travel columns every time he left home or getting inside information from the locker rooms, as Al Lightner did. By 1958, when the full-time Capitol bureau was initiated, many of the next generation were in place; Sprague was building one of the strongest news staffs in the region.[72]

Although the staff had doubled in size since the end of the war, it remained closely knit. The poker parties continued, and in 1959 the newsroom turned out to frame Prange's river cabin on the Little North Fork of the North Santiam, half a dozen miles upstream from Sprague's much grander structure. The volunteers were adequately recompensed for their labor, so much so that when their lone measuring tape was lost they turned to measuring by length of a beer can; keen-eyed visitors later observed that the river wall of the cabin appeared slightly out at the top, which it still is, by the length of one beer can!

During the Columbus Day Storm of 1962, when a hurricane-force wind blew down much of western Oregon, snapped power lines, and toppled trees across roads, the *Statesman* lost power, and the lead pots of the linotype machines went cold. When minimum power had been restored to the print shop, the newsroom operated primarily by flashlight and candlelight, and reporters and photographers made their way gingerly across fallen lines and around trees to produce a newspaper only slightly past its normal deadline. Wet and exhausted, several of them then spent the early morning hours securing emergency plastic tarps to Prange's roof, which had been peeled bare by the gale. It was this combination of professional and personal commitment that marked the paper in this decade.

Sprague was not intimately involved in the newsroom at this point; but when he passed through to give his editorials and columns to the news desk, he would talk to reporters, stop to ask Lightner about his latest officiating escapades, or discuss farm prices with Lillie Madsen. He was seen less often now at *Statesman* parties, where in earlier days he would put in an appearance, declining a drink ("I'll take the Tom but not the Jerry," was his favorite rejoinder) and chatting with employees and spouses. Sprague occasionally supplied news leads, almost always funneled through Webb or Gangware, but the newsroom usually was quite independent from the publisher's office. There were exceptions.

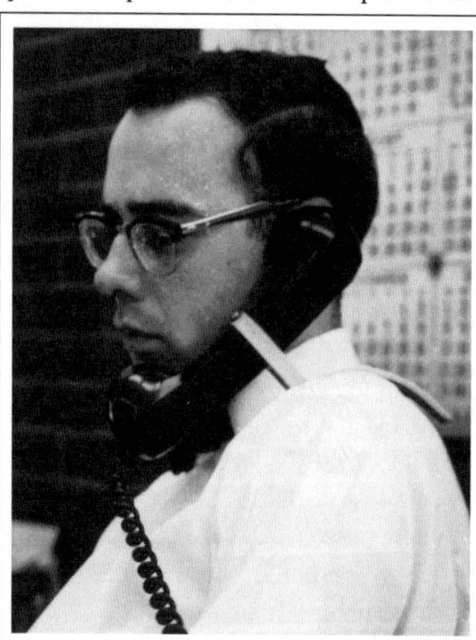

The Statesman's second Nieman fellowship was awarded in 1967-68 to the author, shown here in the Statesman news room (Tom Wright).

Reporter Ken Johnson, seeking to move up from Coos Bay in the early fifties, thought he had been hired by Webb, and was ushered into Sprague's office for a routine introduction. Sprague, who read all the downstate papers, recognized Johnson as the author of an editorial that had castigated Salem's Republican establishment. The dumbfounded Johnson walked out of the office without a job.[73]

Sprague had a reporter's interest in breaking news, and he delighted in beating the competition. "Kick over some outhouses!" he once told a group of reporters. Increasingly, reporters were given time and even travel funds to produce more in-depth articles, and with a single exception the veterans recall no attempt by the publisher to intervene or suggest the slant of a story.

The exception came in the early fifties when Marguerite Wright encountered sources who suggested that a well-placed official of the state training school for girls had some unusual contacts in Portland, and that girls discharged from the school may have been channeled into prostitution. It would have been a very big story, and very embarrassing to the Republican-controlled Board of Control, which supervised the school. Webb wanted to pursue the story, but Sprague ordered it shelved until Wright could present her evidence to the Republicans on the Board, Governor McKay and Secretary of State Earl Newbry. (Treasurer Walter Pearson, a Democrat, did not attend the meeting.) The implicated official resigned shortly thereafter. Whether there was enough solid evidence to run the piece was never determined; Sprague cut it off, for reasons of his own. He may have been unsure of Wright's evidence, he may have wished to avoid embarrassment for the agency and those involved, or he may simply have played partisan politics, protecting Republican office-holders from a scandal.[74]

Sprague took pride in *Statesman* exploits, praising the alertness of reporter Allan (Bud) Morrison, who in 1961 spotted a holdup suspect drinking at the Stagecoach Lounge, where Morrison had repaired after deadline. Morrison's tip resulted in an arrest and confession, and a remarkable set of photos in which the gunman actually posed for the *Statesman* wearing the silk-stocking mask he had used in the holdup. It was, said Sprague, simply an example of *Statesman* reporters going beyond their normal duties. (He conveniently forgot that the story had resulted from Morrison's late-night tippling.)[75]

Sprague was also pleased with the work of his two political reporters, Tom Wright at the Capitol and A. Robert Smith in Washington. The addition of Wright's aggressive Capitol reports and Smith's perceptive national columns put the *Statesman* into a new category, one previously monopolized by the Portland dailies. Wright's and Smith's analyses added to Sprague's columns to give the *Statesman* Oregon's best political coverage in this period. While this paid off in circulation growth and professional prestige, it also ruffled more than a few of the politicians whose exploits were being exposed to more rigorous examination than had been the case in past years. Ultimately, both Smith and Wright came under fire from Mark Hatfield and Wayne Morse, as articles and columns revealed the warts as well as the polished images of the governor and senator.

Smith was a soft-spoken and courtly Southerner who was a scholar of Congress and its ways, and a firm supporter of liberal causes. He began writing for newspapers in Washington state, then expanded his column into Oregon in 1951, first with the *Register-Guard* and *The Oregonian* and the *Statesman*. He later picked up papers in Pendleton, Astoria, Bend and Medford.[76]

Smith was fascinated by the characters Oregon sent to Congress, in particular Senators Morse and Neuberger; when the two broke their alliance and engaged in a series of ever-more-caustic exchanges, Smith was in the middle. Meetings of the Oregon Democratic delegation grew more confrontational, and Smith picked up reports, often from Rep. Charles O. Porter. ("He just couldn't quit talking," Smith recalled.) Morse was irate at the leaks, and tried to determine their origin; Neuberger egged Smith on and slipped him copies of the explosive correspondence. "I loved every minute of it," Smith chuckled later. "It was a helluva story, and Washington reporters live on leaks." In August 1957 Smith's column ripped open the bitter feud and the battle became frequent copy for Smith and others covering the Oregon delegation.[77]

Relations between Smith and Morse ranged over the years from close personal association to outright banishment of the reporter during Morse's period as a self-declared Independent. Smith and Roulhac Hamilton, correspondent for the *Oregon Journal,* were summarily barred from the senator's office because of a disagreement over what Morse had said to the reporters prior to the 1952 Republican National Convention. Bill Tugman in Eugene had used the comments in a prominently displayed story outlining Morse's inconsistencies. Morse lashed back in a Eugene speech, attacking Tugman, the *Guard*, and the two correspondents. The ban lasted until 1955, when the correspondents were once more returned to grace.[78]

Sprague and Tugman took differing approaches to the problem of having their man in Washington cut off by the senior senator. Tugman flared angrily, in a series of emotional editorials attacking Morse on a variety of topics.[79] Sprague's response was predictably less emotional, but he was insistent in his support of Smith. Sprague scolded Morse about his temper, and urged him to reconcile with Smith. During the furor, Morse sent lengthy rebuttals to the *Statesman* and other Smith-served newspapers, and in turn Smith responded to the Morse assertions. Morse suggested that they might "resolve our differences over your Washington correspondent," then went on to solicit Sprague's advice on U.S. policy in Asia, adding, "I feel your writings on American policy in Asia have been very objective."[80]

The reconciliation did not come immediately. Sprague returned to the subject in December, urging resumption on "strictly a professional basis," and adding: "It is both unfair to you and your constituents who are readers of these newspapers not to have Smith enjoy the usual privilege of formal and informal access to you in the course of your public duties." Morse rejected the entreaty, and dictated a four-page memo to his files, detailing his version of the split with Smith. But a few months later the ban was lifted.[81]

In the case of Tom Wright, nothing as dramatic or public took place, and no formal complaint was ever lodged by the Hatfield organization. Wright's probing reporting was complicated by his decision in 1961 to take a part-time job as executive secretary for a legislative interim committee examining the touchy subject of state lands, which were supervised by the all-Republican State Land Board, made up of the top three Constitutional officers. There was precedence for a journalist to attempt this apparent conflict in jobs: Tom McCall had directed the 1957 legislative study of Oregon Native Americans. But it put Wright in an exposed position, and when the interim committee criticized Land Board policies, not only did the Board respond, but Sprague penned a mild rebuttal to the report.[82]

The Hatfield team's dislike of Wright, which extended to Marguerite Wright, who had worked on the Holmes campaign and was deeply involved in Democratic politics, was beginning to be felt at the *Statesman*. Wright himself believed the pressure came from Howell Appling Jr., a tough Texan who had been appointed secretary of state by Hatfield, and from Gerry Frank, whose store was the paper's largest advertiser. But nothing was said directly to Wright. From the beginning, both Wendell Webb and City Editor Bob Gangware were uneasy with Wright at the Capitol because of his known Democratic sympathies and his work on the Holmes staff; it was Sprague who had urged that Wright be assigned to the political beat. And in the end, it was Sprague who took him off the beat. "I just knew my position with the *Statesman* was becoming untenable, and I made offers to Wendell that if it was that bad I would just go, and he said Sprague didn't want it that way," Wright recalled. Finally, in mid-1962, he was told by Webb that he would be reassigned to another reporting beat. Wright chose to accept the new assignment, although he had been looking at other job options. He took on the important task of expanding *Statesman* coverage into the Willamette Valley, a job that had languished under Mervin Jenkins.[83] Advertisers were pressing for more readers in outlying counties, and Wright brought to the task the skills of a photographer as well as those of a fine reporter. *Statesman* circulation growth in the sixties owed a great deal to his cultivation of a presence in Linn, Benton, and Yamhill counties, building on the traditional Marion-Polk base.

Sprague had chosen wisely in selecting Wright and Smith for his expansion into serious political reporting. Although both men were to Sprague's left on most matters, they were solid reporters and certainly not radical in their views. With most sources they were respected and trusted, despite their problems with the governor and senator.

Sprague's role in dealing with the men and their adversaries revealed both his independence and his caution. In both cases, he stood behind his reporters in public and, in Smith's case, in private correspondence with Morse. Within the *Statesman* management circle, Sprague's role is less praiseworthy. He had selected Wright, and also given him approval to take the interim committee job in 1961; he clearly had the final vote on whether to retain him at the Capitol in 1962. How he cast it suggests not so much disagreement with Wright's reporting, which escaped serious criticism, or even concern over Hatfield's opposition, for he was not close to the governor. Rather, it reflects Sprague's caution, and his reluctance to be drawn into a personal conflict. He disliked personal confrontations, and he was getting pressure from the Salem establishment. Without confronting Wright, he cast his ballot with Webb and Gangware.

The decision was painful for all concerned, but it was a pain of growth, and the *Statesman* had made an irreversible decision to staff the state government on a professional basis. With that decision, and with the subsequent expansion into the Valley, the struggling daily of 1929 had become a sophisticated publication that had to be taken seriously for more than Sprague's editorial page.

The growth of the *Statesman* was most spectacular in the period from 1950 to 1969, when circulation grew 111 percent, the fastest growth of any major Oregon daily. From a struggling newspaper holding a poor second in its market, Sprague took the *Statesman* in forty years to the top echelon of Oregon's dailies. In 1969, only the *Register-Guard* among the downstate papers had a larger circulation.[84]

In 1959, printing unions struck *The Oregonian* and the *Journal*, and the publishers set out on a long and costly effort to break the unions. Ultimately that was accomplished, but the strife took a fearsome toll in the newsrooms. Pulitzer Prize winners (1956) Wallace Turner and Bill Lambert were only the most visible of many who left the papers. New talent was discouraged by picket lines and peer pressure. The *Journal* never recovered; purchased by S. I. Newhouse, who also owned *The Oregonian*, the *Journal* was finally put to rest in 1982.[85]

Even before the strike, the Portland papers had been stagnant compared to their downstate counterparts. *Statesman* growth came from expansion into the Valley, but it also came at the expense of *The Oregonian*, the quality and reputation of which had been weakened by the bitter and long-lasting strike. With the addition of more vigorous political coverage, increased photos and features, the *Statesman* was finally a complete newspaper; Salem-area readers could get along without *The Oregonian*, and increasingly many did.

With his news department reaching new levels of competence, Sprague was free to turn his energies to the community. He found outlets for his interest in state government through appointments to three major commissions. As the sixties progressed, he was also thrown increasingly into issues of social and generational conflict. He climbed his last mountain at age 70, but his professional and intellectual striving continued as he moved toward his eighth decade.

10

◆◆◆

An Aging Progressive in a Time of Change

Charles A. Sprague was conservative in the way he approached finances and the basic social structure, but not in the manner of the Republican right, nor in the manner of Democrats like Charles H. Martin and George Putnam. His views were in the mold of Theodore Roosevelt rather than of Eisenhower and Nixon. Sprague had found his niche early in the Progressive Era, and in his lifetime he retained the basic values of the reformers of that time. Progressives did not abhor government, as did the Republican right. Nor did they support the sale of public lands to private interests, generally favoring public ownership of forests, tidelands, and seashores, and often public utilities.

Sprague's strong belief in government as an instrument for progress rather than an enemy of freedom set him apart from many in his own party as the GOP moved rightward, and he found himself increasingly arguing for its soul. If we accept Richard Hofstadter's view that activism is a key characteristic of progressives, then Sprague fit the mold.[1] While he was forced to abandon some of the social engineering of the Progressive Era—Prohibition being the prime example—he put a progressive forestry agenda into law in Oregon, and the zeal he once poured into combating the evils of liquor he later diverted into a battle against intolerance and racism. He accepted social engineering to fight prejudice and bigotry as he had once accepted it to combat the demon rum.

Progressives approached natural resources with what Samuel P. Hays termed "the gospel of efficiency." They wanted wise use and stewardship of soil, water, and trees, and they were willing to use public funds and management to stop private abuse of the land.[2] Sprague began that effort as governor, and continued as adviser to federal forest policies for the remainder of his life. But in his last decade he moved beyond the efficient-use agenda, as he accepted the growing need for wild spaces, whether on a seashore or in the mountains that he knew so well.

He parted ways with most of his party as well as with the important lumber industry when he supported wilderness preservation; he argued for preserving the Oregon Dunes and against asphalting the beaches to straighten Highway 101. Sprague did not initiate or lead these crusades, but his voice of respectability and reason made it difficult for opponents to brand the ideas "radical," for Charles A. Sprague was not a radical man.

In the fifties Sprague accepted Dwight D. Eisenhower, but without enthusiasm. He never accepted Richard M. Nixon, and although Nixon was the heir apparent in 1960, Sprague recommended in the GOP primary a symbolic write-in for non-candidate Nelson Rockefeller. "This columnist confesses to a long-standing hostility to Nixon because of his campaign methods going as far back as 1950 when he ran for the Senate against Helen Gahagan Douglas," Sprague wrote, while giving the vice president grudging approval for "growth in knowledge and in political understanding."[3]

John F. Kennedy was too young and inexperienced for Sprague, and when Nixon won the GOP nomination he got Sprague's support, but it was tepid at best.[4] As Kennedy took over, Sprague warmed to his programs, and was enthusiastic about the Peace Corps. He wrote a letter of endorsement for the Democratic warrior, Howard Morgan, nominated to the Federal Power Commission. He liked the activism in Washington. And Sprague was becoming deeply concerned about the reactionary forces symbolized by the John Birch Society.

Sprague sounded an early alarm as the John Birch Society emerged from its New England base and moved west. His column warned of red-baiting: "Their charges are the eruptions of ignorance and prejudice which appeal only to the gullible." Oregon's home-grown branch was a one-man show: Walter Huss, a fundamentalist minister who sought throughout the sixties and seventies to attain power within the Republican Party. Of Huss, Sprague wrote: "There is no need for self-appointed saviors to take over from the FBI, the intelligence services and local and state police," in the hunt for subversion. Sprague did not see a long-range threat in the Birchers, and certainly not in the zealous but single-minded Huss. He predicted the Birchers would ultimately burn themselves out because of their own excesses.[5] His concern was that extremists would poison the Republican Party; the situation recalled his opposition to Joe McCarthy in the previous decade.

Sprague's concern deepened when the 1964 Republican National Convention in San Francisco engaged in its bitter denunciation of Rockefeller and the press. Rockefeller had campaigned in Oregon accompanied by his new and very pregnant wife, Happy; they were confronted by conservatives affronted by Rocky's divorce and remarriage. When Goldwater declared Rockefeller's Oregon primary win a victory for the "radical left," Sprague observed that, "Republicans here never stray farther left than center field, even to catch a hot political fly." Turning serious, Sprague voiced his deepening concern that Goldwater had "succumbed to the poison spread zealously by the 'radical right.'"[6]

Sprague praised Mark Hatfield's keynote address in San Francisco, in which Hatfield condemned extremism and emerged as one of the promising young leaders of the Republican center. When the convention adopted Goldwater's platform, Sprague mused that "the way is made easier for dissenters to desert the party ticket." That proved to be the case with Sprague. He supported a Democratic ticket for the White House for the first time that fall, pinning much of his reasoning on foreign affairs, an area in which he found Goldwater simplistic and frightening: "(He is) quite beyond his depth as he discusses foreign relations, engaging in many twists and turns. His supporters include the great company who are almost fatalistic in anticipating a final Armageddon or who have such complete distrust of Communist powers as to want no truce with them."[7]

Sprague was certainly not abandoning the party; below the top line, his ballot was almost solidly Republican. In 1968, faced with the resurgence of Richard M. Nixon, Sprague tried again to promote a Rockefeller candidacy, and when that did not happen he again urged a write-in for Rockefeller. Even after Nixon's nomination was apparent, he joined an effort to keep the Rockefeller candidacy alive in Miami Beach.[8]

Despite the party's decline nationally, Oregon Republicans did well in the sixties, with Hatfield and then Tom McCall dominating the state's headlines and politics, and a Republican majority in the House after 1964. A full generation older than the emerging leaders, Sprague was not an active participant in these campaigns, although he was frequently consulted and his column was required reading.

In his dual role as editor and elder statesman, Sprague served as counselor and also as institutional memory. Forest Amsden, who drove Sprague around the state in 1961-62 when Amsden was executive secretary of the Constitutional Revision Commission and Sprague a member, said that these trips were a seminar in Oregon history.

Amsden noted that Sprague's demeanor in meetings could seem detached or disinterested until he spoke, "usually after everyone else had their say, and then he often made you feel a fool when he stated his opinion and destroyed yours, without malice apparent or intended." Amsden, a newsman who had worked for Sheldon Sackett in Coos Bay and who later went to KGW-TV as news analyst, first noted Sprague's influence early in commission deliberations: "Hans A. Linde and Clarence Barton, the former the most brilliant and the latter the most politically able of the members, had the commission stampeded down some policy path or another on a narrow issue, with everyone speaking in agreement, when Governor Sprague quietly said he did not agree, and briefly stated why, and Linde and Barton lost, 15 to 2. Linde was open-mouthed in astonishment. Barton laughed; he always admired a job well-done, even when it was done to him. After that, commission members tried to assure themselves of Sprague's agreement, disinterest, or silence on major questions before advancing them."[9]

The Constitutional Revision Commission was the second major effort in the sixties to modernize the Oregon governmental structure. Sprague had cochaired the first with Robert D. Holmes, an advisory commission appointed by Governor Hatfield. Sprague and Holmes as cochairs were sometimes in opposition; Holmes wanted a more centralized executive. At times the two ex-governors conducted what amounted to a colloquy for their colleagues, Sprague drawing on his remarkable historical sense, Holmes adding the practical views of one who had most recently occupied the office.[10]

Hatfield accepted most of the group's recommendations, but went beyond it in moving toward a cabinet system. Little came of the work; the 1961 session approved only a relatively weak Department of Commerce, consolidating several regulatory bodies. Reorganization was piecemeal over the next twenty years, with most of the progress coming in the administration of Gov. Tom McCall, who had been a member of Hatfield's advisory committee.

The advisory committee, meeting only six times in six months, was primarily a sounding board for Hatfield. The Constitutional Revision Commission drafted its own product, a total overhaul of the Constitution, and Sprague was much more committed to it than he had been to Hatfield's plan. Sprague wrote the preamble to the new Constitution proposed by the seventeen-member committee. In keeping with his views on constitutional matters, it was almost excruciatingly concise:

> *The people of Oregon ordain this Constitution for their government, and by it guarantee to all persons liberty, dignity and equal rights under the laws of the state. The rights herein enumerated are independent of and supplementary to those guaranteed under the Constitution of the United States.*[11]

Sprague did not believe in cluttering the document with items that should be in the statutes, where they could be amended by the Legislature without a vote of the people. In most cases he prevailed; perhaps his most interesting defeat came in an area that would have generated enormous controversy had it been sent to the voters: gun control.

Sprague had never owned a firearm, and took the view that those who did should have a good reason. He moved to strike from the proposal the words, "The people shall have the right to bear arms for the defense of themselves and the state," which he declared "a relic of a hunting economy, [which reminded him] of the Missouri 'minute-men.'" Expressing suspicion of any paramilitary organization, he said the language was not needed, as it was already in the Federal Constitution.[12] The motion failed on a 9-8 vote, most of the negatives cast by legislators, who doubtless realized the difficulty of selling the item to the ensuing Legislature.

Sprague also failed to maintain election of judges, and the secretary of state and treasurer; in each case he argued for more popular involvement in politics. But the commission submitted the so-called "Missouri Plan" under which judges would be appointed by the governor, and run against their records rather than against opponents; and the governor would be the only statewide elected official.[13]

Sprague's views, expressed in both commissions, again reflect the influence of the progressive movement, tempered by his own experience in office. Sprague felt deeply about encouraging people to be active in politics, and he wanted to retain Oregon's greatest contributions to the progressive effort, the initiative, referendum, and recall. He wanted strong, active government, but with an equally strong citizenry to check political wrongdoing.

The 1963 Legislature named a joint Senate-House committee to consider the proposed revision, and at its initial meeting Sprague was the lead-off witness, discussing the revision for nearly an hour. He urged the Legislature to develop an entire revision rather than sending items piecemeal to the voters.[14]

Sprague followed his personal appearance with columns urging support of the document. It required a two-thirds vote of each chamber to be referred to the voters, and it fell three votes short in the Senate. House passage was due in large measure to the skill of Rep. John Dellenback of Medford; the Senate had no similar committed champion, and by its three-vote margin killed hopes for a revised Constitution.[15] Efforts were revived in 1965, but were overshadowed as legislators turned to more pressing daily issues. Sprague was much more successful in the campaign to design an efficient and attractive Capitol Mall, an effort in which he was deeply involved even before he became governor.

When he worked in the thirties to plan what became the Capitol Mall, Sprague had represented the Salem Chamber of Commerce; later, as governor, he gained approval of the Mall's third building, after the Capitol and library. By the time additional Mall problems emerged, Sprague was on the Capitol Planning Commission, appointed in 1952 to replace his longtime associate, Bob Sawyer. Sprague served on the commission until he declined reappointment in 1965.

Two issues dominated: the plans for a new Supreme Court building (for which Sprague strongly favored a site at the north end of the Mall astride Summer Street, facing the Capitol and closing the formal Mall); and the persistent threat to reduce the size of the Mall. The Supreme Court was not built; some jurists preferred the old building, and other needs presented a higher priority. But Sprague prevailed in several instances when legislators proposed trimming the Mall back from D Street to Union Street, the length of two city blocks. In columns and in personal testimony, he led the effort that retained the D Street boundary.[16]

Sprague and Hatfield were generally shoulder-to-shoulder on the Mall, fighting Salem developers to keep the D Street boundary. In 1955, the Marion County legislative delegation split on the issue, with Senator Hatfield holding out for D Street and Senator Lee Ohmart (a realtor) trying to end the Mall at Union. Sprague "would not budge," Hatfield recalled, and this time they defeated the realtor interests. Later, Hatfield and Holmes outvoted Sig Unander on the Board of Control to purchase property beyond Union, with Sprague's support. "He was really fixed on this," Hatfield noted, crediting Sprague's support in overcoming Salem's powerful realtor faction.[17]

Sprague had a strong commitment to the aesthetics of the Mall, beginning with its use of marble and the concept of the Capitol facing the Supreme Court, and he debated Hatfield when the new Labor and Industries Building was constructed in 1961. Hatfield balked at spending $25,000 for a sculpture or fountain to embellish the exterior of the modern construction. Sprague, terming the building "quite austere," argued for a fountain with sculpture at the approach to the building. Hatfield finally accepted a metal sculpture, and Sprague eventually got his fountain; in his will he left $100,000 for a fountain on the Mall, and it sits opposite the L & I Building today.[18]

In the final decade of his life Sprague concentrated on Oregon government and the state's future. He had always identified forest conservation as the major legacy of his governorship. But in the sixties he began moving beyond sustained yield, which had been the core of the old progressive conservation ethic, to limited support of federal wilderness. Sprague loved the mountains and was a hiker and climber, and after he retired from politics he spent an increasing amount of time at Thetford, the family's comfortable lodge on the Little North Fork. At Thetford Sprague could continue to walk in the woods after he was forced to cut back on hiking and climbing. Thetford was in logging country, but it provided a constant reminder of the need for places set aside from commercial harvest.

Sprague built Thetford in 1947 on property leased for $25 a year from the Bureau of Land Management. For thirty years it was a prized retreat where he would chop wood, swim in the icy stream, and read in the quiet evenings as the crystal-clear river rushed below. At its best the North Fork was bitterly cold, and visitors would shiver as Sprague, clad in bright green shorts, dove from a rock into the icy stream. He led hikes in search of beaver dams and initiated grandchildren into the wonders of forest and stream. Summer visits with his family often began at the comfortable house on 14th Street, but the grandchildren always wanted to head for the Little North Fork as soon as possible.[19]

At the river Sprague could slip on old clothes and boots and hike the logging roads and trails of what was still an undeveloped area. The long rambling walks gave him a chance to muse or, when his grandchildren were about, to educate them on the surrounding flora and fauna. The North Fork was close enough to Salem to entertain (friends Alfred and Lucille Schramm had a nearby cabin), yet the atmosphere was informal and there was no pressure to keep up appearances.

Thetford was a combination of Pietro Belluschi architecture and Blanche's old wood kitchen stove and pre-electricity ice box. The house

By 1960, the Sprague family had grown to include five grandchildren, and the family gathered for a summer vacation at Jackson, Wyoming (Sprague Family Archives).

Nestled under firs and along the rushing Little North Fork of the North Santiam, Thetford Lodge was a favorite retreat for the Spragues, built in 1947 and donated to Willamette University in 1963 (Sprague Family Archives).

was powered for many years by a war-surplus generator, but it had a pump organ, which Lucille Schramm would play. The evening solitude, with the river rushing noisily beneath the deck, was perfect for reading and conversation, as wood he had split himself was piled on a roaring fire.[20]

The term "environmentalist" was new in the sixties, and connoted a more militant side to the old conservation movement. Environmentalists placed more emphasis on preserving natural resources than on using them wisely. Sprague had always been a conservationist, and would not have labeled himself an environmentalist; yet as the decade proceeded he found that he shared positions with the emerging environmental movement.

Sprague was a disciple of the Gifford Pinchot school of forestry; he had always advocated blocking out timberland into large parcels, with ownership either public or private, in order to practice scientific forestry. From 1948 until 1967 he was on the Bureau of Land Management's advisory board for the O & C timber lands. The BLM managed the huge O & C forest in Southern Oregon, which had reverted to the counties after a failed railroad scheme. The timber was among the best in the nation.

In 1948 Sprague supported a program of pooling O & C management units with private ownerships, a controversial idea advanced by Assistant Secretary of Interior C. Gerard Davidson.[21] At first Sprague's concern was almost exclusively efficient use of the forest, but by the mid-fifties he was beginning to be increasingly concerned about the rate of cutting on both public and private land. He testified to a Congressional committee that the O & C cutting should be "stretched out" to avoid a future timber crash, and insisted that decisions be made by federal authorities and not by industry-influenced officials of the eighteen affected counties.[22]

Sprague was not an early supporter of federal wilderness legislation, but he did not join the timber industry in opposition. In 1959, commenting on an early bill by Senator Hubert H. Humphrey, Sprague made the important distinction that the term "multiple use" is not applicable to a commercial forest, where "cropping of timber is a permanent use." In 1960, Sprague rejected a Sierra Club plan for a huge national park along the spine of the Cascades from Diamond Peak to Mt. Jefferson as too ambitious to gain public favor.[23] But the next year, he endorsed a wilderness bill in the Senate. Using material from Friends of the Three Sisters Wilderness, Sprague blasted a memorial introduced in the Oregon Legislature to oppose the federal measure. Noting that most of the land involved already carried some type of wild-area designation, he urged permanent protection; the areas, he said, "ought not to be defiled with the accouterments of civilization." In 1963 Sprague returned to the issue, pressing for permanent protection for areas around Mt. Jefferson, an area familiar to him as a hiker and climber.[24]

The Mt. Jefferson Wilderness began its passage three years later, Sprague urging approval and commending the Sierra Club for its efforts. But he backed away from the club's push to expand the Forest Service's 95,450 acres to 125,000 acres. Although he accurately predicted that in the future Jefferson Park would be over-run with backpackers and might require a permit system, Sprague feared the Sierra Club's zeal would result in a breakdown of the compromise needed to pass a law. In later columns, he expressed concern that the "preservationist" view taken by the Club was displacing "conservationists."[25] Sprague was not in the forefront of environmentalists, but his support helped legitimize the movement, for few men had done as much for Oregon's forests and the forest industry. As with civil liberties, Sprague's involvement made it hard to brand the movement as "radical." And Sprague would be heard.

In his final two years, Sprague joined efforts to preserve Oregon's long stretches of sand against incursions from both public and private exploitation. In both cases he sided with State Treasurer Robert W. Straub, a Democrat whom Sprague had earlier decided was too strident and

A view of Sprague seldom seem by the public—unshaven after a day on a forestry tour (Oregon Historical Society Lot 3-2C).

partisan for his tastes. Robert Straub's vigorous campaign against incumbent State Treasurer Howard Belton in 1964 had rubbed Sprague the wrong way, and Sprague was quick to endorse Tom McCall in the important 1966 gubernatorial contest, the first of two pitting McCall against Straub.[26] Straub, however, proved to be an exceptional treasurer, bringing modern money management to the office and to state pension funds. Sprague brought a legal challenge against Straub's investment of pension funds in common stock; the decision went to Straub, and the Oregon system became one of the most profitable in the nation.

Tom McCall brought to the governorship considerable credits as an environmentalist; his documentary for KGW-TV had alerted Oregonians to the pollution of the Willamette River, and he could be counted upon to back most environmental efforts. In 1966, however, he was caught on the horns of a political dilemma: the State Highway Commission, headed by the powerful political king-maker Glenn Jackson, had decided to straighten the narrow, winding Highway 101 along the Oregon coast, by diving directly from a spectacular headlands at Nestucca Bay onto a long unspoiled spit and then along the beach for several more miles. McCall needed Jackson's support in his bid for the governorship, and he plunged full-bore into support for the beach route.[27]

Straub led an angry protest, and a clutch of supporters staged a well-publicized march along the route. McCall and Straub differed on few other issues of importance, and Straub damned the beach highway for all it was worth—which was quite a bit. The *Statesman* ran a series of articles and Wes Sullivan, who was now writing editorials one day a week, persuaded Sprague that the highway alignment was important. The result was a strong statement of opposition, which concluded: "To send all the highway traffic for generations up and down those valuable miles of shoreline would be to carve a scar of noise, fumes and speed through the heart of one of the most beautiful sections of our beach. The Pacific City route should be reopened for study."[28] The route was changed, the headlands and spit remained pristine, and a state park on Nestucca Spit was named for Straub in 1987.

As the beach highway problem moved toward resolution, a Seaside motel owner threatened to fence off a section of beach that he claimed was his property, despite steady public use for more than a century and a general view that the dry sands belonged to the public. The issue was complex and emotional, and tied the 1967 Legislature in knots, with McCall trying to mediate and a host of others lending advice. Legislation emerged, but no one believed the issue was solved.

Straub then led an effort to place one additional cent a gallon on the state's gasoline tax for four years, dedicating the $30,000,000 proceeds to be used to extinguish private claims along the beaches. The powerful Oregon highway lobby—gasoline wholesalers and retailers, truckers, and the AAA motor association—pitched in against the bill, as did coastal developers. Straub, joined by conservationists and belatedly by McCall, was badly out-spent, but he had support from leading editorial writers and other leaders of public opinion.

Sprague, at first preferring legislative action, so that the issue could be debated in an orderly fashion, became convinced by the antics of the 1967 session that legislators might not be able to solve the problem. He came out for the Straub bill, debunking the highway lobby's fear of "diversion of funds," noting that the gas tax was already used for state parks. In two more appeals for the measure, he contrasted Oregon's open beaches with California, and urged commitment to public use.[29] The beach measure lost, however, forcing the Legislature and McCall back to the issue; a compromise solution was finally reached in 1969.

In all of these issues—beaches, forests, a modern structure and location for state government—Sprague's careful logic and reasoning stood him in good stead, and his reaction was predictably that of an aging yet dedicated progressive. It was possible to be above the fray, to weigh and balance and seek compromise, and the views of the elder statesman carried considerable weight among those who still valued mature wisdom. But there was much in the sixties that did not yield to reason, or caution, as the nation was pitched into a state of turmoil that verged at times on revolution.

As he neared his 80th birthday in 1967, Sprague was portrayed by Portland free-lancer Ralph Friedman as:

About two years before his death, Sprague at work in his Statesman office (Sprague Family Archives).

> *a patrician patriarch, with the mien of a Senator in Ancient Rome who looks beyond Caesar. . . . One somehow expects to find a prairie figure, Lincolnesque in phrase, warmth and anguish, but there is a formal aloofness in the man that keeps the eye cool while the lips bend in smile. The simplicity that filters through the poised austerity is not so much earthiness as disciplined conduct in the face of earth. What emerges to the observer is an enlightened conservative, a civilized man who conceals his heart with his brain, a scholar of respectable cloth who despises barbarians but sees beyond them to the farther edge of man's fate in a sea of endless waves.*

Friedman asked Sprague how he thought people saw his role, and how he himself viewed his role in society:

> *"Oh," he said slowly, "I would say primarily as an editorial writer, as an observer of the passing scene.*
>
> *"Perhaps I might see myself more in the role of a moralist, such as Dr. Samuel Johnson." And laughter cascaded out of him.*
>
> *But don't you think, I said, that people tend to regard Governor Sprague as an elder statesman and as a voice of calm reason?*

"That may be," he agreed cordially, "because I'm not inclined to blow a fuse and age always seems to invest a person with a certain aura of authority, and now that I'm the oldest living ex-governor, I suppose it attaches to me, the title of elder statesman."

Do you like that title?

"No, because I try to keep myself contemporaneous. When you are running a daily paper you want to keep the pace."[30]

Few decades posed a greater challenge to keep the pace than the period that began with the assassination of John F. Kennedy in 1963 and really ended only with the sullen resignation of Richard M. Nixon in 1974, which Sprague did not live to see. He was both fascinated and appalled by much of what he witnessed, but he did not lose his faith in the younger generation as it became increasingly militant in Oregon as well as across America.

Sprague wept as he turned in his column on the assassination of President Kennedy; the rare display of emotion jolted reporters in the newsroom. For many Americans, it was a terrible end to a brief moment of glitter and promise, and it ushered in the most traumatic decade since the Civil War. Many Americans of Sprague's generation were swept aside in the tumult, confused and became bitter. In an age of change, more than one writer took refuge in "the good old days." The amazing thing about Sprague's columns in his final decade is that so few looked back, and even those that dealt with the most agonizing turmoil found some

In his later years, Sprague turned to gardening, and was particularly fond of roses (Sprague Family Archives).

Blanche Sprague works at her desk in this sixties-era photograph (Sprague Family Archives).

rays of hope. The major exceptions were Vietnam, a war that Sprague had counseled against but from which he found no exit; and the assassinations.

Sprague was 76 years old when John F. Kennedy was gunned down in Dallas, and 80 when Robert Kennedy and Martin Luther King were killed. Searching as always for some concrete action to take, he argued for gun control in the wake of the second Kennedy assassination. The death of King moved him greatly, for he had been an admirer of the civil rights leader, and quoted him in his editorials and columns. King, said Sprague, was "a modern St. Paul, a Christian missionary to the white community," and Sprague laid his death squarely at the feet of white racism.[31] Building on his service as chairman of the Oregon Advisory Commission to the U. S. Civil Rights Commission, Sprague became a frequent but frustrated apostle for racial harmony.

Sprague's mission in civil rights was primarily that of an educator; with so few minorities in Oregon, readers had little personal basis on which to judge the rapidly unfolding events of the sixties. In 1964 he quoted with approval a United Nations study that pure races do not exist, that intermarriage of races has no proven biological disadvantages, and that differences in achievement must be attributed solely to cultural history. "As a race the Negroes in American have been denied the opportunity to show their potential, and children from Negro homes do suffer from cultural deprivation," Sprague noted, adding that the burden of upgrading the lot of Negro families "is part of the price the white folk pay for three and a half centuries of discrimination against them."[32]

When Congress passed the Civil Rights Act of 1968, Sprague cautioned that with adequate laws now on the book, Americans must turn attention to providing jobs, housing, education and other necessities for all minorities. That, he admitted, would require more federal spending, and he urged readers to support an attack on the economic front. For a man who had bridled at the New Deal and such concepts as Social Security only thirty years before, he had moved a long way indeed, but in reality the support of governmental activism in social reform was a return to his progressive roots.[33]

Sprague shared with most American editors of the sixties a common background: they were white, male, Anglo-Saxon Protestants, university-educated, married, and raising families. All had difficulty dealing with the plethora of "movements" in the decade, whether it was civil rights, feminism, drugs, anti-war, or environmentalism. While others saw their children swept up in crusades they failed to understand or approve, Sprague's grandchildren appeared to be content with their lot. But he saw change all around him, and for once in his life he was not able to suggest remedies. Sprague had always believed that his responsibility as an editor did not end with criticism, and in that belief he differed from editors who unleashed the bombs but did not pick up the wreckage. Whether it was a system to replace Prohibition, an alternative tax plan or a Capitol site, Sprague was at his best when an option was in sight, often of his own devising. Sometimes, the sixties seemed to offer no options; certainly Sprague saw none in Vietnam.

Sprague had not joined in the McCarthy Era's fear of a communistic world, and in 1954 he cautioned against American involvement in Vietnam, where the French were suffering a humiliating defeat. "Not only has the United States no territorial interest in Southeast Asia but its military intervention was never formally asked for either by France or Vietnam, or at least not until the military situation was badly deteriorated," he wrote. "We would enter an area whose peoples have not invited us, to defend regimes we have no duty to underwrite and where our intervention would provoke serious repercussions among other Asian peoples."[34]

Sprague feared an extension of the failed American policy toward China and in 1961, when the outgoing Eisenhower Administration considered sending forces to Laos, Sprague again opposed intervention, concerned that Eisenhower not leave a war in Laos for the new president. Again in 1963 he protested growing American interest in the region.[35]

Less than a year later, Lyndon B. Johnson, the first Democrat ever endorsed by Sprague for president, was drawn toward what Sprague had once termed "the flypaper of Southeast Asia." As Johnson intensified American involvement, Sprague was also caught on the flypaper. Commenting on the president's request for another $125 million for Vietnam, Sprague was in a quandary: "Americans being traditionally actionists [sic] ask, What should we do now? Sen. Morse says 'pull out of Viet Nam.' That would be one solution. . . . [but] The United States has assumed obligations in that area which we can't just walk away from, disagreeable as the task is of carrying them out."[36]

An explanation of his shift in position on Vietnam must be found in Sprague's history in two previous wars. In both, his voice was moderate in the shout of the crowd, but he responded to national authority and the need for unity under fire once troops had been engaged. Commitments, once given, were not to be taken lightly. Perhaps of some importance as well, although almost certainly not determinative, was his endorsement of Johnson in 1964, when Sprague cited Johnson's foreign policy as the major reason for deserting the Republican nominee. Certainly one reason for supporting administration policy was the lack of an acceptable alternative; Sprague simply could not buy Morse's withdrawal policy and, lacking a better idea, he went with authority, not the only American editor to take that road.

Gradually, Sprague attached himself to the flypaper; he felt Wayne Morse was wrong in casting one of only two Senate votes against the Gulf of Tonkin Resolution in 1964, although he did not employ the vitriol against Morse that some editors used. Morse, said Sprague, had raised a question that had to be raised: just how far can we extend the Truman Doctrine of 1947? Morse raised more than that; his attacks cut to the bone of the Johnson Administration's policy in Southeast Asia. But Sprague, with his inherent faith in government, could not accept the depth of Morse's accusations. "Since we are engaged we will have to bear the burden until we can find some way of withdrawal," he reluctantly concluded.[37]

Sprague's experience with previous wars and his deep sense of patriotism made it difficult for him to deal with young men who refused the military draft, and he made a rare break with the American Civil Liberties Union when it challenged conscription. "To allow persons to pick and choose what laws they will obey is merely to invite anarchy," he observed. In an earlier column he worried that Americans might no longer be able to unite for a major war and, although he concluded that they would, he expressed deep misgivings at the divisions being created by the war debate.[38]

Sprague was struggling desperately in his final months to avoid becoming disillusioned with young people because of their rising militancy, and he tried to go beyond the war issue to find positive aspects of the rebellion. But unlike other issues that had claimed his attention in the sixties—forestry and conservation, civil rights, governmental structure—the generational rebellion was one where Sprague was no longer in the vanguard; he was an aging progressive at a time when the term no longer had meaning for most Americans. He refused to surrender the field, however, keeping up a fast pace in what would be his final year.

When University of Oregon students organized a "poverty march" to the Capitol, Sprague went to their press conference and wrote a sympathetic column urging his readers to receive the marchers with courtesy, and to open dialogue. He praised university presidents who worked at compromise with student dissidents, but when radicals occupied and sacked the office of Columbia University President Grayson Kirk, Sprague labeled the actions "anarchy," and pleaded for the pendulum to swing back toward a more reasoned discourse on campuses. Four months later he endorsed lowering the voting age to 18, citing as his reason the positive action of young people in the campaigns of Eugene McCarthy and Robert F. Kennedy. Typically, he looked for positive elements in the turmoil.[39]

He did not avoid the rebellious campuses. He delivered two major speeches in this period at forums that normally attracted nationally known speakers: the Sigma Delta Chi lecture at Indiana University in 1967 and the Eric Allen lecture at the University of Oregon in February 1968. At the former he assessed the work of Marshall McLuhan; at the Eugene conference he called for editors to exert community leadership, to be the "voice of the community." Foreshadowing a 1990s debate over the role of "public journalism," Sprague predicted the revival of small towns and said their publishers and editors must be at the heart of the revival.[40]

At the University of Oregon, Sprague was joined by a grandson, Arthur Hurley, who was completing his degree and serving as a cadet colonel in the Air Force ROTC. Sprague was present when the cadets passed in review at graduation, the ceremony competing with amplified music from war protestors who tried to drown out the ceremonies.[41]

In March Sprague and Blanche took a brief vacation in Mexico with his brother and sister-in-law, this time without the vigorous sight-seeing of most of their other trips. In June, he was off on a grueling flying tour of the Canadian North, joining a group of nearly ninety journalists in a trip organized by the *Wenatchee World*. Sprague's column carried the datelines of Edmonton, Yellow Knife, and Prince George, relaying to readers his fascination with seeing new country.[42]

Blanche was unable to accompany him; she had broken her thigh, and was in the midst of a long hospitalization, requiring two operations. With daughter Martha helping out, she returned home for Thanksgiving, but the homecoming was dampened by Sprague's own treatment for cancer. The marriage that had begun nearly sixty years ago in a tiny farm town in southeast Washington was nearing its end.

Sprague told readers that his own cancer surgery, undergone on his 81st birthday, offered "a favorable forecast for the future." He had entered the hospital just prior to the general election, had tests on November 6, and was operated on for a cancer on one lobe of his lung. It was serious business, but he tried to make light of it in his column, upon returning to work in December:

> *I went to the hospital to let the doctors find out why I had a bad, bad stomachache. They didn't determine that, but did discover a cancer on one lobe of the lung. With no record of smoking or coughing or wheezing, this was the real surprise. (I wonder if I could tap the Tobacco Institute on a testimonial: "Octogenarian, non-smoker, undergoes surgery for lung cancer. Cigarettes innocent.") Anyway, it was a unique experience to start my 81st birthday on the operating table.*[43]

Sprague resumed work, turning out his usual volume of columns, although moving about at a much slower pace.

Sprague took the defeat of Wayne Morse in a very mixed vein. Hospitalized at the time of the vote, he didn't express his opinion until late the following month, when Morse threatened to challenge in the Senate his narrow loss to Bob Packwood. Sprague observed that "There was a degree of pathos," in the Morse defeat, and that it had gone down hard with the Senator to bested by a man a generation younger and with only three legislative terms behind him. Morse, said Sprague, should drop the challenge, accept the results of the recount, and get on with life. At 68, Morse still had plenty to contribute, Sprague noted from his vantage point of 81 years.[44]

The Morse column was part of the usual broad variety of Sprague's columns, which were now his only writing; Wes Sullivan took over the editorial page when Sprague underwent surgery, and continued to write editorials after Sprague's return. In his last month, Sprague's columns commented on Governor McCall's proposed sales tax, the death of

Norman Thomas, legal challenges to the election of Lee Johnson as attorney general, cable television and the Apollo 8 moon landings, which fascinated him.

Then, in his final column, he turned once more to a progressive theme that had long occupied him: the relationship of government to social needs. Commenting in the post-Christmas season, Sprague stated his faith that examples of Christian love more than balanced the forces of hate, "Never before has so much concern been expressed for the poor and the disenfranchised." He noted the trend toward government programs for the elderly, children, the sick and unemployed. "The social conscience has been touched. The debate now is over methods and how to meet the needs. All this is merely an application of the lesson in the parable of the Good Samaritan. . . . even though the agent may be government which professedly is non-religious."[45]

Sprague rested his fingers briefly on the Royal, then reached forward and typed the familiar journalistic ending:

-30-

He walked into the newsroom, handing the column to the desk; perhaps he stopped to visit briefly, asking Al Lightner about a basketball score or sharing with Lillie Madsen news of an old farmer friend. In two days would be a New Year, another beginning in the busy building on Church Street. The next day, Sprague checked into Salem Memorial Hospital.

He began his new year in a private hospital room, undergoing radiation treatment, keeping in contact with the office through Wendell Webb and Wes Sullivan. "It Seems To Me" never appeared again, nor did its author again set foot in the building he had built and dominated.

Charles Arthur Sprague died on March 13, 1969.

11

◆◆◆

Epilogue: The Progressive Legacy

Set aside on the news desk of every daily newspaper are obituaries of living persons of advanced age or great prominence. The standby obituaries await a tragedy or the inevitability of old age; they can appear within hours of the passing of a notable. In the somber *Statesman* newsroom, Sprague's colleagues quietly assembled the material they had prepared.

The obituary of Charles A. Sprague spilled from the *Statesman's* front page onto a full page inside, with an accompanying editorial terming the 81-year-old publisher "lost to us in the prime of his life." The great arbiter of prominence, *The New York Times* obituary page, carried a two-column article with picture, and the subhead described him in a manner he would have approved: "Editor of Paper for 40 Years was Governor for a Term—Column Widely Quoted."[1] Other newspapers joined in the accolades, *The Oregonian* devoting an entire page to his life.

During his final hospitalization, the Salem School Board had named its fourth high school in his honor, and the naming brought tears to the dying editor, the rare show of emotion indicating how strongly he felt about his role as an educator.[2] Later, a lake in the Mt. Jefferson Wilderness would carry his name, as would a forest nursery in southern Oregon.

Sprague's estate was valued at $850,026, including Statesman Publishing Co. stock valued at $420,000. Half of the stock was left to his widow, a quarter each to Wallace A. Sprague and Martha Sprague Hurley, with Wallace designated to vote the family's stock within the Statesman-Journal Co. Grants of a thousand dollars each went to Monmouth College, Willamette University, Lewis and Clark College, First Presbyterian Church of Salem, YMCA of Salem, YWCA of Salem and the Oregon Historical Society.[3]

Sprague had already given Thetford, his Little North Fork cabin, to Willamette University. In his will, he left $100,000 for a fountain on the Capitol Mall: "I choose the Capitol Mall for (a) site because it belongs to all the people of the state, and because of my previous association with its development," Sprague wrote in 1966 as he added the gift to his will, adding, "Also, the Mall needs beautification."[4]

The family and the *Statesman* had been preparing for his death since Sprague's hospitalization in November. Immediately following Sprague's funeral, the new order was announced: Wallace Sprague assumed the title of publisher, with Wendell Webb as editor; Robert Sprague became co-publisher. Wes Sullivan became associate editor in charge of editorials, and Bob Gangware moved to managing editor.

Sprague had made an arrangement in 1940 under which Wallace, Martha and Robert would each purchase 10 percent of *Statesman* stock. At the time of his death, Robert was badly in arrears, and Wallace moved immediately to gain his tenth; the matter became embroiled in controversy, and ultimately wound up in the courts with a cash settlement to Robert Sprague after several years of litigation.[5]

By the time of that settlement, the Statesman-Journal Co. had been sold to the Gannett newspaper group. Gannett opened informal discussions as early as 1970, and the sale was announced in 1973 and completed the following May. It followed four years of increasingly acrimonious relations between Wallace Sprague and the Mainwaring family. Wallace tried unsuccessfully to break the agreement under which the *Statesman* received only 7/13ths of the corporation's news budget despite its increasing dominance, and on several other issues the S-J board split 50-50 along family lines. Wallace and the Mainwarings developed an intense dislike of each other, and the former could not supervise the *Statesman* from Short Hills, New Jersey, where his wife published a weekly newspaper and he commuted to his New York position as vice president of Whitney Communication Company.[6]

The absentee management was causing intense internal strains as well, "an absolute shambles," in the words of Sullivan.[7] The longtime close relationship between Gangware and Webb had deteriorated with their new responsibilities, and key staffers were beginning to look elsewhere. Within perhaps a year of Sprague's death, disposal of his newspaper had become inevitable. As with so many other newspapers of the time, a second generation could not or would not continue the legacy; in this case, the problem was Wallace Sprague's unwillingness to abandon a successful East Coast career to return to a town where he no longer had roots. And Gannett was in an expansion period, paying enormous amounts for newspapers.

"Paul Miller came out and threw a price at us that absolutely astounded us," said Bill Mainwaring of the final discussions with Gannett; as the only member of either family who was interested in personally directing the newspapers, he cast the deciding vote to sell. "I had concluded that I didn't want to spend the rest of my life as Wallace Sprague's partner," he said two decades later.[8] Exact terms of the agreement were not announced, but Gannett issued $15 million in stock to complete a tax-free exchange of stock, according to industry reports. The Statesman-Journal Co. had gross revenues of $6.7 million in 1973, Gannett stated.[9]

In 1950, when *The Oregonian* was sold to the Newhouse chain, Sprague had quizzed E. B. MacNaughton, who managed the sale, as to why it wasn't sold to local owners. MacNaughton's reply indicated that Newhouse was willing to pay some 60 percent more than potential local owners. In the case of the *Statesman*, there had been no local offers.[10]

Many *Statesman* employees, in particular the veterans, felt betrayed. Charles A. Sprague had held intense feelings about local control, Sullivan asserted, quoting Sprague as telling him, "Don't let the ghouls get us," meaning newspaper chains. Some of the older employees believed that Sprague had intended to leave the paper to employee ownership of some type (based on informal comments he had made) but there is absolutely no record that he considered anything other than to leave the *Statesman* to his family. Purchase offers were always politely rejected.[11]

Gannett brought in an outstanding publisher in John McMillan, but the Salem newspapers were cast in the Gannett image, with an emphasis on graphics, short stories, and consumer-oriented features. The *Capital-Journal* was killed in 1980, the morning survivor emerging as the *Statesman-Journal*.

Wendell Webb retired in 1974 after receiving the prestigious Voorhies Award from the Oregon Newspaper Publishers Association. He had become increasingly bitter toward his old boss, feeling that his own efforts had never been adequately recognized. The family awarded Webb an additional $5,000 a year to supplement his inadequate *Statesman-Journal* pension of $245 a month, and Gannett later increased that amount, but Webb died in 1982 stating he had made a mistake in ever joining Sprague.[12]

Blanche Sprague died in 1976, at the age of 95. No family member resides in Salem two decades later, and all of Sprague's colleagues from his 54 years in journalism are dead or retired.

Of the politicians of Sprague's time, the last to retire was Mark Hatfield, who left the U. S. Senate in 1997 after a record-breaking thirty years as an Oregon senator. The progressive political legacy Charles A. Sprague tried so hard to impress on the Republican Party of Oregon was submerged in the nineties by a tide of religious fundamentalism, which would have been anathema to a man who felt that adding the words "under God" to the Pledge of Allegiance was an improper blending of church and state.

With his newspaper cut off from its roots and its editors moving to new causes and challenges, Sprague's name quickly faded from sight. Yet the memory of his service and counsel remained, especially among those who had been close to him in his work or in his public service. Some of them gathered in 1987, joined by members of his family, to note the centennial of Sprague's birth. As they paid respects and considered the impact of this remarkable Oregonian on their own lives, the shape of his legacy appeared, in a quiet but positive way that Sprague would have approved.

The informal ceremony allowed his friends to reminisce. Sprague's funeral in 1969, attended as it was by the political leaders of Oregon and wrapped in the solemnity of the Presbyterian Church, had not lent itself to anecdotes. Now the group laughed easily and often, sharing stories of their common crusades, the days when they had bonded as a newsroom or for the good of civil liberties or sound government.

Sprague's memory had been revived by those whose lives he had affected, and who had found no replacement for the centrality of his thought and leadership. The portly, white-haired Cecil Edwards mingled with Sprague's grandchildren, judges Herb Schwab and Hans Linde recalled constitutional revision debates, and the retired editors Bob Chandler and Bud Forrester remembered the power of Sprague's column. Forest Amsden, who had organized the occasion, referred to Sprague as the leading Oregonian of the century. The stentorian tones of the Oregon Historical Society's Tom Vaughan quoted from Sprague's columns, and Wes Sullivan expressed a "yearning for the contemplative, linear logic of an expert in the printed word . . . in this time when the multiplicity of media, glossed over with emotion-laden immediacy, leaves us unfulfilled and confused."[13]

The Sprague family visited the myrtlewood-paneled office of Gov. Neil Goldschmidt, the first since James Withycombe (1915-19) who had not known or worked with Sprague in some capacity. The intimate private office now housed a computer, its list of electronic messages awaiting the governor's attention on the desk where Sprague's Royal typewriter had sat.

Stretching down the Capitol Mall, the plan Sprague did so much to advance was now in place—his beloved State Library, the office blocks he had proposed or supported and, to the north, the bronze water statuary he had left as a gift to the State of Oregon.

In a state that in the 20th century produced Charles L. McNary, Mark Hatfield, Tom McCall, and Wayne Morse, it may be too much to suggest that a one-term governor and newspaper editor was the state's most distinguished citizen. But it should be beyond challenge that he was its most influential journalist, heir to the mantle worn in the previous century by Harvey Scott of *The Oregonian*. Perhaps only C. S. Jackson of the *Journal* could stake a challenge, for he, like Sprague, had taken a floundering second-place daily and pushed it to greatness by the time of his death.

Sprague, however, was broader than Jackson in his reach—perhaps broader than any Oregonian of the century. His expertise and experience spanned every aspect of state government, took in forestry and agriculture, civil liberties and civil rights, and every level of education. His feet stood atop the Cascade peaks, trod the marble halls of the United Nations, and slogged through Navajo hogans and the ashes of the Tillamook Burn. Each experience was an opportunity to educate. One who read "It Seems To Me" with regularity for 25 years would have ingested a liberal arts education.

The reader would be versed in Oregon history, in the causes and effects of two world wars and the domestic excesses of the Cold War. Personalities seen only at a distance would take form, their strengths and weaknesses revealed. Through the columns passed a parade of Civil War veterans, the smell of a whaling station at Grays Harbor in 1910, the fuzzy feel of special peaches sold by a Polk County farmer, two Parisians dallying over wine at lunch, the joy of discovering a new word or term—all were grist for the daily mill, taking their place alongside the heavy political issues of the day.

When Sprague discovered circadian rhythm or a new theory of the origin of the universe, readers shared his discovery. Fascinated by Charles Darwin and his successors, Sprague moved easily from natural to social science, never "dumbing down" even the most complex topics. Always the educator, Sprague gathered information relentlessly, analyzed it and sent it to his readers in a constant stream of what could only be called civic education.

"It Seems" would have drawn fire from the media consultants who were already feeling for the public pulse, because the column set rather than followed the public agenda, and it never pandered to its audience. A serious man himself, Sprague took readers seriously and addressed them as equals. He resisted suggestions that his columns be collected and reprinted, sure that the passage of time would dim their interest or importance.

While that might be true of comments on the passing legislative or campaign scene, the larger themes remain as his legacy. Read by two generations of Oregon editors and political leaders, they may have been the major intellectual basis of Oregon's image in what is sometimes called the McCall Era. The man with whom the image is inexorably linked knew and admired Sprague for twenty years and, to the extent that the idiosyncratic McCall could be labeled, he was a latter-day progressive.

If the McCall Era was one of toleration and the willingness to accept new ideas while holding to basic values, then Sprague was at least its godfather. He seized leadership in the post-war period as the challenges of human rights demanded response. The dignity of man regardless of color or creed was the theme of dozens of columns and editorials, far surpassing that of any contemporary. In an era of conformist state administrations, Sprague took a leadership role when governors failed to rally to these causes. When stronger governors followed, he was their champion on human rights.

Tolerance had not always been his suit; as a diehard partisan in the thirties, he flailed liberal Democrats and the New Deal and his 1938 campaign stooped to extraneous and mean-spirited Red-baiting in its final days. His decisions regarding Japanese Americans, and the multicultural experience of the United Nations transformed Sprague into a champion of human rights.

Editors, even during the personal newspapering of Sprague's prime years, argued about their proper role in public life. Sprague's active political career was eschewed by most, who argued that an editor should keep his distance to maintain objectivity and credibility. Yet without his service as governor, as United Nations delegate and in a host of other tasks, Sprague might have remained as he was in 1938: a small-town editor of rather rigid political positions and the limited world view of one who had come of age in rural towns of conservative mien. The influence of progressivism had been banked in favor of party regularity in the thirties, and it remained for public service to fan the embers and revive the spirit that had moved him as a young man.

Public service educated him for the task of educating others. Curious rather than gregarious, Sprague went into the larger world to learn, rather than to gain a following. He paid dearly for that as a practicing politician, but as an editor he returned the gift many times over.

Sprague's progressive strain was checked by his personal conservatism; his urge to break from the center was always checked by his fear of excess. The essence of a centrist himself, he urged others to take the plunges from which he was constrained by his own nature. Writing in 1965 for a special section of the *Register-Guard*, Sprague described Oregon as a "middle of the road" state, in which "everything in moderation seems to be the prevailing motto." Perhaps alluding to his own inner conflicts, Sprague quoted Oscar Wilde: "Moderation is a fatal thing. Nothing succeeds like excess." Sprague added, "But Oregonians, I fancy, will adhere to the Middle Way."[14]

Sprague adhered to the Middle Way, but he sought to make of it the way of enlightened progressivism. A nation in turmoil in the late sixties and early seventies could look to Oregon as a bastion of civilized discourse, a state that used government as a force for social and environmental justice. Oregonians who led the way had grown up on Sprague's writing and the writing of others influenced by him.

Oregon, at the time of Charles A. Sprague's death, reflected to a remarkable degree his sense of balance and civility, and it did so in a nation under seige. The last of the progressive editors had stamped his image on the public discourse of his adopted state, and on those who conducted its policies.

◆◆◆

Notes

Abbreviations. The following abbreviations of publications and archival collections will be noted:

AC: Author's collection
CAS: Charles A. Sprague
C-J: The *Capital-Journal*
G-T: Corvallis *Gazette-Times*
ISTM: "It Seems To Me"
J-T: Ritzville *Journal-Times*
MSH: Martha Sprague Hurley
OCF: Oregon Commonwealth Federation
OHS: Oregon Historical Society Archives
OJ: The *Oregon Journal*
Oreg: *The Oregonian*
OS: *The Oregon Statesman*
OSA: Oregon State Archives
OV: *Oregon Voter*
R-G: The *Eugene Register-Guard*
RS: Robert Sprague
SS: Sheldon Sackett
UO: University of Oregon Archives
WAS: Wallace A. Sprague
WS: Wyatt Sprague
WW: Wendell Webb

Introduction

1. A slim volume in the American History Series, Arthur S. Link and Richard L. McCormick's *Progressivism* (Arlington Heights, Ill.: Harlan Davidson, Inc., 1983), summarizes the disparate views and definitions surrounding this period, and provides an exhaustive annotated bibliography. Another summary of progressivism is found in the Introduction to Otis Pease (ed.), *The Progressive Years: The Spirit and Achievement of American Reform* (New York: G. Braziller, 1962), 1-22. More comprehensive examinations of the era include Louis Filler, *Appointment at Armageddon: Muckraking and Progressivism in the American Tradition* (Westport, Conn., 1976); Richard Hofstadter, *The Age of Reform: From Bryan to F.D.R.* (New York: Alfred A. Knopf, 1955); George Mowry, *The Era of Theodore Roosevelt* (New York: Harper & Brothers, 1958).

2. ISTM, 1 Jan. 1950.
3. Mrs. C. A. Sprague to CAS, 7 Oct. 1904, CAS papers, Box 4, OHS.
4. MSH interview with author, Kensington, Calif., 17 Jan. 1998. For Hubbard, see Freeman Champney, *Art & Glory: The Story of Elbert Hubbard* (New York: Crown Publishers, 1968) and Charles F. Hamilton, *As Bees in Honey Drown* (South Brunswick and New York: A. S. Barnes & Co., 1973).
5. Richard Hofstadter, *The Progressive Movement, 1900-1915* (Englewood Cliffs, N.J.: Prentice-Hall, Inc., 1963), 4.
6. Samuel P. Hays, *Conservation and the Gospel of Efficiency: The Progressive Conservation Movement, 1890-1920* (Cambridge: Harvard University Press, 1959), 2 and passim.
7. Robert C. Notson interview with author, Beaverton, 13 June 1994; Forest W. Amsden to J. Wesley Sullivan, 27 Oct. 1987; AC.

Chapter One

1. Diary of CAS, entry for 25 July 1909; CAS papers, Box 5, OHS.
2. CAS to WS, 17 Oct. 1911; CAS papers, Box 4, OHS.
3. From Memorial Day address of CAS, 5 June 1924, J-T.
4. Ibid.
5. George W. Harbin to "Mrs. Sprague," 18 May 1863; transcript in AC.
6. WAS to author, 10 March 1996.
7. MSH interview with author, Kensington, Calif., 17 Jan. 1998.
8. "Oregon Governor Visits Here With Grandmother, Mrs. Brooks, 101," Cedar Rapids (Iowa) *Gazette*, 7 June 1940.
9. "C.A. Sprague Prints Centennial Edition," *Columbus (Iowa) Gazette*, April 1951 (specific date unknown).
10. Figures taken from U. S. Department of Interior, Census Office, Report on the Population *of the United States* (Washington: Government Printing Office); census of 1890, 1900 for State of Iowa.
11. CAS interview by Robert Bruce, 18 July 1962; OHS Tape 92.
12. Ralph Friedman, "Profile of an Ex-Governor," Oreg. Northwest magazine, 29 Jan. 1967: 6-7.
13. CAS note to "*Newslites*," Ainsworth, Iowa, no date; C8 F7, Archives.
14. CAS Rhodes Scholarship application, letters and recommendations, 8 March 1908; Box 4, OHS; CAS diary, entry for 31 Dec. 1909, Box 5, OHS.
15. CAS diary entries for 18 June and 4 July 1910; Box 5, OHS.
16. R. L. Polk and Company, *Polk's Oregon and Washington Gazeteer and Business Directory* (Seattle: R. L. Polk & Co., annually), 1911-12 edition, 299-302.
17. CAS diary entries for 10 Nov. 1910; Box 5, OHS
18. CAS diary entries for 6 April and 8 April 1911, Box 5, OHS.
19. ISTM, 10 July 1953; "Whaling Station," Aberdeen *Herald*, 20 July 1911.
20. "Jackies and Socialists Mix," Aberdeen Herald, 17 July 1911.
21. CAS to WS, 17 Oct. 1911; Box 4, OHS.

22. Blanche Chamberlain Sprague's actual birth date is recorded in David Faris, *The Glasgow Family of Adams County, Ohio* (Baltimore: Gateway Press, Inc., 1990), 89.
23. ISTM, 12 Aug. 1962. Sprague may have actually made two climbs; his daughter recalls that he told of one trip up the mountain with a rescue expedition to recover the body of a man killed on a climb; it is likely that this was a separate climb from his ascent of the peak of Rainier.
24. CAS to WS, 11 Aug. 1912; AC.
25. Blanche Sprague audiotape interview with MSH and Dr. Melvin Hurley, 25 Dec. 1969, Kensington, Calif.; AC.
26. MSH to author, 8 March 1996.
27. MSH interview with author, Kensington, Calif., 25 Feb. 1993.
28. MSH to author, 8 March 1996.
29. Blanche Sprague audiotape.
30. MSH interview, 25 Feb. 1993.
31. "Young Men Form Club," *Walla Walla Union*, 13 Oct. 1912 (Sprague was identified by the *Union* as "A. C. Sprague of Waitsburg."
32. "Progressives Held Rally Last Friday Night," Waitsburg *Times*, 25 Oct. 1912; "Election in this Precinct," Waitsburg *Times*, 8 Nov. 1912.
33. "A Reply to Knute Hill," J-T, 16 Oct. 1924.
34. William T. Kerr Jr., The Progressives of Washington, 1910-1912, *Pacific Northwest Quarterly* 55 (1964): 16-27. See also Dorothy O. Johansen and Charles M. Gates, *Empire of the Columbia: A History of the Pacific Northwest* (New York: Harper and Row, 1957, 1967) 2d ed, 443-476; Carlos A. Schwantes, *The Pacific Northwest: An Interpretive History* (Lincoln: University of Nebraska Press, 1989), 266-287; Gordon B. Dodds, *The American Northwest: A History of Oregon and Washington* (Arlington Heights, Ill: The Forum Press, 1986), 182-197.
35. CAS to WS, 14 Nov. 1919; Box 4, OHS.
36. "C.A. Sprague to be Asst. State Superintendent," Waitsburg *Times*, 10 Jan. 1913.
37. Blanche Sprague audiotape.
38. Sprague Estate, misc. papers file; Box 4, OHS.
39. CAS to WS, 18 June 1915; AC.
40. Inar Pedersen to CAS, 5 July 1916; Box 4, OHS.
41. "Former Assistant Condemns School Head," J-T, 24 Aug. 1916.
42. Preston failed to carry Adams County, however, losing to Democrat Morgan, 1126 to 1047; nor did she carry the county in 1920, although Republicans swept every other office.
43. Jim B. Pearson and Edgar Fuller (eds), *Education in the States: Historical Development and Outlook* (Washington: National Education Association, 1969), 1325.
44. Blanche Sprague audiotape.
45. CAS to WS, 10 Sept. 1915; AC.

46. A number of historical treatments of Russian-Germans in the United States discuss the migration to Washington. See Fred C. Koch, *The Volga Germans: In Russia and the Americas from 1763 to the Present* (University Park: Pennsylvania State University Press, 1977); "Russian-Germans Come to Settle Area," *Adams County Centennial Edition* (Ritzville: *The Outlook* and the *Ritzville Adams County Journal*, December, 1983): 63-67; *History of Adams County, Washington* (Ritzville: Adams County Historical Society, 1986).
47. U. S. Department of Interior, Census Office. *Report on the Population of the United States, State of Washington* (Washington: Government Printing Office, 1911). The highest concentrations of Germans and Russians were Adams County, 31.2 percent; Grant, 18.8 percent; and Lincoln, 16.7 percent. All are rural counties in eastern Washington.
48. ISTM, 11 Jan. 1965.
49. WAS interview with author, New York City, 4 Aug. 1992.
50. MSH interview, 17 Feb. 1998.
51. Ibid.
52. Blanche Sprague audiotape. "C. A. Sprague Notes 50th," J-T, 21 Oct. 1965; "Journal-Times In New Building," J-T, 23 Nov. 1916.
53. MSH, undated manuscript, AC.
54. CAS to WS, 20 May, 2 June and 9 Aug. 1918; contract of sale dated 6 Nov. 1941; Box 4, OHS.
55. CAS to WS, 22 April 1923; Box 4, OHS. Advertisement for Ritzville State Bank, J-T, 3 Nov. 1921. W. H. Martin, president, RSB, to CAS, 7 and 19 March 1933; report to directors of RSB dated 1 Jan. 1937; Box 4, OHS.
56. Among the many publications describing the battle for Grand Coulee, see Bruce Charles Harding, "Water from Pend Oreille: The Gravity Plan for Irrigating the Columbia Basin," *Pacific Northwest Quarterly* 45 (1954): 56-57; Richard L. Neuberger, *Our Promised Land* (New York: Macmillan Co., 1938), 79-83; Dorothy Johansen, *Empire of the Columbia*, 513-519; Murray Morgan, "The Concrete Dream," in Ellis Lucia (ed), *This Land Around Us* (Garden City, N.Y.: Doubleday, 1969), 522-532; Robert Ficken, *Rufus Woods, The Columbia River, and the Building of Modern Washington* (Pullman: Washington State University, 1995).
57. MSH interview, 25 Feb. 1993.
58. "Republican Co. Committee Hold Organization Meeting," J-T, 28 Sept. 1916.
59. "The Break With Germany," J-T, 8 Feb. 1917.
60. Karl J. R. Arndt and May E. Olson, *The German Language Press of the Americas, Vol. I* (Munchen: Verlag Dokumentation, 3d ed, 1976), 642.
61. "A Tribute to Der Beobachter," J-T, 15 Feb. 1917.
62. "To German-Americans," J-T, 5 April 1917.
63. "Ritzville Rouses for Defense," J-T, 29 March 1917.
64. "Wartime Memories," OS, 11 Nov. 1934.
65. "The Lunatic Fringe," J-T, 7 June 1917.

66. "Large Attendance at German Convention," J-T, 14 June 1917; "Conference Meets Here," J-T, 23 Aug. 1917.
67. The original report, by the Leone Valley correspondent, appeared 16 August: "A train passed through Othello Friday containing a carload of Belgian refugees on their way to Oregon to a colony of their own countrymen, where they will make their home. The boys from 6 to 12 years were all marked with the loss of the right hand, a mark of German fiendishness. It is enough to make a strong man weep and to take the slack out of a slacker." The retraction appeared 30 August.
68. Richard Hofstadter, *The Age of Reform* (New York: Alfred A. Knopf, 1955), 270-280.
69. "League Gets Good Start," J-T, 10 Jan. 1918.
70. C. A. Sprague, *History of Adams County in the World War* (Ritzville: *The Journal-Times*, 1920), 19.
71. Ibid., 20.
72. CAS to WS, 19 Jan. 1920, Box 4, OHS.
73. CAS to WS, 27 Nov. 1918, Box 4, OHS.
74. The pledge: "I pledge my assistance to the government in putting down sedition and disloyalty, and consecrate my service to the great cause of Democracy."
75. "How Long? How Long?" J-T, 4 April 1918.
76. "Drop German in Bank Name," J-T, 12 Sept. 1918; "Lutherans to Hold Services in English," J-T, 29 Aug. 1918; "German Use Restricted," J-T, 8 Aug. 1918.
77. "First From County to be Killed in War," J-T, 5 Sept. 1918.
78. "Mill Loses Its License," J-T, 4 July 1918. The minister was released, and all but one sack of flour confiscated. The mill selling him the flour lost its license for a month, however.
79. Advertisement, J-T, 24 Oct. 1918.
80. "Two Men Object to Classification," J-T, 31 Oct. 1918.
81. CAS, *Adams County in the War*, 10.
82. "William Clodius is Arrested," J-T, 17 Oct. 1918; "Found Guilty, Fined $400," J-T, 6 March 1919; CAS, *Adams County in the War*, 34.
83. Ibid., 35.
84. W. Walters Miller interview with author, Ritzville, 9 April 1992. The major historical accounts are *History of Adams County, Washington* (Ritzville: Adams County Historical Society, 1986); and *Adams County Centennial Edition* (Ritzville: *The Outlook* and the *Ritzville Adams County Journal*, December, 1983).
85. "Wartime Memories," OS, 11 Nov. 1934.
86. "Raw Meat for the Jingoes," J-T, 24 April 1924.
87. "Correcting a Wrong Interpretation," J-T, 28 Sept. 1922.
88. "The Ku Klux Klan," J-T, 27 April 1922; "Fanning Old Flames," J-T, 10 Aug. 1922; "Guerilla Warfare," J-T, 6 March 1914; "Klan Holds Meeting Here," J-T, 15 May 1924; "Thousand Hear Klan Lecture," J-T, 4 Sept. 1924.

89. "Government Operation Advisable," J-T, 29 Nov. 1917.
90. "Everett and the I.W.W.," J-T, 9 Nov. 1916.
91. Editorial brief, no headline, J-T, 15 Nov. 1917.
92. See Paul L. Murphy, *The Meaning of Freedom of Speech: First Amendment Freedoms from Wilson to FDR* (Westport, Conn.: Greenwood Press, 1972), 18-46.
93. Blanche Sprague audiotape.
94. WAS interview; MSH interview, 25 Feb. 1993.

Chapter Two

1. MSH unpublished paper, ca 1970; AC. WAS interview with author, New York City, 4 August 1992.
2. The exact number of newspaper casualties is difficult to determine, because there were a number of papers both opening and closing in this period, leaving no net change in number of publications. The estimate of 706 dailies suspending publication was contained in a report to the American Newspaper Publishers Association in 1949 and is quoted in James E. Pollard, "Spiraling Newspaper Costs Outrun Revenues 1939-1949," *Journalism Quarterly* 26 (1949): 270-76.
3. R. J. Hendricks to CAS, 4 May 1928; AC.
4. Hendricks to CAS, 3 May 1928; AC.
5. All circulation figures in this chapter are from *N. W. Ayer & Son Directory of Newspapers and Periodicals* (Philadelpia: N.W. Ayer & Son, annually). Accuracy of figures at this date is generally suspect; a more accurate estimate is found in SS to CAS, 21 Dec. 1928 (AC), in which he estimates actual circulation on 1 Aug. 1928 of only 4100; Sackett insisted, however, that by December circulation had risen to 7000, which he termed "clean circulation."
6. Hendricks to CAS, 9 May 1928, AC.
7. CAS to William S. Walton, 12 May 1928, AC.
8. Roy Hewitt to CAS, 23 Nov. 1928 and CAS to SS, 27 Nov. 1928, AC.
9. CAS to SS and Earl C. Brownlee, 15 Dec. 1928, AC.
10. SS to CAS , 21 Dec. 1928, AC.
11. SS to CAS, 30 Dec. 1928, 2 Jan. and 4 Jan. 1929; CAS to SS, 3 Jan. 1929; AC.
12. SS to CAS, 7, 8 and 9 Jan. 1929; CAS to SS and Brownlee, 7 Jan. 1929; CAS to SS, 10 Jan. 1929; AC.
13. Copies of contracts in AC.
14. She died in 1947 from cancer. "Beatrice W. Sackett Rites at Coos Bay" OS, 20 May 1947.
15. *Capitol's Who's Who for Oregon* (Portland: Capitol Publishing Co., 1937), 476.
16. J. W. Forrester interview.
17. Joseph R. Sand, "Sheldon F. Sackett: Flamboyant Oregon Journalist," Master's thesis (University of Oregon, 1971), 63-64.

18. Sand, "Sheldon F. Sackett," 7.
19. J. W. Sullivan interviews with Cecil Edwards, Paul Harvey, Jr. and others, 16 Aug. 1988, Salem; AC.
20. MSH interview with author, Kensington, Calif., 25 Feb. 1993.
21. ISTM, 3 Sept. 1968.
22. George S. Turnbull, *History of Oregon Newspapers* (Portland: Binfords & Mort, 1939), 74-83.
23. Burton W. Onstine, *Oregon Votes: 1858-1972* (Portland: Oregon Historical Society, 1973), 58-59.
24. *Population of Oregon Cities, Counties and Metropolitan Areas, 1850-1957* (Eugene: University of Oregon, 1958).
25. Turnbull, *History of Oregon Newspapers*, 137-38.
26. "Statesman Charter Member of World-wide Associated Press," OS, 28 March 1951.
27. WAS to the author, February 1993.
28. Quoted in Turnbull, *History of Oregon Newspapers*, 139.
29. George S. Turnbull, *An Oregon Editor's Battle for Freedom of the Press* (Portland: Binfords & Mort, 1952), 3-9.
30. "Progressive Policies Pale," C-J, 14 July 1930.
31. "Harlan and West," OS, 10 Feb. 1929.
32. The short-lived but remarkably successful efforts of the KKK in Oregon are best described in Malcolm Clark, Jr., "The Bigot Disclosed: 90 Years of Nativism," *Oregon Historical Quarterly* 75 (1974): 109-91. The KKK and the Pierce-Patterson rivalry are discussed in Arthur Bone, *Oregon Cattleman/Governor, Congressman: Memoirs and Times of Walter M. Pierce. Edited and Expanded by Arthur Bone* (Portland: Oregon Historical Society, 1981), 149-81 and 306-24.
33. The Progressive Party platform of 1912 may be found in David A. Shannon (ed), *Progressivism and Postwar Disillusionment: 1898-1928* (New York: McGraw-Hill, 1966), 123-36.
34. "A Primer of Taxation," OS, 14 Feb. 1929.
35. "An Act of Impudence," Portland *Telegraph*, 1 March 1929: 18; "Have the People No Will?" Oreg, 28 Feb. 1929: 10; "The Tenth Time," C-J, 28 Feb. 1929; "The Tenth Time," C-J, 2 March 1929. "Their Duty To The State," OJ, 10 Feb. 1929: 6; "As They Grope," OJ, 14 Feb. 1929: 10.
36. "Strife Between the Institutions," OS, 19 Feb. 1929; "The Senate Takes Action," OS, 23 Feb. 1929; "Budget Log-Rolling," OS, 24 Feb. 1929.
37. "Not So Fast," R-G, 23 Feb. 1929; "Where Do We Go?" R-G, 27 Feb. 1929; "The Merger Bill," G-T, 13 Feb. 1929; "What Shall One Say?" G-T, 13 Feb. 1929.
38. "Sips for Supper," C-J, 3 March 1929; "That Miserable Pittance," C-J, 4 March 1929; "A Session of Constructive Labor," OS, 4 March 1929.
39. "Sips for Supper," C-J, 1 Feb. 1929.
40. "Insurgents Plan to Hog-Tie Mayor by Committees Grab," C-J, 21 Oct. 1929.

41. "C-J Group of Council Given Fund Quiz Job," OS, 19 Nov. 1929; "Livesley May Be Given Post on Committee," OS, 21 Nov. 1929.
42. "Dads to Take Final Step in Emancipation," OS, 29 Nov. 1929.
43. "Spite in the Saddle," C-J, 5 Nov. 1929; "'Spite in the Saddle,'" OS, 7 Nov. 1929.
44. "Sips for Supper," C-J, 7 Nov. 1929.
45. "A Lesson in Geography," OS, 9 Nov. 1929.
46. "Just Another Boycott," C-J, 8 Nov. 1929.
47. WAS interview.
48. Jeryme Upston English interview with author, Salem, 3 Sept. 1991.
49. Buren and Upston replaced Jessie Steele, hired in 1931 to replace Olive Doak. Ralph Curtis's spot as sports editor was taken by Paul Hauser in 1934; when Hauser left sports for news in 1937, Ron Gemmel took his spot. Genevieve Morgan was a reporter and Valley editor before going to the state Department of Agriculture as a public information specialist. Winston Taylor's reportorial byline began appearing in 1939, and was interrupted by the war. Others who wrote for the paper in the thirties included Jack Minto, Betty Ohlemiller and Madalene Callen.
50. Others employed in the business office of the thirties were Charles Bier and Baleda Ohmart.
51. Al Lightner interview with author, Salem, 18 Jan. 1994.
52. MSH interview with author, Kensington, Calif., 17 Jan. 1998.
53. Ibid.
54. "On Climbing Mount Jefferson," OS, 24 July 1929.
55. WAS interview.
56. Jeryme English, report to the Capital Card Club, 5 Nov. 1988; AC.
57. "Editorial Correspondence," OS, 9-23 June 1938.
58. Mazie came west in 1929 after her husband, Arch Graham, died; she had two children and lived in Portland until her death in 1947 from a stroke. WAS to author, undated; MSH interview with author, Kensington, Calif., 17 Jan. 1998.
59. MSH interview, 17 Jan. 1998; WAS interview.
60. CAS tax records, AC.
61. "Newspaper Scrip Used in 'Holidays'" and "Letters Tell How Oregon Newspapermen Managed to Keep Wolves From the Door," *Oregon Publisher*, March 1933.
62. "New plant Made-to-order Now Ready," OS, 5 April 1953.
63. All OS financial figures in this chapter taken from copies of OS financial records in AC.
64. RS, "Some Evidence as to the Sales Potential of Oregon's No. 2 Market," undated; AC.
65. RS, undated memo; AC.
66. "Statesman Receives High Rating," OS, 7 April 1936.
67. Jeryme English, OS oldtimers interview.
68. All circulation data taken from N. W. Ayer and Son, *Directory of Newspapers and Periodicals* (Philadelphia: N.W. Ayers and Son, annually).

69. "First Death Claim Filed on Behalf of Statesman Accident Policy Holder," OS, 18 Jan. 1929.
70. "Art for Public's Sake Purpose of Statesman in Starting Campaign," OS, 17 Oct. 1937.
71. "Statesman Show for Housewives Attracts 1200 on Opening Day," OS, 28 April 1938.
72. CAS to SS, Feb. 4, 1930; AC.
73. SS to CAS , Jan. 8, 1937; AC.
74. SS to CAS, Aug. 11, 1938; AC.
75. CAS to SS, Nov. 20, 1938; CAS to SS, Dec. 7, 1938; AC.
76. Joseph R. Sand, "Sheldon F. Sackett: Flamboyant Oregon Journalist," Master's thesis, University of Oregon, 1971: 22-24; "Sheldon Sackett Leaves Statesman," OS, 12 Sept. 1939.
77. WAS interview. Sale of G-T stock was announced in the OS on 3 July 1937: "Selling G-T Interest."
78. Turnbull, *History of Oregon Newspapers*, 139.

Chapter Three

1. ISTM, 21 March 1968.
2. George M. Joseph, "George W. Joseph and the Oregon Progressive Tradition," Senior thesis, Reed College, 1952: 52.
3. Henry Hanzen, unpublished manuscript, "Joseph-Meier campaign of 1930," Chapter 2, page 8; Hanzen papers, OHS.
4. The best narrative of the lengthy and complex maneuvering leading to this point is George M. Joseph, "Joseph and the Progressive Tradition." See also E. Kimbark MacColl, *The Growth of a City: Power and Politics in Portland, Oregon, 1915 to 1950* (Portland: The Georgian Press, 1970), 382-411. Henry Hanzen's unpublished manuscript on the Joseph-Meier campaign is also useful, if colored by Hanzen's own role.
5. Stephen A. Stone, *Stories from the Files of an Oregon Newsman* (Eugene: Parkstone Co., 1967), 150.
6. "Corbett Commands Confidence," OS, 3 May 1930; "Brady Connection Means Norblad Defeat," OS, 30 April 1930.
7. Joseph, "Joseph and the Progressive Tradition," 146.
8. OV, 31 May 1930: 6; and 7 June 1930: 6.
9. "Prejudice Against Jews," OV, 16 Aug. 1930: 14; OV, 1 Nov. 1930: 18-19.
10. "As Long as the Sack Holds Out," C-J, 8 Aug.1930; "Meier, Defender of the Faith," OS, 24 July 1930.
11. "The Barony of Meier and Frank," OS, 30 Oct. 1930.
12. "The Thing Has Happened," OS, 6 Nov. 1930.
13. "Behold the Big Stick," OS, 27 Jan. 1931; "The Conquest of Canaan, Cont.," OS, 28 May 1931; "Julius Meier," OS, 15 July 1937; Ralph Friedman, "Profile of an ex-Governor," *Northwest* magazine of Oreg., 27 Jan. 1967: 7.

14. The best discussion of Oregon Democrats in this period is Robert E. Burton, *Democrats of Oregon: The Pattern of Minority Politics, 1900-1956* (Eugene: University of Oregon, 1970), 61-91.
15. "Midday Ride of 1932 Revere," OS, 3 July 1932.
16. "Thousands Turn Out to Greet Candidate; Brief Address Made," OS, 22 Sept. 1932; "Utility Policy is Outlined by Demo Nominee," OS, 22 Sept. 1932; "Roosevelt Not So Popular As Appeared Here," OS, 25 Sept. 1932.
17. For a discussion of Oregon's Republican preference through the New Deal, see Burton, *Democrats of Oregon*, 61-103; Dorothy O. Johansen and Charles Gates, *Empire of the Columbia: A History of the Pacific Northwest*. 2d ed. (New York: Harper & Row, 1967), 491-586; Carlos Schwantes, *The Pacific Northwest: An Interpretive History* (Lincoln: University of Nebraska, 1989), 288-312; Earl Pomeroy, *The Pacific Slope: A History of California, Oregon, Washington, Idaho, Utah and Nevada* (New York: Alfred A. Knopf, 1965), 215-53; Gordon B. Dodds, *The American Northwest: A History of Oregon and Washington* (Arlington Heights, Ill: The Forum Press, 1986), 226-45; Paul Kleppner, "Politics without parties: The Western states, 1900-1984," in Gerald D. Nash and Richard W. Etulian eds., *The 20th Century West: Historical interpretations* (Albuqerque: University of New Mexico, 1989): 295-338.
18. Richard L. Neuberger, *Our Promised Land* (New York: MacMillan, 1938), 88.
19. Sprague's editorial positions were expressed on several occasions, among them 13 Oct. 1933, 4 Nov. 1934, 28 Oct. 1936, 17 March 1937, and 30 Sept. 1937.
20. "Initiating the Water Plant Purchase," OS, 12 April 1930; "Voting on the Water Amendment," OS, 17 April 1930; "Water Plant Purchase Proposal Carries By Over 2 to 1," OS, 17 May 1930.
21. OS editorials: "Do Not Mortgage Salem," 1 Nov. 1931; "Saving City's Credit," 8 Dec. 1931; "Why We Oppose Bond Issue," 12 Dec. 1931. C-J editorials: "A Great Delusion," and "Baleful In Effect," both 14 Dec. 1931.
22. "Water Bond Issue Carries," OS, 16 Dec. 1931.
23. "Power Distribution," OS, 13 Oct. 1933.
24. "The Grange Power Bill," OS, 4 Nov. 1934.
25. Dorothy O. Johansen, "A Working Hypothesis for the Study of Migrations," *Pacific Historical Review* 36 (February 1967): 1-13.
26. Burton, *Democrats of Oregon*, 78-79.
27. "Martin Enters the Race," OS, 5 Feb. 1934.
28. Burton, *Democrats of Oregon*, 80-82.
29. Richard L. Neuberger, "The Northwest Goes Leftish," *New Republic* 80 (7 Nov. 1934): 357.
30. Sterling to Martin, 5 June 1934; Martin papers, Box 1, OHS.
31. Robert S. McElvaine, *The Great Depression: America, 1929-1941* (New York: Times Books, 1993), 250-64.

32. A good account of this rivalry is William M. Tattam, "Sawmill Workers and Radicalism: Portland, Oregon, 1929-41," Master's thesis, University of Oregon, 1970.
33. "Martin Regards Goon Rout Best," OJ, 1 Jan. 1939: 4.
34. Tattam, "Sawmill Workers," 20-69.
35. "Lumber Mill Wages," OS, 7 May 1935; "The Strike and President Roosevelt," OS, 20 July 1934.
36. "Weekly Report of Communist Activities," Portland Police Bureau to Gov. Charles H. Martin, 30 April 1937; Martin papers, Box 7, OHS.
37. Sergeant Carl A. Glen report to Superintendent of Police Charles Pray, 15 April 1937 and Captain Walter Lansing letter to Pray, 19 April 1937; W. L. Gosslin (Martin's secretary) to John S. Marshall, Marion County Democratic chairman, 23 April 1937; Martin papers, Box 7, OHS.
38. Monroe Sweetland interview with author, Milwaukie, 18 Dec. 1994; Sweetland oral history, tape 5, OHS. See also Jill Hopkins Herzig, "The Oregon Commonwealth Federation: The Rise and Decline of a Reform Organization," Master's thesis, University of Oregon, 1963: 15-20.
39. Ramifications of the appointment are discussed in Monroe Sweetland's letters to J. C. Capt, director, Federal Census Bureau, 10 Oct. 1939 and to James A. Farley, head of the Democratic National Committee, 14 Sept. 1939. OCF papers, Box 12, UO.
40. "Martin on Oregon," OS, 4 Aug. 1934.
41. Burton, *Democrats of Oregon*, 70-71.
42. Paul W. Harvey Jr. interview with author, Salem, 6 Sept. 1991.
43. Charles H. Martin to Paul Kelty, 3 Dec. 1935; Charles H. Martin papers, OHS.
44. "Financial Outlook Held Sound in Local Section," OS, 1 Jan. 1930.
45. "Parades of the Unemployed," OS, 1 March 1930; "Employment in Salem," OS, 26 Nov. 1930; "Employment of Married Women," OS, 5 Dec. 1930.
46. "Marion County's Relief Expenditures," OS, 24 Sept. 1933.
47. E. Kimbark MacColl, *The Growth of a City*, 453-57.
48. Jeff LaLande, "The 'Jackson County Rebellion:' Social Turmoil and Political Insurgence in Southern Oregon during the Great Depression," *Oregon Historical Quarterly* 95 (1994): 406-71.
49. "Progressive Socialism," OS, 5 April 1933.
50. "March 4, 1934," OS, 4 March 1934.
51. "Lippmann for Landon," OS, 17 Sept. 1936; "Major Issue of the Campaign," OS, 21 Oct. 1936.
52. "Forty-eight Solutions," OS, 27 March 1932.
53. "County Republicans Back Prohi Referendum," OS, 10 April 1932.
54. "Liquor Control in Oregon," OS, 18-20 Oct., 25 Oct., 29 Oct. 1933.
55. Warren C. Price, *The Eugene Register-Guard: A Citizen of Its Community* (Portland: Binfords & Mort, 1976), 200-11; Dan Wyant, "William Tugman: Last of the Crusading Editors," *Lane County Historian* 38 (Spring 1993): 16-24.

56. Warren C. Price, *The Eugene Register-Guard,* 249-250.
57. "Frankenstein System of Higher Education," OS, 31 Aug. 1932.
58. R. L. Polk and Company. *Polk's Salem City and Marion County Directory* (Portland: R. L. Polk & Co., annually) 1930-31 edition, 27.
59. Robert Sprague interview with author, Eugene, 16 Jan. 1994.
60. "Capitol Location," OS, 29 May 1935.
61. "Harmony on Capitol Plan," OS, 10 Sept. 1935.
62. "What Happened," OS, 12 Nov. 1935.
63. "Originality of Design Marks Capitol Plans," OS, 27 May 1936.
64. CAS to Miss Grace Wythe, 6 March 1936, and to Jessie Hill Hartman, 23 July 1936; CAS papers, C1 F14, OSA.
65. Robert Sawyer to CAS, 4 Aug. 1939 and Francis Keally to CAS, 11 July 1936; C1 F14, OSA.
66. George Lewis to CAS, 14 May 1937; C1 F14, OSA.
67. "Future State Buildings," OS, 29 Dec. 1936; "State Building Needs," 19 Jan. 1937; "No 'Top Floor' for Library," 4 May 1937.
68. David Eccles interview with author, Portland, 28 Aug. 1991. Eccles to J. Wesley Sullivan, undated; AC.
69. "Sips for Supper," C-J, 1 April 1938.
70. David Eccles letter to editor of Oreg., 14 March 1969.
71. "Dr. Hosch Retiring from Political Field," and "Hosch Quits Contest for Nomination," *Bend Bulletin,* 5 April 1938.
72. Monroe Sweetland telephone interview with author, 30 Sept. 1996.
73. "Goon War Crystallized 'Beat Martin' Movement; Hess Drafted to Run," OJ, 8 May 1938: 1; Sweetland telephone interview.
74. Elton Watkins radio address, KGW, Portland, 27 April 1938; OCF papers, Box 8, UO.
75. Harold Ickes to Henry Hess, 14 May 1938; OCF papers Box 8.
76. George Norris to Hess, 15 May 1938; OCF papers Box 8.
77. E. E. Kelly to Charles H. Martin, 17 May 1938; E. B. Aldrich to Franklin D. Roosevelt, 16 May 1938; see also Alfred Reames to Roosevelt, 18 May 1938; all in Charles D. Martin papers, Box 6, OHS.
78. David Eccles interview.
79. *New York Times* articles: "Martin-Hess Race Is Close In New Deal Test in Oregon," 21 May 1938; "Hess, New Dealer, Winner In Oregon By Narrow Margin," 22 May 1938; "Oregon Vote Cast On National Issues," 22 May 1938; "In The Nation," 24 May 1938.
80. WAS telephone interview; "R. J. Hendricks Signs '30' to 63 Years of Editing," OS, 20 Jan. 1943.
81. Oregon Voter's Pamphlet, Primary Nominating Election, May 1938; Oregon Secretary of State.
82. CAS radio address, 18 April 1938; CAS papers, C8 F9, OSA.
83. Ibid.
84. "Off the Deep End," OS, 1 April 1938.
85. "Back from the Wars," OS, 21 May 1938.

86. Cecil Edwards interview with author, Salem, 15 August 1989.
87. "Democrats Lose an Election," C-J, 23 May 1938.
88. "Candidate Hess," Oreg., 5 June 1938.
89. Ralph A. Moores to Robert Boyd, various dates during General Election campaign; CAS papers, C1 F13, OSA.
90. Moores to Boyd, 20 Sept. 1938; CAS papers, C1 F13 OSA.
91. "Charles A. Sprague's Real Views on Labor," United Brotherhood of Carpenters and Joiners of America; "Sprague—Apostle of Hooverism," OCF papers, Box 13.
92. "The Picketing Bill," OS, 23 Oct. 1938.
93. David Eccles to J. Wesley Sullivan, undated; AC.
94. "Oregon Republicans Swing Left," *New York Times*, 30 Oct. 1938.
95. "Both Candidates for Governor Oppose Anti Labor Bill Number 317," *Oregon Labor Press*, 28 Oct. 1938.
96. Edwards to Boyd, 28 Sept. 1938; CAS papers, C1 F12 OSA. Boyd to Harold Pruitt, 19 Oct. 1938; CAS papers, C1 F13, OSA.
97. Edwards letter to editors, 25 Oct. 1938; CAS papers, C5 F7, OSA.
98. Del Neiderhiser radio address, "election eve" 1938; CAS papers, C8 F9, OSA.
99. "Sprague Confident Voters Will Resent Interference," Medford *Mail-Tribune*, 25 Oct. 1938.
100. "Mr. Ickes Meddles Again," C-J, 25 Oct. 1938.
101. "Sprague Knows Governor's Job," R-G, 16 Oct. 1938.
102. "Sprague Keynotes On 'Square Deal,'" R-G, 15 Oct. 1938.
103. "Cottage Grovers Hear Hess Flay Press, Sprague's Record," R-G, 22 Oct. 1938.
104. "Hess Lambasts Sprague, Press In Speech Here," R-G, 27 Oct. 1938.
105. "Henry Hess Comes To Call," R-G, 29 Oct. 1938.
106. Henry Hess Jr., interview with author, Portland, 18 Feb. 1998.
107. "Veterans' Hess-for-Governor Club" letter; CAS papers, C1 F14, OSA.
108. CAS radio address on KOIN, 24 Oct. 1938; CAS papers, C1 F14, OSA.
109. CAS radio address on KOIN, 1 Nov. 1938; CAS papers, C8 F9, OSA.
110. Robert E. Burton, *Democrats of Oregon*, 87-88.
111. "Washington Merry-go-Round," 3 Dec. 1938, syndicated in various papers.
112. "Successful Candidates Thank Voters," OJ, 9 Nov. 1938.
113. "Prowler Pays Spragues a Visit," OJ, 9 Nov. 1938; "Holman Resigns, Pearson New Treasurer," C-J, 27 Dec. 1938.

Chapter Four

1. "White Hails a 'Revolt' of the Middle Class," *New York Times Magazine*, 20 Nov. 1938: 3, 24-26.
2. "Louis Brandeis," J-T, 10 Feb. 1916.
3. An excellent review of this period's views on conservation is William G. Robbins, *Landscapes of Promise: The Oregon Story 1800-1940* (Seattle: University of Washington Press, 1997), 238-296.

4. Daniel Elazar, *American Federalism: A View from the States* (New York: Thomas Crowell Co.,1966), 89-108 (Elazar names, with Oregon, the New England states, Michigan, Wisconsin, Minnesota, North Dakota, Colorado, Utah and Washington).
5. Ibid.
6. "Inaugural Message of Charles A. Sprague, Governor of Oregon, to the Fortieth Legislative Assembly, 1939," CAS papers, C4 F9, OSA.
7. The Oregon pauper law read: "When any poor person shall not have any relatives or such relatives shall not be of sufficient ability, or shall fail or refuse to maintain such pauper, the said pauper shall receive such relief as the case may require out of the county treasury." quoted in William Mullins, *The Depression and the Urban West Coast, 1929-1933* (Bloomington: Indian University Press, 1991), 40.
8. "Study in Contrasts," C-J, 9 Jan. 1938.
9. Jeryme English interview with author, Salem, 3 September 1991.
10. Jeryme English interview with J. Wesley Sullivan, 14 Aug. 1988, Salem.
11. "Editors Honor Governor-Elect, Wish Him Luck," OJ, 8 Jan. 1939.
12. MSH interview with author, Kensington, Calif., 17 Jan. 1998; Cecil Edwards interview with author, Salem, 15 Aug. 1989.
13. "McCarthy's Fate up to Governor," OS, 18 Jan. 1939; "Sprague Ponders Execution Case," Oreg, 19 Jan. 1939; "Sprague Agreed to Grant Stay if Requested" and "Sips for Supper," C-J, 19 Jan. 1939; "Senate Denies Reprieve Plea by 21-9 Vote," OS, 20 Jan. 1939; "An Obsolete Tradition," C-J, 20 Jan. 1939.
14. In 1949, he supported the death penalty (ISTM, 23 Feb.); but in 1958 he reversed his view, and supported repeal (ISTM, 19 Oct.). His views had grown stronger by 1963 (ISTM, 25 March), and in 1964, supporting the repeal measure that finally passed, he urged voters to "end this debasement of themselves" (ISTM, 25 Oct. 1964).
15. Wallace Sprague telephone interview with author, 26 Feb. 1998.
16. "Two of Sprague's Aides Find Their Salaries Cut," OJ, 3 Feb. 1939 (Eccles was paid $4,000 a year, compared to $5,000 for Wallace Wharton, Edwards $3,000 compared to $3,600 for W. L. "Pinky" Gosslin). The Eccles story was related by Forest W. Amsden in an address to the Oregon Historical Society, 15 Nov. 1987; AC.
17. See CAS letters to Paul Sharp, Webster Jones, Thomas Culbertson Jr., Raymond Staub, 5 Oct. 1939; CAS papers, C1 F1, OSA; Press Release, 5 Oct. 1939, C8 F7, OSA. Correspondence concerning the Forestry action, and reports of Spears Investigation Bureau regarding Ferguson and officials of the Oregon Forest Fire Association are in C3 F11, OSA.
18. The Board of Control was leasing 447 acres from various individuals, including 153 acres at Colony Farm, Eola owned by Doctors R. E. Lee Steiner and J. C. Evans (the superintendent); under terms of the lease the owners got one-fourth of the crops and a crew of some 24 patients and two supervisors was on the premises year-around, clearing land for the owners in addition to other farm duties. See Roy H. Mills to CAS, 5 June 1940, C2

F1, OSA. The 1941 Legislature approved purchase of farm lands to replace the leases.

19. David Eccles interview with author, Portland, 28 August 1991; Harry D. Boivin oral history transcript, OHS; Paul Harvey interview with author, Salem, 6 September 1991.
20. "Sprague Vetoes Pilot Measure," OJ, 21 Feb. 1939; "Clear-Headed Governor," Oreg, 8 March 1939; Governor's veto messages on Senate Bill 52 and 70, House and Senate Journals, 1939 Legislature; "The Veto Messages of Governor Charles A. Sprague," *The Commonwealth Review* 21 (May 1939): 45-59.
21. "Governor's Illness Fails To Halt Control Board," OJ, 16 Feb. 1939.
22. David Eccles to CAS , 28 Dec. 1938; AC.
23. David Eccles interview.
24. OJ editorial page articles by Robert W. Sawyer: "Must Conserve Oregon Timber," 22 Jan.; "The Need For State Forests," 23 Jan.; "State Must Act To Save Timber," 24 Jan. 1941.
25. "Sprague Wants Forests to Be His Monument," OJ, 8 March 1941.
26. John B. Woods, "Forestry Moves Forward In Oregon," *American Forests* 47 (June 1941): 167-269, 292.
27. Robert Bruce, "Interview: Governor Charles A. Sprague Describes His Administration's Proudest Achievement," *Oregon Historical Quarterly* 88 (1987): 403-12.
28. ISTM, 8 Aug. 1945; "Forestry Program," 30 June 1946.
29. WAS telephone interview, 26 Feb. 1998.
30. "Oregon Legislature Ends in Uproar," OJ, 17 March 1941.
31. "Klamath Liquor Licenses Hit," OJ, 16 March 1939; "Klamath Law Enforcement," OS, 15 June 1939; "Proving Their Own Guilt," C-J, 13 June 1939; Lee Bown report to Deputy Superintendent H. G. Maison and CAS to Maison, 25 May 1939; C3 F14, OSA; Richard P. Matthews, "Taking Care of Their Own: The Marine Barracks at Klamath Falls, Oregon, 1944-1946," *Oregon Historical Quarterly* 93 (Winter 1992-93): 343-68. A 1942 report, probably by the federal Division of Social Protection, identified seven houses of prostitution in Klamath Falls, lagging behind only Portland (46) and Pendleton (12) in the state: "Alleged Houses of Prostitution in Cities in Oregon," C7 F5, OSA.
32. Sprague address to Oregon State Bar convention, 28 Sept. 1939; C8 F10, OSA.
33. "Negro Backs Over Bank in Attempt To Start His Car," OS, 15 July 1939.
34. "Collections. Oral History Interview: Kathryn Hall Bogle on the African-American Experience in Wartime Portland," *Oregon Historical Quarterly* 93 (Winter 1992-93): 394-407.
35. Monroe Sweetland report to the OCF Board, 30 June 1937; OCF papers, Box 1, UO.
36. Governor's veto message on SB 11, House and Senate Journal, 1941 Oregon Legislature; Sweetland to Sprague, 9 April 1941 and Sweetland to Roger Baldwin, 17 March 1941, OCF papers, Box 12.

37. Press release, 11 Jan. 1939; OCF papers, Box 3.
38. Press release, undated; OCF papers, Box 3.
39. "Governor Offers Ideas on PUD Laws; Committee Prepares for Final Task," OJ, 23 Feb. 1939; "House Will Act Today Upon PUD Legislation," OS, 10 March 1939.
40. Allan Hart to Paul Raver, 9 Nov. 1940; Herman Lafky to CAS, 16 Sept. 1940; Ormond Bean to CAS, 23 Sept. 1940; CAS to Raver, 19 Dec. 1940; all C11 F14, OSA. "Governor, Raver Disagree on Act," OJ, 20 Jan. 1941.
41. "America's stake in the Pacific," CAS address at the Governor's Conference, Boston, Mass., 2 July 1941. CAS papers, Box 4, OHS.
42. "Let's Keep Our Scrap Iron," Oreg, 3 March 1939.
43. "Astoria's 'Crusade' Threatens to Make International Case," OS, 2 March 1939; "Japanese Consul Urges Action on Ship Tieup," OS, 3 March 1939; "Loading Crews Pass Up Scrap," Oreg, 7 March 1939; "Waterfront Issue," OS, 8 March 1939; "Mass Meeting Hails Embargo," Oreg, 11 March 1939. See also Kenichi Fujishima to Sprague, 2 March 1939 and CAS to Fujishima, 3 March (mis-dated 3 Feb.) 1939, C4 F14, OSA.
44. "Pickets Called Off Scrap Vigil," Oreg, 16 March 1939. See also CAS to E. F. Coates, President, Waterfront Employers' Association, 16 March 1939 and Coates to CAS, 17 March 1939; C4 F14, OSA.
45. Blanche Sprague diary, CAS papers, Box 5, OHS; Blanche in September had christened the *Star of Oregon*, first of the Liberty ships to roll off the ways at the Kaiser yard; she referred to it as "my ship."
46. Paul W. Harvey, Jr. interview.
47. "We, Too, Are Americans," OJ, 14 Feb. 1941.
48. CAS message for *Japanese-American Courier* (November 1940); CAS papers, C4, F14, OSA.
49. CAS to Earl Riley and to Martin T. Pratt, 8 Dec. 1941. C 4 F14, OSA.
50. CAS radio address, 13 Dec. 1941. C8 F13, OSA.
51. Roger Daniels, *Politics of Prejudice* (Berkeley: University of California Press, 1962), 1-7; U. S. Commission on Wartime Relocation and Internment of Civilians, *Personal Justice Denied* (Washington: USGPO, 1982).
52. Census figures cited in U. S. Department of State, *Report of the Honorable Roland S. Morris on Japanese Immigration and Alleged Discriminatory Legislation Against Japanese Residents in the United States*, Reprint edition (New York: Arno Press, 1978), 230-31.
53. For a comprehensive discussion of the legal issues raised by internment see Jacobus tenBroek, Edward N. Barnhart and Floyd W. Matson, *Prejudice, War and the Constitution* (Berkeley: University of California Press, 1954); citizenship is discussed in particular on pp 311-25; see also Sidney Fine, "Mr. Justice Murphy and the Hirabayashi Case," *Pacific Historical Review* (1964): 195-209.
54. *Census of Population: 1940, Volume II, Characteristics of the Population, Part 37, Oregon.* Washington: U.S. Department of Commerce, Government Printing Office, 1941.

55. Clarence E. Oliver to CAS, 11 Dec. 1941; C4, OSA.
56. CAS to Oliver, 8 Jan. 1941; C4, OSA.
57. C. B. Lewis to CAS, 21 Feb. 1941; C4, OSA.
58. Herbert Lundy, "A test for U.S. tolerance," *Sunday Oregonian Magazine*, 4 Jan. 1942.
59. "Japanese-Americans: A symposium," Oreg, 25 Jan. 1942; Herbert Lundy interview with author, Lake Oswego, 9 July 1992.
60. Marvin G. Pursinger, "Oregon's Japanese in World War II: A History of Compulsory Relocation," Ph.D. dissertation, University of Southern California, 1961: 88-126; Morton Grodzins, *Americans Betrayed: Politics and the Japanese Evacuation* (Chicago: University of Chicago Press, 1949), 192.
61. *The Guide*, 19 Dec. 1941; quoted in Pursinger, "Oregon's Japanese," 129.
62. CAS to Attorney General Nicholas Biddle, 17 Feb. 1942; C4, OSA.
63. Frank Bane to Sprague, 8 Feb. 1942; C2 F4, OSA.
64. CAS to Bane, 10 Feb. 1942; C2 F4, OSA.
65. Maj. Gen. J. L. Benedict to CAS, 5 Feb. 1942; C1 F6, OSA.
66. CAS remarks, "Oregon Reports," 13 March 1942, KOIN; C8 F14, OSA.
67. "Sprague Denies Need of Guard at Present Time," OJ, 10 Jan. 1941; Francis J. Murnane, Portland Industrial Union Council, to CAS, 22 Jan. 1941 and CAS to Murnane, 24 Jan. 1941; C7 F1, OSA; CAS to Rogers MacVeagh, 22 Dec. 1941, C7 F1, OSA.
68. Rynerson represented Sprague in resolving a labor dispute involving Western Cooperage Co. in 1940; C2 F3, OSA. Sprague himself was involved in ending an AFL-CIO jurisdictional battle that had shut Columbia Basin Sawmills, Vernonia, in 1939; C7 F5, OSA. For the Oregon Economic Council exchange, see Monroe Sweetland to CAS, 14 Jan. 1940 and CAS to Sweetland, 17 Jan. 1940, also CAS to Sweetland, 21 March 1940; OCF papers, Box 10, UO.
69. "Sprague Gives Hint to Labor," Oreg, 19 June 1940; CAS speech to AFL convention, 17 June 1941, C8 F13, OSA.
70. E. Kimbark MacColl, *The Growth of a City: Power and Politics in Portland, Oregon, 1915 to 1950* (Portland: The Georgian Press, 1970), 571-84.
71. Memorandum to CAS from State Recreation Committee, 2 Nov. 1942; C2 F10, OSA.
72. Quintard Taylor, "The great migration: The Afro-American communities of Seattle and Portland during the 1940s," *Arizona and the West* 23 (Summer, 1981): 109-14, 121; "When Henry Kaiser launched a thousand ships," Oreg, 3 Dec. 1991.
73. "Need for State Defense Council," OJ, 27 Jan. 1941; Minutes of Oregon State Defense Council meeting, 10 June 1941; C2 F8, OSA.
74. CAS to Gov. Culbert Olson, 10 Oct. 1942; C2 F11, OSA.
75. Press Release, Governor's office, 17 March 1942; C8 F8, OSA ; Lt. Col. S. F. Miller, Ninth Army Corps, to Col. Ralph P. Cowgill, 6 April 1941; C7 F1, OSA.

76. Cowgill to Maj. Gen. Kenyon A. Joyce, U. S. Ninth Corps, 25 July 1942; Governor's order authorizing additional units, 15 Sept. 1942; Strength Report, Oregon State Guard, 31 Dec. 1942; all C7 F1, OSA.
77. Acting Gov. Dean Walker to R. T. Harrison, 19 July 1942; C3 F6, OSA; Governor's press release, 2 July 1942, C8 F8, OSA; Joyce to CAS, 10 March 1942; C3 F7, OSA.
78. CAS to Joseph B. Eastman, 2 Oct. 1942; C6 F1, OSA; Letters regarding federal equipment, C2 F9, OSA.
79. Jerrold Owen, "Oregon Prepares for War Emergencies," *State Government* 85, 85-87.
80. Eccles to Ruth Hanna Simms, 13 Nov. 1939; C1 F2, OSA.
81. Paul Harvey interview; "Sprague Adopts Open-Door Policy Toward Capitol Newsmen at Salem," *Oregon Publisher* (April 1939); Herbert Lundy interview.
82. Governor's veto message, HB 259, House and Senate Journal, 1941 Legislature; see also CAS to Tillamook Creamery Association, 5 April 1941; CAS to C. W. Laughlin, April 16, 1941 and Laughlin to CAS, 12 April; Interstate Associated Creameries to Sprague, 21 May 1941; all C8 F3, OSA.
83. David Eccles interview; Robert Notson interview with author, Beaverton, 13 June 1994.
84. Cecil Edwards interview.
85. Robert Sprague interview with author, Eugene, 16 Jan. 1994.

Chapter Five

1. CAS radio address on KGW, 13 May 1942; CAS papers, C8 F14, OSA.
2. Earl Snell radio address, 14 May 1942; Snell papers, C6 F8, OSA.
3. David Eccles interview with author, Portland, 28 August 1991.
4. ISTM, 31 Oct. 1947.
5. "Snell vs. Sprague," OV, 9 Aug. 1941.
6. E. Kimbark MacColl, *The Growth of a City: Power and Politics in Portland, Oregon, 1915 to 1950* (Portland: The Georgian Press, 1970), 570-71.
7. David Eccles interview.
8. "Sprague Administration," analysis by Philip Brandt, July 1941; contained in Brandt to John McCourt, 5 March 1942; C2 F6, OSA.
9. "General Observations," result of public opinion poll, no date or author, Primary Election 1942; CAS papers, C1 F12, OSA.
10. "Confidential Report," 6 March 1942, unsigned; William Walsh to CAS, 2 May 1942; R. W. Hogg to CAS, 23 March 1942; Arthur Beattie to CAS, 9 March 1942; O. E. Crawford to CAS, 12 April 1942; "Confidential Report," 14 March 1942, unsigned. C2 F6, OSA.
11. Travis Cross interview with author, Portland, 27 June 1991; "It's Great to Win," undated clip, OS.
12. "Two-Shot Charlie (He Missed Both) Opens big PITA Trapshoot Here," OS, 21 July 1939; "Hi-Yo! Charley! Governor Now Cowboy," OS, 11 July 1939.

13. Snell advertisement in newspapers during final campaign week, May 5-12 1942; AC.
14. Snell radio address, 12 May 1942, quoted in "Industrial Plan for State Framed," Oreg, 13 May 1942.
15. Snell letter to Republican precinct committeemen and committeewomen, undated 1942; C1 F13, OSA. Excerpts from a speech by Walter Norblad, 6 May 1942, Portland; C6 F8, OSA.
16. CAS radio speech, KOIN, 15 April 1942; C8 F14, OSA.
17. Oregon Business & Tax Research, *Special Bulletin*, 7 July 1941. "No Warning Given, Tax Review Finds," OJ, 14 April 1942; "Taxation Major Talk Theme," OJ, 26 April 1942.
18. Charles V. Galloway, "Fair and Honest Taxation in Oregon," radio address on KGW, 2 May 1942; C8 F14, OSA.
19. McCourt to CAS, 25 Oct. 1941 and CAS to McCourt, 30 Oct.1941; C11 F21, OSA; Galloway radio text; "The Tax Issue In Oregon," OJ, 5 April 1942.
20. Snell radio address, KGW, 11 March 1942; Snell speech, 7 April 1942, C6 F8, OSA.
21. CAS radio address, KGW, 11 May 1942, C8 F14, OSA.
22. Snell radio address, 14 May 1942, C6 F8, OSA .
23. "Sprague vs. Snell," *Coos Bay Times*, 9 May 1942.
24. "Sips for Supper," C-J, 18 May 1942.
25. David Eccles interview. Blanche Sprague diary for 16 May 1942; CAS papers, Box 5, OHS.
26. Forest Amsden, remarks to Oregon Historical Society, 15 Nov. 1987, AC. CAS to Robert Sawyer, 18 May 1942; Sawyer papers, UO.
27. "The Primary Election," *Astorian-Budget*, 16 May 1942; Monroe Sweetland to CAS, 16 May 1942; AC.
28. "Mr. Snell Chosen," Oreg, 17 May 1942.
29. George Aiken to CAS, 14 April 1942; C4 F16, OSA. Minutes of Agriculture subcommittee of State Advisory Committee to U. S. Employment Service, 23 April 1942; C1 F5, OSA.
30. Pursinger, "Oregon's Japanese," 247-53. CAS to Colonel Karl R. Bendetsen, 8 May 1942; Grace G. Tully to CAS, 14 May 1942; CAS press release, 14 May 1942; Milton Eisenhower to CAS, 20 May 1942; Eisenhower to CAS, 20 May 1942; all C4 F16, OSA.
31. Pursinger, "Oregon's Japanese," 259-63.
32. Ibid., 263-72.
33. Ibid., 272-74. Hito Okada to CAS, 25 May 1942; C4 F16, OSA; R. G. Larson to Aiken, C5 F1, OSA.
34. CAS to Elmer L. Sherrell, 2 Oct. 1942; C4 F16, OSA.
35. CAS to Franklin D. Roosevelt, 16 Oct. 1942; C4 F16, OSA.
36. Howard M. Imazeki to CAS, 22 Oct. 1942; C5 F1, OSA.
37. Hugh Ball to CAS, 19 Oct. 1942; CAS to Imazeki, 26 Oct. 1942; C5 F1, OSA.
38. Ichiro Hasegawa, Richard Hikawa and Ken Sekiguchi to CAS, 18 Oct. 1942; C5 F1, OSA.

39. Quoted in Pursinger, "Oregon's Japanese," 269.
40. Ibid., 311-12.
41. Select Committee Investigating National Defense Migration, U.S. House of Representatives, 77th Congress, 2d Session; Part 30, Portland and Seattle hearings, 26-28 Feb. and 2 March 1942.
42. Charles Davis interview with author, Portland, 28 August 1991; Forest Amsden remarks to Oregon Historical Society, 15 Nov. 1987; AC.
43. "Survey reveals Portland favors removal of aliens," Oreg, 12 Feb. 1942.
44. "Mr. Snell Chosen," Oreg, 17 May 1942.
45. CAS to William Walsh, 29 May 1942, C2 F5, OSA; CAS to Robert Sawyer, 27 Aug. 1943; Sawyer papers, UO.
46. Blanche Sprague diary for 13 and 14 Jan. 1943, Box 5, OHS.
47. CAS to Asahel Bush, 28 Jan. 1944; Bush telegram to CAS, 7 Feb. and letter 22 Feb. 1944; AC. ISTM, 27 Oct. 1944. The other Salem journalist killed in the war was Ralph Barnes of the *New York Herald-Tribune*. He died in 1940 when his plane crashed in Yugoslavia. He was the first American correspondent killed in WW II and a Liberty ship was named for him in 1943. "Salem Newspaperman Honored by Launching of Liberty Ship," OS, 11 Dec. 1943.
48. "Editorial Leadership Award Presented to Charles A. Sprague," OS, 20 June 1943; "Newsprint Shortage," OS, 23 Aug. 1943.
49. "Politics and Taxes," OS, 6 March 1943.
50. Sprague spoke for Willkie in 1940 in Washington, Montana, North and South Dakota, Kansas, Oklahoma and Utah. He delivered a major Oregon radio address for the Willkie-McNary ticket on 31 Oct. Material in CAS papers, C8 F11, OSA.
51. "McNary Dies Unexpectedly in Florida," OS, 26 Feb. 1944; the senator's life is described in Steve Neal, *McNary of Oregon: A Political Biography* (Portland: Oregon Historical Society, 1985).
52. Charles W. Ingham to CAS, 24 June and 8 Aug. 1940; CAS to Ingham, 5 Aug.; Morse to CAS, 7 Aug 1940; all CAS papers, C5 F19, OSA. "It Seems To Me," OS, 9 Oct. 1951. A. Robert Smith in his biography of Morse also mentions as potential candidates editors Merle Chessman and Palmer Hoyt; see *The Tiger in the Senate* (New York: Doubleday and Co., 1962), 97-98.
53. "Snell Names Guy Cordon to Fill McNary Vacancy," OS, 5 March 1944; CAS announcement on KOIN, 15 March 1944, CAS papers, C8 F15, OSA.
54. "Guy Cordon Reveals Aims," Oreg, 29 March 1944.
55. "Cordon's Sense of Duty Lauded," Oreg, 11 May 1944.
56. "Holman Charge Lifts Expenses into Spotlight," OS, 2 June 1944.
57. Mason Drukman, *Wayne Morse: A Political Biography* (Portland: Oregon Historical Society, 1997), 120-142; Rex Ellis to CAS, 4 March 1944; AC.
58. Sprague to Wendell Willkie, 22 May 1944; AC.
59. WAS interview with author, New York City, 4 August 1992.
60. MSH, e-mail message to author, 24 Jan. 1998.

Chapter Six

1. Details of WW's early life and a very brief outline of his three decades with the OS are contained in "Journalism—For Food and Fun," an informal autobiography; the original is with his daughter, Marsha Webb Drahn of Eugene. Webb met Sprague when working for the Associated Press in Portland, and inquired about a job when he was assigned to the San Francisco bureau in 1940; WW to CAS, 1 Oct. 1940, AC.
2. Webb autobiography, 79-83.
3. N. W. Ayers and Son, *Directory of Newspapers and Periodicals* (Philadelphia: N.W. Ayers and Son, 1945).
4. Webb autobiography, 79-83.
5. "Statesman-KSLM Spelling Contest Starting Tomorrow, OS, 14 Jan. 1951; Webb autobiography, 85-88.
6. Figures are extrapolated from first-half financial statements only, for the years involved; obviously the unavailability of full-year statements produces less-than-complete records, and the figures must be viewed in that light. But a consistent pattern is quite apparent. Records in AC.
7. Tax records in AC.
8. Financial records in AC.
9. J. Wesley Sullivan, *"To Elsie With Love"* (Eugene: Navillus Press, 1993), 81-83.
10. Among the postwar newsroom staff: Winston Taylor, who had been with the paper briefly before the war; Don Dill, the paper's first photographer; Les Cour, Ron Reeves, Bob Stevens, Larry Hobart, Charles Ireland, John White, Eric Bergman, Vic Fryer, Jim Miller.
11. Marguerite Wright interview with author, Portland, 30 July 1992.
12. The *Statesman* Centennial issue was 28 March 1951. "Hundred-Year Shout," *TIME* (9 April 1951): 49-50.
13. Thomas G. Wright, Jr. interview with author, Portland, 29 Aug. 1989
14. Alfred G. Hill to CAS, 17 Dec. 1939, C7 F1, OSA.
15. CAS United Nations diary, entry for 11 Dec. 1952, AC. CAS to Robert Sawyer, 28 Jan. 1953, Sawyer papers, UO.
16. "Moores Fund May Purchase Venus Statue," C-J, 12 June 1953; "Renoir's 'Venus Victorieuse' to Grace Courthouse Grounds," OS, 13 June 1953.
17. "Venus for the Courthouse," C-J, 13 June 1953.
18. "Pagan Goddess Statue Arouses Writer's Ire," 13 June 1953; "Memorializing Our Pioneers," 13 June 1953; "Protest Grows Against Venus Statue Choice," 16 June 1953; all C-J.
19. "Mayor Offers Opposition to Venus Statue," and "Venus Praised by Architect of Courthouse," OS, 17 June 1953; "Os West Comments Pungently on Venus," C-J, 19 June 1953.
20. ISTM, 17 June 1953.
21. "Venus Abandoned as Memorial to Pioneers," C-J, 20 June 1953.
22. "In Place of Venus," OS, 24 June 1953.

23. "Nude Bronze Venus Shown to Portland," OJ, 3 Oct. 1953; "Dearth Noted in Wolf Calls," Oreg, 3 Oct. 1953.
24. William Mainwaring interview with author, Salem, 17 Sept. 1996.
25. "Oregon Statesman, Capital Journal Reveal Plans for Consolidation of Operation," OS, 28 Nov. 1953; contract of sale, CAS papers, Box 7, OHS.
26. WW to CAS, 7 May and 23 July 1959; RS to CAS, 24 July 1959; William Mainwaring to CAS, undated 1959; "Memorandum of Agreement on News Budgets," 19 July 1959; all AC.
27. CAS letters to eleven daily newspaper joint operations, 16 May 1957, with replies and analysis, undated; AC.
28. William Mainwaring interview.
29. William Mainwaring to Sprague, undated; E. A. Brown to Mainwarings, 6 May 1958; Memorandum of agreement on Statesman-Journal circulation departments, 18 June 1959; all AC. William Mainwaring interview.
30. "Report on Statesman-Journal Newspapers for years 1954-56," undated, AC.
31. Ibid.
32. Ibid.
33. OS wage details from annual news budgets, 1957-68, AC; WW to CAS, 17 June 1959; AC. John L. Hulteng, "Salaries on Oregon Dailies by Experience Levels," *Journalism Quarterly* 42 (1965): 276-78; Edward J. Trayes, "A Survey of Salaries of AP-Served Dailies," *Journalism Quarterly* 46 (1969): 825-28, 891.
34. WAS interview with author, New York City, 4 Aug. 1992
35. "Report on Statesman-Journal Newspapers," undated 1957; AC.
36. Robert Sprague interview with author, Eugene, 16 Jan. 1994.
37. ISTM, 11 and 15 Jan. 1950; "Portland Has a 'Cold War,'" R-G, 13 Jan. 1950; "A Freedom of the Press Issue," C-J, 14 Jan. 1950; unheadlined reprint of Sprague column, G-T, 14 Jan. 1950; "A Statement to Our Readers," Oreg, 14 Jan. 1950; "Up-State Thoughts on M & F Action," Bend *Bulletin*, 21 Jan. 1950. Gerald W. Frank telephone interview with author, 11 Sept. 1996
38. "School Office Building Site Bought by Store," OS, 8 March 1953. Aaron Frank to Sprague, 16 March 1953; AC. Gerald W. Frank telephone interview.
39. Gerald W. Frank telephone interview.
40. Gerald W. Frank oral history transcript, 55-77; OHS.
41. "Flying Pennies Signal End to Cal-USC Tilt, Lightner Rules," OS, 8 Jan. 1956; "No Pass, Ticket—But He's Right in Middle of 'Thrill,'" OS, 9 Aug. 1954; "Landy Confirms Lightner Story," OS, 11 Aug. 1954; "Lightner 'Pinch Hits' Way Into World Series 'Opener,'" OS, 29 Sept. 1955.

Chapter Seven

1. Charles Davis interview with author, Portland, 28 Aug. 1991; "Former Oregon Governor Wins McNaughton [sic] Award," Oreg, 19 Dec. 1962;

"Human-Rights Principles Deep Rooted in Oregon, Says Sprague, Accepting Award from ACLU," OS, 19 Dec. 1962.

2. "Civil Liberties Problem of States," OS, 7 Dec. 1939.
3. "Oregon Statesman," *Presbyterian Life*, 15 Dec. 1960: 14; *100th Anniversary, First Presbyterian Church, Salem, Oregon, 1869-1969"* (Salem: First Presbyterian Church, 1969), 21, 40.
4. "Deport the Japs?" OS, 26 Feb. 1943; "Protest Jap Deportation," OS, 4 March 1943.
5. ISTM, 16 May 1943; "Pierce on Japs," OS, 26 May 1943.
6. "Return of the Japs," OS, 20 Dec. 1944; "No Mass Return of Japs," OS, 22 Dec. 1944. The exact number of Oregon Japanese Americans interned is difficult to determine. An official estimate in February 1942 placed the number in Western Oregon at about 4,000. See U. S. Department of War, *Final Report: Japanese Evacuation from the West Coast, 1942;* Reprint edition (New York: Arno Press, 1978).
7. For Holman, see F. Alan Coombs, "Congressional Opinion and War Relocation, 1943," in Roger Daniels et al. (eds), *Japanese Americans: From Relocation to Redress* (Salt Lake City: University of Utah, 1986), 88-91. For Pierce, see Arthur Bone, *Oregon Cattleman/Governor, Congressman: Memoirs and Times of Walter M. Pierce. Edited and Expanded by Arthur Bone* (Portland: Oregon Historical Society, 1981).
8. An excellent account of Japanese in Hood River is contained in Lauren Kessler's description of the Yasui family, the most prominent of the Japanese families in Hood River, *Stubborn Twig: Three Generations in the Life of a Japanese American Family* (New York: Penguin Books, 1993).
9. "Legion for Exclusion of Japanese," Hood River *News*, 8 Dec. 1944.
10. "Ground for Suspicion," Albany *Democrat-Herald*, 19 Jan. 1945; "Be Americans or Else," *Democrat-Herald*, 25 Jan. 1945; "Why Not Get The Facts?" *East-Oregonian*, 12 Dec. 1944. Arthur Bone, *Oregon Cattleman/ Governor,* 395-99.
11. "Un-American," Medford *Mail-Tribune*, 7 Feb. 1945.
12. "Propose to Bar Japanese," Gresham *Outlook*, 3 Nov. 1944; "Group Organizes Against Japanese," Oreg, 29 Nov. 1944: 1.
13. "Our Japanese Problem," Oreg, 2 Dec. 1944: 18; "Our Enemies at Home," C-J, 4 Dec. 1944.
14. "Be Americans or Else," Albany *Democrat-Herald*, 25 Jan. 1945; "Let's First Win the War," OJ, 6 Dec. 1944.
15. "Enforcement of Land Laws is Demanded," Gresham *Outlook*, 15 Feb. 1945; "Start Drive To Get Funds For Campaign," *Outlook*, 15 March 1945.
16. "Speakers Ask Sane Thought on Japanese," Gresham *Outlook*, 22 March 1945; "Stand Taken on Japanese," Oreg, 17 March 1945: 7; Frank Dillow, "E. B. MacNaughton: Businessman with Soul," Northwest Magazine of *The Sunday Oregonian*, 4 April 1971: 10-11.
17. ISTM, 29 March 1945.

18. "Prefer Homes, But Resigned to Move," Oreg, 27 Feb. 1942: 1; Bill Hosokawa, *JACL: In Quest of Justice* (New York: William Morrow and Company, Inc., 1982), 153-69.
19. "Academic Freedom at OSC," OS, 16 Feb. 1949; "OSC Becomes a Battle Ground," R-G, 19 Feb. 1949.
20. Lionel S. Lewis, *Cold War on Campus: A Study of the Politics of Organizational Control* (New Brunswick, N.J., Transaction Books, 1988), 117-20.
21. "Washington Drops Three Commies," R-G, 25 Jan. 1949.
22. "The Communist Profs," OJ, 25 Jan. 1949: 12; "Tempest in a Teapot," C-J, 16 Feb. 1949.
23. The University of Washington incident, widely discussed at the time, is described by Vern Countryman, *Un-American Activities in the State of Washington* (Ithaca: Cornell University Press, 1951); and Jane Sanders, *Cold War on Campus: Academic Freedom at the University of Washington, 1946-1964* (Seattle: University of Washington, 1979).
24. "Mahoney Will Submit Communist-Hunt Bill," OJ, 11 March 1951: 1.
25. "Red-Hunt for Mahoney?" OS, 12 March 1951.
26. Richard L. Neuberger to E. B. MacNaughton, 12 March 1951; Neuberger Papers, Box 37/5, UO.
27. "An Instrument for Terrorism," R-G, 4 April 1951; "Know this as Tyranny," *East Oregonian*, 14 April 1951.
28. William Tugman to Malcolm Bauer, nd Oct. 1960, Bauer papers, OHS.
29. ISTM, 3 May 1951.
30. Maurine Neuberger interview with author, Portland, 8 July 1992.
31. The professors were Jack Pierce, Stan Ashmer and Alfred Sheets; minutes of House State & Federal Affairs Committee, 3 May 1951.
32. Mark O. Hatfield interview with author, Portland, 13 Feb. 1993; Sprague's last meeting with Hatfield occurred after the final hearing, at which Sprague spoke; Hatfield voted with the majority supporting the bill when it was sent to the House floor after the hearing. Since the bill did not come to a recorded vote in the House, the public record shows no change of position on his part. Had the bill come to a House vote he would have had a chance at that time to vote in opposition.
33. Malcolm Bauer, "The Northwest's Most Influential Editor," *New York Herald Tribune Sunday Forum*, 11 Dec. 1960.
34. Mark Hatfield interview.
35. Maurine Neuberger interview.
36. George M. Belknap to William M. Tugman and Tugman to Belknap, 10 May and 14 May 1951, Tugman Papers, UO.
37. Charles Davis interview with author, Portland, 28 Aug. 1991.
38. Ibid.
39. "McCarthy Not Wrong With Voters," *Enterprise-Courier,* 29 Nov. 1950.
40. "McCarthy and the Election," OS, 2 Dec. 1950.
41. ISTM, 13 Aug. 1951.

42. "This Man McCarthy," OS, 24 Aug. 1951.
43. "How Dangerous Is Senator McCarthy," R-G, 19 Aug. 1951; "Young Republican Protests Senator McCarthy," R-G, 24 Aug. 1951; "McCarthy Comes to Portland, Oreg, 25 Aug. 1951: 6.
44. "Sen. Joe McCarthy Greeted by 'Polite Enthusiasm' at Picnic," OS, 27 Aug. 1951; "President's Record Hit By Senator," Oreg, 27 Aug. 1951: 1, 15.
45. ISTM, 29 Aug. 1951.
46. "Showdown on Joe McCarthy," OS, 18 March 1953; "Showdown on Joe McCarthy," *Mail-Tribune,* 18 March 1953; "Showdown on Joe McCarthy," *Bend Bulletin,* 23 March 1953; "What a Big Boy is Joe," OS, 30 March 1953.
47. "Reed College and Communism," OS, 20 June 1954.
48. A detailed description is Michael Munk, "Oregon Tests Academic Freedom in (Cold) Wartime: The Reed College Trustees Versus Stanley Moore," *Oregon Historical Quarterly* 97 (1996): 262-354. See also Floyd McKay, "After Cool Deliberation: Reed College, Oregon Editors and the Red Scare of 1954," *Pacific Northwest Quarterly* 89 (Winter 1997/98): 12-21.
49. Wright recalled cubicle visits from Tom Dewey and Harold Stassen, from governors and political figures seeking Sprague's endorsement or counsel. Marguerite Wright interview with author, Portland, 30 July 1992.
50. "HST's Power Claim Blasted by Warren," OS, 10 May 1952; "For President: Earl Warren," OS, 11 May 1952.
51. CAS to Richard L. Neuberger, 23 Sept. 1952; Neuberger papers, Box 37, UO.
52. Neuberger to CAS, 17 Sept. 1952; Neuberger papers, Box 37, UO.
53. Political identification of newspapers is listed in the two major industry guides, *Editor and Publisher International Yearbook*. and *Ayer's Directory of Newspapers and Periodicals.* Sprague changed his listing in the E & P guide, used by most editors; it remained "Republican" in the Ayer's guide.
54. ISTM, 26 March 1950.
55. Ibid.
56. Durward V. Sandifer, acting assistant secretary for United Nations affairs, memos to the file; U. S. Department of State, 1952 U.N. session, Box 1282, Federal Archives Center, Landover, Maryland.
57. "Statesman Publisher Named U.N. Delegate," OS, 13 Sept. 1952; ISTM, 21 Sept. 1952.

Chapter Eight

1. Diary of CAS during attendance at Seventh Session of General Assembly of United Nations," entry for 13 Oct. 1952; AC.
2. ISTM, 9 Nov. 1962.
3. CAS UN diary, entry of 19 Oct. 1952.
4. "Problems of Journalism: Proceedings of the 1952 Convention, American Society of Newspaper Editors," Washington D.C., 17-19 April 1952: 126-29.

5. CAS statement to Committee Three, reprinted as "Our Free Press. How Free?" *Nieman Reports* 7 (January 1953): 3-4; "Information Pact Again a U.N. Issue," *New York Times,* 29 Oct. 1952: 4.
6. "Report on the Third Committee of the General Assembly," State Department files, Box 1294, Federal Archives.
7. Ibid.
8. Kathleen Telsch, "Right of Correction Treaty is Advanced," *Editor & Publisher,* 8 Nov. 1952: 11; also Telsch, "UN Asks Signatures on Corrections Treaty." *Editor & Publisher,* 20 Dec. 1952: 8.
9. "U.N. Votes Draft Convention on Right of News Correction," *Washington Post,* 17 Dec. 1952: 3; "U.N. Approves Pact on 'Correcting' News," *New York Times,* 17 Dec. 1952: 1, 19; "A Hazardous Step," *TIME,* 29 Dec. 1952; 52; Telsch, "UN Asks Signatures."
10. "Sprague Advises Aid in Information Pact," *Editor & Publisher,* 27 Dec. 1952: 12.
11. CAS to Eleanor Roosevelt, 13 March 1953; AC.
12. CAS UN Diary, entry for 13 Nov. 1952.
13. Ibid., entries for 15-19 Nov.; "U. S. Bids U.N. Shun Action on Malan," *New York Times,* 16 Nov. 1952: 1, 19.
14. CAS UN diary, entry for 20 Nov.; "South Africa Inquiry Voted in U.N., 35-2," *New York Times,* 21 Nov. 1952: 1, 4.
15. "U. S. to Ask U. N. to Grant Lie Right to Oust American Reds," *New York Times,* 30 Oct. 1952: 1, 12; CAS UN diary, entry for 29 Oct. 1952.
16. CAS UN diary, entries for 21-22 Nov. 1952.
17. Ibid., entry for 22 Dec. 1952.
18. U. S. Civil Rights Commission, "The 50 States Report: Submitted to the Commission on Civil Rights by the State Advisory Committees" (Washington: USGPO, 1961): 528.
19. "Let Little Sambo Alone," OS, 17 Oct. 1951.
20. ISTM, 11 March 1953.
21. "Compulsion Not Democracy," C-J, 17 March 1953; "The No-Discrimination Bill," Albany *Democrat-Herald,* 18 March 1953; "Anti-Discrimination Legislation," Grants Pass *Daily Courier,* 19 March 1953; "Other Editors Say," *Democrat-Herald,* 23 March 1953.
22. Mark O. Hatfield interview with author, Portland, 13 Feb. 1993.
23. Maurine Neuberger interview with author, Portland, 8 July 1992.
24. ISTM, 15 April 1953.
25. "Don't Sign Referendum on Civil Rights Bill," OS, 12 July 1953; ISTM, 18 May 1954; "Civil Rights in Housing," OS, 14 April 1959.
26. U. S. Commission on Civil Rights, "The National Conference and the Reports of the State Advisory Committees to the U. S. Commission on Civil Rights" (Washington: USGPO, 1960): 320. Advisory Committee records, CAS papers, Box 4, OHS.
27. Monroe Sweetland telephone interview with author, 30 Sept. 1996.
28. U. S. Commission on Civil Rights, "The National Conference Reports," 329-30

29. Ibid.
30. Sprague chaired the housing panel at the conference. ISTM, 14 June 1959.
31. U. S. Commission on Civil Rights, 1961 final report, 534-35.
32. Ibid., 531-33.
33. Ibid, 529. "End Discrimination," OS, 10 March 1961; ISTM, 6 May 1962.
34. U. S. Commission on Civil Rights, 1961 final report, 536-38. Marguerite Wright interview.
35. "Sales of Indian Lands," OS, Jan. 1952; "Release Indians from Wardship," OS, 20 Feb. 1952.
36. "Terminating Indian Reservations," OS, 4 March 1954.
37. William A. Brophy and Sophie D. Aberle, *The Indian: America's Unfinished Business. Report of the Commission on the Rights, Liberties, and Responsibilities of the American Indian* (Norman: University of Oklahoma Press, 1966).
38. Minutes of meeting of 12-15 Sept. 1958; CAS papers, Box 7, OHS.
39. Ibid.
40. Ibid.
41. Minutes of Commission meeting of 12-15 Feb. 1958; CAS papers, Box 7, OHS.
42. "Weak Points Found in Klamath Indian Termination Act," R-G, 4 Aug. 1957. The R-G series ran from 4-9 Aug. 1957.
43. Oregon Legislative Assembly, "Report of the Legislative Interim Committee on Indian Affairs: "A Reintroduction to the Indians of Oregon," October 1958: 17-22. Brophy and Aberle, *The Indian*, 140-141, 196-200. Vincent Ostrum and Theodore Stern, "A Case Study of the Termination of Federal Responsibilities Over the Klamath Reservation (1963)," summarized for Commission by Sophie Aberle, undated, CAS papers, Box 7, OHS.
44. Legislative interim committee report, 20-21.
45. "Tentative Plan of Management and Recommended Form of Legal Entity for the Klamath Indian People by the Klamath Management Specialists," Aug. 1957; CAS papers, Box 2, OHS.
46. William Brophy to T. B. Watters, 15 May 1957; Watters to Brophy, 17 May 1957; Watters to William Phillips, 22 May 1957. All CAS papers, Box 7, OHS.
47. Correspondence involving CAS, Bob Sawyer and Kenneth Pomeroy, chief forester of the American Forestry Association, May 11 to June 19 1957, CAS papers, Box 7, OHS.
48. ISTM, 10 March, 26 June and 17 Sept. 1957 and 8 May, 10 July and 18 Aug. 1958; "Passes Klamath Bill," OS, 8 May 1958; "Klamath Bill 'Must' Legislation," OS, 3 July 1958.
49. Brophy and Aberle, *The Indian,* 196-99.
50. Legislative interim committee report, 74-78; Brophy and Aberle, *The Indian*, 211-13.
51. CAS to Commission, 18 July 1957; CAS papers, Box 7, OHS.

52. Report on conference, 15 Feb. 1958, CAS papers, Box 7, OHS.
53. "U.S. Is Cautioned On Indian Pacts," *New York Times*, 16 March 1961.
54. United Press International dispatch, printed in Tulsa (Okla) *Tribune*, 16 March 1961; Joseph Lyford to Lyle C. Wilson, 4 April 1961; Fund for the Republic papers, Box 146, Princeton University library.
55. Sophie Aberle to Edward Reed, 13 Sept. 1962; Fund for the Republic papers, Box 52.
56. Commission preliminary report, 16 March 1961; Fund for the Republic papers, Box 146; Brophy and Aberle, *The Indian*, recommendations appear at chapter endings.
57. CAS to Commission, 18 July 1957; CAS papers, Box 7, OHS. ISTM, 21 Jan. 1959.
58. CAS to Sophie D. Aberle, 22 July 1959; CAS papers, Box 7, OHS.
59. WAS interview with author, New York City, 4 Aug. 1992.
60. Richard Winslow to CAS, 4 Nov. 1955; CAS to Joseph E. Johnson, 21 March 1955; AC.

Chapter Nine

1. Robert E. Burton, *Democrats of Oregon: The Pattern of Minority Politics, 1900-1956* (Eugene: University of Oregon, 1970), 91-101.
2. Mason Drukman, *Wayne Morse: A Political Biography* (Portland: Oregon Historical Society, 1997), 28-45; A. Robert Smith, *Tiger in the Senate: A Biography of Senator Wayne Morse* (Garden City, N. Y.: Doubleday, 1962), 31-38.
3. John Swarthout, "The 1956 Election in Oregon," *Western Political Quarterly* 20 (March 1967): 143.
4. Maure L. Goldschmidt, "The 1952 Elections in Oregon," *Western Political Science Quarterly* 6 (March 1953): 124.
5. "Morse's Candidacy," C-J, 3 Nov. 1944; "Trying to Smear Morse," OS, 4 Nov. 1944; "Morse Smears Himself" and "Let's Look at the Record," C-J, 6 Nov. 1944; "Prominent Republican," OS, 8 Nov. 1944.
6. ISTM, 19 Feb. 1946 and 5 March 1947.
7. ISTM, 21 Jan. 1947.
8. CAS to Morse, 5 June 1952; Morse to CAS, 9 June 1952; Morse papers, UO.
9. CAS to Morse, undated; Morse to CAS, 3 June 1951; Morse papers.
10. Wayne Morse to CAS, 24 Sept. 1944, Morse papers; A. Robert Smith, *Tiger in the Senate,* 120-24; Mason Drukman, *Wayne Morse,* 172-73.
11. ISTM, 26 April 1950.
12. "Morse in Race for President," OS, 1 July 1951; ISTM, 2 July 1951; "A Pivot for Liberals?" OS, 12 July 1951; "Wayne Morse—Best Republican," OS, 16 Aug. 1951.
13. "Hatfield Given Conclave Post Over Senator," OS, 8 June 1952; A. Robert Smith, *Tiger in the Senate*, 135-137; Mason Drukman, *Wayne Morse,* 186-87.

14. "Republican Delegates Spurn Morse," OS, 8 June 1952.
15. Peter Tugman oral history. Oregon Historical Society; see also Warren C. Price, *The Eugene Register-Guard: A Citizen of Its Community* (Portland: Binfords & Mort, 1976), 299-314.
16. CAS to RS, 25 Oct. 1952; AC.
17. "Still, Small Voice of Wayne Morse," OS, 25 Jan. 1953.
18. Robert Blaine Whipple, "The Change and Development of Editorial Attitudes of Selected Oregon Daily Newspapers toward Senator Wayne Morse," Master's thesis, University of Oregon, 1959: 131-61, 250-53, 264.
19. A. Robert Smith interview with author, Bellingham, Wash., 12 Oct. 1995.
20. Robert Notson interview with author, Beaverton, 13 June 1994.
21. Robert Sawyer to William Tugman, 15 Feb. 1954; Tugman papers, UO. Frazier quoted by Robert Chandler, interview with author, Portland, 23 Dec. 1992.
22. Circulation figures from N. W. Ayers and Son, *Directory of Newspapers and Periodicals* (Philadelphia: N.W. Ayers and Son, annually).
23. "Capital-Journal Editor Putnam Killed in Blaze," and ISTM, OS 19 Aug. 1961.
24. For discussion of Aldrich, see Gordon McNab, *The East Oregonian, 1875-1975* (Pendleton: East-Oregonian Publishing Co., 1975).
25. George Turnbull, *History of Oregon Newspapers* (Portland: Binfords & Mort, 1939), 117-33; Frank L. Mott, *American Journalism: A History of Newspapers in the United States Through 260 Years, 1690 to 1950* (New York: MacMillan, 1950), 475-76.
26. Marshall N. Dana, *Newspaper Story: 50 Years of the Oregon Journal* (Portland: The Oregon Journal, 1951).
27. J. W. Forrester interview with author, Astoria, 4 Sept. 1991; Roy Beadle interview with author, Gresham, 13 June 1994.
28. Floyd J. McKay, "With Liberty for Some: Oregon Editors and the Challenge of Civil Liberties, 1942-54," Ph.D. dissertation, University of Washington, 1995: 283.
29. Robert Chandler interview; "Sprague: One-day honor not enough," Bend *Bulletin*, 1 Nov. 1987.
30. J. W. Forrester Jr. interview.
31. Robert Frazier to Jim Welch, 20 June and 1 Aug. 1957; Frazier to Eric Allen Jr., 20 Aug. 1959; Frazier papers, UO.
32. Robert Notson interview; Forest Amsden to J. Wesley Sullivan, 27 Oct. 1987; AC.
33. CAS to WW, 26 Oct. 1952; AC.
34. The political life of the Neubergers is described in Richard L. Neuberger, *Adventures in Politics* (New York: Oxford University Press, 1954).
35. Richard L. Neuberger, *Our Promised Land* (New York: MacMillan, 1938). A good collection of Neuberger's magazine pieces is *They Never Go Back To Pocatello: The Selected Essays of Richard Neuberger*, edited by Steve Neal (Portland: Oregon Historical Society, 1988).

36. Neuberger to Herbert Lundy, 24 May 1953. See also Neuberger to Lundy, 27 Sept. 1952; Lundy to Neuberger, 20 May 1953; Malcolm Bauer to Neuberger, 14 Oct. 1953; Neuberger to Bauer, 16 Oct. 1953. All Neuberger papers, Box 37/8.
37. Neuberger to Donald J. Sterling, 13 Feb. 1948, Neuberger papers, Box 37/7, UO. Maurine Neuberger interview with author, Portland, 8 July 1992.
38. Richard L. Neuberger, "His Pen is Mighty," *The Sunday Oregonian Magazine* (18 March 1951): 8-9, and "Sprague: Conscience of Oregon," *The Nation* (26 Jan. 1952). Maurine Neuberger and J. W. Forrester interviews.
39. Neuberger to CAS, 17 Sept. 1953; Neuberger papers, Box 37/10.
40. "Politics and Prejudice," OS, 12 May 1954.
41. Burton, *Democrats of Oregon*, 130-133; Smith, *Tiger in the Senate*, 211-20; Swarthout, "The 1954 Election in Oregon," 622.
42. ISTM, 6 May 1954; OS editorial brief, 1 July 1954; "The Senatorial Race in Oregon," OS, 20 Oct. 1954; "The Senatorial Race in Oregon-II," OS, 21 Oct. 1954; ISTM, 31 Oct. 1954. J. W. Forrester interview.
43. Maurine Neuberger interview.
44. A. Robert Smith, *Tiger in the Senate*, 218-20; Mason Drukman, *Wayne Morse*, 214-20.
45. A. Robert Smith, *Tiger in the Senate*., 307-19.
46. ISTM, 10 and 12 March and 8 May 1956; "Hitchcock Remains a Candidate," OS, 15 March 1956.
47. Quoted in A. Robert Smith, *Tiger in the Senate,* 317; see also 316-30.
48. "Editorial Comment: 'The Unforgiveable Apostacy of Senator Wayne Morse,'" OS, 22 Oct. 1956.
49. ISTM, 9 Oct. and 4 Nov. 1956.
50. ISTM, 8 Nov. 1956.
51. Morse to CAS, 26 Nov. 1956; Morse papers.
52. Thomas G. Wright Jr. interview with author, Portland, 29 Aug. 1989.
53. ISTM, 18 May 1958.
54. ISTM, 23 March and 11 May 1958.
55. Cecil Edwards interview, Paul W. Harvey Jr., interview, J. W. Forrester interview, Thomas G. Wright, Jr. interview.
56. Mark O. Hatfield, *Between a Rock and a Hard Place* (Waco, Texas: Word Books, 1976), 111.
57. Mark O. Hatfield interview with author, Portland, 13 Feb. 1993.
58. Ibid.
59. "1,200 Attend Formal Wedding of Oregon Secretary of State," OS, 9 July 1958.
60. "Governor: Hatfield or Holmes?" OS, 30 Oct. 1958
61. Ibid.
62. "Morse Claims Hatfield Gave False Evidence," *Medford Mail-Tribune*, 2 Nov. 1958.
63. Mark Hatfield interview.
64. "Dastardly Attack on Hatfield," OS, 2 Nov. 1958.

65. "Salem Shuns Morse Talk as Bitter Campaign Ends," C-J, 3 Nov. 1958; "Senator Hanged in Effigy at WU," C-J, 4 Nov. 1958.
66. Travis Cross interview. A. Robert Smith, *Tiger in the Senate*, 370-78; Kenneth E. Johnson, conversation with author, Salem, September 1996; Mason Drukman, *Wayne Morse*, 311-16; Thomas G. Wright Jr. interview.
67. Mason Drukman, *Wayne Morse*, 240-301.
68. "Sen. Morse to Campaign Against Sen. Neuberger," OS, 28 May 1959; "Morse vs. Neuberger," OS, 29 May 1959; "For U.S. Senator: Maurine Neuberger," OS, 16 Oct. 1960.
69. Thomas G. Wright Jr. interview.
70. Ibid.
71. Conrad G. Prange interview.
72. As the sixties began, Allen (Bud) Morrison and Don Scarborough were beginning reporters; Bob Schwartz was in sports. Others soon arrived who would still be with the OS after Sprague's death: Dan Davies, son of *New York Times* reporter Lawrence Davies; the author was hired from the *Springfield News*, Ron Blankenbaker came from Idaho, and young Lewis Arends was hired as a darkroom technician. Reid English, Jeryme's son, began as a sports reporter, Walt Penk and Jim Woods took news desk positions, Janet Davies began reporting. Isabel Rosebraugh wrote for the women's pages, joined by Kay Apley. Others moved on: reporters Tom Marshall, Ron Reeve, Neil Parse and Joe Morton; sports reporters Gordon Rice and Hal Cowan, news deskmen Garth Fanning and Sam Sinclair and Valley editor Mervin Jenkins. Of those who stayed, many remained into the nineties.
73. Kenneth Johnson personal conversation.
74. Thomas G. Wright Jr. and Marguerite Wright interviews.
75. "Statesman Reporter's Hunch Leads to Arrest of Holdup Man," OS, 29 March 1961.
76. A. Robert Smith interview.
77. Ibid. "Morse-Neuberger 'Honeymoon' Ends With Tiff Via Mails," OS, 15 Aug. 1957; Mason Drukman, *Wayne Morse*, 241-300.
78. A. Robert Smith, *Tiger in the Senate*, 189-201.
79. Warren Price, *The Eugene Register-Guard,* 299-314.
80. CAS to Morse, 28 March 1954; Morse to CAS, 14 April 1954; Morse papers.
81. CAS to Morse, 30 Dec. 1954; Morse to CAS, 6 Jan. 1955; Morse memo to files, undated 1955; Morse papers.
82. ISTM, 17 Feb. 1962.
83. Thomas G. Wright Jr. interview.
84. Circulation figures are from *Editor and Publisher International Yearbook* (New York: Editor and Publisher Co., Inc, annually).
85. The Portland strike is treated by Richard Meeker, *Newspaperman: S. I. Newhouse and the Business of News* (New Haven: Ticknor and Fields, 1983); Robert Notson, *Making the Day Begin* (Portland: The Oregonian Publishing Co., 1976); Donald Lee Guimary, "Strike, problems of the Portland Reporter, 1961-64," *Journalism Quarterly* 45 (1968): 91-94.

Chapter Ten

1. Richard Hofstadter, *The Progressive Movement, 1900-1915* (Englewood Cliffs, N.J.: Prentice-Hall, Inc., 1963), 4.
2. Samuel P. Hays, *Conservation and the Gospel of Efficiency: The Progressive Conservation Movement, 1890-1920* (Cambridge: Harvard University Press, 1959).
3. ISTM, 15 May 1960.
4. ISTM, 15 May and 23 Oct. 1960.
5. "Grass Roots McCarthys," OS, 27 March 1961; ISTM, 8 April 1961; "ISTM, 31 March 1961.
6. "We're the 'Radical Left,'" OS, 19 May 1964.
7. ISTM, 15 and 16 July and 1 Nov. 1964.
8. "Draft for Rockefeller," OS, 10 Jan. 1968; ISTM, 8 March 1968; "Rockefeller Declines to be a Candidate," OS, 22 March 1968; "Presidential Choices Blurred," OS, 19 May 1968; "'Rocky's the One,'" OS, 4 July 1968.
9. Forest Amsden to J. Wesley Sullivan, 27 Oct. 1987; AC.
10. Governor Hatfield's proposal and the report of the Advisory Committee are in "Recommendations for Reorganization of the Executive Branch," 15 Dec. 1960; 1961 Legislature, OSA.
11. First Commission Draft, adopted 14 July 1962; Constitutional Revision Commission records, OSA.
12. Minutes of Commission meeting, 23-24 Feb. 1962; Commission records, OSA.
13. "Constitutional Plan to Go to Legislature," OS, 28 April 1962; Final report of the Constitutional Revision Commission, Commission records, OSA.
14. Joint Senate and House Committees on Constitutional Revision, minutes of 29 Jan. meeting; 1963 Legislature, OSA.
15. ISTM, 6 and 9 May 1963; "Senate Committee 'Revises' Revision," OS, 11 May 1963; ISTM, 27 and 29 May 1963.
16. ISTM, 23 Feb. and 27 March 1961.
17. Mark O. Hatfield interview with author, Portland, 13 Feb. 1993.
18. Minutes of Capitol Planning Commission, 10 Aug. 1961; CAS to Mark O. Hatfield, 24 Aug. 1961; CAS to Capitol Planning Commission members, 31 Aug. 1961 and to Hatfield, 1 Sept. 1961; Hatfield to CAS, 9 Oct. 1961. All CAS papers, Box 1, OHS.
19. Martha and Melvin Hurley had three children and Wallace and Mary Lou Sprague two.
20. In 1960 Thetford was vandalized and robbed; in 1962 the Columbus Day storm caused heavy damage from falling trees. The following year, the Spragues gave Thetford to Willamette University, which still uses it for retreats. MSH and Arthur Hurley interviews with author, Kensington, Calif., 17 Jan. 1998. Transfer deed is in Box 2, OHS.
21. ISTM, 4 June 1948.
22. ISTM, 22 and 23 Nov. 1955.

23. "Saving the Wilderness," OS, 28 June 1959; "'Multiple Use,'" OS, 26 May 1960.
24. ISTM, 19 March 1961 and 25 Oct. 1963.
25. ISTM, 26 Oct.1966; "Mt. Jefferson Wilderness," 6 Oct. 1967; ISTM, 11 March and 21 Sept. 1968.
26. "Retain Belton as State Treasurer," OS, 1 Nov. 1964; "For Governor: Tom McCall," OS, 26 Oct. 1966; "Re-Elect Bob Straub, OS, 24 Oct. 1968.
27. Brent Walth, *Fire at Eden's Gate: Tom McCall and the Oregon Story* (Portland: Oregon Historical Society, 1994), 169-198.
28. "Preserve the Beach," OS, 13 May 1966.
29. ISTM, 20 Oct. 1968; "Governor McCall Favors Beaches Amendment," OS, 26 Oct. 1968; "Beach Tribute from California," OS, 28 Oct. 1968.
30. Ralph Friedman, "Profile of an Ex-Governor," *Oregonian Northwest Magazine*, 29 Jan. 1967: 6-7.
31. ISTM, 8 June and 1 July 1968; "Senate Gun Bill," OS, 20 Sept. 1968; ISTM, 4 April 1968.
32. ISTM, 11 Oct. 1964.
33. "What Didn't Happen," OS, 18 April 1968; ISTM, 23 April 1968.
34. "The United States and Indochina," OS, 4 July 1954.
35. Ibid.; ISTM, 3 Jan. 1961; "Southeast Asia Again," OS, 26 Feb. 1963.
36. ISTM, 21 May 1964.
37. ISTM, 9 Aug. 1964.
38. ISTM, 18 Sept. and 13 April 1968.
39. ISTM, 28 March, 19 May and 15 July 1968.
40. "The Future for Print," Sigma Delta Chi lecture, Indiana University, 17 April 1967; "It Seems To Me," Eric W. Allen lecture, University of Oregon, 16 Feb. 1968. Both AC.
41. Arthur Hurley interview. Hurley went on to fly transports during the Vietnam War and later became a commercial airline pilot.
42. ISTM, 19-25 June 1968.
43. ISTM, 5 Dec. 1968.
44. ISTM, 23 Dec. 1968.
45. ISTM, 30 Dec. 1968.

Chapter Eleven

1. "Charles A. Sprague, Publisher of Statesman in Oregon, Dead," *New York Times*, 14 March 1969.
2. "Fourth Salem High Named for Sprague," OS, 25 Jan. 1969; "Board Won't Rename Sprague Lake," OS, 22 June 1974; J. Wesley Sullivan interview with author, Salem, 12 July 1994.
3. CAS Estate, Marion County Circuit Court; CAS papers, Box 4, OHS.
4. "Memorandum on Fountain," 10 June 1966, attachment to CAS Estate, Marion County Circuit Court and CAS papers, Box 4.
5. Robert Sprague vs Wallace Sprague and Martha Sprague Hurley, U. S. District Court for the District of Oregon, Civil No. 75-742.

6. Minutes of Statesman-Journal Co. board, 28 Sept. 1970, AC. WAS interview with author, New York City, 4 August 1992; Robert W. Sprague interview with author, Eugene, 16 January 1994; William Mainwaring interview with author, Salem, 17 September 1996.
7. J. Wesley Sullivan interview.
8. William Mainwaring interview.
9. "Salem, Oregon dailies purchased by Gannett," *Editor & Publisher*, 27 Oct. 1973; "Gannett to Issue Stock Valued at $15 Million for 2 Oregon Papers," *Wall Street Journal*, 23 May 1974.
10. E. B. MacNaughton to CAS, 13 Dec. 1950; CAS papers, Box 4, OHS.
11. As early as the mid-fifties, newspaper brokers and groups had communicated an interest in the OS, among them broker Jack L. Stoll and Associates, Speidel Newspapers Inc., brokers Joseph A. Snyder, Joseph Mills, Edd Rountree, and Vernon V. Paine; and radio newsman Virgil Pinkley. Correspondence in AC. The OS staffer who most firmly believed that the paper might be left to employee ownership was Al Lightner; Travis Cross, who had discussed sale of the newspaper on behalf of a third party, also believes Sprague considered such a move. Lightner interview with author, Salem, 18 January, 1994; Cross interview with author, Portland, 27 June 1991.
12. J. Wesley Sullivan interview. WW, "Journalism for Food and Fun," unpublished memoirs, 81; manuscript in possession of Marsha Webb Drahn. WW to Al Lightner, 6 Sept. 1981; AC. Lightner and Sullivan interviews; WAS telephone interview.
13. Remarks of J. Wesley Sullivan, Centennial Observance of Charles Arthur Sprague, 3 Dec. 1987; AC.
14. Quoted in ISTM, 28 Feb. 1965.

♦♦♦

Bibliography

Listed here are sources quoted directly, or serving as major sources of information for this work. No attempt is made to list the wide range of works dealing with McCarthyism, the New Deal, progressivism, or American politics in general over the period of Charles A. Sprague's life, although many of these works were consulted during preparation of this book.

Books

History of Adams County, Washington. Ritzville: Adams County Historical Society, 1986.

Adams County Centennial Edition. Ritzville: *The Outlook* and the *Ritzville Adams County Journal*, December, 1983.

"Problems of Journalism." Proceedings of the 1947 Convention. Washington, D.C.: American Society of Newspaper Editors, 1947; also 1952 and 1955 conventions.

Aronson, James. *The Press and the Cold War.* Indianapolis: Bobbs-Merrill, 1970.

Arndt, Karl J. R. and May E. Olson. *The German Language Press of the Americas, Vol. I,* 3d ed. Munchen: Verlag Dokumentation, 1976.

Ayer, N. W. and Son. *Directory of Newspapers and Periodicals*. Philadelphia: N.W. Ayer and Son, annually.

Barrett Jr., Edward L. *The Tenney Committee.* Ithaca: Cornell University Press, 1951.

Bayley, Edwin R. *Joe McCarthy and the Press.* University of Wisconsin, 1981. New York: Pantheon, 1982.

Bone, Arthur. *Oregon Cattleman/Governor, Congressman: Memoirs and Times of Walter M. Pierce. Edited and Expanded by Arthur Bone*. Portland: Oregon Historical Society, 1981.

Brophy, William A. and Sophie D. Aberle. *The Indian: America's Unfinished Business. Report of the Commission on the Rights, Liberties, and Responsibilities of the American Indian*. Norman: University of Oklahoma Press, 1966.

Burton, Robert E. *Democrats of Oregon: The Pattern of Minority Politics, 1900-1956.* Eugene: University of Oregon, 1970.

_____________. "The New Deal in Oregon." In *The New Deal: The State and Local Levels*, vol. 2, edited by John Braeman, Robert H. Bremmer and David Brody, 355-375. Columbus: Ohio State University, 1975.

Capitol's Who's Who for Oregon. Portland: Capitol Publishing Co., 1930-31 and 1936-37.

Carey, Charles H. *General History of Oregon*. Portland: Binfords and Mort, 1971.

Carr, Robert K. *The House Committee on Un-American Activities, 1945-1950.* Ithaca: Cornell University Press, 1952.

Champney, Freeman. *Art & Glory: The Story of Elbert Hubbard.* New York: Crown Publishers, 1968.

Clark, Norman H. *The Dry Years: Prohibition and Social Change in Washington*. Seattle: University of Washington Press, 1965.

Clark, Robert C. *History of the Willamette Valley, Oregon*. Chicago: S. J. Clarke Publishing Co., 1927.

Cleveland, Carl. *Rufus Woods: 'That Dam Editor.'* Wenatchee, Wash: The Wenatchee World, 1973.

Conn, Stetson and Rose C. Engleman and Byron Fairchild. *The United States Army in World War II. The Western Hemisphere: Guarding the United States and Its Outposts*. Office of the Chief of Military History, Department of the Army. Washington: Government Printing Office, 1964.

Countryman, Vern. *Un-American Activities in the State of Washington.* Ithaca: Cornell University Press, 1951.

Dana, Marshall N. *Newspaper Story: 50 Years of the Oregon Journal.* Portland: The Oregon Journal, 1951.

Daniels, Roger. *Politics of Prejudice*. Berkeley: University of California Press, 1962.

_____________. *Concentration Camps USA: Japanese Americans and World War II*. New York: Holt, Rinehart and Winston, Inc., 1972.

Davis, David Brion. *The Fear of Conspiracy: Images of Un-American Subversion from the Revolution to the Present.* Ithaca: Cornell University Press, 1971.

Dodds, Gordon B. *The American Northwest: A History of Oregon and Washington.* Arlington Heights, Ill: Forum Press, 1986.

Drukman, Mason. *Wayne Morse: A Political Biography*. Portland: Oregon Historical Society, 1997.

Duniway, David. *South Salem Past*. Salem: Marion County Historical Society, 1987.

Editor and Publisher International Yearbook. New York: Editor and Publisher Co., Inc, annually.

Elazar, Daniel. *American Federalism: A View from the States*. New York: Thomas Crowell Co. 1966.

Faris, David. *The Glasgow Family of Adams County, Ohio*. Baltimore: Gateway Press, Inc., 1990.

Feinman, Ronald L. *Twilight of Progressivism: The Western Republican Senators and the New Deal*. Baltimore: The Johns Hopkins University Press, 1981.

Ficken, Robert. *Rufus Woods, The Columbia River, and the Building of Modern Washington*. Pullman: Washington State University, 1995.

Filler, Louis. *Appointment at Armaggeddon: Muckraking and Progressivism in the American Tradition*. Westport, Conn.: Greenwood Press, 1976.

100th Anniversary, First Presbyterian Church, Salem, Oregon, 1869-1969. Salem: First Presbyterian Church, 1969.

Frazier, Robert. *Bob Frazier of Oregon.* Edited by Charles Duncan. Eugene: The Register-Guard, 1979.

Freeland, Richard M. *The Truman Doctrine and the Origins of McCarthyism: Foreign Policy, Domestic Politics, and Internal Security, 1946-1948.* New York: Alfred A. Knopf, 1972.

Gellhorn, Walter, ed. *The States and Subversion.* Ithaca: Cornell University Press, 1952.

Goodman, Walter. *The Committee: The Extraordinary Career of the House Committee on Un-American Activities.* New York: Farrar, Straus & Giroux, 1968.

Griffith, Sally Foreman. *Home Town News: William Allen White and the Emporia Gazette.* Baltimore: Johns Hopkins University Press, 1989.

Grodzins, Morton. *Americans Betrayed: Politics and the Japanese Evacuation.* Chicago: University of Chicago Press, 1949.

Gunns, Albert F. *Civil Liberties in Crisis: The Pacific Northwest, 1917-1940*. New York: Garland, 1983.

Halberstam, David. *The Fifties.* New York: Villard Books, 1993.

Hamilton, Charles F. *As Bees in Honey Drown.* South Brunswick and New York: A. S. Barnes & Co., 1973.

Hatfield, Mark O. *Between a Rock and a Hard Place*. Waco, Texas: Word Books, 1976.

Hays, Samuel P. *Conservation and the Gospel of Efficiency: The Progressive Conservation Movement, 1890-1920*. Cambridge: Harvard University Press, 1959.

Hofstadter, Richard. *The Age of Reform: From Bryan to F. D. R.* New York: Alfred A. Knopf, 1955.

__________. *The Progressive Movement, 1900-1915*. Englewood Cliffs, N.J.: Prentice-Hall, Inc., 1963.

Hosokawa, Bill. *JACL: In Quest of Justice*. New York: William Morrow and Company, Inc., 1982.

Johansen, Dorothy O. and Charles Gates. *Empire of the Columbia,: A History of the Pacific Northwest*. 2d ed. New York: Harper & Row, 1967.

Jonas, Frank H., ed. *Politics in the American West.* Salt Lake City: University of Utah Press, 1969.

Joyner, Conrad. *The Republican Dilemma: Conservatism or Progressivism*. Tucson: University of Arizona Press, 1963.

Kennedy, Bruce M. *Community Journalism: A Way of Life.* Ames: Iowa State University Press, 1974.

Kessler, Lauren. *Stubborn Twig: Three Generations in the Life of a Japanese American Family.* New York: Penguin Books, 1993.

Kleppner, Paul. "Politics without parties: The western states, 1900-1984." In *The 20th Century West: Historical Interpretations,* edited by Gerald D. Nash and Richard Etulian, 295-338. Albuquerque: University of New Mexico, 1989.

Koch, Fred C. *The Volga Germans: In Russia and the Americas from 1763 to the Present*. University Park: Pennsylvania State University Press, 1977.

Lewis, Lionel S. *Cold War on Campus: A Study of the Politics of Organizational Control.* New Brunswick, N.J.: Transaction Books, 1988.

Link, Arthur S. and Richard L. McCormick. *Progressivism*. Arlington Heights, Ill.: Harlan Davidson Inc., 1983.

Lofton, John. *The Press as Guardian of the First Amendment.* Columbia: University of South Carolina Press, 1980.

Lowitt, Richard. *The New Deal and the West.* Bloomington: Indiana University Press, 1984.

Lucia, Ellis, ed. *This Land Around Us*. New York: Doubleday, 1969.

Luskin, John. *Lippmann, Liberty, and the Press*. University, Alabama: University of Alabama Press, 1972.

Lyman, W. D. *Lyman's History of Old Walla Walla County*, vol. 1. Chicago: S. J. Clarke Publishing Co., 1918.

MacColl, E. Kimbark. *The Growth of a City: Power and Politics in Portland, Oregon, 1915 to 1950.* Portland: The Georgian Press, 1970.

Malone, Michael P. and Richard W. Etulian. *The American West: A 20th Century History.* Lincoln: University of Nebraska Press, 1989.

McCall, Tom. *Tom McCall: Maverick: An Autobiography with Steve Neal.* Portland: Binfords & Mort, 1977.

McElvaine, Robert S. *The Great Depression: America, 1929-1941*. New York: Times Books, 1993.

McNab, Gordon.*The East Oregonian, 1875-1975.* Pendleton: East Oregonian Publishing Co., 1975.

McWilliams, Carey. *Prejudice: Japanese-Americans, Symbol of Racial Intolerance.* Boston: Little Brown, 1945.

Meeker, Richard. *Newspaperman: S.I. Newhouse and the Business of News.* New Haven: Ticknor and Fields, 1983.

Miller, Douglas and Marion Nowak. *The Fifties: The Way We Really Were.* Garden City, NY: Doubleday, 1977.

Mott, Frank L. *American Journalism: A History of Newspapers in the United States Through 260 Years, 1690 to 1950.* New York: MacMillan, 1950.

Mowry, George E. *The California Progressives*. Berkeley: University of California, 1951. New York: Quadrangle, 1951.

__________. *The Era of Theodore Roosevelt*. New York: Harper & Brothers, 1958. New York: Harper Torchbook, 1962.

__________. *The Progressive Era, 1900-20: The Reform Persuasion.* Washington: American Historical Association, AHA Pamphlets 212, 1972.

Murphy, Paul L. *The Meaning of Freedom of Speech: First Amendment Freedoms from Wilson to FDR*. Westport, Conn.: Greenwood Press, 1972.

Nash, Gerald D. *The American West Transformed: The Impact of the Second World War.* Bloomington: Indiana University Press, 1985.

Neal, Steve. *Dark Horse: A Biography of Wendell Willkie*. New York: Doubleday & Co., 1984.

______________. *McNary of Oregon: A Political Biography*. Portland: Oregon Historical Society, 1985.

Neuberger, Richard L. *Our Promised Land.* New York: MacMillan, 1938.

__________. *Adventures in Politics.* New York: Oxford University Press, 1954.

__________. *They Never Go Back To Pocatello: The Selected Essays of Richard Neuberger*. Edited by Steve Neal. Portland: Oregon Historical Society, 1988.

Notson, Robert. *Making the Day Begin.* Portland: The Oregonian Publishing Co., 1976.

Onstine, Burton W. *Oregon Votes: 1858-1972*. Portland: Oregon Historical Society, 1973.

Orchards, Vance. *Waitsburg: One of a Kind*. Waitsburg, Washington: Waitsburg Historical Society, 1976.

Pearson, Jim B. and Edgar Fuller (eds). *Education in the States: Historical Development and Outlook*. Washington: National Education Association, 1969.

Pease, Otis A. (ed). *The Progressive Years: The Spirit and Achievment of American Reform*. New York: G. Braziller, 1962.

Peirce, Neal R. *The Pacific States of America: People, Politics, and Power in the Five Pacific Basin States.* New York: W. W. Norton, 1972.

Polk, R. L. and Company. *Polk's Oregon and Washington Gazeteer and Business Directory*. Seattle: R. L. Polk & Co., annually.

Polk, R. L. and Company. *Polk's Salem City and Marion County Directory*. Portland: R. L. Polk & Co., annually.

Pollard, Lancaster. *Oregon and the Pacific Northwest*. Portland: Binsfords & Mort, 1946.

Pomeroy, Earl. *The Pacific Slope: A History of California, Oregon, Washington, Idaho, Utah and Nevada.* New York: Alfred A. Knopf, 1965.

Price, Warren C. *The Eugene Register-Guard: A Citizen of Its Community.* Portland: Binfords & Mort, 1976.

Reitman, Alan, ed. *The Pulse of Freedom: American Liberties, 1920-1970s.* New York: W. W. Norton Co., 1975.

Resek, Carl. *The Progressives*. Indianapolis: The Bobbs-Merrill Company Inc., 1967.

Robbins, William G. *Landscapes of Promise: The Oregon Story 1800-1940*. Seattle: University of Washington Press, 1997.

Sackett, Sheldon F. *The Times supports Mr. Roosevelt*. Eugene: University of Oregon Press, 1940.

Sanders, Jane. *Cold War on Campus: Academic Freedom at the University of Washington, 1946-1964.* Seattle: University of Washington, 1979.

Schlesinger, Arthur, Jr. *The Politics of Upheaval.* Boston: Houghton Mifflin Co., 1960.
Schrecker, Ellen W. *No Ivory Tower: McCarthyism and the Universities.* New York: Oxford University, 1986.
Schwantes, Carlos. *The Pacific Northwest: An Interpretive History.* Lincoln: University of Nebraska, 1989.
Seldes, George. *Lords of the Press*. New York: Julian Messner Inc., 1938.
Shannon, David A. (ed). *Progressivism and Postwar Disillusionment: 1898-1928*. New York: McGraw-Hill Book Company, 1966.
Smith, A. Robert. *Tiger in the Senate: A Biography of Senator Wayne Morse.* Garden City, N. Y.: Doubleday, 1962.
Sprague, Charles A. *History of Adams County in the World War*. Ritzville, Wash.: The Journal Times, 1920.
Stein, Harry H. *Salem: A Pictorial History of Oregon's Capital.* Norfolk, Virginia: Donning Co., 1981.
Stone, Stephen A. *Stories from the Files of an Oregon Newsman*. Eugene: Parkstone Co., 1967.
Sullivan, J. Wesley. *To Elsie With Love*. Eugene: Navillus Press, 1993.
Swarthout, John H. and Kenneth R. Gervais, "Oregon: Political Experiment Station." In *Politics in the American West,* edited by Frank H. Jonas, 296-326. Salt Lake City: University of Utah Press, 1969.
tenBroek, Jacobus, Edward N. Barnhart and Floyd W. Matson. *Prejudice, War and the Constitution.* Berkeley: University of California Press, 1954.
Theoharis, Athan. *Seeds of Repression: Harry S. Truman and the Origins of McCarthyism.* Chicago, 1971.
Toy, Eckard V. "The Ku Klux Klan in Oregon." In *Experiences in a Promised Land: Essays in Pacific Northwest History*, edited by G. Thomas Edwards and Carlos A. Schwantes, 269-287. Seattle: University of Washington, 1986.
Turnbull, George. *History of Oregon Newspapers.* Portland: Binfords & Mort, 1939.
__________. *An Oregon Editor's Battle for Freedom of the Press.* Portland: Binfords & Mort, 1952.
__________. *An Oregon Crusader.* Portland: Binfords & Mort, 1955.
__________. *Governors of Oregon*. Portland: Binfords & Mort, 1959.
Walth, Brent. *Fire at Eden's Gate: Tom McCall and the Oregon Story.* Portland; Oregon Historical Society, 1994.
White, William Allen. *The Autobiography of William Allen White.* New York: Macmillan Company, 1946. 2d Edition, edited by Sally Foreman Griffith. Lawrence: University of Kansas Press, 1990.
Wittke, Carl. *German-Americans and the World War.* Columbus: Ohio State University, 1936.
__________.*The German-language press in America.* Lexington: University of Kentucky, 1957.

Articles

Allen, Raymond B. "Communists Should Not Teach in American Colleges." *Educational Forum* (May 1949): 440.

"Communism and Academic Freedom: American Scholar Forum." *The American Scholar* 19 (Summer 1950): 323-54.

Bauer, Malcolm. "The Northwest's Most Influential Editor." *New York Herald Tribune Sunday Forum* (11 December 1960).

Bowles, Dorothy. "Newspaper Support for Free Expression in Times of Alarm, 1920 and 1940." *Journalism Quarterly* 54 (1977): 271-79.

Bruce, Robert. "Interview: Governor Charles A. Sprague Describes His Administration's Proudest Achievement." *Oregon Historical Quarterly* 88 (1987): 403-12.

Chiasson, Lloyd. "The Japanese-American Encampment: An Editorial Analysis of 27 West Coast Newspapers." *Newspaper Research Journal* (1991): 92-107.

Clark, Malcolm Jr. "The Bigot Disclosed: 90 Years of Nativism." *Oregon Historical Quarterly* 75 (1974): 109-191.

"The Veto Messages of Governor Charles A. Sprague." *The Commonwealth Review* 21 (May 1939): 45-59.

Cox, Walter. "The Mighty Pen of Charlie Sprague." *Emerald Empire*, magazine of the *Eugene Register-Guard* (19 May 1968).

Cushman, Kenneth. "Editorials in Oregon Dailies Have Much in Common." *Journalism Quarterly* 42 (1965): 70-72.

Daniels, Roger. "Westerners from the East: Oriental Immigrants Reappraised." *Pacific Historical Review* 25 (1966): 380-81.

Dillow, Frank. "E. B. MacNaughton: Businessman with Soul." Northwest Magazine of *The Sunday Oregonian* (4 April 1971).

"Sprague Advises Aid in Information Pact." *Editor & Publisher* (27 December 1952).

Fine, Sidney. "Mr. Justice Murphy and the Hirabayashi Case." *Pacific Historical Review* (1964): 195-209.

Friedman, Ralph. "Profile of an ex-Governor." *Northwest*, magazine of *The Sunday Oregonian* (27 January 1967).

Goldschmidt, Maure L. "The 1952 Elections in Oregon." *Western Political Science Quarterly* 6 (March 1953): 123-126.

Guimary, Donald Lee. "Strike, problems of the Portland Reporter, 1961-64." *Journalism Quarterly* 45 (1968): 91-94.

Harding, Bruce C. "Water from Pend Oreille: The Gravity Plan for Irrigating the Columbia Basin." *Pacific Northwest Quarterly* 45 (1954): 56-57.

Heale, M. J. "Red Scare Politics: California's Campaign Against Un-American Activities, 1940-1970." *Journal of American Studies* 20 (April 1986): 5-32.

Hook, Sidney. "Should Communists Be Permitted to Teach?" *New York Times Sunday Magazine* (27 February 1949).

Hulteng, John L. "Salaries on Oregon Dailies by Experience Levels." *Journalism Quarterly* 42 (1965): 276-78.

Johansen, Dorothy O. "A Working Hypothesis for the Study of Migrations." *Pacific Historical Review* 36 (February 1967): 1-13
Kerr, William T., Jr. "The Progressives of Washington, 1910-1912." *Pacific Northwest Quarterly* 55 (January, 1964): 16-27.
LaLande, Jeff. "The 'Jackson County Rebellion': Social Turmoil and Political Insurgence in Southern Oregon During the Great Depression." *Oregon Historical Quarterly* 95 (1994): 406-71.
Matthews, Richard P. "Taking Care of Their Own: The Marine Barracks at Klamath Falls, Oregon, 1944-1946." *Oregon Historical Quarterly* 93 (Winter 1992-93): 343-368.
McKay, Floyd. "After Cool Deliberation: Reed College, Oregon Editors and the Red Scare of 1954." *Pacific Northwest Quarterly* 89 (Winter 1997/98): 12-21.
Meiklejohn, Alexander. "Should Communists Be Allowed to Teach?" *New York Times Sunday Magazine* (27 March 1949).
Munk, Michael. "Oregon Tests Academic Freedom in (Cold) Wartime: The Reed College Trustees Versus Stanley Moore." *Oregon Historical Quarterly* 97 (1996): 262-354.
Neuberger, Richard L. "The Northwest Goes Leftish." *New Republic* (7 November 1934).
__________. "It Costs Too Much to Run for Office." *New York Times Magazine*, 11 April 1948.
__________. "His Pen is Mighty." *The Sunday Oregonian Magazine* (18 March 1951).
__________. "Sprague: Conscience of Oregon." *The Nation* (26 January 1952).
Okihiro, Gary Y. and Julie Sly. "The Press, Japanese Americans, and the Concentration Camps." *Phylon* 44 (1983): 66-83.
"Collections. Oral History Interview: Kathryn Hall Bogle on the African-American Experience in Wartime Portland." *Oregon Historical Quarterly* 93 (Winter 1992-93): 394-407.
Owen, Jerrold. "Oregon Prepares for War Emergencies," *State Government* 85, 85-87.
Pollard, James E. "Spiraling Newspaper Costs Outrun Revenues 1938-1949." *Journalism Quarterly* 26 (1949): 270-276.
"Oregon Statesman." *Presbyterian Life*, 15 Dec. 1960: 14.
"Salem's Statesmen-Churchmen," *Presbyterian Life* (15 May 1967): 6-9, 40.
Radin, Max. "The Loyalty Oath at the University of California." *The American Scholar* 19 (1950): 275-84.
Rogers, N. S. "Development of Oregon Forestry." *West Coast Lumberman* 70 (September 1943): 48-49.
Sabine, Gordon. "Oregon Editorial Writers: A Study of Characteristics." *Journalism Quarterly* 28 (1951): 70-74.
Scobie, Ingrid Winther. "Jack B. Tenney and the 'Parasitic Menace': Anti-Communist Legislation in California, 1940-1949." *Pacific Historical Review* 43 (May 1974): 188-211.

Sim, John Cameron. "Community Newspaper Leadership: More Real than Apparent?" *Journalism Quarterly* 44 (1967): 276-80.
Spitzer, Ralph. "Source of Controversy," letter to the editor of *Chemical and Engineering News* (31 January 1949): 306-7.
Sprague, Charles A. "Our Free Press. How Free?" Nieman Reports 7 (January 1953): 3-4.
__________. "The Editor's Job Today." *Journalism Quarterly* 29 (1953): 265-70.
Stevens, John D. "Press and Community Toleration: Wisconsin in World War I." *Journalism Quarterly* 46 (1969): 255-259.
Stone, Stephen A. "Going to Press." *Marion County History* 13 (1979-82): 83-85.
Swarthout, John. "The 1956 Election in Oregon." *Western Political Quarterly* 20 (March 1967).
Tanaka, Stefan. "The Toledo Incident: The Deportation of the Nikkei from an Oregon Mill Town." *Pacific Northwest Quarterly* 69 (1978): 116-126.
Taylor, Quintard. "The Great Migration: The Afro-American Communities of Seattle and Portland During the 1940s." *Arizona and the West* 23 (1981): 109-14, 121.
Telsch, Kathleen. "Right of Correction Treaty is Advanced." *Editor & Publisher* (8 November 1952).
__________. "UN Asks Signatures on Corrections Treaty." *Editor & Publisher* (20 December 1952).
Trayes, Edward J. "A Survey of Salaries of AP-Served Dailies." *Journalism Quarterly* 46 (1969): 825-28, 891.
Webb, Carl C. and George Turnbull. "The Name of William Tugman Added to Honor Roll." *Oregon Historical Quarterly* 45 (1944): 337.
Woods, John B. "Forestry Moves Forward In Oregon." *American Forests* 47 (June 1941): 267-269, 291.
Wyant, Dan. "William Tugman: Last of the Crusading Editors." *Lane County Historian* 38 (Spring 1993): 16-24.

Theses and Dissertations

Cushman, Kenneth. "A Study of Editorials in Selected Oregon Daily Newspapers, January 11 to March 11, 1950." Master's thesis, University of Oregon, 1952.
Evans, David Lloyd. The History and Significance of the Portland Newspaper Strike. Master's thesis, University of Washington, 1966.
Fendall, Bill G. "Oregon's non-Metropolitan Daily Newspaper Publishers: A Socio-Biographical Study of Their Personal and Professional Backgrounds, Activities and Opinions." Master's thesis, University of Oregon, 1958.
Guimary, Donald Lee. "The Decline and Death of the Portland Reporter." Master's thesis, University of Oregon, 1966.

Herzig, Jill Hopkins. "The Oregon Commonwealth Federation: The Rise and Decline of a Reform Organization." Master's thesis, University of Oregon, 1963.
Joseph, George M. "George W. Joseph and the Oregon Progressive Tradition." Senior thesis, Reed College, 1952.
Kennedy, Mary Madge. "Charles A. Sprague: A Study of an Oregon Editor, 1947 to 1951." Master's thesis, University of Oregon, 1970.
McKay, Floyd J. "With Liberty for Some: Oregon Editors and the Challenge of Civil Liberties, 1942-54." Ph.D. dissertation, University of Washington, 1995.
Munk, Michael. "Politics in the Press: A Content Analysis of Portland Press Coverage of the 1954 Senate Campaign." Bachelor's thesis, Reed College, 1956.
Pursinger, Marvin G. "Oregon's Japanese in World War II: A History of Compulsory Relocation." Ph.D. dissertation, University of Southern California, 1961.
Sand, Joseph R. "Sheldon F. Sackett: Flamboyant Oregon Journalist." Master's thesis, University of Oregon, 1971.
Tattam, William M. "Sawmill Workers and Radicalism: Portland, Oregon, 1929-41." Master's thesis, University of Oregon, 1970.
Whipple, Robert Blaine. "The Change and Development of Editorial Attitudes of Selected Oregon Daily Newspapers Toward Senator Wayne Morse." Master's thesis, University of Oregon, 1959.

Manuscripts

Allen, Eric. Papers. University of Oregon Library, Eugene.
Bauer, Malcolm. Papers, Oregon Historical Society, Portland.
Brown, Samuel. Papers. University of Oregon Library, Eugene.
Frank, Gerald W. Oral history, Oregon Historical Society, Portland.
Frazier, Robert B. Papers. University of Oregon Library, Eugene.
Hanzen, Henry. Papers. University of Oregon Library, Eugene; unpublished manuscript, "Joseph-Meier Campaign of 1930," also at Oregon Historical Society, Portland.
MacNaughton, E. B. Papers. Reed College Archives, Portland.
Martin, Charles D. Papers. Oregon Historical Society, Portland; and State of Oregon Archives, Salem.
Moore, Stanley. Files of Reed College regarding his hearing and dismissal, 1954-55. Reed College Archives, Portland.
Morse, Wayne L. Papers. University of Oregon Library, Eugene.
Neuberger, Richard L. Papers. University of Oregon Library, Eugene; Oregon Historical Society, Portland.
Oregon Commonwealth Federation. Papers. University of Oregon Library, Eugene.
Sawyer, Robert. Papers. University of Oregon Library, Eugene.

Snell, Earl. Papers, Oregon Historical Society, Portland; and State of Oregon Archives, Salem.
Sprague, Charles A. Papers. Oregon Historical Society, Portland; and State of Oregon Archives, Salem.
Sterling, Donald J. Papers. Oregon Historical Society, Portland.
Sweetland, Monroe. Oral History, Oregon Historical Society, Portland.
Tugman, Peter. Oral history, Oregon Historical Society, Portland.
Tugman, William. Papers. University of Oregon Library, Eugene.
Webb, Wendell. "Journalism for Food and Fun." Unpublished memoirs. Manuscript in possession of Marsha Webb Drahn, Eugene.

Newspapers and Publications

Oregon newspapers (with circulation in 1950)
The Oregonian, 214,916.
Oregon Journal, 190,840.
Eugene *Register-Guard*, 27,360.
Salem *Capital-Journal*, 17,094.
Salem, *The Oregon Statesman*, 15,798.
Klamath Falls *Herald & News*, 13,306.
Medford *Mail Tribune*, 12,727.
Coos Bay *Times*, 8,033.
Roseburg *News-Review*, 7,512.
Albany *Democrat-Herald*, 7,364.
Astoria *Daily Astorian*, 7,177.
Pendleton *East Oregonian*, 6,513.
Grants Pass *Courier*, 6,124.
Bend *Bulletin*, 5,322.
Corvallis *Gazette-Times*, 5,009.

Washingon newspapers
Aberdeen *Herald*
Seattle *Times*
Seattle, *The Post Intelligencer*
Ritzville, *The Journal-Times*
Waitsburg *Times*

The Forest Log, official publication of the Oregon Department of Forestry.
Oregon Legionnaire, official publication of the American Legion, Department of Oregon.
Oregon Exchanges: For the newspapermen of the State of Oregon. Eugene: University of Oregon School of Journalism, monthly from 1917 to 1932.
Oregon Publisher. Eugene: Oregon Newspaper Publishers Association, monthly since 1932 (continuation of *Oregon Exchanges*).
Oregon Voter. Portland. Weekly journal of political opinion.
Reed College Bulletin, official publication of Reed College.

Government Documents

Oregon Legislative Assembly, *House and Senate Journal* publications of regular and special sessions, 1940-56.

Oregon Legislative Assembly. Minutes of House State and Federal Affairs Committee, 1951 and 1953.

Oregon Legislative Assembly. Report of the Legislative Interim Committee on Indian Affairs: "A Reintroduction to the Indians of Oregon." October 1958.

Oregon Legislative Assembly. Commission for Constitutional Revision, State of Oregon. "A New Constitution for Oregon," 1962.

Oregon Secretary of State. *Oregon Blue Book and Official Directory*. Salem: State Printing Department, annually.

United States Army, Western Defense Command (1943): Final Report, Japanese evacuation from the West Coast, 1942. Washington: USGPO. Reprinted by Arno Press. New York, 1978.

U. S. Commission on Civil Rights. The National Conference and the Reports of the State Advisory Committees to the U. S. Commission on Civil Rights (1960). Washington: USGPO.

__________. The 50 States Report: Submitted to the Commission on Civil Rights by the State Advisory Committees (1961). Washington: USGPO.

U. S. Commission on Wartime Relocation and Internment of Civilians (1982). *Personal Justice Denied.* Washington: USGPO.

U. S. Congress. House. Select Committee Investigating National Defense Migration. *National Defense Migration*. 77th Congress, 2d Session.

U. S. Congress. House. Subcommittee of the Committee on Un-American Activities. *Investigation of Communist Activity in the Northwest Area, Part I*. 82d Congress, lst Session.

U.S. Department of Commerce. *Census of Population: 1950, Volume II, Characteristics of the Population, Part 37, Oregon.* Washington: USGPO, 1952.

U. S. Department of Interior, Census Office. *Report on the Population of the United States*. Washington: USGPO (census of 1980, 1890, 1900 for State of Iowa; 1900 and 1910 for State of Washington).

U. S. Department of State. *Report of the Honorable Roland S. Morris on Japanese Immigration and Alleged Discriminatory Legislation Against Japanese Residents in the United States*. Reprint edition. New York: Arno Press, 1978.

U. S. Department of War. *Final Report: Japanese Evacuation from the West Coast, 1942.* Washington: USGPO, 1921. Reprint edition. New York: Arno Press, 1978.

University of Oregon Bureau of Municipal Research and Service. *Population of Oregon Cities, Counties and Metropolitan Areas, 1850-1957*. Eugene: University of Oregon, 1958.

Work Projects Administration (WPA), Writers Program. *Oregon: End of the Trail*. Portland: Binfords & Mort, 1940. Revised edition, 1951.

Interviews and Oral Histories

Beadle, Roy. Gresham, 13 June 1994.
Chandler, Robert. Portland. 23 December 1992.
Cross, Travis. Portland, 27 June 1991.
Davis, Charles. Portland, 28 August 1991.
Eccles, David. Portland, 28 August 1991.
Edwards, Cecil. Salem, 15 August 1989; interview with J. Wesley Sullivan, Salem, 16 August 1988.
English, Jeryme. Salem, 3 September 1991.
Eyre, David. By telephone, 24 September 1994 and 12 January 1995.
Forrester, J.W. (Bud). Astoria, 4 September 1991 and Portland, 4 January 1996.
Frank, Gerald W. By telephone, 11 September 1996.
Gangware, Robert E. Salem, 3 September 1991.
Harvey, Paul Jr. Salem, 6 September 1991; interview with J. Wesley Sullivan, Salem, 16 August 1988.
Hatfield, Mark O. Portland, 13 February 1993.
Hess, Henry Jr. Portland, 28 February 1998.
Hurley, Arthur. Kensington, California, 17 February 1998
Hurley, Martha Sprague. Kensington, California, 25 February 1993 and 17 January 1998.
Lightner, Al. Salem, 18 January, 1994.
Linde, Hans. Salem, 24 September 1996.
Lundy, Herbert. Lake Oswego, 9 July 1992.
Mainwaring, William. Salem, 17 September 1996.
Miller, Lillian. Ritzville, Washington, 9 April 1992.
Miller, W. Walters. Ritzville, Washington, 9 April 1992.
Neuberger, Maurine. Portland, 8 July 1992.
Notson, Robert. Beaverton, 13 June 1994.
Prange, Conrad. Salem, 31 August 1991.
Smith, A. Robert. Bellingham, Washington, 12 October 1995.
Sprague, Blanche. Interviewed by Martha Sprague Hurley and Dr. Melvin Hurley, Berkeley, California, 25 December 1969.
Sprague, Charles A. Interviewed by Robert Bruce, 18 July 1962. Oregon Historical Society Tape 92.
Sprague, Robert. Eugene, 16 January 1994.
Sprague, Wallace. New York City, 4 August 1992; telephone interviews, 30 September 1996 and 26 February 1998.
Sterling, Donald Jr. Portland, 21 September 1994.
Sullivan, J. Wesley. Salem, 12 July 1994.
Sweetland, Monroe. Milwaukie, 18 December 1994; telephone interview 30 September 1996.
Tugman, Peter. Oregon Historical Society oral history.
Wright, Thomas G. Jr. Portland, 29 August 1989.
Wright, Marguerite. Portland, 30 July 1992.

Index

Numbers in italics refer to photographs